Bridges to Science Fiction
and Fantasy

Bridges to Science Fiction and Fantasy

Outstanding Essays from the J. Lloyd Eaton Conferences

Edited by Gregory Benford,
Gary Westfahl, Howard V. Hendrix
and Joseph D. Miller

McFarland & Company, Inc., Publishers
Jefferson, North Carolina

Library of Congress Cataloguing-in-Publication Data

Names: Benford, Gregory, 1941– editor. | Westfahl, Gary, editor. | Hendrix, Howard V., 1959– editor. | Miller, Joseph D. | Eaton Conference on Science Fiction and Fantasy Literature.
Title: Bridges to science fiction and fantasy : outstanding essays from the J. Lloyd Eaton Conferences / edited by Gregory Benford, Gary Westfahl, Howard V. Hendrix and Joseph D. Miller.
Description: Jefferson, North Carolina : McFarland & Company, Inc., Publishers, 2018. | Includes bibliographical references and index.
Identifiers: LCCN 2018013458 | ISBN 9781476669281 (softcover : acid free paper) ♾
Subjects: LCSH: Science fiction—History and criticism—Congresses. | Fantasy fiction—History and criticism—Congresses.
Classification: LCC PN3448.S45 B75 2018 | DDC 809.3/8762—dc23
LC record available at https://lccn.loc.gov/2018013458

British Library cataloguing data are available

ISBN (print) 978-1-4766-6928-1
ISBN (ebook) 978-1-4766-3193-6

Front cover illustration by Pavel Zhovba (iStock)

Printed in the United States of America

McFarland & Company, Inc., Publishers
Box 611, Jefferson, North Carolina 28640
www.mcfarlandpub.com

Original Publication Information

"Science Fiction as Truncated Epic" by Patrick Parrinder, and "Dialogues Concerning Human Understanding: Empirical Views of God from Locke to Lem" by Stephen W. Potts were originally published in *Bridges to Science Fiction*, edited by George E. Slusser, George R. Guffey, and Mark Rose. Carbondale: Southern Illinois University Press, 1980. 168 pp.

"The Descent of Fantasy" by Eric S. Rabkin was originally published in *Coordinates: Placing Science Fiction and Fantasy*, edited by George E. Slusser, Eric S. Rabkin, and Robert Scholes. Carbondale: Southern Illinois University Press, 1983. 209 pp.

"The Virginity of Astronauts: Sex and the Science Fiction Film" by Vivian Sobchack was originally published in *Shadows of the Magic Lamp: Fantasy and Science Fiction in Film*, edited by George Slusser and Eric S. Rabkin. Carbondale: Southern Illinois University Press, 1985. 259 pp.

"Running Out of Speculative Niches: A Crisis for Hard Science Fiction?" by David Brin was originally published in *Hard Science Fiction*, edited by George E. Slusser and Eric S. Rabkin. Carbondale: Southern Illinois University Press, 1986. 284 pp.

"Effing the Ineffable" by Gregory Benford and "Discriminating Among Friends: The Social Dynamics of the Friendly Alien" by John Huntington were originally published in *Aliens: The Anthropology of Science Fiction*, edited by George E. Slusser and Eric S. Rabkin. Carbondale: Southern Illinois University Press, 1987. 243 pp.

"Nature: Laws and Surprises" by Poul Anderson was originally published in *Mindscapes: The Geographies of Imagined Worlds*, edited by George Slusser and Eric S. Rabkin. Carbondale: Southern Illinois University Press, 1988. 302 pp.

"In the Palace of Green Porcelain: Artifacts from the Museums of Science Fiction" by Robert Crossley, and "Just How Frumious Is a Bandersnatch?: The Exotic and the Ambiguous in Imaginative Literature" by Joseph D. Miller were originally published in *Styles of Creation: Aesthetic Technique and the Creation of Fictional Worlds*, edited by George Slusser and Eric S. Rabkin. Athens: University of Georgia Press, 1992. 271 pp.

"Making the Pulpmonster Safe for Demography: *Omni* Magazine and the Gentrification of Science Fiction" by Howard V. Hendrix was originally published in *Science Fiction and Market Realities*, edited by Gary Westfahl, George Slusser, and Eric S. Rabkin. Athens: University of Georgia Press, 1996. 220 pp.

"For Tomorrow We Dine: The Sad Gourmet in the Scienticafé" by Gary Westfahl, and "Cannibalism in Science Fiction" by Paul Alkon were originally published in *Foods of the Gods: Eating and the Eaton in Fantasy and Science Fiction*, edited by Gary Westfahl, George Slusser, and Eric S. Rabkin. Athens: University of Georgia Press, 1996. 253 pp.

"Longevity as Class Struggle" by Fredric R. Jameson, "How Cyberspace Signifies: Taking Immortality Literally" by N. Katherine Hayles, and "You Bet Your Life: Death and the Storyteller" by Frank McConnell were originally published in *Immortal Engines: Life Extension and Immortality in Science Fiction and Fantasy*, edited by George Slusser, Gary Westfahl, and Eric S. Rabkin. Athens: University of Georgia Press, 1996. 243 pp.

"Revamping the Rut Regarding Reading and Writing about Feminist Science Fiction: Or, I Want to Engage in "Procrustean Bedmaking" by Marleen S. Barr was originally published in *Extrapolation*, 41:1 (Spring, 2000).

"Literary Gatekeepers and the Fabril Tradition" by Tom Shippey was originally published in *Science Fiction, Canonization, Marginalization, and the Academy*, edited by Gary Westfahl and George Slusser. Westport, Connecticut: Greenwood Press, 2002. 182 pp.

"Flying to the Moon in the French *Bande Dessinée*" by Danièle Chatelain and George Slusser was originally published as "Flying to the Moon in French and American Science Fiction" in *Space and Beyond: The Frontier Theme in Science Fiction*, edited by Gary Westfahl. Westport, Connecticut: Greenwood Press, 2000.

"Shapes from the Edge of Time: The Science Fiction Artwork of Richard M. Powers" by Kirk Hampton and Carol MacKay was originally published in *Unearthly Visions: Approaches to Science Fiction and Fantasy Art*, edited by Gary Westfahl, George Slusser, and Kathleen Church Plummer. Westport, Connecticut: Greenwood Press, 2002. 166 pp.

"The Science Fiction of Medicine" by H. Bruce Franklin was originally published in *No Cure for the Future: Disease and Medicine in Science Fiction and Fantasy*, edited by Gary Westfahl and George Slusser. Westport, Connecticut: Greenwood Press, 2002. 184 pp.

"Science Fiction and the Two Cultures: Reflections After the Snow-Leavis Controversy" by Carl Freedman was originally published in *Extrapolation*, 42:3 (Fall, 2001). It was republished in *Science Fiction and the Two Cultures: Essays on Bridging the Gap Between the Sciences and the Humanities*, edited by Gary Westfahl and George Slusser. Jefferson, North Carolina: McFarland Publishers, 2009. 282 pp.

Table of Contents

Introduction

Gregory Benford, Gary Westfahl,
Howard V. Hendrix *and* Joseph D. Miller

The idea of assembling some of the best essays from the J. Lloyd Eaton Conferences on Science Fiction and Fantasy Literature in one volume first emerged in 1999, and since then several individuals have strived to achieve that goal, including George Slusser, founder of the Eaton Conferences, Daniel Bernardi, Eric S. Rabkin, Paul Alkon, and this volume's editors. Now we are pleased to finally be able to present 22 superior Eaton essays (18 accompanied by new afterwords) for some to reread, and others to read for the first time.

The Eaton Conferences began in 1979, designed to both promote science fiction criticism in general and encourage scholars to be aware of, and employ, the resources of the University of California, Riverside's Eaton Collection of Science Fiction and Fantasy Literature, which remains the world's largest institutional collection of science fiction and fantasy texts. These conferences became a unique forum for focused thought and forged a warm community of regular attendees who appreciated their special features. After initial gatherings with broad themes, conferences tightly focused on specific topics; only a relatively small number of relevant papers were accepted for presentation and Slusser sought speakers who were not only literary critics, but also scholars in other disciplines, scientists, and science fiction writers and editors to have key issues addressed from several perspectives and build "bridges" between disparate communities. Conferences had only one track, so participants could hear every paper; presenters and guests were encouraged to attend all sessions and participate in lengthy discussions following each paper, which routinely inspired salutary revisions when papers were prepared for publication. If discussions caused conferences to fall hopelessly behind schedule, Slusser calmly accepted the situation, recognizing the end result would be a significantly improved volume of essays.

Another singular aspect of these conferences: while devoted to serious scholarship, they were also infused with a spirit of fun. This can be attributed to the regular presence of the late Frank McConnell, whose wonderfully witty papers were always a conference highlight. Accordingly, other presenters sometimes felt free to be more playful than portentous: one speaker, discussing science fiction's aliens, donned a pair of antennae; another, describing the weakening of traditional authorities, surprised listeners by having portions of his paper read by unacknowledged collaborators who stood up from the audience. Unusually, Eaton Conferences could be both enlightening and entertaining.

At first, the conferences having done their job, assembling Eaton volumes only involved gathering and arranging each conference's papers. However, as "conference proceedings" became more difficult to publish, the volumes necessarily evolved to become more marketable: to minimize the volumes' length, and only present papers directly related to specific topics, otherwise suitable papers were sometimes excluded. Hence, two of our essays, by Marleen S. Barr and Danièle Chatelain and George Slusser, were presented at Eaton Conferences but appear here for the first time in an official Eaton volume. In other cases, new papers were commissioned to fill gaps in a volume's coverage, so some individuals contributed to Eaton volumes without ever attending an Eaton Conference. But a distinguished record of publication was nonetheless achieved, as the first 20 Eaton Conferences all produced published volumes.

Eventually, however, due to changing circumstances, Slusser's productive model for Eaton Conferences was abandoned, as later conferences offered expediently diffuse themes, increasingly large numbers of speakers, fewer participants who were not literary scholars, multiple tracks, and tight schedules allowing little time for discussion. Conference coordinators of the twenty-first century, confronting vast numbers of unrelated papers of uneven quality, usually did not even attempt to assemble a conference volume, and only one additional Eaton volume appeared presenting essays from one of the final conferences.

Still, for many years, Slusser admirably maintained what was effectively an ingenious machine for generating cohesive, provocative volumes of essays that made the Eaton Conferences, as many noted, the field's most prestigious gatherings. We had hoped this volume might provide an impetus to stage new Eaton Conferences following Slusser's original pattern; instead, since it now appears unlikely there will be any future Eaton Conferences, this volume can only serve as a memorial to Slusser's vision and accomplishments. Still, we are using the Eaton format for a George Slusser Conference in April 2018 at the University of California, Irvine, with Jonathan Alexander and three of this volume's editors as coordinators, which may revive the Eaton tradition.

From another perspective, it is perhaps appropriate to bring the Eaton Conferences to an end, because they have manifestly achieved Slusser's original goals: science fiction criticism is now thriving and widely accepted, and its increasingly numerous scholars are familiar with the Eaton Collection and regularly examine its holdings.

In the informal discussions that engendered this volume, the planned compilation was called a "best of Eaton" volume; but all Eaton Conferences featured several papers that might be counted among the best, and no single volume could present them all. So, our title promises only to offer some "outstanding essays" from the conferences, acknowledging there were other fine Eaton essays that, for a variety of reasons, we could not include, or chose not to include.

We offer these essays exactly as first published, with minor copyediting to standardize their format (though we retained the original format of Westfahl's idiosyncratic essay). They are arranged in chronological order, according to when they were presented, to provide a picture of how science fiction criticism evolved in recent decades. When there was relatively little science fiction criticism, early essays tended to examine science fiction from a broad perspective, drew information and ideas from a limited number of resources, and dealt largely with major themes and "canonical" texts. Later essays focused more on particular topics and authors, could reference a broad range of secondary texts, and began addressing matters that traditional scholars ignored—like fictional food, science fiction art, and marketplace issues that concern authors more than critics but unquestionably influence the genre.

In planning this volume, we considered incorporating additional features, like Westfahl's *Extrapolation* essay about the Eaton Conferences, "Science Fiction and the Playing Fields of Eaton" (2006), other participants' memories of past conferences, and all conference programs and the contents of all Eaton volumes. Ultimately, however, we resolved to devote virtually all our space to essays and afterwords, though we include an "Eaton Roll of Honor" to acknowledge the numerous individuals who contributed to the Eaton Conferences and Eaton volumes. We also hope to post other ancillary materials online, as informal supplements to this volume, and should remind interested readers that 12 of the 21 Eaton volumes remain in print, and all volumes can be found in university libraries throughout the world. This book, then, offers only samples of the scholarly riches that emerged from the Eaton Conferences.

Science Fiction as Truncated Epic

(1979 Eaton Conference)

Patrick Parrinder

Far from being settled long ago, the questions of the definition of science fiction and of its relation to other literary forms remain controversial and confused. Perhaps the earliest of the literary theorists to have taken notice of science fiction was Northrop Frye, who categorized it in *Anatomy of Criticism* (1957) as a mode of romance.[1] More recently critics have sought a definition that would yield an account of the genre's relationship to science; Darko Suvin's view of it as a "literature of cognitive estrangement" is a much-discussed example.[2] My premise in this essay is that science fiction, like the novel itself, is a typically modern literary form both in its self-consciousness about generic matters and in its evasion of any simple generic definition. Thus I shall not argue that all science fiction is or should be epic, but rather that a number of familiar science fiction texts are significantly related to the epic form. The same texts—not to mention other science fiction works—may also be related to certain of the other traditional forms such as romance, fable, and parody. That is, the traditional generic categories offer a series of overlapping perspectives that may be combined to make up a composite picture of the science fiction genre. Both fable and parody will be invoked later on in this argument; my starting point is the distinction between the epical and the romantic.

The epic has been defined in modern terms by Ezra Pound as a "poem including history."[3] The inclusion of history marks the contrast between the epic and the romance, since the latter form tends to present an absorbing, coherent, and yet arbitrary vision of the world, which the reader can only enter at the price of a willing surrender to the writer's authority.[4] The desirable (including the deliciously horrifying) takes precedence in romance over what is realistically plausible. The author, in Robert Louis Stevenson's words, sets out to

> satisfy the nameless longings of the reader, and to obey the ideal laws of the day-dream. The right kind of thing should fall out in the right kind of place: the right kind of thing should follow; and not only the characters talk aptly and think naturally, but all the circumstances in a tale answer one to another like notes in music.[5]

While this is an evocation of the romance as an ideal type, hence greatly oversimplified, it would seem that the term "scientific romance" as used for early science fiction is something of a misnomer. Pure scientific romance is to be found in some of Nathaniel Hawthorne's tales, where an exotic twist is given to a doomed love match by the labors of a demonic scientist. This is very different from the science fiction of H.G. Wells and Jules Verne. Criticism of the romance tends to stress, not its verisimilitude, but its orchestration of emotional effects, viewing it alternatively as a recapturing of some archetypical essence and as a machine for the production of literary pleasure. Yet the solemnity that the myth critic and the structuralist—and even, for that matter, the "aesthetic" critic such as Stevenson—bring to the romance is far from being endemic to this most purely diverting of narrative forms.[6]

The purpose of epic writing is never simply to hold its audience spellbound. The dignity and seriousness of the classical *epos* reflect the fact that the heroic deeds it recounts are supposed to have really taken place, whereas the secondary epics of Dante and Milton lay claim to a profound religious and symbolic truth. Where the romance may be written in a whimsical and parodic manner, drawing attention to the imaginary nature of the world it depicts, epic writing postulates a historical or eschatological continuity between the events it narrates and the reader's situation. These events have both a specified time and place in the historical world, and a permanent national or religious significance for the social group to whom the epic belongs. And although the intervention of gods and goddesses in human affairs is a regular feature of traditional epic, this is portrayed in terms of recognizably human motivations of pity, affection, benevolence, jealousy, and spitefulness rather than as part of an undifferentiated supernatural. The epic is thus a secular or historical narrative of events and deeds that constitute the heritage, or provide the key to the destiny, of the people for whom it is written.

A debased use of the term "epic" is a commonplace of the promotional material on science fiction put out by publishers and film companies. It may, indeed, be the mindless reiteration of the term on paperback covers and movie posters that has led to its comparative neglect by critics of the genre. "Epic" science fiction in the commercial sense invariably involves space travel, since space is the last natural frontier and thus the appropriate setting for a new heroic age of exploration, adventure, and imaginary wars. The story of how the Earth, or some other homeland, was saved is a plausible substitute for the old national epic, concerned with the establishment and defense of the realm. Nevertheless, the run-of-the-mill space epic is usually decked out with the stock figures and situations of conventional romance: villainous monsters, enchanted landscapes, plucky young heroes, and princesses born to send brave men to their deaths. The new heroic age of exploration repeats the discovery of America (we may even end up on a beach with the ruins of the Statue of Liberty, as in the film of Pierre Boulle's *Planet of the Apes* [1968]), and the story of how the Earth was saved turns into a cosmic game of cops and robbers or a rerun of World War II. The presence of detailed technical descriptions may help to give the impression of verisimilitude, and thus of a genuine approximation to epic form. The hard technology of *2001: A Space Odyssey* (1968) might be compared to Homer's itemization of military equipment, and the purely decorative spacecraft of *Star Wars* (1977) are reminiscent of the horses and armor of chivalric romance. However, the principal ground for calling some science fiction "epic" as opposed to "romantic" is that it deals with future or alternative history. The plausibility such stories share with realism is as essential as the heroic deeds and fateful contests they share with modern fantasy.

The events portrayed in epic fiction must be of a certain magnitude. Though they need not be noble deeds in the old sense, they must involve the fate, not of individuals, but of whole societies or of the human race, its collaterals or descendants. Science fiction is often closer than realistic fiction to the old epics by virtues of its universal scale, the scope it allows for heroic enterprise, and its concern with man's confrontation with non-empirical and extraterrestrial forces. Nevertheless, science fiction that takes the form of a fictive history has often been likened to realism.[7] Robert A. Heinlein once tried to define science fiction as a whole as "realistic future-scene fiction."[8] Wells suggests that the "futurist story ... should produce the effect of an historical novel the other way round."[9] He was referring to the illusion of reality it ought to sustain. Though both are related to traditional epic, the idea that the future history and the historical novel are mirror images of one another is to some extent a chronological illusion. Bad historical novels and bad science fiction tend to resemble one another, since both rely on the stereotypes of the romance genres; the essential difference, however, between the fictional bringing-to-life of a past world and the invention of a future one is the difference between historiography and speculation or prophecy.

The great Marxist critic Georg Lukács follows Georg Hegel in arguing that all the modes of modern realism are descendants of the ancient epic. The progressive alienation of man from his fellow men since the dawn of Greek civilization accounts, in his view, for the passing away of the primitive epic form with its direct expression of the "extensive totality of life." The bourgeois novel attempts to recapture the unity of Homer's "rounded universe" through its portrayal of the social trajectory of the "problematic hero."[10] In *The Historical Novel* Lukács argues that the novelists whom he calls "critical realists" are able to evoke the process of social development by means of their portrayal of conflict between typical individuals. (The concept of characters as representative types, it should be noted, is a modern innovation that implies a combination of the epic form with allegory or fable.) The pioneer of the modern realist epic, in Lukács's view, is Sir Walter Scott. Lukács's key distinction between the classical form of Scott's historical novels and the naturalistic costume drama exemplified by Gustave Flaubert's *Salammbô* (1862) is helpful in considering the nature of science fiction's historical narratives. Scott's novels, according to Lukács, have as their underlying theme the social transformations that have led to the emergence of modern Britain. He shows these historical crises as they were experienced within the being of the age—the broad sweep of everyday life. The conflicts undergone by Scott's middle-of-the-road heroes are those that, in retrospect, may be seen as constituting a decisive parting of the ways in national development. These conflicts are portrayed with a degree of necessary anachronism, since Scott allows his characters to express "feelings and thoughts about real, historical relationships in a much clearer way than the actual men and women of the time could have done."[11] In this way the period in which the novel is set is revealed as part of an essential history leading up to the present.

Flaubert in *Salammbô* portrays a society (that of ancient Carthage in conflict with the Barbarians) that has no organic connection with his own. His novel expresses a "scientific" attitude in its reliance upon historical and archaeological research and in its elimination of any sort of anachronistic historical awareness on the part of its characters. The attractions of *Salammbô* for the reader lie simply in its exoticism and in what Lukács calls its "pseudo-monumentality." However, the exoticism is only superficial, since the emotional conflicts of the protagonists are characterized by an implicit modernization:

> Artists have admired the accomplishment of Flaubert's descriptions. But the effect of Salammbô herself was to provide a heightened image, a decorative symbol, of the hysterical longings and torments of middle-class girls in large cities. History simply provided a decorative, monumental setting for this

> hysteria, which in the present spends itself in petty and ugly scenes, and which thus acquired a tragic aura quite out of keeping with its real character.[12]

The mode that Lukács is describing here is that of the historical costume drama, in which characters in alien settings and exotic dress are shown pursuing desires of a basically familiar and conventional kind. The pseudomonumentality that Lukács detects is all too familiar in "historical" science fiction, whether the futures it depicts are embodiments of glittering rationality or of neofeudal brutality and splendor. Indeed, the great majority of really lengthy science fiction novels and so-called epics are costume dramas of considerable banality.

Is there, however, a classical form of epic science fiction comparable to that which Lukács discovered in the historical novel? Since there are no credible equivalents to Scott's Waverly novels or Tolstoy's *War and Peace* (1869), it has sometimes been suggested that the great epic of science fiction has yet to be written.[13] Yet it must be remembered that future histories differ profoundly from the historical novels of the nineteenth century in that their basis is not history but speculation or prophecy. The concepts of speculation and prophecy require some clarification at this point.

In our secularized societies the idea of prophecy has declined from an article of faith to a strong but residual metaphor. The social prophet is recognizable as such partly by his Old Testament literary manner (as with the so-called Victorian sages) and partly by his concern to direct readers' attention to the future and to anticipate social and technological innovations. Even the most visionary modern thinkers are prophets only by metaphorical courtesy. Nevertheless, modern society combines skepticism about the possibilities of foretelling with a great hunger for intimations of what the future will hold. Science fiction authors of future histories very frequently gain a reputation as prophets. Conversely, any secular attempt to speculate about the future is a hypothetical exercise and may, if we wish, be described as fictional.

The science fiction that I shall call "prophetic" invokes the authority of the modern cognitive sciences for its speculations about the far future. (We are not concerned here with Verne-like speculations about the very *near* future, in which the vast majority of social data remain unchanged.) The major problem of this mode of writing—one identified by Wells in his remarks about the futurist story—is that while the future history may be convincing in outline, it is very difficult to keep it convincing in detail. The greater the wealth of fictional incident, the greater the reader's awareness is likely to be that he is faced not with logical necessity but with hypothetical and, often, gratuitous fantasy. For this reason, science fiction writers have good reason for steering away from traditional epic construction in their narratives of the future. The characteristic relationship of many science fiction stories to the older epics is, it would seem, one of truncation or frustration. If the events that they portray are of epic magnitude, the manner of their portrayal is brief and allegorical, reminiscent not of the poem in twelve books but of the traditional fable. A major example of the truncated epic in science fiction is Wells's *The Time Machine* (1895), the story of a voyage of thirty million years into the future that is told in little over 30,000 words. The (unnamed) Time Traveller, a representative nineteenth-century scientist and inventor, comes, as he tells us, "out of this age of ours, this ripe prime of the human race, when Fear does not paralyse and mystery has lost its terrors."[14] He embarks on a Promethean mission since, from the viewpoint of post–Darwinian evolutionism, knowledge of the future could transform man's sense of the meaning and possibilities of his existence. Wells does not disappoint us in his promise to give a comprehensive and prophetic account of the future. It might be objected that his brevity in doing so was determined by the publishing conditions of the 1890s, but in fact Wells was exploiting a newly-won freedom to publish short fiction rather than being forced to confine himself to a certain length. The prospect of *The Time Machine* in three volumes did not appeal to its author and does not appeal to the reader.[15]

The reason for this brevity lies not only in Wells's didactic intentions, but also in the nature of the scientific thought on which the story is based. The plausibility of *The Time Machine*'s prophecy of the future is proportional, in large part, to the abstract and inhuman nature of the laws of evolution, thermodynamics, and class struggle invoked by the Time Traveller to explain what he sees. Wells could have invented more episodes to show the various intermediate stages of the future and especially the epoch of man's supremacy—a period that he passes over in virtual silence. In fact, as he revised the story, he actually suppressed one episode. The story as it stands has an air of historical inevitability, from which further fanciful invention could only detract.

There are two major prophecies in *The Time Machine*: that of the degeneration of human civilization as represented by the Eloi and the Morlocks, and that of the gradual regression of all life on Earth to the point reached in the final scenes on the beach. The episode of the Eloi and Morlocks, although a demonstration of evolutionary decline, seems to embody a warning of the possible consequences of the greed, complacency, and rigid class divisions of present society. Wells here is satirizing both the society in which he grew up (the stratification of the country house in which his mother was housekeeper) and the effete but prosperous societies that utopians such as William Morris foresaw in the near future. The effect is to make sense of man's possible future, since this future appears as the outcome of social choices made in the present. It may be questioned whether the same logic applies to the final scenes, where the progressive extinction of all higher forms of life as a result of planetary cooling is an unforgettable expression of cosmic pessimism. In theory it is possible for mankind to avoid the fate reserved for life on Earth—by migrating into space—but this possibility is not mentioned in the story. Rather, the vision of implacable biological necessity confronting man fulfills the prophetic intimations that came upon the Time Traveller as he gazed, fascinated, upon the "winged sphinx" at the moment of his entry into the world of 802,701:

> A colossal figure, carved apparently in some white stone, loomed indistinctly beyond the rhododendrons through the hazy downpour. But all else in the world was invisible.... It chanced that the face was towards me; the sightless eyes seemed to watch me; there was the faint shadow of a smile on its lips. It was greatly weather-worn, and that imparted an unpleasant suggestion of disease. *I stood looking at it for a little space—half a minute, perhaps, or half an hour.* It seemed to advance and to recede as the hail drove before it denser and thinner. At last I tore my eyes from it for a moment, and saw that the hail curtain had worn threadbare, and that the sky was lightening with the promise of the sun.
>
> *I looked up again at the crouching white shape, and the full temerity of my voyage came suddenly upon me.* What might appear when that hazy curtain was altogether withdrawn? What might not have happened to men? What if cruelty had grown into a common passion? What if in this interval the race had lost its manliness, and had developed into something inhuman, unsympathetic, and overwhelmingly powerful? I might seem some old-world savage animal, only the more dreadful and disgusting for our common likeness—a foul creature to be incontinently slain [my emphasis].[16]

It is only after his trancelike examination of the sphinx that the Time Traveller is able to make out any other details of the future world. (It is notable that Wells does not describe him taking his eyes off the sphinx the second time; rather, the whole landscape becomes visible behind and around the sphinx.) The statue of the sphinx is an embodiment of the awesomeness of the prophetic vision, which the Time Traveller himself experiences as "the full temerity of my voyage." His fear of finding himself in the grip of overwhelming power is not realized in the world of 802,701 (in which he appears almost godlike to the Eloi, and is able to meet the Morlocks on more or less equal terms), but in the "Further Vision," where he confronts not the descendants of humanity but the "inhuman, unsympathetic, and overwhelmingly powerful" force of entropy that is bringing about the death of the solar system. The epic quality of the story results not only from its projection of future history but also from the Time Traveller's courage in facing the evidence of mankind's futility and in bringing it back to his hearers. He is committed to observing what lies in store for humanity (although he can do no more than observe it), however appalling that knowledge may be. His personal heroism is finally proved by his readiness to embark on a second journey in time—the one from which he never returns. The ambivalence with which a more ordinary humanity must regard such heroism and such prophecy is implied by the narrator's remarks in the Epilogue:

> He, I know—for the question had been discussed among us long before the Time Machine was made—thought but cheerlessly of the Advancement of Mankind, and saw in the growing pile of civilisation only a foolish heaping that must inevitably fall back upon and destroy its makers in the end. If that is so, it remains for us to live as though it were not so. But to me the future is still black and blank—is a vast ignorance, lit at a few casual places by the memory of his story.[17]

The final phrase is a reminder of the difference between prophecy and historiography and, also, of the tentativeness that afflicts all modern epic writing (whether or not it is science-fictional), since there is always a level at which the hero's deeds seem gratuitously inflated and the narrative is "only a story." The fact is that no artist's vision today can mold his society as inescapably as Homer did his.

The Time Machine, then, is a narrative of heroism and prophecy in which the degree of dramatization exactly corresponds to the authority of the "laws of future history" that it invokes. While it is the element of dramatization that constitutes the difference between science-fictional prophecies and those of "futurology,"[18] it remains true that *The Time Machine* would not exist were it not for the anticipative and eschatological tendencies inherent in the scientific thought of Wells's time. The process of extrapolation from the present into the future reflects the basic promise of science, which is that all things can in principle be known because they are subject to "natural law." Yet it has already been argued that "anticipations" belong in the category of fictions and hypotheses, rather than in that of scientific knowledge. Logically they do not differ from models of the world based on premises admitted to be fantastic, provided that the latter models are self-consistent. The most that can be said of them is, in Isaac Asimov's words, that "sometimes such extrapolations are fairly close to what happens."[19] In addition, our response to them is often a factor in determining whether or not they are close to what happens.

Apart from simple assumptions of the order of "if this goes on," twentieth-century science fiction has two basic rational methods of projecting the future—technological determinism and evolutionism. Technological determinism is the belief that man's future will be transformed by technological innovations whose impact it is possible to predict. Evolutionism is the belief that all life is subject to irreversible change under the operation of natural laws such as the need to adapt to its environment or perish. Predictions based on these two beliefs claim the impersonal authority that comes from viewing the future as a process of natural, rather than man-made, history. Such authority, however tentative its actual foundations, has had an almost irresistible attraction for certain science fiction writers.

The basis of technological forecasting is that man's life will be materially transformed in the future as radically, if not far more radically, than it has been in the past. Evolutionism, however, suggests what must be irreparably lost in this process; whether or not mankind is destined to die out like the great dinosaurs, such prophecies invariably involve fundamental changes in the human ecology. These prospects have been explored in a growing literature of scientific anticipation, which received great impetus in the earlier twentieth century both from the work of Wells (in fiction and nonfiction) and from the popular writings of such eminent scientists as J.B.S. Haldane and J.D. Bernal. Haldane's *Daedalus: Or, Science and the Future* (1924) and Bernal's *The World, the Flesh and the Devil* (1929) are two seminal works in this tradition. In the present context, Haldane's fictional essay "The Last Judgment" (1927) will serve as a classic example of pure prophecy involving both technological determinism and evolutionism.

"The Last Judgment" is an eschatological speculation on "the most probable end of our planet as it might appear to spectators on another."[20] Haldane begins by discussing possible causes of the eventual catastrophe—the sun might become a supernova, a huge meteor might collide with the Earth, or planetary cooling might take place—but he concludes that a man-made disaster is far more likely. The disaster he envisions is an unforeseen, long-term consequence of man's greatest technological triumph—the harnessing of tidal power as an energy source—which brings about prosperity and happiness on Earth. But, as his future historian writes in what now seems a manifestation of high optimism, "it was characteristic of the dwellers on earth that they never looked more than a million years ahead, and the amount of energy available was ridiculously squandered."[21] The eventual result is that the speed of Earth's rotation begins to diminish, causing unprecedented climatic severity and the extinction of virtually all nonhuman species. Alarmed by these events, a group of humans band together and set off to colonize Venus. Disease, crime, and unhappiness reappear among them, but they also evolve new senses, one of which is a form of telepathy. Their biological development is so fast that the crew of the last projectile to reach Venus are discovered to be incapable of fertile unions with the existing colonists; as a result (and this is typical of the ruthlessness of the new Venusian breed) the latecomers are used for experimental purposes. Meanwhile, the Earth's moon splits up, and some of its fragments strike the mother planet, destroying the remnants of terrestrial humanity. The Venusians prepare to recolonize Earth as well as the remainder of the planets of the solar system, breeding specially equipped races to accomplish each task. Their eventual goal is the conquest of the whole galaxy and then—since the galaxy may not survive for more than eighty million years—of the further limits of the universe. The death of the Earth is a negligible event in this process.

The substance of Haldane's prophecy is that man faces a choice between emigration to other worlds and extinction on Earth. The prospect of galactic imperialism that he introduces at the end of "The Last Judgment"—and that is also present in Bernal and the later Wells—was simultaneously providing an "epic" subject matter for the contributors to Gernsback's and other science fiction magazines. The climax of the Wells–Alexander Korda movie *Things to Come* (1936) is one of many places in which the choice of whether or not to colonize the galaxy is posited as a fundamental parting of the ways in future history:

> PASSWORTHY: My God! Is there never to be an age of happiness? Is there never to be rest?
>
> CABAL: Rest enough for the individual man. Too much of it and too soon, and we call it death. But for MAN no rest and no ending. He must go on—conquest beyond conquest. This little planet and its winds and ways, and all the laws of mind and matter that restrain him. Then the planets about him, and at last out across immensity to the stars. And when he has conquered all the deeps of space and all the mysteries of time—still he will be beginning.[22]

Today's reader may well be tempted to moralize about the trail of destruction and sheer wastage of natural and human resources that a race spreading throughout the universe and dedicated to overcoming every challenge of the environment seems likely to leave behind it. Yet, in literary terms, one might as well lament the despoliation in the *Iliad*. In the decades before the achievement of space flight, galactic imperialism was both a credible prophecy of man's destiny and an ideal framework for the narratives of heroic conflict and resolution that are the legacy of traditional epic. The result was the proliferation of science-fictional costume drama (space opera) and the attempts by writers such as Olaf Stapledon, Arthur C. Clarke, Asimov, Heinlein, and Walter M. Miller, Jr., to create a more serious mode of future history.

Stapledon was not a professional novelist in the usual sense, and *Last and First Men* (1930), through all its inordinate length, follows the method of factual historiography. At the same time, it pioneers the projection of a cyclical history, which has become commonplace in more recent science fiction. In *Last and First Men* humanity and its descendants rise and fall no less than thirteen times. As Robert H. Canary points out in his discussion of fictive histories, cyclical theories of history serve to familiarize the future, since they entail the repetition of patterns found in the past.[23] The theme of the rise and fall of civilizations has a powerful appeal to historically minded writers; nevertheless, it deserves to be treated with some suspicion. The idea that civilizations reaching a certain stage *must* go into decline, though widespread in the post-Darwinian period, is a capitulation to antiscientific irrationalism. Though the organic analogy for society is valid for some purposes, a society is not a living organism, any more than it is factory for producing identical china dolls. The popular future histories based, for example, on Oswald Spengler's *Decline of the West* (1918)[24] express the fatalistic attitude that the future will be just like the past, if a bit more exotic—and there will be far, far more of that future—rather than anything proper to scientific speculation.

Cyclical histories such as Asimov's trilogy *Foundation* (1951–1955) and Miller's *A Canticle for Leibowitz* (1959) typically consist of a series of disjointed episodes, each introducing a new set of characters and loosely tied together by an overall theme. In *A Canticle for Leibowitz*, for example, the theme is the Catholic church's survival and preservation of fragments of knowledge through the dark ages that succeed each epoch of scientific development. The novel ends with a second nuclear Armageddon on Earth and the departure of a small group of monks in a spaceship. This closure of the cyclical history at the moment of destruction and possible new beginning is one way of ending such a story. Alternatively, as in Clarke's *Childhood's End* (1953), the story may lead to a final mystical apocalypse. (Even the physicist Bernal indulges in such an apocalypse when, in his speculative essay *The World, the Flesh and the Devil*, he speaks of humanity's "becoming masses of atoms in space communicating by radiation, and ultimately perhaps resolving itself entirely into light."[25]) Both cyclical repetition and ultimate mysticism are ways of shedding light on the "black and blank" future and serve, in fact, as a means of extending the truncated epic to what writers and publishers may consider a proper length. We have seen that technological determinism and evolutionism appear to speak to us with some certainty about the future, but in terms that are brief and cryptic in the extreme. At most, they suggest a number of crises that humanity is bound to confront in the future while saying very little about the order and combination in which these crises will occur. The actual events are bound to be drastically modified by these contextual factors. I should suggest that these considerations have a bearing on the disappointing thinness of the heavyweight histories (notably, those of Stapledon and Asimov) that have been cited. Conversely, they may also account for the excellence of some of science fiction's short stories. The epic strain in science fiction may be present to its greatest advantage where a single future crisis is portrayed with precision and economy. In stories like Clarke's "The Sentinel" (1951), Murray Leinster's "First Contact" (1945), and Clifford D. Simak's "Huddling Place" (1944), the possibilities of a future heroic age of space exploration are examined through the medium of what might be termed "epic fables."

Heinlein's early future history series is a sequence of stories and novellas, some of which are merely trivial diversions and some of which present a serious view of future crises. The two culminating stories in the sequence, "Universe" (1941) and "Common Sense" (1941), despite the banalities of their literary style (they were first published in *Astounding Science-Fiction*), are an effective portrayal of the relapse into barbarism following a mutiny aboard a spaceship on a 500-year voyage to Proxima Centauri. Several generations after the mutiny, a small group of men is able to defy the superstitious tyranny that has been established aboard the ship and to recover the knowledge of the mission's nature and purpose. Though much of these stories (reprinted as *Orphans of the Sky* [1963]) hardly bear rereading, the hero's realization that there is a universe outside the ship and his final landing with his followers on a virgin planet fleetingly capture both the strangeness of seeing things for the first time that is essential to science fiction and the noble simplicity that nineteenth-century critics associated with Homer. Here are the closing paragraphs of "Common Sense":

> The sun had crossed a sizable piece of the sky, enough time had passed for a well-fed man to become hungry—and they were not well fed. Even the women were outside—that had been accomplished by the simple expedient of going back in and pushing them out. They had not ventured away from the side of the Ship, but sat huddled against it. But their menfolk had learned to walk singly, even in open spaces. Alan thought nothing of strutting a full fifty yards away from the shadow of the Ship, and did so more than once, in full sight of the women.
>
> It was on one such journey that a small animal native to the planet let his curiosity exceed his caution. Alan's knife knocked him over and left him kicking. Alan scurried to the spot, grabbed his fat prize by one leg, and bore it proudly back to Hugh. "Look, Hugh, look! Good eating!"
>
> Hugh looked with approval. His first strange fright of the place had passed and had been replaced with a warm deep feeling, a feeling that he had come at last to his long home. This seemed a good omen.
>
> "Yes," he agreed. "Good eating. From now on, Alan, always Good Eating."[26]

This is, of course, very transparent writing. One could go through it separating the authentic primitivism of a new beginning in human history from the bogus, tribal primitivism of Heinlein's *macho* imagination. In addition, how lucky it is that this unsurveyed planet on which Hugh has made a blind landing just happens to be full of trees and juicy small animals! However, the ridiculous improbability involved is something to which Heinlein carefully draws the reader's attention. He can afford to do so, much as Wells could afford the suggestion that the Time Traveller's adventures were no more than a made-up story. "Common Sense" is a prophetic speculation about man's future that satisfies the epic requirements of realism, universality, heroic enterprise, and confrontation with forces beyond man's control. If "Universe" and "Common Sense" together make up a slim book of little over 120 pages, and if even at this length they contain a good deal of superfluous violent action, this should be taken as evidence that the one aspect of the traditional epic that science fiction does not inherit is its amplitude—except in the forms of romantic costume drama and, as well shall see, parody.

Orphans of the Sky and similar works may be used to exemplify one of the classic modes of science fiction: the truncated epic based on the prospect of galactic imperialism, and its associated themes of leaving Earth, colonizing the planets, and meeting with aliens. It remains to be noted that early twentieth-century optimism about the conquest of the universe has now receded, so that these themes can no longer be successfully treated with the epic simplicity that Heinlein found possible. The urge to write the epitaph of the space age is strong in such influential writers of the 1960s as Kurt Vonnegut, Jr., J.G. Ballard, and even perhaps Stanislaw Lem. Both Vonnegut in *The Sirens of Titan* (1959) and Ballard in many of his stories offer deliberate parodies of the future history. Ballard's "Thirteen to Centaurus" (1962) is a neat reversal of *Orphans of the Sky*, in which a precocious adolescent on board a multigenerational spaceship manages to deduce, not only that there is a world outside the ship, but also that "outside" is not deep space but a psychological laboratory on Earth. The simulated space voyage began as a courageous experiment to provide the necessary data for actual voyages; after two generations, during which public opinion has decisively turned against the space program, it has turned into an embarrassing anachronism. As one of the psychologists monitoring the experiment reflects, "What began as a grand adventure of the spirit of Columbus, has become a grisly joke."[27] The joke is at the expense not only of the brainwashed crew—and of the psychologists who believe that men can be kept in ignorance indefinitely—but also of galactic imperialism as a whole. In this and other stories Ballard deliberately takes the form of the truncated epic and turns it inside out.

When the old epics lost their primary authority over their readers, they gave rise to the various modes of mock epic, comic epic, satire, and burlesque. Lucian's *True History*, the earliest surviving narrative of interplanetary travel, begins as a parody of the *Iliad* and the *Odyssey*. In recent years, comic fantasy has become a prominent science-fictional mode; one thinks not only of *The Sirens of Titan* but as well of Italo Calvino's *Cosmicomics* (1965) and of the seemingly inexhaustible episodes of Lem's *The Cyberiad* (1965) and *The Star Diaries* (1957–1971). Other recent science fiction shows not so much an inversion of the epic mode as its fusion with different generic elements. The representative science fiction novels of the 1960s and 1970s are, by and large, not future histories but stories of parallel worlds created by changing or simply stepping outside man's actual historical world. Philip K. Dick's *The Man in the High Castle* (1962) and Kingsley Amis's *The Alteration* (1976) are well-known examples of this mode, but, at a more complex level, there is Lem's *Solaris* (1961), in which the development of the science of Solaristics is analogous to, rather than being a plausible extension of, present-day scientific thought. *Solaris* is a "novel including history," but the history is that of an alternative future in which the unique and remarkable qualities of a simple, remote planet have become a human obsession. The Solaris ocean is a "godlike" being at least to the extent that it makes mysterious interventions in human lives. Epic heroism enters the novel through Kelvin's struggle (which may or may not be successful) to conquer his scientific and emotional immaturity and to carry on the work of his great predecessors in Solaristics. The ending of the novel, in which he at last completes his long voyage from Earth by landing on the surface of the alien planet, is epic both in its dramatization of Kelvin's bold decision to stay on Solaris and in its prophetic intimation that "the time of cruel miracles was not past."[28] Yet, although *Solaris* thus ends with a prophecy, it is one with no more than a distant analogical relationship to scientific anticipation in the world in which we live.

Science fiction since the end of the 1950s has become more self-conscious, more freely speculative, and more intellectually ambitious. It would be tempting to think that its Homeric primary epics might now give way to secondary epics. Yet I suspect that a more fruitful approach—which I have no space to develop here—would be to examine a contemporary masterpiece such as *Solaris* as an intriguing combination of epic, fable, romance, and parody elements. The argument of this essay has been that epic science fiction has arisen where writers have most responded to those scientific anticipations that may be studied in the literature of so-called popular science.[29] Where such anticipations seem likely to affect the whole of man's future—even though they can do no more than to illumine a few casual places in the blackness and blankness of that future—science fiction has responded by dramatizing them in the form of the truncated epic.

Afterword

In 1979, Jimmy Carter was President and America was a remarkably benign place to spend an exchange year, an experience unforgettably captured in David Lodge's comic novel *Changing Places* (1975). *Star Wars* and *Close Encounters of the Third Kind* (1977) had just been released: America was science fiction. It was also, for a British professor like myself, a country where you could actually *teach* science fiction alongside Shakespeare, Milton, and other literary giants. In the University of Illinois's English Department, I was giving my second science fiction course (the first was at Concordia University in 1977). I felt part of the new wave in literary studies, and the book I was writing, published the following year, was *Science Fiction: Its Criticism and Teaching* (1980).

A new wave, yes, but one that still sought justification in the eyes, and to some extent the terms, of the old. Hence, perhaps, "Science Fiction as Truncated Epic." Cultural Studies was only just beginning, and the inclusion of sf in the curriculum seemed to demand some fairly strenuous intellectual and aesthetic justification. Although this artform was popular and hugely influential, that was not sufficient. A few years earlier, a student of mine at Cambridge (who later did Cultural Studies under Stuart Hall at Birmingham) had been widely quoted in the British press complaining, "My supervisor wants me to read Pope. I want to read comics." I was the hapless supervisor.

"Science Fiction as Truncated Epic," then, seeks to outline what in those days—following Suvin and, before him, Frye—we would have called a "poetics" of sf. (Suvin's "cognitive estrangement" theory was first advanced in his referenced essay "On the Poetics of the Science Fiction Genre.") My decision to emphasize sf's epic qualities was in conscious reaction against Frye's categorization of it as romance, together with all-too-familiar promotions of the genre as "modern mythology" motivated by the "sense of wonder." Admittedly, I carefully argued that sf was best understood through a series of overlapping perspectives, of which the epic was only one; but I felt (and still feel) most strongly attracted to the epic form and the genre's relationship to literary prophecy. What strikes me as questionable today is not the value and significance of epic science fiction, but whether—and, if so, why—its epic form should preferably be "truncated."

I now find it telling that I was so quick to condemn the "mindless reiteration" of the term "epic" on paperback covers and movie posters in the 1970s: there was no mention of *Close Encounters*, and *Star Wars* was (correctly) dismissed as romance. In retrospect, "Science Fiction as Truncated Epic" can be criticized as an essay in aesthetic rationalization, making a literary virtue out of the material necessities that determined the evolution of sf at two specific periods in its history. The first was the late nineteenth century, with the collapse of three-volume novels and sudden arrival of mass literacy in Britain; the second was America's "Golden Age," characterized by sf's reliance on, and eventual emergence from, the pulp magazine market. I acknowledged these material conditions, citing, for example, Locke's pioneering essay "Wells in Three Volumes?" (1976), which clearly influenced my approach. I should also have given Locke's subtitle, "A Sketch of British Publishing in the 19th Century." (The fact that an article with this subtitle appeared in *Science-Fiction Studies* suggests the extent to which, like sf, the discipline of publishing history then was also marginalized. Subsequently it became more mainstream and is now commonly known as "book history," a highly prejudicial term of relation to sf.)

In the late nineteenth century, Wells and most of his contemporaries established themselves as professional writers by their readiness to enter the market for short stories and magazine fiction. Even *The Time Machine*, originally a newspaper serial, was (as I noted) only 30,000 words long in its book version. To describe *The Time Machine* as Wells's first novel (like one recent critic) is anachronistic and therefore misleading. It is worth repeating Locke's conclusion: "I see Wells' science fiction as the product of the publishing trends of his time. Wells in three volumes? I shudder to think of the alternate universe where that might be so."[30] With that sentence Locke moves abruptly from the material to the aesthetic level, a move that "Science Fiction as Truncated Epic" seeks to justify with its claim that "Wells was exploiting a newly-won freedom to publish short fiction rather than being forced to confine himself to a certain length."

The fiction of "Golden Age" writers like Asimov, Clarke, and Heinlein was equally molded by material necessities. Nowadays I would want to look closely at the process of "novelization" by which, typically in the early 1950s, magazine stories were expanded and rewritten to reach what would be seen as their "classic" form at the length demanded by the new paperback market. As I discovered recently in relation to Ray Bradbury's *Fahrenheit 451* (1953), the processes of composition that went into even the best-known sf novels of this time are still far from being exhaustively researched: a mixture of publishing history with close textual comparison and scrutiny is needed. In "Truncated Epic" I identify some specific weaknesses (cyclical repetition and the retreat into mysticism) that may have been introduced in the process of novelization, and argue that the prophetic impact of sf is necessarily weakened when stories are prolonged. Implicitly, prophecy is necessarily cryptic, on the Delphic model, with the most powerful prophetic fiction taking the form of "epic fables," but that position needs—to say the least—a fuller defense than I could give it when writing this essay.

By that time, the period of novelization was long past and publishers were happy to commission sf novels at lengths that in an earlier age would have more than justified publication in three volumes. I see this as aesthetically damaging since it tends to compromise sf's epic ambitions. There are, of course, any number of counterexamples a hostile critic could cite; the one I find most challenging is Kim Stanley Robinson's *Mars* novels (1992–1996) which actually do form a trilogy. Yet—since my definition of prophetic sf excludes speculations about the very near future—the theory of "truncated epic" does not, strictly speaking, apply to this trilogy. Robinson's "first hundred" colonists reach Mars in 2027; the trilogy ends in 2212. To add to the sense of temporal imminence, both here and elsewhere Robinson invokes the device of increased longevity to allow the same characters to bear witness to changes occurring over more than a hundred years. In other future histories such as Clarke's *3001: The Final Odyssey* (1997), cryonics is used to the same effect. The typical sf portrayal of the next millennium (as I argued in a 2003 essay) shows the "intermediate future" as a time of prolonged stasis rather than the almost unimaginable changes we would be wise to expect.[31]

Finally, if writing "Truncated Epic" today, I would use terms such as "humanity" and "humankind" instead of the generic "man" which I inherited from the scientific enlightenment—the species term flagged up for what are now seen as ideological reasons by Wells, Darwin, Haldane, and others who inspired the notion of scientific prophecy underlying the truncated epic. In 1979 the feminist critique of language had yet to make its mark. I also wish to record a specific linguistic debt, to the late George Guffey, who suggested the word "truncated," having heard my original paper at the Eaton Conference under a slightly different title. It is to George, and those other colleagues who made my brief trip from the depths of the Midwestern winter to Riverside, California, in February 1979 an unforgettable and (dare I say it?) epic experience, that I would now rededicate this essay.

Notes

1. Northrop Frye, *Anatomy of Criticism* (Princeton: Princeton University Press, 1957), 49.
2. Darko Suvin, "On the Poetics of the Science Fiction Genre," 1972, *Science Fiction: A Collection of Critical Essays*, ed. Mark Rose (Englewood Cliffs, NJ: Prentice-Hall, 1976), 57–71.
3. Ezra Pound, quoted in Paul Merchant, *The Epic* (London: Methuen, 1971), 1.
4. Gillian Beer, *The Romance* (London: Methuen, 1970), 8.
5. Robert Louis Stevenson, *Memories and Portraits* (London: Heinemann, 1924), 122.
6. For myth criticism, see Frye; for examples of literary structuralism, see Vladimir Propp, *Morphology of the Folktale*, 1928, trans. Lawrence Scott (Bloomington: Indiana University Press, 1958), and, in an American context, John G. Cawelti, *Adventure, Mystery, and Romance* (Chicago: Chicago University Press, 1976).
7. See Robert H. Canary, "Science Fiction as Fictive History," *Extrapolation*, 16:1 (December, 1974), 81–95, an article I have found particularly useful.
8. Robert A. Heinlein, "Science Fiction: Its Nature, Faults and Virtues," *The Science Fiction Novel: Imagination and Social Criticism*, ed. Basil Davenport (Chicago: Advent, 1959), 22.
9. H.G. Wells, "Fiction About the Future," typescript, Wells Collection, University of Illinois Library. Unpublished talk broadcast over Australian radio, December 29, 1938.
10. George Lukács, *The Theory of the Novel*, trans. Anna Bostock (London: Merlin, 1971), 46, 78–81.
11. Lukács, *The Historical Novel*, trans. Hannah and Stanley Mitchell (London: Merlin, 1969), 63.
12. Lukács, *The Historical Novel*, 189.
13. See Mark R. Hillegas, "Second Thoughts on the Course in Science Fiction," *Science Fiction: The Academic Awakening*, ed. Willis E. McNeely, supplement to *CEA Critic*, 37 (November, 1974), 17.
14. Wells, *The Time Machine* (1895; London: Heinemann, 1949), 90.
15. See George Locke, "Wells in Three Volumes? A Sketch of British Publishing in the 19th Century," *Science-Fiction Studies*, 3:3 (November, 1976), 282–286.
16. Wells, *Time Machine*, 30–32.
17. Wells, *Time Machine*, 143–144.
18. See Charles Elkins, "Science Fiction Versus Futurology: Dramatic Versus Rational Models," *Science-Fiction Studies*, 6:1 (March, 1979), 20–31.
19. Isaac Asimov, quoted in John Huntington, "Science Fiction and the Future," *Science Fiction: A Collection of Critical Essays*, 165.
20. J.B.S. Haldane, *Possible Worlds and Other Essays* (London: Chatto and Windus, 1927), 292.
21. Haldane, 295.
22. Wells, *Things to Come* (New York: Macmillan, 1935), 154–155.

23. Canary, 85.

24. See R.D. Mullen, "Blish, Van Vogt, and the Uses of Spengler," *Riverside Quarterly*, 3 (August, 1968), 172–186.

25. J.D. Bernal, *The World, the Flesh and the Devil* (1929; London: Cape Editions, 1971), 46.

26. Heinlein, *Orphans of the Sky* (1963; New York: Berkley, 1970), 127–128.

27. J.G. Ballard, "Thirteen to Centaurus," 1962, *The Best Short Stories of J.G. Ballard* (New York: Holt, Rinehart and Winston, 1978), 159.

28. Stanislaw Lem, *Solaris*, 1961, trans. Joanna Kilmartin and Steve Cox (London: Arrow, 1973), 204.

29. For further discussion of the literature of scientific anticipation, and a brief bibliography, see Parrinder, "Science Fiction and the Scientific World-View," *Science Fiction: A Critical Guide*, ed. Parrinder (London: Longman, 1979), 67–88.

30. Locke, 286.

31. Parrinder, "'You Must Have Seen a Lot of Changes': Fiction beyond the Twenty-first Century," *Envisioning the Future: Science Fiction and the Next Millennium*, ed. Marleen Barr (Middletown, CT: Wesleyan University Press, 2003), 173–190.

Dialogues Concerning Human Understanding

Empirical Views of God from Locke to Lem

(1979 Eaton Conference)

Stephen W. Potts

Science fiction, as a genre, has traditionally supplied its readers with plenty of confrontations with the unknown; indeed, there would be little to science fiction without them. Like science itself, however, science fiction has also traditionally had a low tolerance for that which remains unknown. Most readers of science fiction expect, and receive, answers to all questions raised; most science fiction, true to its roots in scientific empiricism, presents the triumph of human reason over the irrational, the alien, the mysterious, the initially mind-boggling. To treat of the unknowable, to raise more questions than one can answer, has been the conventional territory of the philosophical and literary mainstream. Yet even general relativity is in part an admission of the limitations of human knowledge. As cosmologists strain to translate the story the quasar tells and as physicists seek the ultimate order of all things in the elusive subnuclear realm of the quark, an old question resurrects: is there a limit to what human reason can known and do? Can man understand the nature and purpose of the cosmos, or through reason achieve unity with what has historically been known as God?

Stanislaw Lem deals with these very questions in a number of his works, the best known of which is *Solaris* (1961). The ostensible plot of *Solaris* concerns a small group of men on a scientific station orbiting the planet Solaris, which is covered, inhabited one could say, by an organic "ocean" that regularly manifests indications of intelligence and self-direction, the most recent of which, and the one that motivates the plot, is its incarnating in humanoid form the subconscious guilts of those on the station. In the case of the narrator, Kris Kelvin, that means the unshakable presence of his young wife, Rheya, who killed herself years before as a result of Kelvin's withdrawing love from her. But this plot is in fact only a metaphor for the theme of the work, which weaves overtly in and out of the chapters.

At three points in the course of events, the narrator seeks answers—refuge—in the station library, where he explores the tomes that record the century-long history of Solaristics. What unfolds is a pathetic account of humanity's endeavor to understand the utterly alien life form of the planet, of man's struggle to achieve that consummate cosmic goal—Contact. But the Crusade is frustrated time and time again; new theories of the ocean's nature and behavior give way to new disillusionments when they prove false, and humankind's attitude toward Solaris and Solaristics gradually evolves from empirical curiosity to mystified reverence to cynical despair. There remains little question that the endeavor is doomed, hopeless. Lem also leaves little doubt as to why.

The first broad clue appears in a conversation between Kelvin and the Solarist Dr. Snow, when the latter is informing Kelvin about the subconscious origins of the visitors sent by the ocean. Dr. Snow is old, a longtime resident of the station, driven to cynicism and alcohol by the latest turn of events and by the overall failure of Solaristics to accomplish its original goal. As he tells Kelvin, "We don't want to conquer the cosmos; we simply want to extend the boundaries of the Earth to the frontiers of the cosmos.... We think of ourselves as the Knights of the Holy Contact. This is another lie. We are only seeking Man. We have no need of other worlds. We need mirrors."[1]

However, it is throughout the various histories and texts that Kelvin studies that the reasons for humanity's inability to understand the ocean—to achieve Contact—are most explicitly set forth. Man insists on viewing the ocean with the reflective lens of anthropomorphism. During his researches Kelvin refers to "our compulsion to superimpose analogies with what we know" and to "giving way to the temptations of a latent anthropomorphism" in describing the ocean's behavior. At one point, after reviewing in one text several attempts of scientists to comprehend the complex abstractions constantly created from the ocean's surface in terms of terrestrial forms, he notes, "There was no escaping the impressions that grew out of man's experience on earth. The prospects of Contact receded" (132).

These conclusions are underlined and elaborated upon in a pamphlet Kelvin later comes across, the work of one eccentric autodidact named Grastrom, who asserts that all of humanity's most abstract achievements in science, such as the theory of relativity, have been no more than projections of our own physiological limitations. Therefore, man could never truly understand anything in the cosmos beyond himself, and "there neither was, nor could be, any question of 'contact' between mankind and any nonhuman civilization" (178). Yet, despite the growing awareness of Solarists and of the human species in general that the hopes of eventual contact are fruitless. despite the metaphysical pain that results from that knowledge, the endeavor to understand the ocean of Solaris doggedly, if much less enthusiastically, continues.

Contact in fact, is less a scientific than a religious goal. One of the more cynical Solarists that Kelvin reads and explains to us is Muntius, who describes Solaristics as "the space era's equivalent of religion" or "faith described as science." As evidence, he points to a number of parallels between the two—the refusal of Solarists to acknowledge arguments that undermine the foundation of their belief, the effort to discover in the ocean some body of ultimate meaning that is by its nature untranslatable in human terms, and thus incommunicable. In Kelvin's paraphrase, "unconsciously it is Revelation itself that they expect, and this revelation is to explain to them the meaning of the destiny of man! Solaristics is a rival of longvanished myths, the expression of mystical nostalgias which men are unwilling to confess openly. The cornerstone is deeply entrenched in the foundations of the edifice: it is the hope of Redemption" (180).

Originally, Kelvin notes, still paraphrasing Muntius, Contact, which Solarists had always avoided defining, was to be a beginning. Over the years it had become an end in itself—"the Mission of Mankind." The tragedy of Solaristics, and the theme of the novel, is that though everyone loves a mystery, human nature cannot bear one that insists on remaining a mystery.

A similar theme threads through another of Lem's novels. In *The Investigation* (1959), Scotland Yard is given the task of explaining the apparent resurrections of a number of corpses in a particular region of the English countryside. The inspectors assume, logically, that a human perpetrator is behind the disappearance of the bodies and then attempt, through logic, to make the empirical facts fit their conclusion. Even when it seems clear that no human being could have committed the alleged crimes, the obvious supernatural conclusion remains impossible to accept. Refusing to believe in miracles, the protagonist, Inspector Gregory, goes so far as to assign the behavior of the corpses to an intelligent microbe, "a microbe with the ability to think ahead the way a human being does."[2] Finally, Gregory conspires with his superior to explain away the "crimes" as the work of a truck driver who had, conveniently, died in an accident shortly after the incidents ceased. In other words, if the facts do not permit an anthropocentric conclusion, create one.

No image better sums up the novel's theme than that in which Gregory, wandering through London in search of explanations, stumbles into a shopping arcade where he confronts a dark figure that will not let him pass. On the verge of violence, he suddenly realizes he is facing a mirror in a dead end; the figure is his own reflection. Ultimately, all Man can know is Man.

It should be clear that the questions raised by the investigation, as by the failure of Solaristics, go much beyond the novels themselves. Indeed, these questions—the limitations of human reason and its capability to comprehend God, the supernatural, the Absolute—have preoccupied metaphysicians and theologians in one form or another since the Hellenic dawn of Western philosophy and with specific reference to empiricism since the beginning of the scientific age in the seventeenth century. In fact, in these works, and in *Solaris* in particular, Lem adds another chapter to a dialogue that finds its source among such philosophers as John Locke and David Hume and that comes to us after centuries of alternating belief, skepticism, paradox, and dispute.

In his afterword to the Berkley edition of *Solaris*, Darko Suvin provides the reader with a helpful overview of Lem's philosophical roots and suggests his interest in seventeenth- and eighteenth-century thought. It is no coincidence that during those centuries empirical materialism first flourished, challenging the long-accepted faiths of Christian idealism.

The empiricists themselves resisted identification with skepticism and atheism, attempting to prove through their new rationalism the existence of God and the inherent presence of a recognizable moral order in the universe. In *An Essay Concerning Humane Understanding* (1689), Locke argued that knowledge depended on the evidence of the senses, on the impressions of solid facts and observations on the human mind. Like his immediate predecessor René Descartes, however, he bent his thesis somewhat in order to prove the existence of the Deity. Locke asserted: "To show, therefore, that we are capable of *knowing*, i.e., being certain that there is a God, and *how we may come by* this certainty, I think we need go no further than *ourselves*, and that undoubted knowledge of our own existence."[3] He offered as proof that man and creation could not exist—and the evidence of our senses manifestly demonstrates that these do exist—without a preexisting Absolute, since to imagine something created from nothing is absurd; and this preexisting something has to be a reasoning being because man is a reasoning being and could not have been created by matter insensate. Locke, therefore, using his empirical method, managed to create God once again in man's image, utilizing the impressions that have grown out of man's experience on Earth.

Less than a century later, Hume carried the discussion forward in his *Dialogues Concerning Natural Religion* (1779). In this work the spokesman for empiricism, who ultimately receives the narrator's stamp of approval, defends himself against two disputants, one a Platonic idealist left over from the earlier Age of Faith and the other a skeptic doubting the capabilities of human reason. The empirical position as stated here is that the order of the universe can be inferred from the order of the human mind, that the laws by which the cosmos operates are much the same as those one can observe in operation on Earth, and that the characteristics of the Deity are evident in the highest ideals and noblest qualities of man. The idealist argues that God and the cosmos are beyond the ken of mere mortals, since human understanding is earthbound and therefore flawed. The reply of the skeptic to the empiricist is even more pointed. After insisting that man and all he knows on Earth is only one tiny portion of the universe and not the model for the whole of it, he inquires, "Why select so minute, so weak, so bounded a principle as the reason and design of animals is found to be on his planet? What peculiar privilege has this little agitation of the brain which we call *thought*, that we must thus make it the model of the whole universe?" And he asks, "Is there any reasonable ground to conclude, that the inhabitants of other planets possess thought, intelligence, reason, or anything similar to these faculties in men?" and later, with reference to God, "And will any man tell me with a serious countenance, that an orderly universe must arise from some thought or art, like the human; because we have experience of it?"[4]

Throughout the *Dialogues* the skeptic and the idealist are frequently able to agree on the remoteness and incomprehensibility of God. In the opinion of both, the major philosophical sin of the empiricist is his anthropomorphic view of God and the universe. Even though, with many reservations, the skeptic ultimately concedes "that the cause or causes of order in the universe probably bear some remote analogy to human intelligence," he still maintains that his empirical opponent is an "anthropomorphite" (94). The skeptic argues his point well and the charge seems to stick. Even the narrator must accord some wisdom to the skeptic's position when the dialogue ends. Yet, as we know empirical materialism, anthropocentric though it was, eventually triumphed, making our age of science possible while carrying its anthropocentrism with it.

Platonic idealism, which had retired in defeat from Hume's work. nevertheless had not given up the struggle. A century after the *Dialogues*, it went on the offensive again in the metaphysics of Søren Kierkegaard, whose *Fear and Trembling* (1843) explored the limitations of human understanding in confronting the mysteries of the divine. Written in part as a reply to two Hegelian materialists of his own day, *Fear and Trembling* is built around the Old Testament tale in which God, to test the faith of the patriarch Abraham, commands him to sacrifice his son Isaac. Kierkegaard repeatedly points out that by any human ethical standard God's request is outrageous, wholly offensive to any concepts of right and good, and that Abraham, in demonstrating his willingness to obey, shows himself by human standards an infanticide and an immoral beast. But he makes clear that human standards are not divine standards and that, in exercising his faith despite the horrified awareness of what he is doing, Abraham proves himself the holiest of men. Because of the absolute nature of the Deity, an absoluteness implicit by definition in the concept of deity, human understanding can only fall hopelessly short; the more the human mind attempts to comprehend the ultra-Platonic divine will through rational means, the further it will find itself enmeshed in paradox, since the Absolute is not accessible to human reason. Thus, Kierkegaard concludes, man, if he wishes to be one with the meaning and purpose of the universe, must embrace the irrational, the paradoxical, the absurd; he must take a "leap of faith" over and beyond reason.

If this leap was difficult for thinkers in Kierkegaard's time—a fact manifested as well in the work of Herman Melville and of Fyodor Dostoyevsky—it had become virtually impossible by the beginning of the twentieth century. Nowhere is the resultant metaphysical angst better expressed than in the morose, complex work of Franz Kafka. An avid reader of Kierkegaard, Kafka pursued theological paradox in his parables and longer fiction. While much controversy continues to permeate Kafka criticism, there remains little doubt that the religious content of Kafka's work, if not the sole aspect of it, is at least an important one. Some have gone so far as to see in Kafka's two major novels, *The Trial* (1925) and *The Castle* (1926), the individual's pursuit of, respectively, divine justice and divine grace. The already complicated works are made even more problematic by the fact that neither was finished. Kafka's parables, however, may provide some clue to the meanings of these novels.

One central concern is best demonstrated by the parable *Vor dem Gesetz*, translatable as "Before the Law" or "Before the Court," which appears near the climax of *The Trial*. It relates the history of a man who comes to the gateway of absolute authority only to find his ingress blocked by a stern and sturdy gatekeeper. The man tries to reason with the guard, but repeatedly fails to get permission to pass. He cannot overpower the guard, who warns that, even if the man could, there are many gates beyond, each with a mightier gatekeeper than the last. The man, wanting nothing but to enter the Court of the Law, spends his lifetime alongside the gate, unable to persuade the gatekeeper or even the fleas in his fur collar. The gatekeeper himself becomes the sole object of the man's attentions, and all beyond the gate is forgotten. At his death the man is told by the guard that this entrance was meant only for him, and with that the guard closes it.

Of similar import is the parable "An Imperial Message," in which the Emperor, the bright Imperial sun, has sent a message to the reader, the most microscopic of his subjects, from his deathbed. The message, of singular, even divine, importance, is whispered into the ear of his strongest and most trusted messenger, who makes his way through the crowd that jams the Emperor's chamber. But after forging his way through one crowd, he has to confront a crowd in the next chamber, and another in the one after that. And even if he can get through the chambers of the innermost palace, he still has to fight his way through stairways and courtyards, then still another palace. And if after the sands of years he has managed the impossible and arrived at the outermost gate, he still has the overflowing throngs of the capital city to push through. The message can never reach its destination across so many insurmountable barriers.

In both parables the goal—ultimate understanding, presumably of the cosmos—is frustrated by the presence of man-made or manlike barriers, gates and gatekeepers, walls and courtyards. In the novels these serial obstacles are created by bureaucracies of infinite complexity, consisting of layer upon layer of officials, clerks, messengers, servants, and other human operatives; in each the protagonist barely gets beyond the first obstruction before his strength gives out or he is defeated. In both parables the walls, the gates, and the bureaucracies established to protect the Truth finally prevent anyone from reaching it. Unable to comprehend the cosmos, yet unable to abandon that quest, man reaches an impasse; his striving for redemption degenerates into a hopeless struggle with a single human obstacle—a stubborn guard or an apathetic clerk.

One of the strongest arguments posed in opposition to the religious interpretation of Kafka's novels is that the institutions supposedly embodying divine law and acceptance are disgustingly corrupt, venal, and all too fallibly human. The metaphysical critics have fallen back on Kierkegaard, pointing up the ethical distinctions he makes between the unknowable laws by which the Deity operates and the moral laws of man. But it is more likely that Kafka's bureaucracies, mistaken by humanity for the Absolute, are in fact merely human constructs, paradigms of man's reason.

Unfortunately, in recreating the universe in his own image and in modeling the Truth on the machinations of his own mind, man has unwittingly sacrificed his ability to make Kierkegaard's "leap of faith." Unable to transcend empirical anthropocentrism, man is left with unfulfilled hopes and the endless, doomed continuation of the search. For—and herein lies the source of much of Kafka's angst—the hope and the search continue, must continue, though they become ends in themselves and lead ultimately to despair, defeat, and death.

Kafka remains a part of the literary soil of Eastern Europe; in Poland he is, in fact, now celebrated as a master of the absurd.[5] A number of scholars have noted his influence on Lem,[6] particularly in regard to *Memoirs Found in a Bathtub* (1961), which depicts a man struggling through a multilayered bureaucracy called "the Building" in pursuit of his Mission, primarily trying to discover what it is. Official after official thwarts the agent; clerk after clerk delays him. He stumbles from level to level, room to room, every step leading him further from the goal of ultimate comprehension, of understanding his role in the order of things—or the order of things itself. Certain scenes and images come directly out of Kafka. For instance, when one secretary refuses him immediate entry to an important official, the narrator must wait in the outer office. Following repeated subsequent refusals, he commences pleading with her, plying her with questions and confessions, at one point screaming into her indifferent ear. Eventually, he has no choice but to give up and go elsewhere. This secretary is by no means the only gatekeeper in the novel; indeed, one character is even called Gatekeeper. Yet at the end, despite the agent's repeated failures, despite everything he suffers, he discovers that "against, entirely against, my better knowledge—I still held on to my faith—like a last hope, a hope against hope—in that accursed, that thrice accursed Mission of mine."[7] Though defeated by the indecipherable snarl of contradictions and paradoxes, by the flawed constructs of humankind's pretentious rationality, he finds himself unable to discontinue his search for purpose.

Attempting to achieve redemption, to comprehend the ultimate purpose and meaning of the universe, Lem's Solarists have met the same fate as the seeker in *Memoirs Found in a Bathtub* and for the same reason: the imperfect nature of human reason. Yet, in the closing chapter of *Solaris*, Kelvin perhaps finds a solution to this problem. With Rheya and the other visitors finally gone, Kelvin engages in philosophical discussion with the weary Snow. They consider the possibility that the ocean may be an imperfect god, a supernatural child just learning to handle its power. Darko Suvin takes the suggestion seriously; David Ketterer observes that it is probably just one more anthropomorphic theory.[8] Kelvin insists, however, that his imperfect god is neither the ocean nor another reflection of man; it is, instead, "the only god I could imagine believing in, a god whose passion is not a redemption, who saves nothing, fulfills no purpose—a god who simply is" (206).

To understand the nature of this god as Lem intends it to be understood, one must turn—as with Kafka—to one of the author's shorter parables. In "The Twenty-First Voyage" of Ijon Tichy in Lem's *The Star Diaries* (1957–1971), the planet-hopping protagonist comes upon a community of robot friars living in catacombs under a world in which all logical support for belief has been made impossible by the infinite possibilities of science. For centuries this planet's humanity, like our own empiricists, had endeavored "to accumulate arguments and proofs for God's existence and, when those inevitably crumble, to take the bits and chips and raise them up anew."[9] But the more empirical knowledge and material power one accumulates, as the mechanical prior points out, the further away God becomes. Reason and faith are irreconcilable, and the former cannot be used to strengthen the latter.

The robots believe simply because "belief is the only thing that cannot be taken from a conscious entity, so long as that entity consciously cleaves to it." Their faith is "completely naked ... and completely defenseless." According to the prior, "We entertain no hopes, make no demands, requests, we count on nothing, we only believe" (230). And a passage of striking significance follows:

> If someone believes for certain reasons and on certain grounds, his faith loses its full sovereignty; that two and two are four I know right well and therefore need not have faith in it. But of God I know nothing, and therefore can only have faith. What does this faith give me? By the ancient reckoning, not a blessed thing. No longer is it the anodyne for the dread of extinction, no longer the heavenly courtier lobbying for salvation and against damnation. It does not allay the mind tormented by the contradictions of existence; it does not smooth out those edges; I tell you—it is worthless! Which means it serves no end. We cannot even declare that this is the reason we believe, because such faith reduces to absurdity: he who would speak thus is in effect claiming to know the difference—permanently between the absurd and the not absurd, and has himself chosen the absurd because, according to him, that is the side on which God stands. We do not argue this. Our act of faith is neither supplicating nor thankful, neither humble nor defiant, it simply is, and there is nothing more that can be said about it [224–225].

The faith of the robot friars pointedly counters empiricism's anthropocentric dependence on logic and reason and the Kierkegaardian idealist's pridefully humble surrender to the absurd.

Following his experience with Solaris, and shortly before declaring his possible belief in this god, Kelvin asserts: "I shall never again give myself completely to anything or anybody.... I shall remember my follies and my hopes. And this future Kelvin will be no less worthy a man than the Kelvin of the past, who was prepared for anything in the name of an ambitious enterprise called Contact. Nor will any man have the right to judge me" (203). Like the friars, Kelvin has not necessarily renounced empiricism, but he has renounced mankind's foolish endeavor to comprehend rationally the nonhuman with human models. He has at the same time renounced the idealist's absolute god of judgment and redemption. In so doing he has avoided the despair that Kafka perceived in the unbridgeable gap between man and the Absolute; he has turned his back on the ultimate transcendence that Kierkegaard saw in God and that the Solarists saw in Contact. In fact, Kelvin much resembles Hume's skeptic, who also argues convincingly for the necessity for an imperfect God, an agnostic's God, the god of the robot friars. Having broken the tenuous link between scientific empiricism and mankind's yearning for redemption, Kelvin has cleared the way for a new kind of commitment, an open-ended commitment.

After his dialogue with Snow, Kelvin descends to the planet to meet the ocean on its own territory. Arriving on the shore of an old mimoid—a floating scab of an island—Kelvin reaches out toward an oily, organic wave. It envelops his hand without touching him—contact, but not quite. After Kelvin tries the same experiment with the same results a few times, the ocean grows indifferent and avoids his still-extended hand. Although he had read several accounts of this phenomenon, he says, "none of them had prepared me for the experience as I had lived it, and I felt somehow changed.... I had never felt the ocean's gigantic presence so strongly, or its powerful changeless silence, or the secret forces that gave the waves their regular rise and fall. I sat unseeing, and sank into a universe of inertia, glided down an irresistible slope and identified myself with the dumb, fluid colossus; it was as if I had forgiven it everything, without the slightest effort of word or thought" (210).

Having lost Rheya, his own single anthropomorphic link with the ocean, he asks himself why he should stay, probing the ocean, seeking the purpose it appears to have. "I hoped for nothing," he says. "And yet I lived in expectation. Since she was gone, that was all that remained.... I knew nothing, and I persisted in the faith that the time of cruel miracles was not past" (211). His unseeing, unreasoning identification with the ocean certainly seems like a Kierkegaardian leap of faith. But, if indeed a leap into the irrational, it is an existential leap, not in pursuit of God or the Absolute, but with a mind wholly open to all experience, with no judgments or anthropocentric conclusions preordained. Like Kafka's protagonists, Kelvin preserves his sense of expectation while understanding nothing; unlike them, but like the friars of Tichy's "Twenty-First Voyage," he hopes for nothing either. Ironically, at this point he has become the logical extrapolation of the earlier empiricism, an empty slate ready to receive the universe on its own terms, to accept—to quote the friars—"existence in its entirety," a conclusion implied long ago in the well-argued stance of the skeptic in Hume's *Dialogues*. It would not be unlike Lem's active wit to have hinted at this eventuality in a pun; like the scale of temperature that bears his name, Kelvin now begins at absolute zero.

In *Solaris*, in *The Investigation*, and more pointedly in "The Twenty-First Voyage," Lem deals directly with the issues raised by Locke, Hume, and Kierkegaard, and in terms that could only come out of a familiarity with the work and thought of these philosophers. Lem not only extrapolates—in the honored fashion of science fiction writers—from scientific theory; he calls into question the entire set of assumptions underlying any naively positivistic thought. To accept without question the empirical principles that inform our age—as so many readers and writers of science fiction have done—is to commit the sin of Solaristics and to create the universe in the image of Earth, to see in the multifarious faces of God no more than a reflection of ourselves. In going deeper into Western tradition than many modern science fiction writers are willing to go, Lem unearths a richer vein of material and, pursuant to the law of geological succession, one with sources further back in time. Lem's work reminds us that, after all, our scientific tradition grows out of our philosophical tradition.

Afterword

I produced this essay while completing my Ph.D. at the University of California, Berkeley. At the time (1979), studying science fiction was not an option in my department, although in that decade critical trends were evolving toward interdisciplinary and broader cultural interests. The popular culture of the West had long been institutionalized through the Bancroft Library, while New Historicism was newly being applied to Renaissance studies. My dissertation—in process in 1979—focused on popular American magazines of the 1920s and 1930s, but only through the lens of F. Scott Fitzgerald's career.

When approached about republishing this article, I was flattered but a little unnerved that my "best" work might have appeared so early in my academic career. After all, I have published much since then, including two other Eaton Conference papers. Upon rereading it—as I had not done for decades—I encountered such early interests as empirical philosophy and Kafka's fiction, along with my discovery of Lem and other Slavic science fiction authors. Happily the essay fulfilled the theme of that and many subsequent Eaton conferences: bridging the cultures of science and the humanities through imaginative literature. Furthermore, it laid the foundation for most of my critical career, such as my 1993 monograph on Arkady and Boris Strugatsky and my continuing interest in the cultural context of scientific ideas, especially those framed by science fiction.

In short, 38 years later, this essay remains seminal in my own theoretical approaches to literature, popular culture, and science studies.

Notes

1. Stanislaw Lem, *Solaris*, 1961, trans. Joanna Kilmartin and Steve Cox (New York: Berkley, 1971), 81. Parenthetical page references are to this edition.
2. Lem, *The Investigation*, 1959, trans. Adele Milch (New York: Avon, 1976), 111.
3. John Locke, *An Essay Concerning Humane Understanding*, 1689, ed. Alexander Campbell Fraser (1894; New York: Dover, 1959), 2:306–307.
4. David Hume, *Dialogues Concerning Natural Religion*, 1779, ed. Henry D. Aiken (New York: Hafner, 1948), 22, 34. A parenthetical page reference is to this edition.
5. Heinz Politzer, *Franz Kafka: Parable and Paradox* (Ithaca, New York: Cornell University Press, 1966), 371.
6. To mention only two: Darko Suvin, "Afterword" to *Solaris*, 222; and Jerry Jarzebski, "Stanislaw Lem, Rationalist and Visionary," *Science-Fiction Studies, Second Series*, ed. R.D. Mullen and Suvin (Boston: Gregg, 1978), 226.
7. Lem, *Memoirs Found in a Bathtub*, 1961, trans. Michael Kandel and Christine Rose (New York: Seabury, 1973), 186.
8. A brief response to Suvin's credulity appears in David Ketterer, "Solaris and the Illegitimate Suns of Science Fiction," *Extrapolation*, 14 (December, 1972), 84.
9. Lem, *The Star Diaries*, 1957–1971, trans. Michael Kandel (New York: Avon, 1977), 206. Parenthetical page references are to this edition.

The Descent of Fantasy

(1981 Eaton Conference)

Eric S. Rabkin

"All art," according to Oscar Wilde in his preface to *The Picture of Dorian Gray* (1891), "is quite useless."[1] Indeed, all the qualities especially associated with verbal art are customarily dismissed as insignificant: specious arguments are just rhetoric, popular misconceptions are only myths, and impossible longings are mere fantasies. Nonetheless, we all acknowledge the universal occurrence of stories in general and of fantasies in particular: as the ancients knew, all leadership involves force of rhetoric; every culture founds itself on its own creation myth; and fantasies include both the socializing tales of insubstantial Faery and the breathless visions of humankind's highest hopes. In the face of such ubiquity, I reaffirm the utility of art and wish to uncover at least part of what that utility might be. This subject, of course, is vast, as various as the forms of art and the myriad arenas of artistic production and consumption. And yet, if a phenomenon is universal, one supposes either parallel evolution of an extraordinary kind or descent from a common source or condition. This essay into what might be called semiobiology[2] is my initial attempt to sketch in the merest stages in the descent of fantasy. My speculations here are trials, attempts to lay out lines of inquiry and articulate areas of investigation without at this point marshaling the full data from those areas. Like Freud's primal myth, this cartoon is offered in the hope that it will draw forth debate and help in the posing of useful questions. I begin with the notion that if this fantastic story has use, as in eliciting useful questions, then other fantasies may have a use in common with it and that the telling of the story may suggest reasons why the story, and stories the world over, need to be told.

The first use of anything, or perhaps its last, is survival. The cacophony of modem biology opens every strain with random variations and ends each tune with a funeral dirge. Those of us who survive dance to whatever tune the piper plays. In social beasts, such as us, the piper's music symbolizes our most powerful tool for survival: sociality. Bees find pollen by communicating with bees, deer protect their young from lions by grazing in herds, and men defend their safe territories by pledging allegiance to a flag. While the young of sea turtles hatch alone and march wobbly legged to the sea, the offspring of primates cling to their parents and gaze into their eyes. Among the competing hordes of our ancestors, those races with the chance capacity to employ more signals more subtly held their territory best, hunted most efficiently, and beat or starved other hordes into extinction. The roaring lion coordinates the movements of his pride and holds sway over resources otherwise more easily run to ground by the swift but often solitary cheetah; the yapping canines flourish in far greater numbers—and biomass—than the stealthy felines; and the *Homo sapiens* who teaches his offspring to wield a club and circle in on prey to the sound of a beating drum defeats them all. Men, in number and in biomass, overgrow every other single species. Our groups are the most efficient groups, the largest groups, the most stable and subtle and adaptable groups, and we rule the world. The making of groups, the bringing of young into effective roles within groups, and the continual trimming of the life courses of individuals in groups make our potent sociality possible. The single most flexible tool for the creation, adjustment, and use of human groups is language. To be capable of language is to have a survival advantage; to be incapable of language is to abandon this particular field. The gorilla withdraws to ever smaller plots of Kenyan forest while our species hurls itself at the stars.

No human infant, dropped in the most equable climate, could survive alone. While this is true of some other animals, such as most primates, the interdependency of humans extends throughout life. Even the atavistic Natty Bumppo circulates about the fringes of society, tied to the rest of humanity by his need for shot and powder and, more important, his needs for companionship and sharing of values. To have been raised to human adulthood means to have been socialized, to have heard the stories of the sacrifice of one's own deity and the tales of origin of the plants one eats, to have acknowledged authority in the persons claiming your parentage, and to have chosen to take on your human mantle by speaking the formulaic words. The liar is cast out; the hypocrite is demoted; the tongue-tied are ignored; and the autistic do not reproduce at all. The greatest survival mechanism evolved by our species is sociality itself and the greatest tool evolved by our species for sociality is language.

Virtually all human functions necessary for survival are beyond much conscious control. Although we can choose one sort of food over another, few of us, in the presence of food, could or would starve to death; none of us could hold our breath to the point of death; almost all of us feel strong and frequent urges toward activity that results in tending the body and reproducing it. Most people, most of the time, succumb to these urges. In fact, human happiness seems to arise from the satisfaction of these urges to eat, to exercise, to rest, and even to tell and hear stories. I propose that such happiness is our reward for cooperating with the urges evolution has built into us. When we are tired, sleep feels good; when we are hungry, food feels good; when we are grappling with problems of understanding, storytelling and listening feels good. I am glad to be able to tell this story to you.

In larger or smaller degree, those functions crucial to our group survival, which of course include functions that preserve the individual members of the group, all employ processes of exchange among members of the group. No human being could survive long, and certainly not reproduce and raise young, outside a functioning human economy. You feed the child while I gather the berries; you draw water while I hunt for meat; you stand guard while I sleep and in turn I will later guard you. Safety is not only in numbers but in communication used to organize the relations among those separate numbers. We will exchange your child-rearing services for my berry-gathering services, your water for my meat, our guardianship for each other's. Thus through exchange is sociality reinforced repeatedly and pleasurably in the daily necessities of human life.

In fairy tales, as Max Luthi points out in *Once Upon a Time: On the Nature of Fairy*

Tales (1962), no one ever says "I love you"; instead, food is given and taken.[3] Luthi was referring to mother love, as when Red Riding Hood's mother gives her cakes and wine. But something is amiss in that story since the food is to be passed not to the child but by the child to the grandmother, that is, to the mother of the food provider. That social deformity manifests itself in Red Riding Hood's own desire to receive pleasure; she readily gives in to the wolf's suggestions that she stop and enjoy the woods. The girl's disobedience to her mother's instructions not to tarry compounds the social disorder. As the story proceeds, the consequences of this deformity grow: the girl is unsafe even in her own grandmother's house. Now the consequences of wishing oneself out of maternal control are traumatically clear; instead of eating the cakes and wine the mother gave her, the girl is in turn eaten. But social order is strong; the huntsman passes by and divines the difficulty. He slices open the wolf's belly and the girl gets the chance to be born again, this time much more obedient. In the Grimm brothers' version, "Red-Cap thought to herself, 'As long as I live, I will never by myself leave the path, to run into the wood, when my mother has forbidden me to do so.'"[4]

This small story has much to tell us. Note first that it ends in obedience, that is, in the delineation of the exchange relations between parent and child: I give you food, you give me service. This obedience is established, or more properly reestablished, against expectable pressures. Mothers do sometimes show love to others than their children; children do sometimes have desires of their own. It is normal for some human affairs to tend against obedience. This is dangerous and wrong, the story seems to say to its little child listener, but, despite initial appearances, not necessarily fatal. One can easily imagine a grandmother lulling a granddaughter to sleep with this story, assuaging the child's guilt on a day that included some single but understandable childish act of self-motivated desire. The story itself becomes a good for exchange: through the telling at the bedside, the grandmother is providing psychological pleasure in this story of heightened and then ameliorated fear; she is also providing the occasion to attend the child as sleep comes on, performing her grandmaternal guardianship. In return, the child is drawing the psychological sustenance that perhaps earlier it had been denied or feared it might lose as Red Riding Hood had to carry but not eat the cakes and wine. In drawing this sustenance, the child listener is going to sleep as requested, being a good little child, and giving due obedience. By the telling of the story, then, the child is given one more opportunity at the end of the busy day to perform the required obedience. It can fall off to sleep now secure in the knowledge that it has been good and that the big people will therefore protect it. Society and its children rest secure on a base of known relationships.

This fairy tale is hardly unique. The relationship between mother love and food exchange is common. Witches are anti-mothers and known to be witches, as in "Hansel and Gretel," by their desire not to feed children but to eat them. When Snow White's evil stepmother can express her hate and envy no other way, she feeds the girl a poisoned apple. Cinderella's role in her stepmother's house is obviously topsy-turvy since it is the child who must do the cooking for the adult. Fortunately, the fairy godmother, doubtless the spirit of the dead true mother, provides help, just as other god figures in all cultures demonstrate their parental care by providing loaves and fishes or manna or cargo or, through their own ultimate sacrifices, the seasonal renewal that is life itself, a sacrifice we participate in by retelling the god's story, by performing again the rituals of painful initiation, by taking the host into our own mouths and consuming the god in obedience to him. By this exchange, performed often with the help of such powerful tale bearers as educated priests or epileptic shamans, human sociality is extended to the fullness of the awesome universe engulfing us and thus the realm of the overpowering is made the realm of our parents and our right relation to it is defined. Through the story, we become able to sleep in comparative peace.

There are other kinds of love than mother love. Cinderella dances in the embrace of the Prince; Sleeping Beauty is awakened with a kiss; Rapunzel bears her lover twins. Put bluntly but truly, the phrase "I love you" is omitted from these stories not to be replaced by an exchange of food but by an exchange of physical contact. Seen most oppressively, the exchange of genital contact defines, at least for Susan Brownmiller,[5] a social order dependent on constant rape. I will give you my daughter if you will give me her bride-price. Seen less oppressively, the ordering of allowable exchanges of genital contact is not only the concern of these stories but of marriage rites, law, and courtship rituals—including a young couple's self-revelation through presentation of autobiographical narratives. Exchange of genital contact, like the exchange of food and guardianship, is crucial for the survival of our species and is, in our species, accomplished with and through the employment of language in general and stories in particular.

Language can be used for many purposes. Each phrase made and attended to participates in the continual jostling within the web of sociality that maintains and develops our human groups. Aggressive competition, strongly suggestive of territorial posturing, plays out the social drama through the weapons of promise and threat. Promises and threats are made of language and are exchange items. Social relations may be revealed in part by discovering whose threats have sway with whom, whose promises are relied on by whom, the nature of the reciprocity or asymmetry of those relations and so on. The king's promise and threat are the law of the land; he need rely on no one's word. The serf extends all promises of loyalty if required to do so, including even acknowledgment of the *droit du seigneur*, relying on the promise of protection and believing the threat of dissociation from the human economy by sanction or by death. Thus the hierarchy of feudal society comes in focus. Tristan is bound by his oath. Nowadays the exchange of food that means "I love you" (or is it the other way round?) does not go only from female to male and the exchange of protection marked by the marriage ring does not go only from male to female. Women often pay for men at restaurants and men often wear wedding rings. Tristan and Isolde each drank the magic love potion and created a symmetrical social order between themselves that was insupportable in the inevitable and overwhelming network of the hierarchical society they both more generally inhabited. The result was death. Tristan had no offspring.

Language obviously has exchange value. It is worth much to some people to have the right person say "I dub thee knight," "He is my friend," or "You may now kiss the bride." Unlike money or cowrie shells, however, language does not have only exchange value. The exchanges of language may be used to warn, cajole, coordinate. All of these activities, done by us to each other, keep producing our social world.

What world do we inhabit? My world, to take an example with which I am acquainted, floats tiny in the emptiness of space. Yet this was true of no one's world until 1643, the year in which Evangelista Torricelli deduced by experiment that the air around us was a local phenomenon and that most of the distance to the moon must be truly empty. How did he deduce this? I can only say by telling you what he did: he took a tube, sealed at one end and filled with mercury, and inverted it into a bath of mercury. The mercury began to flow out of the tube but then stopped, producing in the top of the tube a partial vacuum and suggesting to the early physicist that air had weight. Given this hint, he quickly discerned that the weight of air necessary to hold up the column of mercury, what we now call barometric pressure, would be produced by a column no more than five miles tall if the air did not attenuate. And the moon was known to be a quarter of a million miles away. Suddenly, nature preferred a vacuum. Outer space was discovered.

This little story, like the tale of Red Riding Hood, also has, I think, much to tell us. First, it has a human interest, the happy conjunction of accident and genius, the satisfactory correction of error. Second, it must once have—in fact did—reshape people's beliefs about the nature of their world. Aristotle's assertion that nature abhors a vacuum was dealt a hard blow. This story is the current basis for my own belief in the vacuum of space although I did not know the story until many years after I had already been taught of the vacuum. I believed my teachers and they believed their teachers, or so I suppose, back to Torricelli. This story about Torricelli explains their belief, at least to my satisfaction, and thus my sense of the world conforms to the story. Yet I must admit that I have never felt nor seen the vacuum of space nor have I ever seen Torricelli's experiment before: my belief rests on the reliance I place on the tale and on the plausibility of the tale given all else I have come to accept. It is true that so-called scientific facts take their places within a web of observations and assertions which have implications for each other and so no single experiment need be personally experienced in order to assent to science. Yet it is equally true that the vast majority of what we know we know only by report, relying on a few tests having proved true and thus having established the probable believability of individuals. When scientists are found to have distorted their results, they are fired and ostracized. Believability is not simply a matter of the truth of one's assertions but of one's place in the social fabric, a place defined by one's own experience and attested to by one's own life story. When you apply for an academic job, you send your vita—the summary of your life—before you. I did a few experiments in school, and many of them worked out much as the books said they would, but my belief in outer space really rests on my belief in the social order, a continuous and evolving thing that extends back over three centuries to Torricelli and over the eons to our mute ancestors on the ancient plains.

All explanations, I would suggest, are at bottom narrative. Not only does scientific explanation require faith in the telling but all matters of human fact are established by testimony and history. Not only will the sun rise because it has always risen but the sacred symbol will lead us to victory because it has always done so. The most immutable narratives, the explanations for the most profound aspects of our world, are told in a time out of time, the time of ever-repeatable scientific experiment and the time of myth and fairy-land; the times, in short, of permanent reality and of untouchable fantasy. We learn by conditioning: once bitten, twice shy. For a social animal, there an obvious survival advantage in being able to understand and believe someone else's experience. Events happen to us all. Language can report these events. Narrative is the exchange of the report of events. A full theory of narrative would clearly need to ask who exchanges what sorts of reports of what sorts of events with whom in what contexts for what purposes. That is a massive project; let us focus this first effort on the story at hand.

My telling the story of Torricelli does have exchange value. It may, for example by its oddity perhaps or its satisfactory resolution, strike you as a good story and hence one you are glad to have heard. That would make me, in consequence, a bit more of an individual whom you might credit, to whom you might extend believability. In addition to simple exchange value (I'll tell you a joke for five dollars) a storytelling performs other social functions. The telling may well help define the status of the teller and of the hearer in the sociality, the nature of the world beliefs they may share, and may give happiness or in some other way cooperate with some fundamental urge. The fundamental urges we might spot operating in the telling of this story are several: curiosity has survival value and so does its exercise; its assuagement by this narrative ought to give some pleasure. Order and regularity are well worth perceiving for they help us predict future conditions and hence prepare for them; stories with perceivable form assuage the desire for order. But once we have come to the idea of stories serving us by their very order, we have come to the point of suggesting that part of the true use of a story is its aesthetic value. I would suggest that the telling of proper tales, well made and rhetorically interesting tales, in a social world so dominated by language exchange as is ours, signals social success and the likelihood of social position. He who can produce good language has a constant supply of items for social exchange. Just as grebes delight potential mates with displays of plumage and acrobatics, we delight our potential mates, or curry our employers or dominate our inferiors, by displays of language. The development of an aesthetic sense has survival value and one ought to wonder little that, in varying degrees, all humans share it.

The most brutal narratives simply assert social order on the basis of that order: "Do this because I am your father" or "The law is the law." In other words, there are other words, older words that recount earlier events such as intercourse or legislation and these earlier events are to be taken to institute and explain our worlds. Yet it is not the events which institute our world but our belief in the report of the events. This belief comes in part from our experience in social exchange—we know teachers and doctors and parents are trustworthy by experience and by failure to disconfirm our earlier belief in them; this belief also comes in part from our capacity to test some of the reports against our own experience; and this belief finally comes in part from our aesthetic sense. To tell a well made story is to move up in the social scale. Priests and poets have often dominated soldiers and stonecutters. The pen, we have all said, is mightier than the sword. For a species for which the question of the well-madeness of language is and should be central to survival and reproduction, an aesthetic sense is a tool for survival. How shall we exercise that aesthetic sense?

Narratives are but one class of language as used that might be tested aesthetically, but they are a significant class. Some utterances are primarily adjunct to accomplishing physical deeds. We warn people to duck a flying object, command platoons into battle in the most deadly manner, and teach apprentices how to wield their tools. These utterances are judged in part by their well-madeness, but mostly they are judged by their effect. A vulgar, mispronounced order that nonetheless carries the day was a good order. In narratives, different sorts of events may be reported. Some of those events, like what happened when Torricelli did what to which, are testable and may be judged good or bad according to their accuracy. Such tales, however, fit less completely into the realm of physical consequence of military commands and more into the social fabric of believability. The tale might be better or worse told. Narratives that are the least susceptible to physical test must be judged most by their well-madeness. There is minimal specifiable content to the great assertions of religion, like "God is love," and there is minimal testable report in the great narratives of creation. The same is true of fairy tales. But these tales are great despite their untestability because they assuage, in a broad and powerful way, our aesthetic sense. While the theories of caloric and phlogiston are no more, the story of the Fall still touches us. In part this is so because the content accords with something in our own lives, of course, but in part because the story handles that something in ways to create potent order, aesthetic order. The more the particular, realistic content in a narrative, the more susceptible it is to disconfirmation; the less the particular, realistic content, the more its value rests on aesthetic considerations. Fantasies are special narratives made of unfalsifiable events in part so that the reports of these events can be exchanged long after particular reality changes. The exchanging of reports of fantastic events shapes the world of *Homo sapiens*. And it is by well made fantasy that *Homo sapiens* shapes the world. Put another way, displaced as they are from our time and our world, fantasies are the richest field for the growth and display of the human aesthetic urge, an urge inherited through the accidents of survival and competition and remaining with us as a crucial capacity for our group struggle on toward the future. The descent of fantasy mirrors the descent of man.

Afterword

When George Slusser reached out to me to participate in the first Eaton Conference, I had no idea he had begun what became a mainstay collaboration in my professional life and, for me, a lifetime of exciting participation with an evolving international group of pioneering scholars and critics. When I offered "The Descent of Fantasy" at the third Eaton Conference, I made what seemed to me and others a new and unexpected claim about the pro-adaptive significance of fantasy as a mode of thought and cultural production. Since then, the essay has been reprinted a number of times not only for its priority but because, retrospectively, one sees the time for its thesis had come, and it came at the Eaton Conference.

Evolution offers both a conceptual framework and explanatory model in field after field. Today the term is most commonly associated with biology, and takes Darwin's *On the Origin of Species* (1859) as a key founding document. However, evolutionary thinking actually entered science with the German-born English organist-turned-astronomer William Herschel (1738–1822). Thanks to his keen mind and technological leaps forward in designing and fabricating telescopes, he dispelled the notion that there exists a luminous "fluid" in the heavens, resolving nebulae (from the Greek word for "clouds") as collections of individual stars. He called these collections "island universes." We now call them "galaxies" (from the Greek word for "milk"). Herschel saw that the density of stars varied among these universes and so hypothesized that the stars in any island universe attracted each other through gravity. Therefore, the denser the star field, the older the island universe. Not only did Herschel multiply the number of stars—literally—astronomically, but his foundation of the science of sidereal astronomy for the first time brought evolution into scientific thinking. The objects in the universe we observe today reflect both the nature of Nature and workings of time.

The workings of time, and competition for survival—whatever survival may mean in any given field—have become ubiquitous foundational concepts. They were not when "The Descent of Fantasy" was written. Now, however, there is a whole field sometimes called evolutionary aesthetics. Through Eaton, I had the privilege of exchanging ideas with early notable evolutionary aestheticians like Brett Cooke and Ellen Dissanayake. The field is now fully established.

Also through Eaton and the workings of time, I found many relationships; among those was that with the late George Slusser, my dear friend and the visionary who conceived and led the Eaton Conference for decades. On the occasion of this gathering of Eaton essays, I am grateful and honored to stand with others in acknowledging that the memory of George and the descent of Eaton continue to enrich the world.

Notes

1. Oscar Wilde, *The Picture of Dorian Gray* (1891; New York: Dell, 1968), [6].

2. The term "semiobiology" was suggested by Wladyslaw Godzich at a "Conference on Theories of Narrative" held in Bloomington, Indiana, 24–26 October 1980, under the auspices of the Department of English of Indiana University and Society for Critical Exchange. It was at that conference that I first began to organize diverse ideas I had had into a form that led to this essay. I wish to thank many people for their stimulation and comment at that conference, especially David Bleich, Ralph Cohen, Jonathan Culler, Paul Hernadi, Mary Louise Pratt, Gerald Prince, Leroy Searle, and James Sosnoski. In addition, much of my thinking about evolution in particular and science in general has been stimulated by conversations with colleagues at the University of Michigan and in particular with Richard Alexander, Gordon Kane, Matthew Kluger, and Roy Rappaport. I thank them all.

3. Max Luthi, *Once Upon a Time: On the Nature of Fairy Tales*, 1962, trans. Lee Chadeayne and Paul Gottwald, with Luthi's additions (New York: Frederick Ungar, 1970), 111.

4. Jacob Grimm and Wilhelm Grimm, "Little Red-Cap," 1812, *Grimm's Household Tales, with the Author's Notes*, Volume 1, trans. and ed. Margaret Hunt (London: George Bell, 1884), 113.

5. Susan Brownmiller, *Against Our Will: Men, Women and Rape* (New York: Simon & Schuster, 1975).

The Virginity of Astronauts

Sex and the Science Fiction Film

(1982 Eaton Conference)

VIVIAN SOBCHACK

Human biological sexuality and women as figures of its representation have been "repressed" in the male-dominated, action-oriented narratives of most American science fiction films from the 1950s to the present. Semiotically linked, insofar as each in our culture is conventionally reversible and may stand as a signifier for the other, sex and women and the significant connection between them is denied all but a ghostly presence in the genre. It is as if such a potent semiotic relation poses a threat to the cool reason and male camaraderie necessary to the conquest of space, the defeat of mutant monsters and alien invasions, and the corporate development and exploitation of science and technology. Thus, biological sexuality and women are often absent from science fiction film narratives, and when they do turn up they tend to be disaffiliated from each other, stripped of their cultural significance as a semiotic relation, carefully separated from each other so that biological sexuality is not linked to human women and human women are not perceived as sexual.

More than any other American film genre, then, science fiction denies human eroticism and libido a traditional narrative representation and expression. Sex and the science fiction film is, therefore, a negative topic. It points to a major absence in the genre, rather than a minimal presence. It surrounds a purposeful—if unconscious—repression. And it also suggests that such a marked—that is, noticeable—absence at the narrative level has left its trace, carved out its hollow, elsewhere in the films. Usual critical discourse, however, is not tuned to the analysis of negatives, of absences, of traces left by repression. Generally, it looks at what is there, at what is represented as present. Psychoanalysis, on the other hand, looks at what is there but represented as absent. As a mode of critical investigation that differs in focus and direction from other kinds of critical analysis, psychoanalysis, Michel Foucault tells us, "points directly ... not towards that which must be rendered gradually more explicit by the progressive illumination of the implicit, but towards what is there and yet is hidden, towards what exists with the mute solidity of a thing, of a text closed in upon itself, or of a blank space in a visible text."[1] A psychoanalytic approach to the topic of sex and the science fiction film would therefore seem an appropriate way to redeem the repressed to the realm of critical discourse and to explore its significance to the genre as a represented absence. Borrowing upon the psychoanalytic techniques of free association and dream analysis, such an approach should allow us to see how human sexuality and women return to the science fiction narrative in displaced and condensed forms, in an emotionally-charged imagery and syntax that bears relation to the cryptic but coherent language of dream. And it should also help us to understand how—in their repressed and potent combination as a sign evoking male fear and desire—sex and women figure significantly, if covertly, in shaping the basic structure of the genre and initiating its major themes.

Let us return to what is represented as present in American science fiction films. (I should point out here that my recurrent cultural qualification is less patriotic than indicative of some particular conflicts localized in the American psyche and centered around the opposition of biology and technology. Science fiction films from other countries do not seem to base themselves in a semiotic system in which biological reproduction and the female are linked as a sign opposed to the sign constituted by linking technological production to the male.) Certainly, at the overt level of plot and narrative, there are some human erotically articulated women. Human heterosexual relations are relatively important to the development of plot and narrative in *Forbidden Planet* (1956), *The Incredible Shrinking Man* (1957), *Colossus: The Forbin Project* (1970), and *The Stepford Wives* (1975). Becky, in *Invasion of the Body Snatchers* (1956), immediately comes to mind as a female character who functions centrally and erotically. But these are exceptions. For the most part, human heterosexual relations in the science fiction film are tepid—more obligatory than steamy. Indeed, those few science fiction films which deal overtly with sex and the sexuality of human women—their erotic appeal and their procreative function—generally do so outside the articulated context of human heterosexuality and within that of racial and spatial miscegenation. Hence we have not only films like *I Married a Monster from Outer Space* (1958) and *Mars Needs Women* (1967), but also films like *The World, the Flesh and the Devil* (1959) and *Demon Seed* (1977). Surely, in these latter two films, the titles say it all. Women who are erotically attractive or biologically fertile are subject only to an alien embrace—in the one instance (however liberal the film's surface message) to a black male, and in the other to a bronzed machine.

Generally, then, in the various overt dramas of science fiction film, the nature and function of human heterosexuality are either muted or transformed. While there are numerous boy-meets-girl encounters across the galaxy and the genre, they tend to be chaste and safe in their dramatization and peripheral to narrative concerns—no matter when the films were made. One gets the feeling that they are included either to satisfy the vague demands of formula or to answer the unspoken charges of homosexuality that echo around the edges of the genre. Science fiction films are full of sexually empty relations and empty of sexually full ones. In concert with this narrative de-emphasis on human sexuality and women, biological sexual functions—intercourse and reproduction—are avoided in their human forms and, instead, displaced onto mutant and alien life forms and into technological activity. In this way, women characters are narratively deprived or any problematic connection with sexuality. They rarely exist in the films to "be made" or "to make," as sexual objects or as sexual subjects. Think, for example, of the chaste "seduction" of Alta in *Forbidden Planet*, so safe that it is charming rather than erotically compelling. Alta's lack of passionate response to Lieutenant Farman's cheerfully comic "kissing lesson" looks no different than her supposedly passionate response to Commander Adams. And the men do not seem particularly aroused either. Thus, even in a film in which male rivalry between prospective suitors and between father and lover are central to the plot, sexuality and eroticism are absent at the level of human representation. They are drained from the female character and missing from the male characters as well—despite the lip service they are given in the ritual wisecracking and wooden flirtations common to such sf film encounters.

Throughout the genre, human female biological difference from the male is literally covered up. (Women represented as alien, however, are often scantily and sexily-clad.) The 1950s films are peopled by women restrained by shirtwaist dresses, Peter Pan collars, and occasional lab coats. Again, the only exception that comes immediately to mind is Becky in *Invasion of the Body Snatchers*—her strapless dresses and push-up bra a bold declaration of sexuality which perhaps forces the script to put her to sleep and turn her into a pod. Indeed, a telling echo of Becky occurs in a brief sequence in *It Came from Outer Space* (1953), where the alien and threatening quality of female sexuality appears in the transformation of the amateur scientist/hero's girlfriend. In her normal state, her clothes are unrevealing and indicate an unerotic and sensible partner for rational John Putnam. However, when her body is borrowed and "taken over" by the stranded aliens, she appears against a barren hill in a black, strapless evening dress—a chiffon scarf fluttering in some chill and ill-begotten wind. She has literally become the alien—and the marker of that transformation is her sexually provocative clothing (which has no logical source in the narrative) and its revelation of her as a woman. With rare exception, then, female biological difference is de-emphasized in the films. The question it asks, the response it demands, the need and desire it evokes in the male are hidden and defused by sensible and functional attire, by rational occupations, and by the unprovocative, unquestioning "fulfilled" sexuality of a peripheral and occasional wife and mother.

This diffusion of difference, this visual and narrative "coding" of women in the science fiction film as not only peripheral but also asexual, might seem to be a function of the chronological and cultural context in which the films were made. We tend to think of the 1950s as conservative, as lived in some mythic miasma of unremarkable normality, as cautious and gray, as neutral and neutered. It bears remembrance, however, that the 1950s were also the time of Marilyn Monroe—of the image of blond sexuality, of female fullness and fertility. Although she appeared in *film noir*, thriller, musical and western, Marilyn never made a science fiction film. (One can hardly count *Monkey Business* [1952].) Indeed, it is by virtue of its patent absurdity that the idea is so wonderfully appealing. Whether in the 1950s or now, the genre could not have possibly contained her body, and she would have destroyed the impact and iconic potency of any technological marvel or activity, of an alien being or threat, simply by the awful truth of her visual presence. That female body, those full breasts and rounded belly, that amplitude and plentitude of flesh, would have distracted both male characters and the narrative alike from their generic course. Why build machines when that biological marvel that is the female body mocks the male desire for autonomous creation and demands babies? Why get one's rockets off when that body invites an earthbound penetration and offers the deep space and infinitude of the womb? And why fear alien invasion and destruction when that alien is clearly here and already triumphant—in the awesome body of the Woman, that different body of the Other. Such a monumental female screen presence as Marilyn could only stop the genre in its narrative tracks and expose the imitative function of technological production, space travel, and alien encounters—their structural and visual mimicry of biological intercourse and birth, or impregnation and reproduction.

The de-emphasis on human female sexuality in the science fiction film, then, is not limited to a particular period, but rather seems particular to the genre—at least sufficient if not necessary. Although less obvious than in the 1950s films, this generic cover-up of biological difference is still present in recent films which feature central and narratively active female characters. Women are sexually defused and made safe and unthreatening by costume, occupation, social position, and attitude—or they are sexually confused with their male counterparts and narratively substituted for them. Princess Leia of *Star Wars* (1977) and Ripley of *Alien* (1979) exemplify these alternatives which both serve the same repressive ends—the disaffiliation of women and sexuality and its corollary, the disguise of biological difference. For all her aristocratic presence as a princess, Leia is also represented as one of the boys. Whatever her narrative relations with Han Solo, her tough and wisecracking character is not about to let her tightly coiled hair down nor expose her female flesh. It is only against her will that Leia wears the scanty costume of a harem slave in *Return of the Jedi* (1983). And it is not Han Solo, but Jabba the Hutt—an alien—for whom she stands as an unwilling erotic sign. She is simultaneously protected and desexed by her social position (princesses are to fight for, not to sleep with) and by her acerbic and pragmatically critical attitude. While she might be compared in some ways to the Hawksian heroine, who through true grit and stoicism gains acceptance by a male community, Carrie Fisher certainly has none of the erotic presence of a Lauren Bacall. Leia, then, is sexually defused and it seems safe to presume that no matter how involved she gets with Han Solo in episodes to come, she will still come off as chaste as her white robes.

Ripley in *Alien*, however, is subject to another sort of representation. Narratively active as she is, she is no more a sexual being than are *2001: A Space Odyssey*'s Bowman or Poole. It is telling that the original script of *Alien* conceived Ripley as a male, and that few changes were made to accommodate the differences that such a sex change in the character might present. Ripley, indeed, is hardly female (and considered by her shipmates as hardly human). Unlike Leia, Ripley is not so much defused in her sexuality as she is confused with her male companions and denied any sexual difference at all. Instead of white robes that mark her both as a woman and chaste or off-limits sexually, she wears the same fatigues as the community of astronauts of which she is—from the beginning—a part. She is not marked as either a woman or sexual—except for one sequence at the climax of the film, a climax which has double meaning and function since it is both narrative and sexual. It is truly disturbing and horrific when Ripley takes her clothes off toward the end of *Alien*, not only because, given the rules of genre, we suspect that her complacent belief that she has destroyed the alien creature is unfounded. It is also horrifying because she exchanges one kind of power for another, her sudden vulnerability at the narrative level belied by her sudden sexual potency as a visual representation on the screen. In becoming a woman at the level of the narrative, Ripley is clearly marked as a victim; however, in becoming a woman as a fleshy representation of biological difference, Ripley takes on the concrete configuration of male need, demand, desire and fear, and she commands power at a deeper level of the film than that of its story. Stripping her narrative competence with her uniform, Ripley no longer represents a rational and asexual functioning subject, but an irrational, potent, sexual object—a woman, the truly threatening alien generally repressed by the male-conceived and dominated genre. It is no wonder that at the narrative level, the represented alien emerges phallic and erect and seeks to destroy and consume the fearsome difference that Ripley has so suddenly exposed. (And can one, then, forget that the alien was not of woman born—but erupted in violence and fury from a male belly?)

Sexuality, however, is not denied only to the few women characters in science fiction films. The male heroes who dominate almost all science fiction films are also remarkably asexual. Indeed, most of them are about as libidinally interesting as a Ken doll; like Barbie's companion, they are all jaw and no genitals. This sexlessness spans the occupational possibilities of the genre—from lab scientist to doctor, from amateur astronomer to geologist. It seems particularly radiant, however, in the superb physiques, wooden movements, hollow cheerfulness, and banal competence of science fiction astronauts. Certainly, although all science fiction films are—in one way or another—about space travel and the transgression of those established boundaries and markers which give shape and identity to mind, body, and place, not all science fiction films have astronauts in them. Yet, astronauts are clearly those figures who centralize and visually represent the values and virtues common to all the male protagonists of the genre in a single archetypal presence. They are cool, rational, competent, unimaginative, male, and sexless. These qualities make them the heroes of the genre, as they are heroes of our popular culture, and they embody in their cinematic and social presence all that Marilyn's body would subvert. Whereas the semiotic link between biological sexuality and women has been repressed or broken by the genre, the semiotic link between biological asexuality and men has been forged by it and allowed a full range of representation. Thus, much as one can productively free associate around the absence in the science fiction film that Marilyn represents, the virginal astronaut presents an opportunity to free associate around a dominant and significant presence.

Certainly, although it provides a provocative title for this essay, the virginity of astronauts is not to be taken literally. Given their average x½ children, we all know that real astronauts (and some cinematic ones) engage in sex—even if it is difficult to imagine them in or enjoying the act. Rather, my virginal astronauts are visual signs that systemically and systematically function in a conscious and unconscious narrative syntax. That is, they are simultaneously icon, index, and symbol. In their visual representation and narrative activity, they embody, dramatize, and stand for the science fiction film's secondary and conscious—or textual—conflict. And they also embody, dramatize, and stand for the genre's primary and unconscious—or subtextual—thematic problem and the narrative momentum it generates. The major generic problem centers around the male desire to break free from biological dependence on the female as Mother and Other, and to mark the male self as separate and autonomous. The realization of this desire—certainly at the level of science fiction narrative—necessitates the rejection and repression of female difference and its threat to male autonomy as being, indeed, the difference which makes a difference. In the genre, only women represent difference and so are outcasts at the edges of the narrative or are covered up in overalls and lab coats so they might share a bit of narrative space. This connection of the female with difference, sexual difference and biological power, suggests perhaps why we tend to think of astronauts in the plural. They usually come in teams, representing similitude on the screen rather than difference. Maleness in its clear-cut asexuality is visually coded as assembly-line sameness. (Discussing the matter, a colleague aptly commented that this visual representation of male similitude made films not homosexual, but homotextual.[2]) It is not surprising, then, that one cultural critic has remarked, "Who wants to talk to *one* of the astronauts?"[3] And Pauline Kael, in a negative review of *Marooned* (1969), precisely identifies the point as she misses it when she asks, "Who in his right mind would cast the three leads with Gregory Peck, Richard Crenna, and David Janssen, when anybody can see they're all the same man?"[4]

My virginal astronauts, then, tend to be more corporate than corporeal. Indeed, it is their interchangeable blandness, their programmed cheerfulness, their lack of imagination, their very banality (think of that reductive language they all use), that makes them heroes, that gives them that aura of mechanical and robotic competence which insists that nothing can go wrong, that everything is A-OK. They all look as if they can accomplish the unthinkable without ever having to think about it. They are a team, all the same—and certainly never separated by real sexual rivalry. Offscreen or on, these men who figure in our public myths neither appeal to prurient interest nor really seem to have any. They are never "sexy." Their wooden postures and—dare I say it—tight-assed competence disallows any connection with the sexual and sensuous. *2001*'s astronaut Poole, basking nearly naked under a sunlamp, is hardly a piece of beefcake. Thus, whether named Buzz or Armstrong, Buck, Flash, or Bowman, our public astronauts reek of locker room camaraderie, but hardly of male sweat or semen. As if in training for the big game, they have rejected their biology and sexuality—pushed it from their minds and bodies to concentrate on the technology required to penetrate and impregnate not a woman but the universe.

The virginal astronauts of the science fiction film are a sign of penetration and impregnation without biology, without sex, and without the opposite, different, sex. They signify a conquering, potent, masculine and autonomous technology which values production over reproduction, which creates rather than procreates in a seeming immaculate conception and a metaphorically autocratic caesarian birth. As signs, my asexual astronauts give concrete form and presence in both culture and film to this public—if unspoken—disaffiliation of rational technological enterprise from human biological activity. Not only does technological man want to make his own babies, but he wants to do so without the hormones and flesh, without lust and arousal, and his most heroic representatives, the astronauts, embody this distrust of women, of the biological, and of the irrational dependencies of the flesh.

It is understandable, then, that women pose a particular narrative threat to science fiction heroes and their engagement with technology. They are figures who—as mothers, wives, girlfriends—arouse male need, demand, and desire. They represent the Mother and the Other whose very presence points to the puny and imitative quality of male endeavor, of technological creation and its inanimate products. Their power to originate life is envied and emulated. Thus, their absence from a central position in science fiction narrative creates an indelible and deeply significant space. Women cannot be avoided in the science fiction film no matter how many spaceships leave them behind. They also serve who only stand and wait—or who actively emerge from narrative exile to occupy the paradigmatic space of the imagery. Thus, if human females and Mother Earth are abandoned, if male heroes escape them, it is to yet another female presence: the dark womb of space both beckons and menaces—yielding and receptive to phallic exploration and reunion, or as consuming and destructive as a black hole in its eradication of male potency and presence. Women do not disappear from the science fiction film—nor does sex. They may be repressed, but they return to the narrative in what Foucault called "the mute solidity of a thing," in the condensed and displaced imagery and action of the genre that are themselves sensuous and sexual though no longer human in their overt and articulated form of signification.

Repression is the psychoanalytic term for the "active process of keeping out and ejecting, banishing from consciousness, ideas or impulses that are unacceptable to it."[5] An attempt is made to push the entire painful and emotionally-charged idea—the whole being called an "instinct-presentation"—into the realm of the unconscious. Psychoanalysis tells us:

> It is possible to reduce to a minimum the influence of such an instinct-presentation by first breaking it up into its two basic components: the idea and the affective charge. This means that there are three things that are subject to repression: (1) the instinct-presentation; (2) the idea; (3) the affect. In many instances, when the entire instinct cannot be successfully repressed, either the ideational or the affective part may be. If the idea is repressed, the affect with which it was associated may be transferred to another idea (in consciousness) that has no apparent connection with the original idea. Or, if the affect is repressed, the idea, remaining, so to speak, alone in consciousness may be linked to a pleasant affect. Finally, if the whole instinct-presentation is repressed, it may at some later time return to consciousness in the form of a symbol.[6]

This psychoanalytic description describes precisely what has been entertained here about the presence and absence of women in the science fiction film. The instinct-presentation is comparable to what I have earlier described as the complete sign of sexual woman, the semiotic bearer—in her bodily difference—of a biological power which demands the painful male recognition of dependence and impotence and their corollaries, desire and envy. The influence of this instinct-presentation is minimized when the films break down the semiotic connection between its two parts, when they separate biology and sexuality from women, the affective charge from the idea. When human women are present in the narrative, when they remain as an idea but their affect, their biological difference and sexuality, is repressed, they are merely pleasant or indifferent presences and representations. When biological difference and sexuality are present in the narrative, when they remain as an affect but their idea, their traditional semiotic representation as female, is repressed, they are usually transferred to another idea that seems unrelated to the original one. Thus, sexuality can be transferred to a giant mutant insect about to lay eggs, or to the biologically different sexuality of an alien creature like the Thing which can breed from its hand and whose offspring we see pulsating tumescently during a sequence of the 1951 film version. (Consider the film's counter to this: the hero's human male hands are literally tied by his very aware girl friend, because in their last encounter he couldn't keep those hands off her.) Nearly all of *Alien*'s imagery is organic and/or sexual, whereas the humans are not—except for Ripley's climactic emergence as female toward the end of the narrative.

Finally, as I have suggested, if both women and human sexuality are repressed from the narrative as a whole, as a sign, as the entirety that is the instinct-presentation, then that whole may return in another form to the narrative—in some symbolic representation. The narrative enterprise of space exploration and its accompanying visuals may be viewed as a symbolic representation of birth and/or intercourse: the expulsion from the body as well as the penetration of space, the infant's separation from the Mother or the adult male's reunion with the Mother in the form of the female Other. Similarly, the alien invasion of the planet or the alien mind/body "takeover" may be viewed as the symbolic enactment of the fear of femaleness—both as all-consuming, castrating, possessive, and potent (having the power of breast *and* penis), and as an "inverted" rape fantasy in which the invasion of the planet, mind, and body represents the negative, passive, vulnerable, and female side of penetration, represents "being screwed" rather than "screwing." And, of course, female sexuality may return symbolically in the representations of the alien or mutation. These representations return the repressed to the narrative, then, but they are returned in visual disguise—transformed by the semiotic processes of the unconscious known as condensation and displacement.

Condensation is the term given by psychoanalysis to that process in which a single idea, word, or image "is made to contain all the emotion associated with a group of ideas," or a conversation, or a lived scene or experience.[7] Thus, one representation comes to stand for many. A single signifier is substituted for a number of signifiers and comes, therefore, to have attached to its manifest form a number of meanings—multiple signifieds. In addition, it condenses and compresses all the emotion connected with each of the individual signifiers and signifieds for which it alone has come to stand. The similarities that are perceived between single ideas, words, or images, between emotional associations and life experiences, provide the attraction which brings a particular group of signifiers and signifieds together under the symbolic umbrella of a single super-charged representation. This process is certainly characteristic of all dreams, but it can be seen also in the metaphorical nature and function of conscious language—a structural and functional similarity which has been emphasized by French neo-Freudian Jacques Lacan, and which allows me to justify the pertinence of condensation to the science fiction film without going so far as to claim that film is identical to either dream or human psyche.[8] Rather, we are looking at cinematic signification of a particular type. We are looking in most science fiction films at a powerfully charged or cathected imagery that is not consciously articulated as metaphorical, at an imagery which is meant in the narrative to denote precisely that for which it iconically stands.

Think, for example, of the Rhedosaurus in *The Beast from 20,000 Fathoms* (1953). At the denotative level of the narrative, the creature is a signifier—an image or visual representation—of a single signified: a prehistoric giant reptile. However, that visual representation carries a great emotional charge—and not only because it wrecks Coney Island. It has the visual force it does because it represents other things and ideas and associations in addition to its denotative function. It also signifies primeval origins, the primal sink and slime from which life first emerged. It also signifies atomic force and destruction and extinction (it was aroused by an atomic blast), and the fear of an avenging nature which has been disturbed by technology. It signifies, too, something unnameably alien, inhuman, unknowable in its scaliness and reptilian being, something Other (perhaps the female Other, the bad Mother—since the creature's destructive path leads to its ancient breeding ground). While each of these semiotic connections could be argued and cannot be supported without an analysis of the entire film, the idea of condensation as it relates to science fiction imagery should be a little clearer. In addition, insofar as this particular film never overtly articulates these signifieds at the level of the narrative, never deals with the origins of life or the perils of atomic power or the hideousness that mere difference represents (be it of species or sex), we can see how condensation emerges as an imagery of the repressed.

Displacement similarly emerges as an expression of the repressed, and it too is characteristic of dreams. Lacan has likened it in structure and function to the metonymic nature and function of conscious language, to the way in which signifier follows signifier in a contiguous chain of substitutive movement. Displacement is the "transference of the emotions ... from the original ideas to which they are attached—to other ideas."[9] Emotion or psychic energy can be transferred from its source in an original event and that event's original representation to something else, something less originally meaningful. In such a manner, psychoanalysis tells us, the emotions "may be able to gain the realm of consciousness, attaching themselves to ideas to which the patient is ordinarily indifferent. By such an arrangement the patient is spared the pain of knowing the original source of the affects."[10] Often, in the science fiction film, the emotions generated by the narrative and the visual imagery in regard to being, for example, in a spaceship are those of confinement, of discomfort, of dependence (upon the ship and computer to sustain life support—think of the lifeline and the "umbilical" which links technological man to the mother machine). Powerlessness is also evoked, visualized in the helpless and dependent sleep of those aboard. It is more than likely that the original source of these emotions—not attached to technology—comes from a deeper level than the narrative and can be related to the original and repressed representation of human biology and its process: the passage from womb to tomb, the infantile intimations of original being and not-being that merge in the biological space travel which results in birth and also, finally, in death.

Displacement also involves not only the transference of emotion from an original to a secondary representation, but also "the shifting of id impulses from one pathway to another."[11] Someone who is civilized is not supposed to hit an antagonist and so will curse him roundly. In the science fiction film, someone who is rational is not supposed to destroy things irrationally or ravage them—and so will raise a creature or machine who can do it for him. Of particular interest to biology, sex and science fiction, displacement often involves transferences at the level of the body, in relation to both the organic and erotogenic. We are told: "The instincts shift, for example, from the oral to the anal, to the genital zones, or to any other erotogenic zone. In conversion hysteria a psychic complex may be displaced upon a potentially organic structure. Or, all the issues connected with genitality may be displaced to the oral zone. Displacement 'from below upward' is a common phenomenon."[12]

In *Invaders from Mars* (1953), one sequence of images shows a woman about to be "taken over" (that is, possessed, taken) by the aliens. She is shown lying on a platform, the nape of her neck about to be penetrated by some long, tubular sort of mechanical mind probe which will place the red crystal it holds at its tip into her body. Supervising this enterprise is the "head" alien creature—who is, literally, a head encased in a glass ball and moved about by mutants who obey its telepathic commands. In this film (as in many other science fiction films), the head—narratively the place of reason as opposed to libido—has become the representation of the penis. The nape of the neck in this instance (which is an erotogenic zone in some cultures) has become the representation of the womb and anus (it is, after all, the back of the neck). The action, what we see on the level of the narrative as an alien invasion, an appropriation of the mind, is a displacement of sexual erotic activity, particularly in its negative implications as rape and sodomy. While it is never consciously articulated in the films, such displacements "from below upward" are articulated in the absolutely sensitive—if vulgar—locutions of such phrases as "giving head" or "mind-fuck" or even in such an innocent synonym as "conception" for "idea."

In a sense, everything I have tried to say here about condensation and displacement as the means by which the repressed figure of the sexual female can return from its relegation to the science fiction film's unconscious to the conscious articulation of the narrative has already been cinematically demonstrated. Woody Allen has hilariously performed a psychoanalysis of the genre, decoding and exposing its repression of sexuality and its primary scenario as the play of fear and desire around female potency and biological difference. In two episodes from his *Everything You Always Wanted to Know About Sex* (*But Were Afraid to Ask)* (1972), Allen overtly links the genre to sexual conflict and to body imagery. He also plays out explicit dramas of sexual encounter and redeems the repressed relation between sex and women to the conscious level of the narrative, revealing how they function together as a sign of some hidden and mute reality that both attracts and threatens the male. What Allen does, finally, is point directly to the processes of condensation and displacement through which the unconscious speaks the repressed to consciousness—processes which are always active usually concealed in the science fiction film.

As a model of condensation, Allen provides "Are the Findings of Doctors and Clinics Who Do Sexual Research and Experiments Accurate?"—a narrative in which a forty-foot high breast terrorizes the landscape and the populace until scientists and military finally capture it by constructing a giant bra. The repressed Marilyn Monroe does return in a fashion to the genre, then. What is usually condensed either further into a visual representative of a creature which appears to have no overt relationship with sexuality or women is presented—in the flesh—in Allen's film. Woman here—in an awesome synecdoche—becomes literally the "bad object," the bad Mother and female Other. Describing the death of a little boy, the hero says, "The cream slowed him up and the milk killed him. We're up against a very clever tit. It shoots half and half." This is the breast that would smother and consume and annihilate, that rejects its nurturing function while fulfilling it. This is also the breast with the awful power to sustain life, to nourish and feed, to provoke desire, to answer or reject infant demand, to fulfill basic need. A billboard in the film shows a bikini-clad pinup and announces that "Every body needs milk." This breast clearly has power and reflects not only infantile need and the fear of rejection, but also the infantile confusion of the breast with the penis, the confusion of male and female power. This breast is, indeed, clever. It shoots half and half—both semen and milk. It is the baddest of bad objects.

As a model of displacement, Allen gives us another segment entitled "What Happens During Ejaculation?" The sexual and orgasmic activity that is ordinarily displaced in the genre onto sending rockets into space is exposed by Allen, as is the process of displacement itself. Allen uses the firing of a rocket as an explicit metaphor for the ejaculation of a sperm about to be sent to the womb. Allen plays the skeptical, fearful, reluctant sperm/astronaut who says, "You hear rumors about this pill these women take." And the drama of the male body is played out by white overalled technicians operating flashing electronic consoles. What is so consummate (the pun is certainly intended) is the parody's truth in relation to the real and hidden concerns of the genre, its recognition of the surrogate sexuality of the concentrated effort and tension and release of science fiction's visualization of men shooting their rockets off into space. Think, for example, of a parallel "serious" scene in *Marooned*; as the rocket lifts off, all the technicians in the NASA control room stand up from their consoles, look at the big monitoring screen, and chant "Go, go go!" in a rhythmic and ascending crescendo. The connection between the basic asceticism and asexuality of male characters in the science fiction film and their constant orgasmic release in a public and communal male technological effort which transcends the earthbound corporality of flesh and dependence upon women is made central and overt in the Allen parody.[13] The desire to impregnate and penetrate the womb of space is visually articulated—and so is the fear. Allen's sperm/astronaut fears a hostile space (one which has taken the pill), a space which may destroy him, reject him as readily as he may penetrate it. The sperm/astronaut is at once afraid and desirous, both potential newborn and incestuous mother-fucker.[14]

Just as metaphor and metonymy form the basic axes of linguistic representation, so too do condensation and displacement form the basic axes of the unconscious representation as it is given manifest form and utters the repressed to consciousness. Both, thus, work at once. In the ejaculation sequence, for example, not only does Allen make explicit how the genre traditionally displaces biological and sexual affect from women onto some other technological representation (rockets), but he also makes explicit how the idea of woman becomes part of a visual condensation and returns in disguised form, in this case (and others) as space itself. The point to be made here is that both displacement and condensation work at once in the entirety of the narrative and concentrate their efforts on the complete or partial repression of the instinct-presentation and its component parts: female sexuality and fertility, female biology and its representation in a body that is different, that is difference itself. What results is a basic structure which informs the genre—a kind of push-pull configuration in which what is repressed will return in disguise to become overtly articulated. The basic structure, however, is also able to accommodate historical and cultural change—for what will be repressed (the sexual female, or sexuality itself) will alter with the times and will also emerge in a disguise that responds to historical concerns. While these changes may be marked, however, the structure itself remains constant. Displacement and condensation will occur or the genre will not exist—in the same way that metonymy and metaphor exist or there can be no language.

Earlier I suggested that all science fiction films were about space travel whether or not they had rockets or spaceships in them, whether or not they were manned by my virginal astronauts. By space travel, I was referring to the passage across known and marked boundaries that give identity to the world and to ourselves—as earth and space, as inside and outside, as self and other, as male and female. Borders and markers in the science fiction film are seen as extendable—and their contents as spilling over into each other, possibly merging. This is what is so thrilling about the genre, and what is so threatening, what structures its narratives as a play of fear and desire. It is also what affixes the genre to infantile and pre-Oedipal dramas in which the female—as Mother and Other—becomes the focal point and origin of questions the infant must answer regarding its own sexuality, its selfness, its very identity as human and biologically gendered. In representing women and sexuality, in a culture which semiotically links biology and sexuality to women and technology to men, most American science fiction films play out scenarios which focus on infantile experience while pretending to adult concerns.

Sigmund Freud, Melanie Klein, and others have noted the following features which characterize infantile experience. One can see immediately how they are paralleled by the action and imagery of the American science fiction film in its various dramatic manifestations. The infant feels a sense of helplessness, impotence, and dependence; a sense of insignificance and smallness in relation to the monstrous size and physical importance of the mother. The infant has a confused image of gender identity, its own and its mother's, and tends to collapse the penis and breast into a bisexual imagery in which body parts and power are interchangeable. The infant has difficulty in distinguishing boundaries between itself and its mother, between inside and outside, mind and body, body and tool or toy. It has extreme ambivalence toward maternal power in its relation to the infant's own limited power, resulting in a tension between its sense of its own desire and destructive potential and its dependent demands upon one who can destroy. Thus, the infant has a tendency to introject or project maternal power, to see itself as powerful and potent and autonomous like the other or to fear the other as monstrous, destructive, and all-powerful. As well, the infant is both curious and afraid in its lack of knowledge—it wants to know, but is afraid of what it does not know or what it may find out. And this lack of knowledge is most focused around sexual and body imagery and concern for its own origin.[15] "Where did I come from?" is a question penultimately connected with another: "Who or what am I?"

These questions lie repressed in the narratives of the science fiction film. At the level of conscious representation, the one is articulated as "Where are we *going*?" or "Where did *It* (or *They*) come from?" The first is a positive and the second a negative disguise for the infant's "Where did I come from?" The second question takes the disguised form of "Who or what is *It* (or *They*)?" instead of "Who or what am I?" If these questions were exposed in their original form, in the "true speech" that Lacan sees as the unconscious, the genre could not exist at the narrative level as the kind of exploration it is. Thus, these questions of origin and identity and the conventional sign of the sexual female which provokes these questions must be repressed. Marilyn Monroe could never have made a science fiction film; she would have destroyed it if it could not desex her. And, insofar as American culture observes and perpetuates the semiotic linkage of biology to woman and technology to male, astronauts will always be represented as virginal no matter how much they screw around.

Afterword: After Ripley, After 9/11

It has been interesting, if also frustrating, to respond to an essay I wrote about sex, gender, and American science fiction films in 1985. So much has changed in our world and the genre that it seems like a century has passed (which, indeed, it has). I could write a lengthy essay on the topic—and I have.[16] However, constrained by the brevity of an "afterword," all I can do here is address some of the changes that challenge the present generic and cultural relevance (or not) of my essay's most important aspects: the central metaphor and screen image of "virginal astronauts"; the general on-screen absence or marginalization of women and human biological sexuality and their paradoxically important function in shaping the genre; and the psychic and narrative structures emergent from this functional absence or marginalization through processes (both psychic and poetic) of displacement and condensation. I claimed these structures are "able to accommodate historical and cultural change," but only in passing and without illustration. In this regard, the essay sometimes seems ahistorical and essentialist—particularly in solely focusing on "repression," as if that were the only psychic structure sufficient to generating sf screen narrative and imagery. As many contemporary sf films demonstrate, however, others might do the same, if with significant differences.

Indeed, hindsight charges one's vision with historicity. Today, I would hold to my essay's claims about the sf film's basic narrative structure—and poetics—of condensation and displacement; but precisely "what" gets condensed and "where" it is displaced onscreen is not a psychic constant but a collective, if not unanimous, response to historical and cultural change—and, in extremity, to collective trauma that may be "irrepressible."

Generated by a seemingly neverending, cumulative, and grim parade of catastrophic historical, cultural, and natural events beginning on 9/11, the dominant psychic structure now informing films (and American culture) has changed from "repression" to "abjection." Moreover, this change significantly reconfigured the ideational and affective relations of sex and gender that earlier dominated the genre's narrative structure and imagery.

Certainly, after Ripley's 1979 appearance in *Alien* amidst second-wave feminism, increasing numbers of women in both significant and minor roles have broken up the homosociality of the genre, and by their onscreen presence put structural pressure on the central oppositions that informed sf film. Most constant were those between male/female and technology/biology—the first terms hierarchically dominating and "repressing" the second, which "returned" to narratives in affectively-charged, displaced form and imagery. However, after 9/11, the successful, low-tech "alien" castration of a monumentally phallic American erection produced a more general detumescence of confidence in the exceptionalism and potency of American masculinity. The "idea" of masculinity (emblemized in the 1960s by NASA astronauts), that condensed rationalism, technological "know-how," and optimistic belief in "man's" ability to control both his destiny and emotions, was belied by the "affect" associated with the "irrational," terrifying events of 9/11: an overwhelming sense of grievous loss, personal vulnerability, pervasive fear, and feelings of powerlessness—collectively experienced across sex and gender differences but psychically processed as "feminizing" and devastating to the self-image of American men. Thus, the opposition of male and female both in the culture and sf cinema became less oppositional, the boundaries between them permeable, and their respective "qualities" confused.

Indeed, along with generating a sense of "perpetual danger," as Julia Kristeva writes, abjection is above all "marked by ambiguity,"[17] emerging in response to an overwhelming threat that "tends to destroy the fragile equilibrium where heterogeneous contradiction is maintained and returns [us] to the state in which differences are effaced."[18] Abjection psychically internalizes the breakdown of the symbolic order: those "ideas" constituting the boundaries and coherence of the categories we collectively perceive as self, system, and social order. Moreover, "emanat[ing] from an exorbitant outside or inside, ejected beyond the scope of the possible, the tolerable, the thinkable,"[19] this threat collapses boundaries between surroundings and self—the Twin Towers literally, the body politic psychically. Overwhelmed by the irrationally impossible, intolerable, and unthinkable, the abject subject dissociates and "splits" between affirmation and negation of the self, and (the stuff of science fiction) between the existence and extinction of "humanity." However, in most contemporary sf films (at least until recently), the affirmation of self and collectivity seemed unprecedentedly weak in comparison to the strong negativity emerging from 9/11's effect on "American masculinity"—that "idea" and "image" which previously generated the primary (affirmative) subject and "self" of the genre, assuring the obligatory but "happy ending" of a heterosexual coupling and the now-male (re)production of a collective future.

This abjection of male protagonists had significant effects across the genre. The dissociative splitting of abjection is most explicit in the self-affirmation and negation of the (always) male protagonists of contemporary time travel narratives—and not just in films that involve forms of onscreen "duplication" like *Primer* (2004), *Looper* (2012), and *Coherence* (2013), wherein characters assert and affirm themselves through, dare I say, a host of "selfies," but ultimately negate and annihilate them. There are also significant "do-over" films like *Déjà Vu* (2006), *Source Code* (2011), and *Edge of Tomorrow* (2014). To borrow again from Kristeva, their protagonists are narratively "dissociated [and] shattered into [the] painful territories" of different timelines as they compulsively relive traumatic events, dying at least once and often more trying to prevent catastrophe.[20] As the promotional tagline for *Edge of Tomorrow* synopsizes: "Live. Die. Repeat"—until you get it right. However, there is no getting it right in a "do-over." Because of time travel's "self-consuming" determinist structure, the protagonist's success and affirmation are only superficial. The catastrophe is predestined and cannot be prevented in all timelines where it has already happened; all the protagonist does is create another where it does not.

A subtler (if more spectacular) display of male abjection and the split between affirmation and negation is seen in the marked retrenchment of narrative and psychic scope in "disaster" cinema. The once-intrepid "hero" attempting to save the world, backed by the military and advanced technology, is negated and replaced by a lone (often widowed, separated, or divorced) "ordinary" guy who is affirmed by saving (without fire power) a small group of people, most frequently his children and (usually) broken family. That is, despite their grand spectacle, these films' narratives have been reduced to more personalized and domestically-focused dramas. One need only watch *Knowing* (2012) and *2012* (2009), or compare the original *War of the Worlds* (1953) to its 2005 remake, released with the proudly reductive tagline, "As Earth is invaded by alien tripod fighting machines, one family fights for survival." It is also telling that the nurturing function generally associated with women is now affirmatively attached to male parents. "Survival" thus centers around the male (re)production of the biological family. Nonetheless, wives and mothers generally are (still) in absentia in these films: not repressed and displaced as breeding creatures, they have died or left irresponsible husbands to be replaced by "feminized" men, affirmatively transformed by disaster into responsible and nurturing males (not weak and impotent ones) able to save the next generation.

Women are usually absent or marginalized in these time travel and disaster films, which still foreground a male protagonist, even if now abject—either dissociating himself from himself in time, or feminizing himself as himself over time. Elsewhere in the genre, however, women are not only present in narratives but dominant protagonists. In a small number of recent films like *Ex Machina* (2014), women and female sexuality are clearly "othered," although unlike earlier films they are not narratively repressed and their onscreen displacement is thematically deconstructed and critiqued. In this regard, despite being disembodied as an operating system in *Her* (2013), embodied as an alien in *Under the Skin* (2013), subject to—then subject of—mental and physical transformation in *Lucy* (2014), and cyborgized in *Ghost in the Shell* (2017), Scarlett Johansson's women were not only their films' central "I" but overtly interrogated their generic power over abject and/or ineffectual men.

Indeed, few American sf films feature female protagonists who, like male counterparts, are abject or even depressed. Regarding abjection, I can cite only *Another Earth* (2011), wherein the literal—and planetary—dissociative "splitting" of the protagonist's "I" actually makes possible her affirmative psychic atonement for a reckless act that ruined someone else's life. As for depression, female protagonists in *Gravity* (2013) and *Arrival* (2016) grieve the death of a daughter (one in the past, the other in the future), yet even these "mothers of sorrow" affirmatively opt for both a personal and collective future.

However, the most future-oriented, optimistic, and confidently affirmative sf women live in dystopic and/or post-apocalyptic worlds, becoming rebel leaders out to negate an untenable social structure and elite government. The first of these female-centered films is *V for Vendetta* (2005), but they become most prevalent (and popular) in two recent series: *The Hunger Games* (2012, 2013, 2014, 2015) and the progressively-titled *Divergent* (2014), *Insurgent* (2015), *Allegiant* (2016), and forthcoming *Ascendant*. In both franchises, female protagonists significantly look toward a viable future, but one that is responsive to human need and not dependent upon a science and technology that has been co-opted for oppression. Thus Appalachian-like music is thematic for Katniss Everdeen, and Tris Prior is born into the homespun-clothed "faction" of Abnegation, an affirmative word for "selflessness" that, under a rigid regime, becomes more like self-negation. Underlying these films, and possibly their popularity, is a prelapsarian impulse to establish the generation—and generations—of family and the security of "home" as supreme values. The last—and gauzy—shot of the final *Hunger Games* film shows Katniss and her heretofore chaste love interest, Peeta, years later, watching their children playing in the sunshine and grass.

Beyond the demographic and economic appeal that enables a movie franchise, it seems no psychic accident that these films derive from "young adult" novels. Both the films and their confident world-changing protagonists suggest that adults have screwed up the present and are ultimately "hopeless" and incapable of (re)producing a viable future. Though they provide roles for women actors of a "certain age," these adults unfortunately include powerful women holding high (and villainous) government positions, like Oscar winners Julianne Moore (*Hunger Games*), Kate Winslet (*Divergent*), and Jodie Foster in *Elysium* (2013), one of the few films of social rebellion and liberation wherein an abject male transforms self-negation into collective affirmation. The recent exception is Charlize Theron, who in *Mad Max: Fury Road* (2015) plays the battle-scarred Imperata Furiosa, an adult woman of few words and extreme action. Furiosa becomes the driving force behind a more just—and matriarchal—social reconfiguration to produce a viable, if post-apocalyptic, future.

SF films after 9/11, then, increasingly put their faith in women to produce both a familial and collective future while traumatized men try to undo the past or are limited in response to present disasters. In either case, however, time is of the essence—as both a narrative device and existential imperative. Thus, despite the emphasis of its title, *Interstellar* (2014) dramatizes how the gravity of time, in relation to our now-tenuous survival, has come to outweigh the expansiveness of space. Cooper, widowed father and astronaut-turned-farmer on a polluted, dying Earth, tells his father-in-law, "We used to look up in the sky and wonder at our place in the stars; now we just look down and worry about our place in the dirt." In Cooper's future world (which is ours, only earlier), history books assert the Moon landing was a hoax and NASA, long discredited, has gone underground. Looking inward as well as upward and outward out of desperation, *Interstellar* is a cry against abjection and a call to affirmative action involving both space and time travel and requires not only men but women—particularly Cooper's daughter Murph, who, from pre-teen girl to aged, dying adult older than her father, is the alpha and omega of initiating and resolving the unsolved problems of gravity's relation to space-time, gender inequality, and the conflicts between scientific rationalism and human emotion, and between the security of "home" (even as it's dying) and the existential risks of leaving it to explore possible new homes. Overbearing because overused in its rejection of abjection, the film's anthem was "Rage, rage, against the dying of the light." *Interstellar* was a harbinger of things to come.

Years after suggesting the possibility "of rebirth with as well as against abjection,"[21] Kristeva, in a 2002 interview for an anthology (published shortly after 9/11) poignantly titled *Hope: New Philosophies for Change*, calls this a "joyful revolt"—not only a radical "questioning of identities and values," but also a "symbolic deconstruction [...] and renewal, which comes from creation—psychic creation, aesthetic creation, rebirth of the individual." The antidote to abjection is not symbolic repetition but symbolic renewal. She reminds us, from the distance of France, what took more than a decade for both our culture and sf cinema to acknowledge in the face of extinction: "it's up to us to transform reality, but the transformation depends on our mental state, on the forms of discourse we adopt, and if our symbolic disposition leans more towards [...] that of optimism, we have a stronger hold on reality than if our disposition is that of lamentation and melancholy. [...] It is only by traversing our grief that there can be any possibility of hope."[22]

Kristeva's words might have been dialogue in *Tomorrowland* (2015) which echoes her thought. Although criticized as overly didactic in narrative insistences on less pessimism about the future (primarily voiced by a teenage girl who tries to subvert the demolition of a decommissioned NASA launch pad), whatever its faults, the film follows upon *Interstellar* as an "unremitting manifesto of hope."[23]

This returns me to the confident, chauvinistic, unimaginatively optimistic and pioneering spirit of the astronauts I described (and skewered) more than thirty years ago, who linger as national emblems of American exceptionalism and masculinity. Rereading my essay, what astonishes me (but shouldn't) is remembering that in 1985, there was little public interest in astronauts and manned space flight either in the culture or cinema. Indeed, it wasn't until 1995 (ten years after my essay's publication) that astronauts were foregrounded in extremely popular movies: *Apollo 13*, the celebratory docudrama of an aborted moon mission, and *Toy Story*, with its parodic, if loving caricature Buzz Lightyear (all jaw and no genitals) who returns, impersonated as a throwback and phantasm by George Clooney, in *Gravity*. In 2000 there was *Space Cowboys*, a wry, reflexive swan song that both deconstructed and honored astronaut mythology. Tellingly, as this chronology unfolds, astronauts become the "last of their kind"—not surprising given the last American manned space flight was in 2011.

Only recently have there been signs of a revolt both against and within abjection. Led almost single-handedly by Elon Musk (albeit with NASA's help), the relationship between the lack of time before self-extinction and resumption of "manned" space travel has again generated public interest. So did the stranded astronaut played with humility but self-sufficiency by Matt Damon in 2015's popular *The Martian*. Nonetheless things have changed over thirty years: Damon's astronaut only survives because of his faith in his astronaut captain—now an intrepid, "can-do," and optimistic woman.

Notes

1. Michel Foucault, *The Order of Things* (New York: Vintage, 1973), 374.
2. The colleague cited here is Zoë Sofoulis, a doctoral student in the history of consciousness program at UC Santa Cruz, who was instrumental in broadening my exposure to pre-Oedipal symbolism and to literature of pertinence to this essay. Indeed, her own work—of mammoth import and needful of the book-length study she is engaged in—has been a great influence on my own.
3. Anne Marie Cunningham, "Forecast for Science Fiction: We Have Seen the Future and It Is Feminine," *Mademoiselle* (February, 1973), 140.
4. Pauline Kael, review of *Marooned, Deeper into Movies* (New York: Bantam, 1974), 107.
5. Leland E. Hinsie, and Robert J. Campbell, *Psychiatric Dictionary*, Fourth Edition (Oxford: Oxford University Press, 1970), 660.
6. Hinsie and Campbell, 660.

7. Hinsie and Campbell, 149.

8. The book most recommended for a clear explication of Lacan and his semiotic psychoanalysis is Anika Lemaire's *Jacques Lacan*, trans. David Macey (Boston: Routledge, 1979).

9. Hinsie and Campbell, 219.

10. Hinsie and Campbell, 219.

11. Hinsie and Campbell, 220.

12. Hinsie and Campbell, 220.

13. Much of this section is taken from my *The Limits of Infinity: The American Science Fiction Film* (Cranbury, NJ: A.S. Barnes, 1980).

14. Articulating this idea in terms of the vulgar "mother-fucker" was the "brain-child" of Bruce Kawin and brought up at the Eaton conference.

15. Again, I thank Zoë Sofoulis who brought these characteristics to my attention in a presentation, "Science Fiction, Psychoanalysis and the (M)Other," for my Film Genre course at UC Santa Cruz, Fall, 1981.

16. Sobchack, "Abject Times: Temporality and the Science Fiction Film in Post-9/11 America," *Reality Unbound: New Departures in Science Fiction Cinema*, ed. Aidan Power, Delia González de Reufels, Rasmus Greiner, and Winfried Pauleit (Berlin: Bertz + Fischer, 2017), 12–33.

17. Julia Kristeva, *Powers of Horror: An Essay on Abjection*, trans. Leon Roudiez (New York: Columbia University Press, 1982), 9.

18. Kristeva, "The Subject in Process," *The Tel Quel Reader*, trans. and ed. Patrick Ffrench and Roland-François Lack (London: Routledge, 1998), 152.

19. Kristeva, *Powers*, 1.

20. Kristeva, "Subject," 152.

21. Kristeva, *Powers*, 31.

22. Kristeva, "Joyful Revolt: Interview with Mary Zournazi," *Hope: New Philosophies for Change*, ed. Zournazi, trans. Peter Cowley (Annandale, NSW: Pluto Press, 2002), 76, 75.

23. Marjorie Baumgarten, Review of *Tomorrowland*, *Austin Chronicle*, May 22, 2015, at https://www.austinchronicle.com/calendar/film/2015-05-22/tomorrowland/.

Running Out of Speculative Niches

A Crisis for Hard Science Fiction?

(1983 Eaton Conference)

David Brin

There is a question that is often heard at science fiction conventions these days.

"Is hard sf dead or dying?"

Certainly from the number of panel discussions devoted to the subject, it would seem that there is some concern out there among the readers, editors, and writers. Whether or not it is true that the subgenre is experiencing problems, it cannot be denied that there is a widespread feeling that hard sf has seen better days.

Of course there is always the question of definition. If by hard sf we mean "boy engineer" stories in which a pair of Aryan-type male heroes—chaste, innocent, and yet wise—come up with a chain of ever more unlikely techno-wizardries to defeat alien bad guys, then few would mourn the loss. But not many modern readers would use such a definition when discussing hard sf.

A more appropriate stab at a criterion to the subgenre might be that in a hard sf story or novel, "science" itself—the body of knowledge which encompasses verifiable, predictable patterns in our universe—is a major character. In other words, while science or a scientific question need not be all there is to the plot of a hard sf story, it must participate substantially in motivating the characters to do what they do. Also, the science in a hard sf piece must be as consistent as possible with accepted scientific paradigms, straying from what is currently accepted only in purposeful speculation having directly to do with the story. And those departures must be few and rigidly defined.

At its best, hard sf must also be good literature. That almost goes without saying. Well-written hard sf must fulfill the same standards of characterization, setting, plot consistency, drama, and good writing that other varieties of fiction strive to attain. The requirement of having "science as a character" is in addition to all else.

It is arguable that the hard sf subgenre can be further divided. For instance, there is clearly a difference between "engineering sf," such as Steven Barnes and Larry Niven's *The Descent of Anansi* (1982) and scientific sf, such as Gregory Benford's *Timescape* (1980). The two subcategories share a common heritage, but face different problems.

We shall speak more of this division within hard sf momentarily. However, for now, let us discuss the goals of hard sf writers themselves.

It is betraying no fraternity secret to say that to some degree hard sf writers write for each other. That is, in addition to wanting their works to be good stories for the sake of the broad audience (and even critics), these writers also tend to be aware of the other hard sf authors as they work out the details of their plots and universes.

There is, at a low, good-natured level, a certain competition among hard sf authors to come up with the most startling and original—yet obvious—possible departures from reality and to present these altered settings or situations in logical and consistent ways.

(Use of the word *obvious* is significant. For, like the writer of a murder mystery, the hard sf author likes nothing better than to have a peer smack himself in the forehead and exclaim, "Of course! Now why didn't I think of that!")

There is some pride in being the first to write about life on a neutron star, or a physically possible world in the shape of a ring, or communications through time in a manner not inconsistent with known physics. Indeed, so many of our recent advances in science and technology were predicted by the hard sf of the forties and fifties that one is compelled to wonder which hard sf speculation of the eighties will be vindicated by history.

Hard sf is, in essence, the portrayal of what "might" happen. In this way it is a little like playing what-if games with the future—excluding what we know to be impossible, but exploring Arthur Conan Doyle's range of the improbable in minute detail.

It is even possible that hard sf may someday serve humankind at a critical moment. In its library of well-thought-out situations and plots, hard sf offers a catalogue of scenarios which might shorten our reaction time if and when some truly dramatic event—such as contact with an alien race—ever occurs. The hard sf library has already been influential (e.g., Aldous Huxley's *Brave New World* [1931], Eugene Burdick and Harvey Wheeler's *Fail-Safe* [1962], George Orwell's *Nineteen Eighty-Four* [1949], Michael Crichton's *The Andromeda Strain* [1969]). Someday it might prove invaluable.

[2017 Note: the author later developed this concept, writing about the role of science-fictional warning fictions in creating "self-preventing prophecies."[1]]

Why, then, all this murmuring over the "death" of hard sf? The hard stuff appears to be well motivated, even useful. It remains popular. Yet, talk to the fans, and one might imagine that hardly any is being written anymore.

It may be that what we now call *Hard Sf* has begun to suffer from a double-bind. The subgenre seems to have entered new ground where it is simply more *difficult* to write, making many new authors unwilling to chance its slippery surface.

One of the deterrents to dabbling in hard sf might be discomfort with the very same "peer-review" I mentioned above. Few science fiction authors really have substantial educations in science. While in the old days it may have been possible to buy an engineer friend a few beers and come away with the technical details needed for a go-to-the-moon story, the depth of research called for in a truly innovative modern hard sf tale may seem daunting to many writers. Certainly awareness that there is a community of hard sf readers and writers "out there," ready to judge a work by very exacting standards of verisimilitude, may have frightened some away from working in the subgenre. (This seems verified from discussions with several sf authors.)

As Robert F. Forward discusses in his article "When Science Writes the Fiction" (1986),[2] the science often writes all or part of the plot for the author of a hard sf tale. While few carry out this rule with the devotion of Dr. Forward, it is true that hard sf authors must bow to an outside master. They abdicate to Reality some of the storycasting role that most writers jealously preserve for their own imaginations. Not all authors can, or wish to learn this partnership.

All in all, it is easier to craft a dragon than a good spaceship.

But there is an additional factor that I believe is having a major impact on hard sf today. It is implicit in the discussion given above. It has to do with the ferocious nature of speculation itself.

Hard sf may face a crisis simply because the knowable universe may be *finite,* and hence we may be filling in the gaps faster than we think.

Such a broad statement needs some explaining. I shall try.

In Western civilization we have adopted a number of points of view which are so commonly held that they take on some of the aspect of religious dogma. Yet these assumptions are not labeled dogmatic because they are considered "modern" opinions.

For instance, the famous "Principle of Mediocrity" of astronomy—also called the Copernican Principle—holds that there is nothing special about our place and time—that the earth is a mundane world circling a mundane star among trillions in this corner of the universe alone. The Mediocrity Principle was a daring and revolutionary idea when broached during the Renaissance. It took years to supplant the earlier, anthropocentric, geocentric worldviews and become a bulwark of modern astronomy.

Yet the notion of Mediocrity is now under assault by an upstart theory called the "Anthropic Principle," which dares to say that Earth may, indeed, be special. Major evidence given is the total absence of any sign of visits to earth by extraterrestrial civilizations in geologic history. This is a topic getting a lot of attention in certain intellectual quarters today.

Another example of a major assumption that was once revolutionary, but which now is under attack as "conservative," might be called the Principle of the Endless Scientific Frontier. It proposes that there is no limit to what can be learned about nature, and that natural law has no boundaries. The implication is that there will be waves of scientists without end, and that each generation can stand on the shoulders of its predecessors to learn more.

But will there always be exciting new frontiers of knowledge? Is it possible that we are closing in on the borders of the knowable?

Certainly this was thought to be true around the turn of the last century, when professors of physics actually discouraged new graduate students, stating blithely that everything of real value had already been determined!

Of course we now know that quantum mechanics, relativity, radioactivity, and numerical analysis would blow that contention apart just a short time later. The Principle of the Endless Frontier was reaffirmed in the 1920s.

Yet, we are now beginning to hear the refrain of "limits" once again. Science-philosophers, such as F.W. Atkins and P.C.W. Davies, contend that late twentieth-century mankind is on the verge of filling in more than 50 percent of the landscape of physics. If this is so, the other sciences must, perforce, follow.

It is a disconcerting idea to a native of that twentieth century. One is tempted to hearken back to the failed Cassandras of 1890, and indeed, we might be on the verge of discoveries which will open up the endless horizons once more.

But because the Cassandras of science were proven wrong once doesn't necessarily mean they will be again. Physicists are far more sophisticated today. When they say that the gaps are rapidly being filled, they must, for the time being at least, be taken at their word.

If science itself has a boundary, then, must not hard science fiction, as well? We spoke of what almost amounts to a competition among hard sf authors to find thematic gaps where a topic worthy of speculation has not been treated before. The goal is to find and describe such virgin territory—telling a good yarn in the process—before anyone else gets the idea. Once a subject has been treated well by one author, others tend to shy away from covering it again (at least in the same way), seeking to do something original, instead.

Is it possible that this competition is *dangerous* to the profession—almost "Malthusian" in a way? Are hard sf authors gobbling up a finite resource ... the Possible? If science itself is due to plow its last fallow fields, can hard sf be far behind?

It's a debatable question. However, the *appearance* of limits is sufficient, perhaps, to cause some sf authors to fear the hard branch, without entirely knowing why.

In this matter of Limits to the Possible, we must return to the distinction between "engineering sf" (ESF) and "science sf" (SSF), two branches of hard sf in which, respectively, engineering and science are themselves major characters of the story, having something new to say.

What I have called SSF is the sub-subgenre which faces this quandary of the speculatively possible head on. An author of SSF says "what if?" in a big way, having to simultaneously satisfy both originality and scientific believability. The muses of sf are demanding. They don't pay well if the ideas aren't grand, and they are unforgiving if either originality or believability are lacking.

Engineering sf suffers gentler constraints. *Analog* magazine prints no lack of entertaining stories that are, indeed, *hard* sf, and there seems to be no dearth of ideas. The only difference between ESF and SSF is that originality is not so severely judged in ESF. An ESF story does not cover the grand topic of life on the surface of a neutron star, but rather a neat way in which the space shuttle might be used to rescue a doomed cosmonaut. It doesn't worry over the cosmological implications of Black Holes, but plays instead with how to pull off a successful revolt in a space colony with a 98 percent independent recycling system.

Engineering sf faces no shortage of "possibilities" to be exploited. Many sf authors may stay away from it because of some of the other reasons we have discussed here, but not because there are few gaps left to be filled.

However, scientific sf—the hard sf having to do with the very nature of reality—may be entering an era of hard times. It is a common truism that there will never be a shortage of good and original new ideas. But is it wise to count on a truism always being true?

As one who earns his living in part by writing SSF ... and who enjoys reading it ... I hope these fears are unfounded. Yet they go a long way toward explaining some of the reluctance many talented sf authors seem to feel toward stepping into the heartland of science fiction—hard sf itself. Not only has the hard stuff become more difficult, with time. But its essence, the idea, also has grown precious and may become more so as time goes on. (In truth, does not this help to explain why critics and scholars of sf shy away, as well?)

It sounds like a tract from some strange ecological exposé. "Will future generations forgive us if we carelessly, thoughtlessly, squander a rare resource ... the very imagined Possible itself ... without packing some away for a rainy day?"

It might make a good plot for a story....

Author's Note: Some months after delivering this talk, I saw a piece in *Analog*, entitled "Melancholy Elephants" by Spider Robinson.[3] It was about this very topic of the "mining out" of ideas themselves. I had put off writing my own story on the subject, and there it was. "Melancholy Elephants" won a Hugo Award for best short story. I crumpled my own early draft and threw it away. Rats.

Notes

1. David Brin, "The Self-Preventing Prophecy: How a Dose of Nightmare Can Help Tame Tomorrow's Perils," first posted at AOL's *iPlanet* (1999), then at http://www.davidbrin.com/nonfiction/tomorrowsworld.html.
2. Robert F. Forward, "When Science Writes the Fiction," *Hard Science Fiction*, ed. George Slusser and Eric S. Rabkin (Carbondale: Southern Illinois University Press, 1986, 1–7.
3. Spider Robinson, "Melancholy Elephants," *Analog: Science Fiction/Science Fact*, 52 (June, 1982), 132–143.

Effing the Ineffable

(1986 Eaton Conference)

Gregory Benford

Their light of pocket-torch, of signal flare,
Licks at the edge of unsuspected places,
While others scan, under an arc-lamp's glare,
Nursery, kitchen sink, or their own faces.
—Kingsley Amis

There is probably no more fundamental theme in science fiction than the alien. The genre reeks of the desire to embrace the strange, the exotic and unfathomable nature of the future. Often the science in sf represents knowledge—exploring and controlling and semisafe. Aliens balance this desire for certainty with the irreducible unknown.

A lot of the tension in sf arises between such hard certainties and the enduring, atmospheric mysteries. And while science is quite odd and different to many, it is usually simply used as a reassuring conveyor belt which hauls the alien on stage.

Of course, by alien I don't merely mean the familiar ground of alienation which modern literature has made its virtual theme song. Once the province of intellectuals, alienation is now supermarket stuff. Even MTV knows how commonly we're distanced and estranged from the modern state, or from our relatives, or from the welter of cultural crosscurrents of our times.

Alienation has a spectrum. It can verge into the fantastic simply by being overdrawn, as in Franz Kafka's "The Metamorphosis" (1915), which describes a man who wakes up one morning as an enormous insect. Only one step beyond is Rachel Ingalls's recent *Mrs. Caliban* (1983), in which a frog man appears. He simply steps into a kitchen, with minimal differences from ordinary humans. He is merely a puppet representing the "good male," and in fact can be read as a figment of the protagonist's imagination. The novel isn't about aliens, of course; it's a parable of female angst.

We don't describe our neighbors as alien just because they drive a Chevy and we have a Renault. What sf does intentionally, abandoning lesser uses to the mainstream, is to take us to the extremes of alienness. That, I think, is what makes it interesting.

I deplore the *Star Trek* view, in which aliens turn out to be benign if you simply talk to them kindly; this is Hubert Humphrey in space. That fits into a larger program of some sf, in which "friendly alien" isn't seen for the inherent contradiction it is. Friendliness is a human category. Describing aliens that way robs them of their true nature, domesticates the strange.

Yet much early sf was permeated with the assumption that aliens had to be like us. In *Aelita, or The Decline of Mars* by Alexsey Tolstoy (1923), the intrepid Soviet explorers decide even before landing that Martians must necessarily be manlike, for "everywhere life appears, and over life everywhere man-like forms are supreme: it would be impossible to create an animal more perfect than man—the image and similitude of the Master of the Universe."[1] Plus the Martians are Marxists!

We've come a long way since such boring certitudes—through the marauding Martians of H.G. Wells, the inventive and Disney-cute Mars of Stanley Weinbaum's 1934 short story "A Martian Odyssey," and into hard sf's meticulously constructed worlds for fantastic creatures. Aliens have been used as stand-in symbols for bad humans, or as trusty native guides, as foils for expansionist empires, and so on.

Yet for me, the most interesting problem set by the alien is in rendering the alienness of it. How do you set the ineffable in a frame of scientific concreteness? This is a central problem for sf. Very seldom has it been attempted in full, using the whole artistic and scientific arsenal.

Artful Aliens

Of course, we all know that one cannot depict the totally alien. This is less a deep insight than a definition. Stanislaw Lem's *Solaris* (1961) asserts that true contact and understanding is impossible. It was a vivid remainder twenty years ago. As genre criticism, it seems nowadays ponderously obvious.

Since then, its targets—anthropomorphism, the claustrophobic quality of intellectual castles, and cultural relativism—have become rather cold meat. Indeed, everybody now assumes without discussion that, in writing about the very strange, we must always gesture toward something known, in order to make analogies or provide signs. So we're careful, because unless we keep reminding the reader that this creature is to be taken literally, it readily becomes (surprise, surprise) a metaphor.

In the mainstream, walk-on aliens come with metaphors and labels worn on the sleeve. How could they not? In "realistic" fiction, aliens can't be real. Sf insists that they are—and that important issues turn upon admitting alien ways of knowing.

Even in sf, though, I must inveigh against the notion that we make statements about the alien in the form of a work of art.

Not so. While this reductionist view is useful for inquiring into epistemology, or diagnosing contemporary culture, or other worthy purposes, it has little to do with what happens when we confront the alien in fiction.

Naturally, there are always people who want to put art to use for some purpose—political, social, or philosophical. But it is so easy to forget, once we're done using art, that it is not only about something, but that it is something.

The alien in sf is an experience, not a statement or an answer to a question. An artistic—that is, fulfilling, multifaceted, resonant—rendering of the alien is a thing in the world itself, not merely a text or a commentary on the world.

All the deductions we can make from a story about the truly alien give us conceptual knowledge. So does science. But the story should—must—also give us an excitation, captivating and enthralling us. When sf works, it gives us an experience of the style of knowing something (or sometimes, as I'll discuss, not knowing).

This means that a prime virtue in depicting the truly alien alien is expressiveness, rather than "content"—a buzzword which provokes the style/substance illusion in criticism. We don't read Wells's *The War of the Worlds* (1898) for its views on Martian biology or psychology, but for the sensations of encounter.

This may well be the most original thing which sf does with the concept of irreducible strangeness. It's worthwhile inquiring into the underlying ideas and approaches scholars and writers take in pursuit of it.

Science and "Sensawonda"

Most sf which takes the idea of the alien seriously (though not necessarily solemnly) deploys a simple strategy:

First, use scientifically sound speculative ideas to construct either the background or the actual physical alien. Garnish the strange planet with whatever ecology looks workable, always favoring the more gaudy and spectacular effects.

Next, deploy a logical sequence of deductions about how an alien would evolve in this place. Stick to concepts like Darwinian evolution, or some later modifications ("punctuated equilibria" in evolution, for example). Then make the alien behave in keeping with this world. Present his/her/its actions, getting the maximum effect of the detailed world view. Only slowly make known how the alien got that way. This guarded unfolding spices the story with mystery.

This usually works well to make a situation strange and intriguing to the reader. Isaac Asimov's *The Gods Themselves* (1972) uses a speculative physics and well-rendered oceanic imagery to evoke strangeness. Larry Niven and Jerry Pournelle's *The Mote in God's Eye* (1974) has three-legged Moties with well-thought-through implications. On the other hand, Hal Clement's classic *Mission of Gravity* (1953) uses a gargantuan planet of crushing gravity; yet the aliens come over more like midwesterners. (Maybe this was necessary at the time. The planet was so *outré*, Clement may have used ordinary aliens to keep things manageable.)

An obvious pitfall of this whole class of approach is that the reader—who may be quite technically adept and can catch the author in a lapse of world building—may find all this apparatus merely clever and engaging, a fresh kind of problem story. He'll get no sense of strangeness.

What writers are after here is what the fans call "sense of wonder"—an indefinable rush when beholding something odd and new and perhaps a bit awesome. "Dat ole sensawonda" is the essential sf experience. No alien should leave home without it.

Beyond this approach there are refinements. Chad Oliver's *The Shores of Another Sea* (1971) treats a chilling alien form which is never more than glimpsed, but whole strangeness slowly comes across, through the way it uses animals in Africa. Some writers have tried to render alien perceptions, grounding their effects in the sciences. Damon Knight's short story "Stranger Station" (1956) treats the anguish of a human trying to enter into an alien's way of thinking. The human emerges with a provisional explanation of how a vastly powerful alien society sees us. (There is a strong hint, though, that he has merely projected his own childhood traumas on the huge creature, so this is really another failed attempt at real contact.)

What I find most interesting about this area is the tricky way it can make so many of our cherished ideas disappear up our own assumptions.

Alien Chat

Scientists often say that communication with aliens could proceed because, after all, we both inhabit the same physical universe. We should agree on the basic laws—gravitation, electromagnetism, stellar evolution, and so on. This is the gospel of the universal language. I'm not so sure. After all, we must frame our ideas in theory, or else they're just collections of data. Language can't simply refer to an agreed-upon real world, because we don't know if the alien agrees about reality.

There's an old anthropologists' joke about this. In the outback, one anthropologist is trying to learn a native's language by just pointing at objects until the native tells what the object is in the language. He wanders around pointing and gradually getting more excited. He tells a colleague that these people have built into their language the concept that nature is all one essence, because whatever he points to, the native says the same word.

It is a great discovery. Only much later do they discover that the word the native used is the one for "finger."

So we can't just rely on raw data. We must somehow convey concepts—which means theory. And in science, theory inevitably leads to mathematics.

Indeed, the standard scenario for communicating by radio with distant civilizations relies on sending interesting dit-dah-dit patterns, which the receiving creatures dutifully decompose into pictures. Those sketches show us, our planetary system, some physical constants (like the ratio of the proton mass to the electron mass), and so most confidently on and on.

Let's play with some notions that go against this grain. Suppose the aliens don't even recognize the importance of dit-dah-dit? Why not? Their arithmetic could be non-numerical, that is, purely comparative rather than quantitative. They would think solely in terms of whether A was bigger than B, without bothering to break A and B into countable fragments.

How could this arise? Suppose their surroundings have few solid objects or stable structures—say, they are jelly creatures awash in a soupy sea. Indeed, if they were large creatures requiring a lot of ocean to support their grazing on lesser beasts, they might seldom meet even each other. Seeing smaller fish as mere uncountable swarms—but knowing intuitively which knot of delicious stuff is bigger than the others—they might never evolve the notion of large numbers at all. (This idea isn't even crazy for humans. The artificial intelligence researcher Marvin Minsky told me of a patient he had once seen who could count only up to three. She could not envision six as anything other than two threes.)

For these beings, geometry would be largely topological, reflecting their concern with overall sensed structure rather than with size, shape, or measurement, à la Euclid. Such sea beasts would lack combustion and crystallography, but would begin their science with a deep intuition of fluid mechanics. Bernoulli's Law, which describes simple fluid flows, would be as obvious as gravitation is to us.

Of course these creatures might never build a radio to listen for us. But even land-based folk might not share our assumptions about what's obvious.

Remember, our concepts are unsuited to scales far removed from those of our everyday experience. Ask what Aristotle would've thought of issues in quantum electrodynamics and you soon realize that he would have held no views, because the subject lies beyond his conceptual grasp. His natural world didn't have quanta or atoms or light waves in it. In a very limited sense, Aristotle was alien.

Perhaps only in the cool corridors of mathematics could there be genuinely translatable ideas. Marvin Minsky takes this view. He believes that any evolved creature—maybe even intelligent whorls of magnetic field, or plasma beings doing their crimson mad dances in the hearts of stars—would have to dream up certain ideas, or else make no progress in surviving, or mathematics, or anything else. He labels these ideas Objects, Causes, and Goals.

Are these fundamental notions any alien must confront and use? We've cast a pale shadow of doubt over Objects, and I wonder about Causes. Causality isn't a crystal-clear notion even in our own science. There are puzzles about quantum cats and, as I elaborated in my novel *Timescape* (1980), fundamental worries about the sequence of time, too.

Why should Objects, Causes, and Goals emerge in some other-worldly biosphere? Minsky holds that the ideas of arithmetic and of causal reasoning will emerge eventually because every biosphere is limited. Basically, it's economics—eventually, some inevitable scarcity will crop up. The smart bunny will turn into a fast-track achiever since he'll get more out of his efforts. Such selection will affect all his later biases. Minsky has framed technical arguments showing that these notions must turn up in any efficient (and, presumably, intelligent) computer.

I have my doubts, but others have gone a long way toward making math alone carry the burden of communication. Hans Freudenthal's LINCOS is a computer language designed to isolate the deepest ideas in logic itself and to build a language around it. It uses binary symbols typed out in lines. LINCOS stands ready the moment we run into something green, slimy, and repulsive, and yet with that restless urge to write.

Math is central to the whole issue of communication because it allows us to describe "things" accurately and even beautifully without even knowing what they are. Richard Feynman once said, to the horror of some, that "the glory of mathematics is that we do *not* have to say what we are talking about" (emphasis his).

This is quite a threat to the humanists, who often wish that scientists would become more fluent in communicating. Feynman means that the "stuff" that communicates fields, for example, will work whether we call it wave or particle or thingamabob. We don't have to have cozy pictures, as long as we write down the right equations.

I'm reasonably comfortable with this idea. As David Politzer of Caltech once remarked, "English is just what we use to fill in between the equations." Maybe scientists will themselves make useful models for aliens.

Delving into the artistic pursuit of alienness always brings up the problem of talking. As I've sketched here, there are sound reasons to believe that some aliens are genuinely unreachable. We must share a lot to even recognize aliens as worth talking to—note how long it's taken us to get around to thinking about whales and dolphins.

But suppose we finesse the communication card for a moment. How does a writer assume that some chat can occur and then create the sensation of strangeness?

The Trapdoor Moment

One of my favorite sf stories is Terry Carr's "The Dance of the Changer and the Three" (1968), in which a human visiting a world remarks that he "was ambassador to a planetful of things that would tell me with a straight face that two and two are orange."[2]

This reminds me of surrealism in its deliberate rejection of logic. Notice, though, that even while it is commenting on the fundamental strangeness of the aliens, this sentence tries to impose a human perspective—why should the natives have a "straight face" at all? Or any face?

The story deals with creatures on the rather ordinary world of Loarra, and their folk legends are shown in loving detail. This takes most of the text and the unwary reader thinks he is reading a pleasant bit of pseudoanthropology. Then the aliens suddenly kill most of the expedition. Why? "Their reason for wiping out the mining expedition was untranslatable. No, they weren't mad. No, they didn't want us to go away. Yes, we were welcome to the stuff we were taking out of the depths of the Loarran ocean. And, most importantly, no, they couldn't tell me whether they were likely ever to repeat their attack" (52).

The story concludes two paragraphs later, with the humans unable to decide what to do next. Notice that the use of "mad" can be read here as either colloquial for angry, or else genuinely crazy. And through the aliens' rejection of prediction they deny the very notion of science as we would hold it. This seems to rule out the universal language dogma.

I like the story because it strings the readers along and then drops the trapdoor just as we're lulled into a pleasant sensation of Loarran pseudopolynesian simplicity. The ideas revealed this way are startling, but the core of the story is that sideways lurch into the strange.

For contrast, consider one of the most famous stories about alien encounter, Fredric Brown's "Arena" (1944). A man is trapped inside a desert-floored dome and told he must fight it out with an implacable alien foe for mastery of the galaxy. In their struggle, the alien "roller" reaches the man telepathically (avoiding the whole language problem).

> He felt sheer horror at the utter *alienness*, the *differentness* of those thoughts. Things that he felt but could not understand and could never express, because no terrestrial language had the words, no terrestrial mind had images to fit them. The mind of a spider, he thought, or the mind of a praying mantis or a Martian sand-serpent, raised to intelligence and put in telepathic rapport with human minds, would be a homely familiar thing, compared to this.[3]

But if the roller were utterly alien, it would be incomprehensible. As the critic John Huntington has pointed out, it is *understandable* alienness that so horrifies the human. In fact, it is horrible because it stimulates difficult, inexpressible feelings in the man. He understands the alien by reading his own feelings. He can't deal with them, so he attacks their origin.

"Arena" is usually read as a paean to hard-boiled, Campbellian rationality. I think you can read it as covertly pushing unconscious emotionality. This program is completely different—intellectually and emotionally—from Carr's.

Modernist Aliens

Oscar Wilde remarked that in matters of supreme moment, style is always more important than substance. So, too, here. We cannot know the true deep substance of the totally alien, but we can use conscious and conspicuous style to suggest it. Some of the best sf takes this approach. It is quite different from the careful scientific explanations in the style of Hal Clement.

In Robert Silverberg's short story "Sundance" (1969), the text surges back and forth between points of view, changes tenses, and ricochets between objective description and intense personal vision—all to achieve a sense of dislocation, of reality distortion, of fevered intermittent contact that one cannot quite resolve into a clear picture. "It is like falling through many trapdoors, looking for the one room whose floor is not hinged."[4]

The story culminates in rapidly reflecting and refracting visions of the same "reality," seeing slaughtered aliens for one moment as objects and then experiencing them from the inside. The narrative voices lurch and dive and veer, always pulling the trapdoor from under any definitive view. The story concludes "And you fall through" (473). There is no solid ground.

This is one of the best examples of how sf has used styles and approaches first developed in the dawning decades of the twentieth century, in what the critics term modernism. Breaking with the whole nineteenth-century vision, modernism evolved methods to undermine consensual reality and achieve a more personal, dislocated view. In the Joycean stream of consciousness, in the Faulknerian wrenchings of *The Sound and the Fury* (1929), literary devices dynamite cozy assumptions.

When science fiction uses such methods, they have different content. This is, I think, one of the most important contributions the genre has made to literature as a whole. Run-on sentences don't merely mean internal hysteria, flooding of the sensorium, runaway ennui, and so on. Instead, the method suggests genuinely different ways of perceiving the world, emerging not from psychology and sociology, but from evolution, genetics, even physics.

Unnoticed, sf has taken "mainstream" methods of breaking down traditional narrative and turned them to achieve uniquely sf ends. (I'd almost term it—delving into jargon myself—using modernism to achieve a kind of sf postrealism.) Nor has this ground been fully explored. I believe it is only now being pioneered. One of the most interesting uses is that, in sf, these can translate as a rendering of the scientifically unknowable—or, at least, unfathomable by humans. The blizzard-of-strangeness motif is a persistent notion, even among hard-science types.

Time and again in sf, encounters with the alien swamp mere humans. In Fred Hoyle's *The Black Cloud* (1957), Chris Kingsley, the eccentric and brilliant scientist protagonist, is driven into a kind of overloaded insanity when he attempts full contact with a huge, intruding superintelligent cloud. To accommodate the immense flood of new ideas and perceptions, Kingsley "decided to accept as rule that the new should always supersede the old whenever there was trouble between them."[5] This is an sf article of faith. But in the end, contradictions are unmanageable. The new information settling into the same neural brain sites makes life itself impossible. Kingsley (an echo of Kingsley Amis?) dies. Hoyle is no stylist, but I find it significant that he is drawn to the same notion of contact. Others later expanded on this insight.

Thus, one underlying message in sf is that the truly alien doesn't just disturb and educate, it breaks down reality, often fatally, for us. Here sf departs quite profoundly from the humanist tradition in the arts. Science fiction nowhere more firmly rejects—indeed, explodes—humanism than in treating the alien. Humanist dogma holds that man is the measure of all things, as Shakespeare put it. Sf makes a larger rejection of this than did modernism or surrealism, because it even discards the scientists' universal language and the mathematicians' faith in Platonic "natural" ideas. Sf even says that the universe may be unknowable, and its "moral" structure might forever lie beyond humanity's ken.

This makes Albert Camus and Jean-Paul Sartre and nihilism seem like pretty small potatoes. If you're shopping for literary alienation, sf offers the industrial-strength, economy-size stuff. Yet it also contains the symbols of certainty, through science.

I suspect that the longstanding antagonism between the literary world and the sf community isn't merely the old story of the stylish effetes versus the nerd engineers. Instinctively, without much overt discussion, the two groups dispute the fundamental ideals behind humanism. Sf writers take different views of the universe and can't be reconciled by a few favorable notices in the *New York Times Book Review*.

Erotic Strangers

Writers as diverse as Philip Jose Farmer ("The Lovers" [1952]), James Tiptree, Jr. ("And I Awoke and Found Me Here on the Cold Hill's Side" [1972]), and Gardner Dozois (*Strangers* [1978]) have dwelled upon the erotic component in the alien. It turns up in such drive-in movie classics as *I Married a Monster from Outer Space* (1958).

In discussing as personal a subject as sex, I might as well drop the convenient cover of dispassionate critic and write about my own work. At least this approach minimizes the number of potential lawsuits.

When I began thinking about the alien in detail, one of the first stories I wrote was "In Alien Flesh" (1978). I constructed it more or less unconsciously, piecing the story together from parts written at separate times over a period of months. For a long time, I didn't know where the tale was going.

In it, a man named Reginri has been hired to crawl up into a huge, beached whalelike alien on the shore of an alien sea. He is an ordinary worker, not a scientist. He simply finds sites to plunge sensors directly into the inner reaches of the being, called the Drongheda. Direct contact floods him with images, feelings—that sensual overload. It provokes ineffable thoughts. And he gets trapped inside the beast.

I wrote most of the story, but had no ending. So I retreated, building a frame around the central tale, which makes the main narrative a flashback. In the frame, Reginri is looking back on his nearly fatal encounter with the Drongheda. I put into this part an approaching fog which humans must avoid, a damaging mist of another planet. Only after I wrote the last lines of the story did I suddenly see what the end of the flashback portion had to be: "There was something ominous about it and something inviting as well. He watched as it engulfed trees nearby. He studied it intently, judging the distance. The looming presence was quite close now. But he was sure it would be all right."[6]

That done—though not understood, at least by me—I quickly retreated to the point where Reginri is smothered in the alien mountain of flesh and in desperation taps directly into the Drongheda's nerves. I started writing again, filling in action without thinking or planning very much.

Shaken by the flood of strange mathematics and sensation he has gotten from the Drongheda, Reginri finds his way out. Standing in the wash of waves as the Drongheda moves off on its inexplicable way, Reginri learns that one of his fellow workers has been crushed by the alien. Looking back, he sees that the hole he had used to crawl up into the Drongheda, pushing and worming his way in, was not "something like a welt" (26)—the description I'd written before and let stand—but in fact was quite obviously a sexual orifice!

Until I wrote those lines, I had no clue what the story was really about. What a field day for Freudian analysis! A critic's playground! Effing the ineffable!

I decided to let the frame stand. Having written the thing by intuition, I didn't dare tinker with it in the cool light of a critical eye. There's always a point in writing when you have to let go, for fear that you'll tinker away all the life in a piece. So, whatever the tale means, or says about my own disquieting interior, there it is.

Although I have now applied the reductionist hammer—which I scorned at the beginning of this essay—to one of my own works, I must say that I think post-readings do tell part of the story. Still, once you've dissected a salamander, you know more about it, sure—but it's dead.

As for my own way of assembling the story, I prefer this manner of pondering, shuffling back and forth, and by bits and pieces trying to artistically render the alien—intuitively, not seeking final answers, and with a certain lack of embarrassment, as well.

I'll return to my first assertion, too, and maintain that performing the usual critical slice-and-dice on "In Alien Flesh" misses the thrust of it. Rendering the alien, making the reader experience it, is the crucial contribution of sf. Such tales can argue over communication, spring trapdoors, inundate the reader with stylistic riverruns—all to achieve the end of a fresh experience. That's what the alien is really about.

Afterword: Aliens and SETI

This essay reflects my literary thoughts, which I later turned to scientific ends. I mentioned Minsky's ideas, and treated this in detail in reinspecting traditional Search for Extraterrestrial Intelligence (SETI) strategies. With my brother and nephew I published two papers in *Astrobiology*, extending that Minsky view to a new searching strategy for radio telescopes. To get the flavor I here provide an adapted passage from those papers:

We assume that if aliens are social beings interested in SETI conversations or passing on their heritage, they know about tradeoffs between social goods, and thus, in whatever guise it takes, *cost*. But what if we suppose, for example, that aliens have very low-cost labor, i.e., slaves? A finite number of slaves can be used to do a finite number of tasks, so you pick and choose by assigning value to tasks, balancing the equivalent value of the labor used to prosecute those tasks. Choices are still made on the basis of available labor; hence, labor has no value only where labor has no limit. That might be if aliens live forever or have limitless armies of self-replicating automata, but such labor costs something, because resources, materials, and energy are not free.

Our point is that *all* SETI search strategies must assume something about the Beacon builder, and that cost may drive some alien attempts at interstellar communication.

Beacon-Builder Motives

Through most of its history SETI assumed a high-minded search for other lifeforms. But other motives are possible.

What could motivate Beacon builders? Here we can only reason from our own historical experience. Other possible high intelligences on Earth (whales, dolphins, chimpanzees) do not have significant tool use or build lasting monuments. Sending messages over millennia or more connects with our own cultures. Human history suggests[7] there are two major categories of long-term messages that finite, mortal beings send across vast time scales:

- *Kilroy Was Here* These can be signatures verging on graffiti. Names chiseled into walls survive from ancient times. More recently, we sent compact disks on interplanetary probes, bearing people's names and short messages that can endure for millennia.
- *High Church* These are designed for durability, to convey the culture's highest achievements. The essential message is *this was the best we did; remember it.*

A society that is stable over thousands of years may invest resources in either path. The human prospect has advanced enormously in only a few centuries; the lifespan in advanced societies has risen by 50 percent in each of the last two centuries. Living longer, we contemplate longer legacies. Time capsules and ever-proliferating monuments testify to our urge to leave behind tributes or works in concrete ways (sometimes literally). The urge to propagate culture quite probably will be a universal aspect of intelligent, technological, mortal species (as Minsky often remarks).

Thinking broadly, high-power transmitters might be built for various goals other than two-way communication driven by curiosity. For example:

- *The Funeral Pyre:* A civilization near the end of its life announces its existence.
- *Ozymandias*: Here the motivation is sheer pride; the Beacon announces the existence of a high civilization, though it may be extinct and its Beacon tended by robots. This recalls the classic Percy Shelley lines,

> And on the pedestal these words appear:
> "My name is Ozymandias, King of Kings;
> Look on my works, Ye Mighty, and despair!"
> Nothing beside remains. Round the decay
> of that colossal wreck, boundless and bare,
> The lone and level sands stretch far away.

- *Help!* Quite possibly, societies acknowledging time scales over 1000 years will foresee physical problems and wish to discover if others have surmounted them. An example is a civilization whose star is warming (as ours is), which may wish to move their planet outward with gravitational tugs. Many others are possible.
- *Leakage Radiation*: These are unintentional, like objects left accidentally in ancient sites and uncovered long after. They do carry messages, even if inadvertent: technological fingerprints. These can be not merely radio and television broadcasts radiating isotropically, which are fairly weak, but deep space radar and beaming of energy over solar system distances. This includes "industrial" spaceship launchers, beam-driven sails, "planetary defense" radars scanning for killer asteroids, and cosmic power-beaming, driving interstellar starships with lasers or microwaves. There are many ideas about such uses already in the literature.
- *Join Us*: Religion may be a galactic commonplace; after all, it is here. Seeking converts is common, too, and electromagnetic preaching fits a frequent meme.

Whatever the Beacon builders' motives, we should periodically reassess our SETI assumptions in light of how our own microwave-emitting technologies develop. Since the early SETI era of the 1960s, microwave emission powers have risen orders of magnitude and new technologies have altered how we emit very powerful signals. Given Beacon ranges of over 1000 light years, EIRPs (Effective Isotropic Radiated Powers) greater than 9×10^{16} watts are needed. These high powers suggest all possible motivations will succumb to economics, however. Is cost/benefit analysis arguably universal?

Parsimony and Beacons

Traditional SETI research takes the point of view of *receivers*, not *transmitters*. This neglects the implications of what signals should look like *in general*, and especially the high emitting costs, which receivers do not pay.

We assume, like conventional SETI, that microwaves are simpler for planetary societies, since they can easily outshine their star in microwaves. Microwaves are probably better for Beacons, not radio.

Whatever the lifeform, evolution will select for economy of resources—an established principle in evolutionary theory. Further, Minsky in 1985 maintained that, as a general feature of intelligence, it selects for economy of effort. Biologist Gordon Tullock argued in 1994 that social species evolve to an equilibrium, with each species unconsciously carrying out "environmental coordination" following rules like those of a market, especially among plants. He gives many such examples. Economics will matter.

SETI broadcasters will face competing claims on resources, some from direct economic competition. Standing outside this, SETI beaming will be essentially altruistic, since replies will take centuries if not millennia, or else are not even an issue. SETI need not tax an advanced society's resources. The power demands we assume are for average powers in the gigawatt range (10^9 watts), far less than the 17 terawatts (10^{12} watts) now produced globally.

But even altruistic Beacon builders, like humans, will have to contend with competing altruistic causes. They will confront arguments that the response time for SETI is millennia, and anyway, advanced societies leak plenty of microwaves, etc., into deep space already. Clearly, only by minimizing cost/benefit will a Beacon builder's efforts succeed. This is parsimony, meaning "less is better," a concept of frugality, economy. Philosophers use this term for Occam's Razor, but here we mean the press of economic demands in any society that contemplates long-term projects like SETI. On Earth, advocates of METI (*M*essaging to *E*xtra*t*errestrial *I*ntelligence) also face economic constraints.

Note that parsimony directly contradicts the Altruistic Alien Argument that Beacon builders will be vastly wealthy and make everything easy for us. An omnidirectional Beacon, radiating at the entire galactic plane, for example, would have to be enormously powerful and expensive, and so not be parsimonious.[8]

My point is that literary ideas can have scientific consequences. Perhaps this is a good example of the interplay of science and sf, a facet that sets the genre apart from the rest of literature. It also shows that sf comes from the dance of these cultures, and thus has become a major way humanity contemplates its future.

Notes

1. Alexsey Tolstoy, *Aelita, or The Decline of Mars*, translator unidentified (1923; Ann Arbor: Ardis, 1985), 30.

2. Terry Carr, "The Dance of the Changer and the Three," 1968, *Nebula Awards Stories Four*, ed. Poul Anderson (1969; New York: Pocket, 1971), 50. A parenthetical page reference is to this edition.

3. Fredric Brown, "Arena," 1944, *The Science Fiction Hall of Fame, Volume I*, ed. Robert Silverberg (1970; New York: Avon, 1971), 307.

4. Silverberg, "Sundance," 1969, *The Road to Science Fiction, Volume 3: From Heinlein to Here*, ed. James Gunn (1979; Clarkston, GA: White Wolf, 1996), 472–473. A parenthetical page reference is to this edition.

5. Fred Hoyle, *The Black Cloud* (1957: New York: Signet, 1959), 188.

6. Benford, "In Alien Flesh," 1978, *In Alien Flesh* (New York: Tor, 1986), 29. A parenthetical page reference is to this edition.

7. See Benford, *Deep Time: How Humanity Communicates Across Millennia* (New York: Avon, 1999).

8. Adapted from James Benford, Gregory Benford, and Dominic Benford, "Searching for Cost Optimized Interstellar Beacons," *Astrobiology*, 10:5 (July, 2010), 491–498; "Messaging with Cost Optimized Interstellar Beacons," *Astrobiology*, 10:5 (July, 2010), 475–490.

Discriminating Among Friends

The Social Dynamics of the Friendly Alien

(1986 Eaton Conference)

John Huntington

Let me begin by emphasizing a distinction that underlies everything I have to say. The problems posed by the imagined alien are quite different from those posed by the actual alien. The imagined alien is a gratuitous invention, a complication that someone, for reasons that bear investigation, has added to the world. The actual alien is not gratuitous, and it has to be dealt with as it is. Of course, there is necessarily some overlap between the two. Actual aliens stimulate fantasies about aliens.

It does not seem unreasonable to view the imagined hostile alien as a projection onto "the other" of qualities of ourselves that we wish to deny.[1] This basic dynamic of the hostile alien is exquisitely rendered in Fredric Brown's "Arena" (1944) when Carson, the human hero, caught in what he claims is telepathic rapport with the hostile alien, describes his sensation as "Things that he felt but could not understand and could never express."[2] Having attributed his unacceptable feelings to the alien, Carson can then exclude it from the category of creatures requiring moral consideration and can attack it without reservation or qualm.

I have argued elsewhere that once a writer sets up such a system of exclusion as is required by the hostile alien story, the writer is trapped in it, and even an attempt to correct the exclusionary system fails to do anything but reverse the polarities and leads to anthrophobia in the place of xenophobia. Ursula K. Le Guin's *The Word for World Is Forest* (1972) is a clear instance of this process by which a strong attack on the xenophobic proclivities of humanity finds its satisfaction in scapegoating the prejudiced human.

As we have come to understand the stark exclusions of the hostile alien story, we have tended to disregard the more subtle dynamics of the benign alien. In imaginative literature, the phrase "friendly alien" becomes an oxymoron: the imagined friendly alien achieves its benignity by approaching the familiar and conventionally valued, that is, by not being truly alien. Such alienness is a superficial costume hiding a familiar personality.[3] But having observed this aspect of contradiction in the benign alien, we may ask why an author should undertake such an imaginative exercise in the first place. The motives for imagining the hostile alien seem clear enough; what motive would one have for imagining the friendly alien? I will suggest that the benign alien has at its core a social fantasy: that of radical individualism that would deny the meaning and power of social groups altogether.

In an essay attacking the xenophobia of American sf, Le Guin credits the "invention" of the "sympathetic alien" to Stanley G. Weinbaum's "A Martian Odyssey" (1934).[4] I wish to focus my inquiry on the fairly complex social dynamics of this elementary story. The story is probably familiar. Its plot is simple: Jarvis, a human separated from his expedition on Mars, saves the life of Tweel, a tall, birdlike alien; they become friends of sorts and have a series of adventures, in the last of which, when the humans arrive to save the day, Tweel disappears. Tweel is a charming character who verges on the incomprehensible. His language seems to keep changing; a thing is never called by the same word twice. He displays pleasure by soaring seventy-five feet into the air and descending like a javelin, nose first, to stick quivering in the earth. But behind such comic eccentricities, we see an essentially human figure: bipedal, rational, tool-using, capable of emotion and loyalty. Toward the end of the story, when Tweel has helped him escape the Martian barrel people, Jarvis says, "Thanks, Tweel. You're a man!" (38–39). Out loud he wonders whether that is really a compliment, but in the next breath he acknowledges that it is the highest form of praise he can conceive.[5] Thus, Tweel's differentness is superficial; he is an eccentric who, despite his oddities, is valued for the way he approaches a human ideal.

But Tweel is admittedly odd, and once we grant his difference, we find that "A Martian Odyssey" pays for its generosity toward him by an excessive anxiety about all other differences, even differences which seem absurdly trivial in the Martian context. The humans in the story are men of different nationalities, and while their comradeship is acknowledged, the story repeatedly points to the differences in their language and understanding. The difficulty even humans have understanding each other is rendered by confusions of pronunciation at the beginning of the story: Harrison (who is American) tells Jarvis, "Spill it, man." Leroy (who is French) asks, "Speel.... Speel what?" to which Putz (who is German) easily answers, "He means 'spiel.' ... It iss to tell" (14). A clumsy understanding is attained here, but it is by false etymologies and mispronunciations. Throughout the story, Leroy and Putz mangle idiomatic English. One has to be struck by Weinbaum's attention to this level of ethnic difference when the main theme of the story seems to be the areas of identity between aliens. This sense of the minor gaps between people can shade easily into hysterical and exclusionary discriminations.

Tweel aside, the other forms of Martian fauna—the living grass, the silicon bricklayer, the dream monster, and the barrel people—involve common clichés of alien exclusion of the sort we expect to find in hostile alien stories. The dream monster is the most conventionally hateful: like the Roller in Brown's "Arena," it is tentacled; it can be described a number of times simply as "one of those writhing, black rope-armed horrors" (30). Like the Roller, it has a telepathic capability that renders it particularly dangerous to the open, goodnatured human. The only way to deal with it is to destroy it. The barrel people belong to a slightly different set of clichés. They are laborious, self-oblivious, organized automatons who learn from Jarvis two phrases, which they repeat frequently: "We are v-r-r-riends. Ouch!" (35) The final revelation that Jarvis has stolen the shining thing that removes warts and may cure cancer places us casually in the imperialist tradition. It is taken for granted that Jarvis is in the right and that his theft is heroic; the barrel people's hostility turns out to be justified, but it is also disregarded.

We can observe here how casually a story which at one level has tried to be sympathetic to the alien can settle back into conventional postures. The effort to appreciate

Tweel cannot entirely change underlying discriminatory structures, and the more generous the story is toward Tweel, the more necessary it is for it to reinforce its essentially chauvinist base at other points in the story. One alien can be accepted as benign only by discovering another creature which can absorb the xenophobic charge. We can see this mechanism in the recent film *E.T.: The Extra-Terrestrial* (1982): as the alien gains our sympathy (by behaving in recognizably human ways), hostility is generated against such adult authorities as scientists and policemen. Sigmund Freud observes that "it is always possible to bind together a considerable number of people in love, so long as there are other people to receive the manifestations of their aggressiveness." He calls this phenomenon "the narcissism of minor differences," a phrase he admits does not do much to explain the phenomenon.[6]

If the differences in language and pronunciation repeatedly remind us of the potential distances between humans, they do not thereby settle the issue of friendship, for distance here may be a source of affection as well as hostility. On the one hand, there is a superficial bad-temperedness in the story: Harrison, the captain, repeatedly accuses Jarvis of being crazy; Jarvis himself makes a crack about the apparition of a woman being "as solid as Putz's head," and simply ignores Putz's confused "Vot?" (30). Such moments, while denotatively hostile, are also rituals of friendship. As the stereotype of the slow foreigner is developed, it is also being transformed from simple exclusionary mechanism into a language of a kind of affection. It is an affection, however, made possible by condescension. And just as the humans' seemingly hostile banter covers affection, so does the barrel people's rendering of "We are friends" conceal indifference and hostility.

The affection-hostility confusion parallels a confusion between superior and inferior intelligence. Harrison keeps trying to attribute Tweel's actions to craziness and to see his intellect as inferior. Jarvis prefers to see him as sane and intellectually superior: he observes that Tweel is able to learn some English while Jarvis himself can learn nothing of Tweel's language. The possibility that nouns keep shifting in Tweel's language may be evidence of confusion or of a superior antinomian awareness of radical individualism.[7] The barrel people render this enigma of intelligence even more acutely. Jarvis points out that Tweel's description of them is ambiguous.

> Their intelligence was not of our order, but something different and beyond the logic of two and two is four. Maybe I missed his meaning. Perhaps he meant that their minds were of low degree, able to figure out the simple things—"One-one-two-yes!"—but not more difficult things—"Two-two-four-no!" [34].

Although Jarvis finally concludes that Tweel meant the first, there is good reason for us to see these perhaps intelligent creatures as limited, as comic, mechanical, and routinized zombies. They imitate language without attaining it. In a late scene, we see them sacrifice themselves dispassionately.

These apparently epistemological problems (How can we evaluate alien intelligence? How can we tell affection from hostility?) may be misleading, however. Clearly, Jarvis's affection for Tweel exists regardless of the level of his intelligence, and, just as clearly, his affection for Putz and Harrison exists despite the hostile language. The difficulty is not one of knowing affection, but one of expressing it openly. For reasons that will become clear, desire is the issue here, and it is repeatedly blocked in this story.

The scene in which Jarvis sees the image of Fancy Long becomes central. As in a nightmare, behind the woman Jarvis finds the "black rope-armed horror" of the dream monster. But if Jarvis has a deep dread of the woman, he also desires her. The conflict leads to some bizarre moments. When Jarvis lets Tweel shoot the vision of the woman, we get one of a number of instances of narrative indecision. "I don't know why I stood there watching him take careful aim, but I did" (30). Clearly, Jarvis has realized that the image is false, that this is not really Fancy Long. His declaration of ignorance about his motives is necessitated by the atrocity his abstention sanctions: he has to deny that he allowed a woman to be shot. But he is also caught in a moment of passionate desire so strong that it is in danger of distorting his rational understanding of the situation even in the retelling.

The dream monster apparently "uses its victim's longings and desires to trap its prey." Jarvis cautions the crew to watch out. "We can't trust even our eyes," he warns. "You might see me—I might see one of you—and back of it may be nothing but another of these black horrors!" (31). Such a conviction justifies repression of all affection. The danger of the dream monster is that it might lure the men by their desire for one another. The important issue, however, is not anxiety about homosexuality, but anxiety about all desire.

When Tweel disappears toward the end of the story, Jarvis says, "He'd gone, and damn it! I wish—I wish he hadn't!" (39). What strikes one here is the quite extraordinary flatness of the obviously deeply felt line. In part, the hesitation after "I wish" and the tepid "hadn't" are formulas of the era (just like the phrase "just friends, get me?" [29] said earlier of Fancy Long), but they are also further signs of difficulty with feelings. Earlier, we see another instance of Jarvis' ability to say what he really feels and means when he stops himself in midsentence. Jarvis is talking:

> "Yet, in spite of all difficulties, I *liked* Tweel, and I have a queer certainty that he liked me."
> "Nuts," repeated the captain. "Just daffy."
> "Yeah? Wait and see. A couple of times I've thought that perhaps we—" he paused, and then resumed his narrative [21].

This last incomplete sentence is different from the usual narrative device in which the reader is able to fill in the words the speaker cannot say; here it is impossible to determine what Jarvis might have said. The break does not reveal what meaning the character is repressing.

If we cannot know exactly what Jarvis meant to say, we can nevertheless speculate on some of the issues he might discuss at this point. His concern with liking Tweel may lead him to generalizations about human affection. Or Jarvis might be responding to Harrison's accusation of craziness and intending to generalize about sanity and alienness. Or he might be about to comment on Harrison's general attitude and language, on the slandering of those we actually like.

Whatever the subject of his meditation, it breaks off on the enigma of the pronoun "we." The ambiguity of the "we" leaves it open whether his comment would be restricted to just Tweel and himself or would include Harrison, to whom he has just responded, or the rest of the crew, or perhaps larger generalizations (we men, we humans, we communicators, we explorers). By breaking where it does, the sentence emphasizes the problem of the constitution of the group, the "we."

This enigmatic gap in the story is a moment at which the story comes up against the real social dilemma posed by imagining the friendly alien. Try as it will to imagine forms of desire independent of social groups and conventions, the story finds itself inevitably forced to confront the crucial issue of the group. Even the unique couple, old as it may be, constitutes a social group and thereby changes or distorts the larger, more conventional social field. I am reminded of the extraordinary moment in Yevgeny Zamyatin's *We* (1921) when, as the revolutionaries surge into the city, one jubilantly exclaims, "We are acting!" D-503, caught between his love for I-330 and his still deeply ingrained social allegiance to the Benefactor, can only wonder in dismay, "Who are we? Who am I?"[8] The fantasy that we can define ourselves outside of the group is a powerful one, but it rather quickly comes up against the fact that the individual is defined, is only meaningful, against the background of a group. No sooner has the group been transcended than it must be reconstituted. Jarvis' dilemma is that he cannot—nor can any of us—"think" the contradiction of the individual and the group.

The question that arises is how much of the elaborate economy of love and hate in "A Martian Odyssey" is inherent in the formula fiction of America in the thirties and how much is structurally inherent in the act of imagining the friendly other. It would be naïve to think that we could settle the question precisely and finally. Clearly, some of Weinbaum's mechanisms are historically local. But if we consider Ursula K. Le Guin's "Nine Lives" (1969),[9] a much more self-conscious story published thirty-five years later, we can see that some aspects of this system of balances are common to efforts to imagine the sympathetic alien.

Le Guin's story is conscious of the difficulties we have been examining. In "Nine Lives," two miners, Martin (Argentine) and Pugh (Welsh), who have spent two years of irritable isolation on a volcanic planet, greet their assistance team, a "tenclone" consisting of five men and five women, all nearly identical. Relations between the two miners and the highly integrated tenclone are tense. When nine of the members of the tenclone are killed in an eruption, the survivor has to learn to trust and gain emotional strength from men different from himself. The story's thesis is, roughly, that the harmony that exists among members of the tenclone shows up as a kind of isolation ("Incest is it, or masturbation?" [313] asks Pugh when two members of the clone make love), while the friction caused by the difference between Martin and Pugh shows up as a negotiated contact which can achieve love. The gruff words that seem to point gratuitously to differences, while initially signs of disharmony in the human ranks, by the dialectical process that Le Guin makes explicit, finally become signs of affection.

We all know perfectly well, however, that differences do not necessarily breed affection. Le Guin's squabbling humans can finally declare their love for each other, but in other situations and with other people such petty nagging can be the obvious expression of deep antipathy. In the Weinbaum story, the system remains explosively undischarged of both possibilities. The love of the alien, whether Tweel or Martin, is in part a fantasy of overcoming obstacle to love.

But, if both stories are in favor of "love," we should also note that in both stories it is the harmonious group that is a major object of distrust. In Le Guin, the tenclone, while admirable for its efficiency, is too narcissistic (if one can use that term for a group) to engage in genuine social interaction. It substitutes good manners for true engagement with others. In Weinbaum's story, the barrel people are an allegory of social coherence; their mindless greeting, "We are v-r-r-riends! Ouch!" is in the same social category as the tenclone's good-mannered obliviousness to Pugh and Martin.

Tweel is, so far as we know, not part of a larger group. He is the only creature of his type Jarvis ever meets. The humans in the story seem to take it for granted that Tweel is a Martian, although he may be no more aboriginal than they are. After Jarvis tries to signify that Earth is his home, "Tweel set up such an excited clacking that I was certain he understood. He jumped up and down, and suddenly he pointed at himself and then at the sky, and then at himself and at the sky again. He pointed at his middle and then at Arcturus, at his head and then at Spica, at his feet and then at half a dozen stars, while I just gaped at him" (20). This is a confusing message, but after it one might expect Jarvis to investigate Tweel's origins more thoroughly. Instead, he just repeats the message about his own origins. The bond between Tweel and Jarvis is, therefore, not a sign of social integration, but rather the opposite: they represent individuals free from all social bonds and definitions who, in this state of isolation, find meaningful connection. At the moment Jarvis is reunited with his human comrades, Tweel is lost to him. Both of these stories aspire to finding bonds of loyalty and affection between individuals apart from and unrelated to the larger groups to which they belong. If "A Martian Odyssey" runs up against the problem of who "we" are, it also fantasizes a friendship that makes questions of who "we" are irrelevant.

We observe here a dialectical process that will belong to any consideration of the alien. If the story of the hostile alien is often an exercise in excluding individuals because of their group type, the story of the benign alien is often an exercise in finding a bond that transcends groups. It isolates the individual and emphasizes his or her difference from the rest of the species. This rejection of the group, while it may lead to a readiness to accept the individual alien, may also lead to a disregarding of social factors that generate discrimination in the first place. Just as the phrase "Some of my best friends are X" is often the preface for a discriminatory generalization about X, this claim to transcend group categories by finding the alien individual friendly, far from obliterating the categories, allows them to operate with impunity, beyond the control of rational awareness.

I would therefore suggest that the story of the benign alien may not be any more socially constructive than that of the hostile alien. The Freudian bond of "the narcissism of minor differences" is based on a strict emotional economy. Freud argues that the injunction to "love they neighbor as thyself" entails a disastrous contradiction: I can love so indiscriminately only if I disregard or devalue the very qualities and virtues that earn love. Similarly, I can love the extraordinary alien only by abandoning the social conventions which allow for rational exchange and understanding.

Afterword

I think the essay speaks for itself. I would only add that in the current national and global situation the implications of imagined aliens and understanding who "we" are seem even more immediately relevant than they did thirty years ago.

Notes

1. See Patrick Parrinder, "The Alien Encounter, Or, Ms. Brown and Mrs. Le Guin," *Science-Fiction Studies*, 17 (March 1979), 46–75; Gregory Benford, "Aliens and Knowability: A Scientist's Perspective," *Bridges to Science Fiction*, ed. George Slusser, George R. Guffey, and Mark Rose (Carbondale: Southern Illinois University Press, 1980), 53–63; Robert G. Pielke, "Humans and Aliens: A Unique Relationship," *Mosaic*, 13 (1980), 29–40; Mark Rose, *Alien Encounters: Anatomy of Science Fiction* (Cambridge: Harvard University Press, 1981), 77–81; and John Huntington, "Impossible Love in Science Fiction," *Raritan*, 4 (1984), 85–99.

2. Fredric Brown, "Arena," 1944, *The Science Fiction Hall of Fame, Volume 1*, ed. Robert Silverberg (New York: Avon, 1970), 307.

3. Pielke, 30.

4. Ursula K. Le Guin, "American Science Fiction and the Other," *Science-Fiction Studies*, 2:3 (November 1975), 208–210. Weinbaum's "A Martian Odyssey" has been frequently anthologized. I have used the text in *The Science Fiction Hall of Fame, Volume 1*, 13–39. Parenthetical page references are to this edition.

5. Parrinder discusses this compliment in "The Alien Encounter," 54.

6. Sigmund Freud, *Civilization and Its Discontents*, trans. James Strachey (New York: Norton, 1961), 68.

7. Jarvis has a typical Western condescension to thought processes he cannot follow. He plays with (and discards) the idea that Tweel's language may be like of the Negritos who have "No word for food or water or man—words for good food and bad food, or rain water and sea water, or strong man and weak man—but no names for general classes. They're *too primitive to understand* that rain water and sea water are just different aspects of the same thing" (22—emphasis added). There are, of course, other possible explanations besides "primitive" understanding for such linguistic behavior.

8. Yevgeny Zamiatin, *We*, 1924, trans. Mira Ginsburg (New York: Viking, 1972), 219.

9. "Nine Lives," first published in 1969, is also much anthologized. I have used the text in *World's Best Science Fiction 1970*, ed. Donald A. Wollheim and Terry Carr (New York: Ace, 1970), 302–327. A parenthetical page reference is to this edition.

Nature

Laws and Surprises

(1987 Eaton Conference)

Poul Anderson

I take "mindscapes" to mean imaginary settings—geographies of the mind as used in fiction. As a writer, I would like to discuss the construction of such imaginary settings, with reference, but not exclusive reference, to the role that natural law and scientific discovery play in their making.

I am not a literary critic nor a literary historian. What I can do or have done is make constructs of this kind. I propose to look at imaginative literature from that viewpoint, from the side where the nuts and bolts are. Needless to say, my remarks will be highly personal, and many of my fellow practitioners will probably disagree with some or all of them. Furthermore, for reasons both of time and of ignorance, I will necessarily omit a great deal. If your all-time favorites do not get mentioned, please forgive me.

Let us go straight to the subject. It seems to me that the setting of a story is as important in fiction, any kind of fiction, as it is in real life. There is the social setting, of course, the whole intricate web of human conditions, assumptions, and ways of going about things. Personalities in one kind of society differ in ways that are often very basic from personalities in another kind. But that is a separate large matter.

There is also the physical setting, the geography. Here on Earth, geography has had a powerful, pervasive, often decisive influence on societies. Civilization itself appears to have begun as a set of responses to a set of environmental challenges. Civilizations have had enormously different characters of their own, and much of this appears to be due to environment. For example, Karl August Wittfogel argued that despotic government originated in the Orient with what he called the hydraulic civilizations, where the work of building and maintaining irrigation systems required organization of mass efforts.[1] A quite similar form of despotism evolved in the Andes, culminating in the empire of the Incas, although there the labor undertaken was of a different kind. Be this as it may, a farmer on arable land and a nomad in the desert not only live differently, they think differently. There are subtler influences too. For example, being blessed with ample space and resources, Americans developed concepts of individualism and privacy far beyond those of Europe and still more beyond Asia. To this day, from an American viewpoint, they seem lacking, or rudimentary, in Japan. And yet the Japanese have a strong, creative, altogether admirable civilization. It simply is not the same as ours, and much of the difference appears due to the fact that the Japanese have less elbow-room than we do.

Environment may work on even deeper levels than this. Oswald Spengler developed a quasi-mystical concept of societies as organisms, each with its unique "soul," its inherent capabilities, drives, limitations, ways of understanding the world. He suggested that these arose from the landscape of the Urheimat, the country in which the core society came into being. For instance, the Apollonian Classical society, with its sense of order and boundedness, was born in the narrow valleys of Greece, while Faustian Western society, infinitely ambitious, was born on the great plain and in the great primeval forests of central Europe.[2] This may strike you as pretentious twaddle, and I will agree that it goes far beyond any verifiable facts, but it does have a certain suggestiveness. And in any event, there is little doubt that the settings in which all of us grew up and in which we now live have had much to do with making us the kinds of people we individually are.

Imaginative literature can make this interaction vivid. The author is free to construct radically strange environments, put people there, simplify social factors, and thus show us societies, with the individual persons in them, that are clearly shaped by their settings. An obvious example is the late Frank Herbert's novel *Dune* (1965). He imagined a planet that is one vast desert but nonetheless has been colonized. In the course of generations, human beings there have had to adapt all their institutions and ways of thinking to the harsh conditions around them. One might raise various technical quibbles about the likelihood of this or that feature of Arrakis and its civilization, but there is no disputing that Herbert did a marvelous job of visualizing his world in so much detail that while we are reading *Dune* we are lost in it, utterly convinced.

Apropos desert worlds, here I would like to put in a word on behalf of Edgar Rice Burroughs. He may not have been much when it came to style or characterization, but he knew how to tell a story, and he was also an uncommonly conscientious workman where it came to building his settings. Too many planets in science fiction are lazily made exactly like Earth, except for having neither geography nor history. Burroughs's Mars of the hurtling moons and dead sea bottoms and dying canal-side cities has no more to do with astronomy than does Ray Bradbury's Mars. It has serious logical flaws, such as the coexistence of swords and ray guns. But damn it, there is a lot of colorful and coherent stuff to explore on Barsoom! Likewise for Burroughs's Venus and Pellucidar.

I will come back later to the importance of sound construction as the basis for even the highest-flying fantasy. Here let me mention that in science fiction we also have the interesting option of letting our imaginary worlds bring forth intelligent beings of their own, nonhumans. Thereby we can speculate on how not only society but evolution may depend on setting.

As an example, allow me to bring in a novel of my own, *The Man Who Counts* (1958; originally published as *War of the Wing-Men*). It is not the greatest thing of its kind ever done—Hal Clement is the unchallenged dean of world builders—but this is a piece of construction that I know from the inside out. We have a planet large but poor in metals, therefore of low density. The result is that gravity at the surface is about the same as on Earth, but the gravitational potential is considerably higher. Therefore, the planet has hung onto more gas than ours has; the atmosphere is a great deal denser. This means that it can support winged, flying creatures more or less the size of a human, hence big enough to have large enough brains for intelligence. In addition, the planet has an axial tilt about like that of Uranus, rotating almost in the plane of its orbit, so that winter means total darkness over an entire hemisphere.

For lack of metals, nowhere on the planet have our flying natives gotten beyond the Stone Age, though some of them have invented some pretty sophisticated things. Even before there was intelligence, their ancestors had to make annual migrations between hemispheres. This conditioned the reproductive pattern and therefore the entire psychology. However, in recent centuries one society among them has partly liberated itself from the requirement by taking to the sea on huge rafts and catamarans. Normally the effort of making the migration works through the glands to release a sexual impulse, so that the migrant majority breed only at one time of year.

However, the sailors work hard on their vessels all the time, and therefore are subject to a milder but constant sexual impulse, like humans. You can see how profoundly alien these two kinds of society become to each other, and the potential for conflict between them. Religion, morality, law, custom—everything traces back directly or indirectly to the environment.

Now, of course, the more people advance in technology, the more they make, or even become, their own environment. This is not always for the best. Look at what we are doing to Earth and its biosphere, as well as to ourselves. Not that I want to sound like an ecofreak. Ignorance and conclusion-jumping, not to speak of hysteria, are far too common already. I remember some twenty years ago, following an Apollo mission on television, hearing the commentator solemnly declare that the Moon has no environment.

Having been a farm boy, I harbor no illusions about the so-called simple, natural life. But I do point out that already much of the human race, including those of us here today, spend most of our lives on what amounts to an alien planet. We are surrounded by man-made things, materials and objects and conditions never found in nature.

Science fiction has been looking into this business of man-made and man-modified worlds for a long time. Captain Nemo's *Nautilus* is a classic artificial environment. It also enabled Jules Verne to introduce readers to the wonders and strangeness of the undersea world, long before Jacques Cousteau. The spaceship *Enterprise* of *Star Trek* continues this tradition. It was thought out with some care; you can actually buy plans of it. To be sure, I wonder if it has an organizational chart at all. An officer on an aircraft carrier, which is an environment not so unlike that of the *Enterprise*, once told me in some detail how little those entertaining adventures have to do with any real-world naval operations. But never mind.

In a story called "Universe" (1941) and its sequel, Robert A. Heinlein did a marvelous job, also in this tradition. Probably many of you know the stories, perhaps, under their joint title *Orphans of the Sky* (1963). A giant spaceship, limited to speeds less than that of light, was built to go to Alpha Centauri. Since the voyage would take generations, the interior of the ship must be a self-renewing, fully recycling environment. A mutiny broke out, order collapsed, the survivors degenerated into barbarians and savages. At last nobody even knew they were in a spacecraft. Its interior was their entire universe. They had only dim, mythic traditions about "the Trip," and the more thoughtful among them interpreted these in a mystical or symbolic way. Since the only "gravity" they knew was due to the rotation of the gigantic cylinder they lived in, they also developed some curious notions about the physical nature of things.

Larry Niven's *Ringworld* (1970) and its sequel *The Ringworld Engineers* (1980) come close to giving us an ultimate artificial environment. You surely recall his astronomically huge annulus spinning around its sun, the inner surface with many times the area of Earth, possessing any number of unique regions and local phenomena. The development of the implications of a concept is one of the very special delights found in science fiction.

To be sure, it also has its special dangers—for the author, at any rate. He or she has thought of the basic idea, worked out the details as logically and thoroughly as possible, described them in a story, and gotten the story into print. Now there it sits, an irresistibly tempting target for anyone who suspects it contains mistakes of either fact or logic. Hal Clement calls this "the game." It is played between author and readers. The author's moves are all made beforehand, with the object of having zero flaws in the construction. (Purely literary quality is something separate.) The fewer scientific nits readers can pick, the higher the author scores.

It is more fun for him or her than it sounds, actually. Learning and argumentation are among the great pleasures of life, after all. This experience can be enlightening, and even profitable. In Niven's case, certain fundamental difficulties with the Ringworld as described were pointed out to him. So he wrote the sequel, mainly to deal with these matters, and it too was a highly successful book.

Heaven knows I have made my own share of blunders. Once I had some characters in a novel waiting out a crisis, meanwhile sipping the best wine in the house, which I specified. Somewhat later I got a letter from a gentleman in France: "Pretty good story, but as for that wine—oh, no, no, monsieur, that was a very bad year for it."

Another time, in a story set in Ice Age Europe, I made mention of a saber-toothed tiger. Another Frenchman, my late friend the paleoanthropologist François Bordes, told me this was an error. Although sabertooths were still around in America at that time, they were long extinct in Europe. Remarked he: "It seems long-toothed carnivores always survive later in America."

In a lengthy series of stories, all set in the same future universe but covering centuries of time and scores of planets, I have made considerable effort to keep things consistent; but inevitably, on occasion I have heard from some eagle-eyed fan to the effect that something in one story did not jibe with something in another. My standard reply to this has come to be: "Perfect consistency is possible only to God Himself, and a close study of Scripture will show that He doesn't always make it."

But of course, even though we often will fail, the ongoing effort to get things right is of fundamental importance. I really see no excuse for sloppy workmanship. A literary genius of the first rank may, once in a while, erect a splendid edifice on foundations of sand, but literary geniuses of the first rank are few and far between. Frankly, I doubt that any are alive at this moment, in any branch of literature. Whether this is true or not, I do not see that careful construction ever does any harm; and in most cases it makes all the difference.

By this I do not mean that absolute scientific accuracy is a *sine qua non* of good imaginative literature. For one thing, the scientific picture is always changing. We can still enjoy C.S. Lewis's *Out of the Silent Planet* (1938), for instance, in spite of what our space probes have since told us about Mars. Much of the cosmology in Olaf Stapledon's *Star Maker* (1937) is now obsolete, but his magnificent cosmic vision has lost nothing thereby. Yet I do invite you to note how solidly timbered these works are.

In fact, to name a few other tales, I remember sitting next to Jerry Pournelle at a meeting of the American Association for the Advancement of Science quite a few years ago, when the findings of the Pioneer One mission to Jupiter were first publicly described. Afterward we compared notes and found we had been thinking the same thing. As one revolutionary discovery after another came forth, we had thought: "There goes *Farmer in the Sky*. There goes 'Meeting With Medusa.' There goes 'Desertion.' There goes 'Call Me Joe.' There goes 'Bridge.'"[3] And so on for every memorable story ever written about Jupiter. Regardless, most of them are still remembered, still alive in reprint. Meanwhile, here we have been presented with this whole absolutely wonderful new world to write new stories about.

Besides the mutability of what we knew, or believe we know, there is the fact that often a story requires a nonscientific or counterscientific assumption. Travel faster than light is an obvious example. If ever we find that this is possible after all, we will probably find it within the context of a physics totally different from any that we have any hint of today, a physics in which general relativity is just a special case. The upheaval that that implies is beyond imagination. Nevertheless, when we need to get our hero from star to star in a reasonable time, we go ahead and use "hyperspace" or whatever. This is legitimate enough in itself, provided we respect the body of well-established fact otherwise. Indeed, speculation about the nature and characteristics of, say, hyperspace can form quite an interesting element in the story.

Scientifically preposterous environments are acceptable when really necessary to the author's purpose. Bradbury's Mars comes to mind. Here, though, we border on out-and-out fantasy, about which I would like to say a few words later on.

First I would like to return to planet building. It exemplifies the literary riches to be found in science, riches almost entirely neglected by the so-called mainstream. There are other uses of hard science in science fiction, for instance in creating imaginary biologies, but planet building is closest to our topic of environments. Besides, I have spoken on it and written about it repeatedly in the past, and so can claim to know some aspects of it pretty well. I am by no means alone in this, of course, and can name Greg Bear, Gregory Benford, and David Brin, all of them masters of the craft.

This is not the place to repeat myself. I simply want to skim over the subject as a way of showing that when we abide by the findings of science as best we can, we do not constrict ourselves. Rather, we get inspiration, and the tools with which to do a job that inspires and excites readers. I have sometimes called science fiction the tribal bard of science. Like a bard of old singing of the exploits of heroes, science fiction sings of wonders and possibilities revealed to us by our quest for knowledge. This is not the only thing science fiction does, of course, or even what it mostly does, but I do submit that it is something no other literary form ever really gets into.

Let us consider constructing an imaginary planet. First, unless it is wandering free in space, it has a sun. What kind of sun? There is a broad variety of types, not all of them well understood yet. Some are too unstable or otherwise short-lived, some too dim and cold, some too surrounded by lethal radiation, to be plausible hearth fires of life. However, a writer sufficiently imaginative and well informed may take this as a challenge, and go on to provide some such star with organisms that look plausible but that are quite alien to anything earthly.

Even with more conservative assumptions, we have to think of just what our sun is like in temperature, color, mass, and so on. Is it a single, a double, a triple star? If it is a multiple, how stable an orbit is a planet likely to have, and of what shape? How does that orbit precess, and otherwise change with time?

From a few assumptions, many consequences flow with mathematical inevitability. For instance, take a star of a given mass. If it is on the main sequence—an astrophysical technicality of great importance—then that mass and the age determine how bright it is, within a fairly narrow range. Set a planet revolving about it at some given mean distance. This immediately determines the length of the year and the irradiation received—in other words, the range of temperatures, the color of light, the basic patterns of climate and weather, and so on for a long list.

The sun is not the only factor in these calculations, of course. The planet itself has a great deal to do with them. Just for openers, its own mass and density tell you about its gravity field, which in turn gives you important clues to what sort of atmosphere and hydrosphere it may have, which in turn begins to give you a little insight into conditions down on the surface. I have already mentioned rotation, the tilt of the axis, and naturally the rate of spin as crucial factors. They are to at least some degree involved with any satellites the planet may have and now you start getting into things like tides and ocean currents and their effects.

I could go on at great length, but you get the idea. The end product is a set of dry-looking numbers. Few or none of them will get directly into the text of the story. And yet they are vital numbers—nuts and bolts, if you will, but also ribs and foundations, integral to the creation and to whatever sense of reality it may have.

Needless to say, this is the bare beginning. One must go on to geography, life forms, societies, eventually individual characters and their destinies. About these, obviously, there is progressively less and less inevitability, less precision, until in the end we reach those questions of life itself where calculation is impossible and only intuition can take us farther.

Even when it comes to the nuts and bolts, I do not want to get dogmatic. If I have sounded that way, it was mainly in order to save time. Right down at the elementary level of physics and chemistry, high school stuff, there is an immensity we do not understand. For instance, our ideas about how planets form are still vague and controversial. Lately it has turned out that even if we know all the laws and have all the data, we are often inherently unable to predict how a system will behave. In other words, we do not have to invoke quantum mechanics; we can think entirely in terms of differential equations and Newtonian determinism and still find the course of events unforeseeable in principle. The study of this is known as chaos theory, and I for one consider it to be of fundamental philosophical significance.

Then there are the remaining unknowns in our underlying concepts of the physical universe itself. Earlier I mentioned faster-than-light travel as an impossibility, unless we make such discoveries in the future that we must revise our entire physics. Well, that was another oversimplification. Frank Tipler has shown that a kind of faster-than-light travel, and for that matter a kind of time travel, are logically compatible with general relativity. They still seem to be physically impossible, but perhaps someday we will learn that here and there the conditions are actually met. In any event, this is an enormously exciting development, out of which I got a novel myself. I steal only from the best sources. It illustrates how marvelous, how profoundly meaningful, modern science really is.

By postulating natural phenomena and laws beyond our present-day ken, a number of writers have been enabled to work out some fine, fully conceived, soundly carpentered imaginary environments. Doubtless the foremost creator in this area is Philip Jose Farmer, who has probably given us more distinct settings than everybody else put together. Just think of the Riverworld stories, with a single river many thousands of miles long, looping all around its planet and running into itself, on whose banks awakens recreated every human being who has ever lived and died. Superscience is allegedly responsible for all this, but we know it is really magical omnipotence and that we are on the boundaries of pure fantasy here. Likewise, Farmer's multitiered "pocket universes," with their own laws of nature to fit the requirements of the story, allow the introduction of actual gods.

This is reminiscent of the grand old *Unknown Worlds* tradition of fantasy relentlessly and often hilariously following out the logic of its own premises. Thus, in the Harold Shea stories by L. Sprague de Camp and Fletcher Pratt, if there is an infinity of parallel but distinguishable universes, everything one can imagine must exist somewhere among them. The hero finds a way to travel to whichever he chooses, but the method does not always work, and even when it does, the place is never quite as he had envisioned it, whether it be the world of Edmund Spenser's *The Faerie Queene* (1590, 1596) or the world of Irish heroic sage. In each of the stories, the plot depends on just these carefully worked-out details of the setting.

Before going on to really pure fantasy, I might mention one more extraordinary set of environments generated by what is ostensibly a science fiction device. The book is *Eye in the Sky* (1957), by the late Philip K. Dick, and the settings, one after another, are the minds of the principal characters. Each comes out as a kind of landscape, special, weird, and yet deeply convincing. C.S. Lewis did something of the kind too, in a short story called "The Shoddy Lands" (1956).

But let us continue briefly to pure fantasy. I do not much like that term. It suggests there is some clear-cut boundary with science fiction, which of course there is not. For that matter, I do not think it makes sense to fence off either kind of literature, or any other, from the *soi-disant* mainstream. All fiction is fantasy, in the sense that it deals with unreal people and events. However, we can in a rough fashion mark off those stories that are not obliged in any way to take the facts of science into account. We visualize it, perhaps, as writing that makes more use of the right brain than of the left.

Yet I do not think its settings are any more exempt from the requirements of thought and care than any others. Certainly, to the extent that they use ordinary, nonmagical things, they should make sense. I once wrote an essay on the absurdities that disfigure so much heroic fantasy, such as having the hero swing a fifty-pound broadsword, gallop a horse all day, or go somewhere by sailing ship as steadily as he might if he had a motor. The supernatural element is different, of course. It can be spelled out with complete logic in the *Unknown Worlds* manner, but it does not have to be. In fact, I would say that except for humorous purposes, it is generally better to leave something mysterious, some questions unanswered and unanswerable. Nevertheless, the author does need to have a good understanding of the magic and the elven folk and the gods and so forth. He or she needs a kind of feel for them, if the reader is to get any.

Turning from generalities to the question of settings, one rather surprising feature appeared to me as soon as I started thinking about this. One would suppose the environments of fantasy are usually more strange, more evocatively set forth, than those of science fiction. But actually, the reverse is the case. Most fantasy stories take place on Earth of the present or the past, or a thinly disguised version of it. In fact, most fantasy characters are rather familiar and prosaic compared to the aliens or the far-future humans of the best science fiction.

Why is this? I suspect the reason is largely what I was discussing earlier, that science fiction draws much of its inspiration from science, from the vast and complex natural world that science reveals, and this always holds far more than the merely human can. As the Psalmist cried a long time ago: "When I consider thy heavens, the work of thy fingers, the moon and the stars, which thou hast ordained; What is man, that thou art mindful of him? and the son of man, that thou visitest him?"[4] (Psalms 8:3–4). By making an imaginative effort, we can create some wonderful fantasy settings. Such efforts can be cumulative over generations, and this is why nobody has ever bettered the environments of myth and folklore. At least, I do not know of anything that beats the places in the *Odyssey* or those that Sinbad the Sailor visited, nor that entire cosmos the Eddas put in and around the world tree Yggdrasil, nor a number of others. There are some splendid environmental touches in the Chinese classic known as *Journey to the West* (1592), such as a river of quicksand three hundred miles wide, but its authorship is uncertain and it amounts more to a compilation of legends than to an entirely new creation.

It is therefore understandable that modern writers often use ready-made settings with little or no modification. There is our present-day world for a start, and heaven knows, as I remarked earlier, it is quite weird enough. One thinks of H.P. Lovecraft's New England towns or Fritz Leiber's marvelously eerie phantoms rising from the smoke and grime and electricity of great cities.

There used to be remote, unexplored parts of the world, used by such imaginative writers as H. Rider Haggard, but jet aircraft and Earth satellites have taken those away from us. In this connection, I would like to put in a good word for another underrated writer, A. Merritt. His style was no doubt a bit florid, but his lost lands were beautifully visualized and worked out in loving detail.

You can go back into the past in search of a glamorous setting. Consider the current popularity of novels about King Arthur; most of them have a fantasy element. Currently my wife Karen and I are finishing the last volume of a novel that grafts the city Ys of Breton legend onto a late Roman Empire as realistic as a jot of research can make it.

There is also the pseudohistorical setting, in which the world much resembles something like, say, medieval Europe but is not identical. I am not putting down this class. Among other great works, it includes J.R.R. Tolkien's *The Lord of the Rings* (1954–1955) and Leiber's tales of Lankhmar.

The author can take over a mythical cosmos and play things out in it. Mark Twain did this in both a witty and touching way for the universe of the Bible, in his stories "Eve's Diary" (1905) and "Extract From Captain Stormfield's Visit to Heaven" (1907). Later writers have used various pagan mythologies, though some of these have gotten rather overworked.

It is more challenging to create one's own mythology, but also apt to be more rewarding when it does come off. Three cases in point are the Zimiavia books of E.R. Eddison, the Earthsea books of Ursula K. Le Guin, and Tolkien's *The Silmarillion* (1977).

In creating an imaginary world or a new mythology, it helps mightily to have a good ear, a gift for inventing names that are strange and evocative and right. For instance, in Fletcher Pratt's *The Well of the Unicorn* (1948), the battlefield Skogalang sounds as if there just has to be a battle there. In Eddison's *The Worm Ouroboros* (1922), the harshness of the name "Eshgrar Ogo" makes an enemy stronghold seem all the more forbidding. Lord Dunsany was an absolute master of the singing name—Merimna, Rhistaun, Perdondaris. So, currently, is Jack Vance—Starbreak Fell, AerUth, Embelyon, Kaiin.

We are moving on into realms where there is less of the known world and more of the author's sheer imagination. L. Frank Baum's various places in the land of Oz may have their sources, but they are all uniquely his. Still more splendidly themselves are the countries Alice found in Wonderland and Through the Looking-Glass.

I have mentioned dreamscapes in a science fiction context. We find a superbly visualized fantasy one in Rudyard Kipling's story "The Brushwood Boy" (1895). The trick is much harder to pull off than one might suppose. I once spent a week on quite a short story attempting it, "The Visitor" (1974), and still cannot judge the degree of its success or failure.

There is nothing overtly supernatural, but there is everything eerie and dreamlike, in Mervyn Peake's Titus Groan novels. That huge, moldering mansion is as original and unforgettable a setting as I have ever seen.

Lord Dunsany's stories of imaginary realms and of the borderlands of Faerie are equally haunting, because they are equally well realized. The author knew them. By far my favorite Lovecraft story is "The Dream-Quest of Unknown Kadath" (1943), which is strictly a Dunsany pastiche. Then there are all those lovely little touches elsewhere in Dunsany, like falling off the edge of the world, or opening a manhole, looking down, and seeing the stars.

I could go on, but this is quite enough. At that, I have omitted any number of fine writers and excellent works. I have scarcely touched the vast realm of science fiction and fantasy in languages other than English. But I have not been trying to review the subject, only to discuss, a little bit, one aspect of it, the importance of a good foundation beneath the edifice, a strong skeleton behind the flesh and blood and glamour. In the effort to make such a groundwork, we will find ourselves harking back again and again to the real world, to nature, the infinite permutations of her Jaws and the endless, enlightening surprises she keeps springing on us.

Afterword (by Karen Anderson)

Poul called science fiction the tribal bard of science. But bards make history into tales of wonder; *poet* means *maker*, not merely rhymer. Homer's Troy was rediscovered by a grocer with a poet's vision. Science fiction writers see the physicist and chemical engineer as heroes, like Jason's shipmates or King Arthur's knights, seeking—instead of gold or grail—technologies so advanced that they cannot be distinguished from magic.

Notes

1. See Karl August Wittfogel, *Oriental Despotism: A Comparative Study of Total Power* (New Haven: Yale University Press, 1957).

2. See Oswald Spengler, *The Decline of the West*, two volumes, 1918, trans. Charles Francis Atkinson (London: Allen & Irwin, 1926–1928).

3. The works referenced are Robert A. Heinlein's *Farmer in the Sky* (1950); Arthur C. Clarke's "A Meeting with Medusa" (1971); Clifford D. Simak's "Desertion" (1944); Anderson's "Call Me Joe" (1957); and James Blish's "Bridge" (1952).

4. Psalms 8:3–4.

In the Palace of Green Porcelain

Artifacts from the Museums of Science Fiction

(1989 Eaton Conference)

Robert Crossley

Recall these scenes from a short list of science fiction masterpieces: A twenty-first-century Englishman, the last human being on Earth, finds relief from loneliness by studying "the Diorama of ages" in the monuments, libraries, and galleries of Rome. A traveler, seeking his stolen time machine, takes an afternoon off to explore the darkened corridors and ruined exhibits in a derelict museum. An unhappy mathematician feels his imagination disturbingly liberated as he walks through a preserved ancient house of the nineteenth century, "completely enclosed in a glass shell" like an enormous museum exhibit. Ten million years from now a crew of engineers in Siberia unearths a vast underground archive of scientific and historical records carved on stone tablets by the survivors of an ancient atomic disaster. A former graduate student, having escaped a devastating plague in North America, wanders the stacks of a deserted university research library, reverently handling its books. A stowaway on an intergalactic starship is given a guided tour of the local city museum of an alien world, with special attention to a gallery of art reproductions and natural history models from Earth. In an era of profound climatic change, a pirate in a white suit hauls treasures up from the tropical waters covering the cities of Europe and installs them in his own floating museum. A visiting professor of physics from the Moon, touring a museum of decorative arts in a sophisticated capital on the mother planet, sickens at the sight of a royal ceremonial garment made from the tanned skins of human beings. A self-taught reader in an illiterate future America sits in the film archive at New York University painstakingly deciphering the printed speeches of twentieth-century silent films. A visionary in a post- industrial tribal society examines the stone pillars that once supported a vanished cathedral before an atomic detonation destroyed Canterbury hundreds of years before. A twenty-first-century Australian in a world impoverished by the cumulative effects of the greenhouse phenomenon steps into the museum of Melbourne's cinematographic society and views the slapstick comedies of his great-grandparents' culture.[1]

This preliminary catalog of artifacts from the museums, libraries, and archives of science fiction provides variants of a scene that gets reconstituted with astonishing frequency in science fiction narratives. The spectacle of an observer examining an artifact and using it as a window on to nature, culture, and history permits that convergence of anthropological, prophetic, and elegiac tonalities that science fiction handles more powerfully than any other modern literary form. The building itself, as much as the artifact, is important in such scenes. A museum operates as a place that is at once social, impersonal, and contemplative; it also, necessarily, constitutes an artificial world that disorients spectators in space and time. As a locale, therefore, the museum is ideally suited to science fiction, that form of fantastic literature most concerned with the speculative and the epistemological, most focused on humanity at large rather than the private self, and most at home on other worlds and in times to come. When a science fiction protagonist experiences an epiphany in a museum the event enacts in a very precise way the preoccupations of the genre itself.

Every public museum is a repository of some portion of the past and an act of faith in the future; it is a laboratory for humanistic or scientific research; it is an organized record of cultural differences and continuities; it stands as a secular and populist alternative to the private collections of churches and social elites. Similarly, science fiction is specially concerned with temporality and change, with the representation and analysis of cultural difference, with experimental constructions of hypothetical realities, with the intersections of natural history and human history, and with the development of countercultural and popular audiences; in all these respects it has functional affinities with the museum. Above all, both the museum and the science fiction text have a paradoxical relationship to time. "Virtually all the best science fiction is, explicitly or implicitly, a kind of time travel," one recent historian of the genre has argued.[2] The same might be said of the best museums. A museum is never wholly a monument to the past any more than science fiction is narrowly or exclusively a literature of the future; while the museum typically represents the past (even if only the recent past), its interest in preservation makes it profoundly committed to the future, and while science fiction is usually oriented to the future it rarely looks ahead without also glossing the present and the past. A museum may not be precisely a time machine, but it is a contrivance that collapses linear time and encourages the tourist who visits it to shuttle back and forth imaginatively among temporal worlds. Before looking more closely at the uses of such temporal disjunctions in a few of the fictional scenes in museums summarized in my preliminary list, I want first to sketch a very brief institutional history of the museum as it bears on the aesthetic concerns of science fiction.

The opening of museums as public buildings rather than private "cabinets of curiosities" roughly parallels the historical rise of science fiction. Both the public museum and the genre of science fiction are emblems of the nineteenth century's experiment in the democratization of culture. It is true that one may find suggestive anticipations of science fiction in Lucian or Milton or Jonathan Swift, and so too there are prefigurings of the modern museum in ancient and Renaissance collections of natural objects and cultural artifacts. Nevertheless, most historians of science fiction find the genre achieving its authentic identity only in the nineteenth century—either with Mary Shelley, if you follow Brian Aldiss's account of Gothic origins, or somewhere in the latter third of the century if you accept Mark Rose's argument that the genre is emphatically postromantic[3]—and similarly most cultural historians see the public museum as essentially a nineteenth-century creation. Ancient collections with limited access, like those housed in the Library at Alexandria, were more akin to the private holdings of the royal houses of Europe than to the museums and libraries of the past two centuries. The treasure hoards of feudal lords have far more in common with the contemporary market for "collectibles" as a form of investment than with the museum's functions of conservation, arrangement, and public display of artifacts. Of other possible prototypes for the modern museum, the most viable is the medieval cathedral, which in its architecture and crafts (if not always in its manuscripts and art treasures) could make limited claims to be "people's buildings," open to all.[4]

When the first London College of Antiquaries was founded in 1572 its members celebrated their personal collections of rarities—often the loot from so-called voyages of discovery—more as trophies of wealth and as hobbies to be shared with fellow antiquarians than as bases for museums of science or of art; but in the eighteenth century a reformed Society of Antiquaries began to articulate the principles on which future public museums would be established. Collectors of scientific and artistic curiosities, the Society maintained in initiating its journal *Archaeologia* in 1770, might help prevent the darkness of ignorance from descending on a future age:

> The only security against this and the accidents of time and barbarism is, to record present transactions, or gather the more ancient ones from the general wreck. The most indistinct collection has this merit, that it supplies materials to those who have sagacity or leisure to extract from the common mass whatever may answer useful purposes.[5]

By the end of the eighteenth century the connoisseur was in the ascendancy over the indiscriminate collector, although not every putative rarity could live up to the Society's grand claims. The century could boast Sir Hans Sloane's extraordinary 100,000 specimens that eventually formed the core collection of the British Museum, but there were also such whimsical sideshows as Pontius Pilate's wife's chambermaid's sister's hat in the collection of James Salter—a useful reminder that the connoisseur and the con artist often roam the same territory.[6] But the Society of Antiquaries, while championing the scholarly value of even "the most indistinct" of its members' holdings, was not proposing to open the collections to any but those few suitable people of "sagacity or leisure."

The Ashmolean is widely recognized as the first modern museum, in which natural history specimens, antiquities, and various "curiosities" were arranged for display, for teaching, and for public inspection at a charge of six pence, so that country folk arriving in Oxford on market-day could crowd in to examine Roman burial urns, St. Augustine's crozier, or the famous stuffed dodo.[7] In fact, the *Oxford English Dictionary*'s first two recorded usages of "museum" in its modern sense of "a building or portion of a building used as a repository for the preservation and exhibition of objects" are references to the Ashmolean.[8] But the Ashmolean was not typical of eighteenth-century museums, and its location in a university town ensured that its primary audience would be scholarly. The British Museum, established in 1759, took nearly a century to begin to admit the public in significant numbers on a regular basis.[9] The model public art museum in the early nineteenth century was the Louvre—which managed to combine the populist principles of the Revolution with the rich plunder gathered up during the Napoleonic wars—and the Pennsylvania Academy of Fine Arts had similar intentions of being a "people's palace." But London took several decades to catch up with these democratic tendencies. The reopening of the British Museum in 1829 at its new location in Bloomsbury, the completion of the domed reading-room in 1857, and the siting of the Natural History, the Science, and the Victoria and Albert Museums in South Kensington in the second half of the century are vital signs of the coming of age of the English public museum. The dramatic potential for the emerging museum as a locale in science fiction can be illustrated by comparing two nineteenth-century futurist texts, one published when the fascination with museums was just beginning to catch the public imagination and one published later when museums were enjoying their heyday.

The final scenes of Mary Shelley's 1826 eschatological novel *The Last Man* are played out in the palaces and churches of Italy as Lionel Verney and a diminishing circle of companions seek consolation for the impending extinction of humanity by contemplating "master-pieces of art," "galleries of statues," and other "antiquities."[10] Arriving in Venice, the survivors climb the tower of San Marco for a prospect view of the tumbledown condition of the city's famous buildings, the paintings defaced by salt water and mud, and the seaweed draped over marble artifacts. "In the midst of this appalling ruin of the monuments of man's power," Verney writes with romantic gloom, "nature asserted her ascendancy, and shone more beauteous from the contrast" (319). Alone after the deaths of his last two companions during a storm, Verney takes a grim satisfaction in imagining how, if the earth should ever be repopulated by some other intelligent species, our artifacts might offer a window on to human civilization and "we, the lost race, would, in the relics left behind, present no contemptible exhibition of our powers to the new comers" (331).

The Last Man's ultimate destination is Rome, "the capital of the world, the crown of man's achievements" (335). Its "storied streets, hallowed ruins, and stupendous remains" (335) make the whole city the great outdoor exhibit of European culture. Wandering among the sculptures of Phidias and Praxiteles, touring the Coliseum and the temple of Jupiter, Verney wants to validate the grandeur of human aspiration and achievement. But when he sees a buffalo walking along the ancient Roman avenues he understands that the age of human dominance is gone, that already other creatures have begun to occupy the space we called "Rome." He takes to sheltering in an abandoned palace, where he can pass his sleepless nights with splendid paintings; in a Keatsian gesture he embraces and kisses the cold marble of statues representing passionate lovers; and mimicking papal pomp he solemnly ascends the steps of St. Peter's to carve the numbers 2100 in stone, the date of humanity's last year. In the absence of any social context, both the artifacts and the beholder appear ludicrous or pitiful. At the end Verney harbors no more illusions about "eternal Rome"; he feels himself a living anomaly, his body "a monstrous excrescence of nature" (340), and Rome becomes both physiologically and psychologically a deathtrap: a breeding-place for malaria and a shrine to the dead-end of human aspiration.

Few of the buildings Shelley's Verney visits can be properly called "museums." The power of this climactic scene resides in its focus on monuments, urban architecture, and artifacts which belong to the public perception, even myth, of imperial and ecclesiastical Rome. It is Verney's consciousness, rather than the design of a curator, that organizes these disparate artifacts and displays them to the reader as a lesson in the glory and the boundaries of artistic achievement. When H.G. Wells attempted a similar didactic episode seventy years later in *The Time Machine* (1895) he was able to do so with greater concentration and a more impressive art because he could draw upon the idea of the public museum and the experience of museum-goers in ways not quite yet available to Shelley. "At the first glance," the Time Traveller recalls of his stepping through the main door of a still-imposing though disused building 800 millennia from now, "I was reminded of a museum."[11] The familiarity of the design of its entrance ("the customary hall, a long gallery lit by many side windows" [82–83]) leaves him in no doubt about the building's purpose and signals to the reader that the function of this episode will be in some way analogous to our familiar museum experiences. In this instance, as in many others in the early history of science fiction, Shelley and Wells seem almost to work in tandem: she pioneering an intellectual strategy and he discovering its most streamlined narrative form; she articulating the archetype and he imagining the fictional prototype. If Shelley found a way to turn all Italy into a museum as a way of fabricating a *memento mori* for the human species, Wells succeeded in creating the most memorable of all science-fictional museums, the eerie, deserted, ruinous Palace of Green Porcelain.

Inside that vast structure of metal, glass, and tile the Time Traveller explores galleries of paleontology, mineralogy, botany, zoology, chemistry, military history, ethnography, industrial history, and many others unspecified in the course of a long and wearying afternoon. Excepting some sketchily described futuristic machines in one gallery, all of the exhibits might have been found in London in 1895. Wells's Palace is almost certainly a composite of the several branches of the British Museum in Bloomsbury and South Kensington as they existed at the close of the nineteenth century. In uniting these separate buildings into one "Palace" Wells accomplished in fiction and in the future what Prince Albert dreamed of at mid-century: a single grand institution that would acknowledge the interdisciplinary nature of anthropological study and that would not separate natural history from human artifacts in the study of culture. Surviving photographs suggest that some details of Wells's Palace are drawn directly from the Victorian museums he knew: the enormous fossil of a brontosaurus at the entrance to the Palace is reminiscent of the brontosaurus that dominated the East Dinosaur Gallery of the Natural History Museum and "the old familiar glass cases of our own time" (83) duplicate those that the trend-setting British Museum had just installed in its ethnographic galleries. The cracked and smashed "white globes" (85) the Time Traveller sees hanging from the ceiling of an interior gallery undoubtedly reflect the recent installation of electrical lighting in the buildings at Bloomsbury and South Kensington.[12]

Many commentaries on *The Time Machine* either ignore this chapter, or view it as a kind of interlude in the narrative, or give it short shrift as a supply depot out of which the Time Traveller can arm himself to recover his machine and so advance the plot to its proper culmination in the year thirty million.[13] But Wells and his traveler have to go out of their way to get to the Palace of Green Porcelain—eighteen miles, the Time Traveller estimates—and there may have been more convenient ways to get fire and a club into the Time Traveller's hands if that was all Wells was after. The Palace is a locale central to the aesthetic and moral design of *The Time Machine*, I suggest, because Wells saw the institution of the museum as an immediately accessible icon for the narrative's philosophical concerns with nature and culture, time and change. In what he calls "this ancient monument of an intellectual age" (84) the Time Traveller, alternately exhilarated and dismayed, receives a vision of mortality, of the inexorable processes of time, of the frailty of human culture second in power only to his more famous apocalypse in the year thirty million. If that later vision of the world's end offers the definitive view in *The Time Machine* of the hostility of the cosmos to terrestrial life, the epiphany in the Palace of Green Porcelain is the book's most concentrated lesson in the vanity of human wishes and the brevity of mind.

Any catalogue of artifacts from science fiction's many museums would have to give pride of place to the contents of Wells's Palace: the sealed camphor and matches, the bulky corroded machinery, the Eloi necklaces fashioned out of fossilized bones, the dummy dynamite caps, the inoperable guns, and the easily vandalized stone idols arranged in what the Time Traveller names "the ruins of some latter-day South Kensington!" (83) But the most spectacular moment in the Palace of Green Porcelain comes when the Time Traveller enters a room hung with "brown and charred rags." At first mistaking them for decayed military banners, he quickly grasps that he has happened upon the museum's library and that the rags are what survive of its books. Staring at the empty bindings, he wryly places the fate of his own seventeen published scholarly papers on optics into the framework of a universal disintegration of texts: "They had long since dropped to pieces, and every semblance of print had left them. But here and there were warped boards and cracked metallic clasps that told the tale well enough. Had I been a literary man I might, perhaps, have moralized upon the futility of all ambition." In his epiphany in the museum Wells's Time Traveller, not for the last time in the narrative, marks the end of a world. The "sombre wilderness of rotting paper" (87) in the Palace's library furnishes an elegiac commentary on the fantasy of the triumph of will over time, of art over nature. Precisely because the Time Traveller does not speak out of the wishful sensibilities of "a literary man," the episode amounts to a matter-of-fact repudiation of the bravado that opens Shakespeare's fifty-fifth sonnet:

> Not marble nor the gilded monuments
> Of princes shall outlive this pow'rful rhyme.

Tellingly, what survive best in the Palace are the means for destruction—sulfur and camphor and matches, rusty hatchets and a mechanical lever recycled into a mace; the works of intellect and imagination are only as durable as their materials. Poetry, philosophy, criticism, scholarly journals, scientific romances, the printed words you are reading right now: these are far more fragile.

Wells's successor as historian of the future, Olaf Stapledon, imagined more durable textual artifacts surviving time's processes, but foresaw an equivalent fragility in the mental and moral stability of future users of the materials preserved from the past. One entire stage of *Last and First Men* (1930) can be described in terms of a pair of crucially placed archives. Stapledon's Patagonians, struggling to contrive a human civilization some 100,000 years from now, are psychologically devastated when a team of archaeologists discovers in the basement of a derelict building in China metal plates from which twentieth-century books were printed. Decoding this futuristic Rosetta Stone, Patagonian linguists and cultural anthropologists realize that their own culture, at a stage roughly equivalent to the European Renaissance of the sixteenth century, had been long since surpassed and that their human ancestors had not been primitive but highly and dangerously developed. Everything the Patagonians thought they were discovering and inventing was in fact a recovery. Some of them find this revelation a deterrent to initiative and become reactionaries incapable of facing the future because paralyzed by the past; others take the evidence of a lost high civilization as reason to hope that such a level of material comfort and intellectual vigor might be achieved again.

In the upshot this "progressive" mentality wins out, though the triumph is as problematic and as compromised as that of our familiar twentieth-century progress. The Patagonians restore civilization at the price of nationalism, global warfare, economic rivalries, class stratification, squandering of planetary resources, and at last the unleashing of the djinn in the bottle of atomic energy. A chain reaction scalds the planet and destroys all but thirty-five members of the human species, and thus the ruined Chinese depository of printing blocks predicts the cycle of human risings and fallings central to the aesthetic and psychological design of *Last and First Men*; the artifacts miraculously preserved from the twentieth century serve only to stimulate the cataclysm of the hundred-thousandth century. Out of that cataclysm the survivors in Siberia, before sinking after several generations into subhuman barbarism, create a stone archive preserving as much knowledge of the Patagonian civilization as they can on carved tablets, along with a pictorial dictionary and grammar. The project falters when newer generations begin to resent "the hardship of engraving endless verbiage upon granitic slabs."[14] Inevitably, several million years later, that stone museum is unearthed, its artifacts decoded, and its ideals recycled into the evolved human species Stapledon calls the Second Men. The condition of the literary artifacts in Wells's Green Palace and the uses made of the historical records removed from Stapledon's archives testify to both the grandeur and the ironies in the human project of composing imperishable monuments, whether in stone, in metal, or in words.

In George Stewart's *Earth Abides* (1949), the library at the University of California at Berkeley has a similarly pivotal role in defining an attitude toward civilization. Initially Isherwood Williams cherishes the library as a cultural temple and a bulwark against a reversion to barbarism in the aftermath of a global epidemic. "Here rested in storage the wisdom by which civilization had been built, and could be rebuilt," we are told after Ish carefully breaks into the building.[15] But as a new Arcadian society forms, the library's treasures, at first invested with a taboo status by Ish, come to seem largely irrelevant to the future. Books, after all, are "mere wood-pulp and lamp-black" (268) in an unlettered culture. When a great fire burns most of the San Francisco Bay area near the end of the novel, the elderly Ish observes among the gutted buildings of the university campus the still-intact library, its million volumes amazingly spared from the flames. He feels he should rejoice in this preservation but is no longer sure that the accumulated wisdom of earlier ages will matter to the future. Guiltily, he turns his back on the literary and scientific culture embodied and entombed in the library: "Will I dream of a million books passing in endless procession, looking reproachfully upon me because after so long I have begun to have doubts in them and all they stood for?" (309).[16]

As Ish stands in the reader's near future pondering a more distant future, he loses confidence in the ability of a bankrupt past to offer any usable guidance for those who will shape the new society. "History repeats itself," according to one of the central aphorisms in *Earth Abides*, "but always with variations" (176), and therefore the relation of past and future will always be problematic. In a later post-catastrophe novel which imagines a less attractive illiterate society than the neo-Amerindian one Stewart projected, Russell Hoban has staged an epiphany in the closest thing to a museum in southeastern England to survive the nuclear holocaust that ended twentieth-century civilization. At "CambrySenter," the latter day mystic Riddley Walker discovers a crypt that once sat beneath Canterbury Cathedral. Entering the hole in the ground where, as it seems to him, stone trees grow out of the earth, he is shaken by his perception of a saner ancient world whose artisans carved pillars with such cunning art and out of an instinctive sense of the wholeness of things:

> it come to me what it wer wed los. It come to me what it wer as made them peopl time back way back bettern us. It wer knowing how to put therselfs with the Power of the wood be comestoan. The wood in the stoan and the stoan in the wood. The idear in the hart of every thing.
>
> If you cud even jus only put your self right with 1 stoan. Thats what kep saying its self in my head. If you cud even jus only put your self right with 1 stoanyouwd be moving with the girt dants of the every thing the 1 Big 1 the Master Chaynjis. Then you myt have the res of it or not. The boats in the air or what ever. What ever you done wud be right.
>
> Them as made Canterbury musve put therselfs right. Only it dint stay right did it. Somers in be tween them stoan trees and the Power Ring they musve put therselfs wrong.[17]

In *Riddley Walker* (1980) these relics from medieval culture outline the tragedy of Riddley's world and ours but they also define the aesthetic of the artifact Riddley is making as he struggles with a degenerate language to write the autobiographical and anthropological narrative that we read, a text in which Riddley attempts to put himself—and the world—right again.

In Arthur C. Clarke's *Childhood's End* (1953), the epiphany takes place on another world, although as in *The Time Machine* from the moment the protagonist enters the alien building of the Overlords there is no doubt in his mind that the structure must be a museum. The stowaway Jan Rodricks, stunned by the radical strangeness of daily life on another planet, gets "a much needed psychological boost to find himself in a place whose purpose he could fully understand."[18] But if he finds the physical layout of the interstellar museum familiar and reassuring, Jan does not find his actual tour of the museum an antidote to culture shock. Far from it. In an interview with the Curator for Earth, he is distressed at how few of the terrestrial specimens he can identify and at the magnitude of his ignorance of human culture. His pride chastened, he then is given a further jolt when he sees the model of an enormous eye of a "cyclopean beast" from a distant stellar system (197), an eye so frighteningly alien that it further reduces the stature of human beings in the midst of a Nature infinitely inventive and profoundly inhuman.

J.G. Ballard's *The Drowned World* (1962) is enacted on our own planet but its physical environment is in many ways as alienating as anything in *Childhood's End*. The most spectacular site in *The Drowned World* is the submerged London planetarium to which the biologist Robert Kerans descends in diving gear, but the essential museum-locale in the novel may be Strangman's "treasure ship," a mobile monument to kitsch and rapacity. Strangman, the leader of a gang of vandals who plunder the abandoned cities of Europe, has installed meretricious pseudo-art in the form of fake marble columns, peeling gilt banisters, gold-colored draperies and tassels that, we are told, give the ship's decor the look of "a bad film set of Versailles."[19] The ship's cataloguing room contains a miscellany of good and bad pieces looted from museums: stone limbs and torsos, an ornamented altar piece, stacks of gilt-framed pictures, pairs of huge cathedral doors, pieces of armor, equestrian statues, ceremonial ink stands, and other assorted bric-a-brac. Strangman, walking his visitors through the storeroom, identifies this mass of stuff with a single identifying phrase about its original home: "Sistine Chapel" or "Medici Tomb." One of the tourists on this pirate ship murmurs, "Aesthetically, most of this is rubbish, picked for the gold content alone" (93). Another member of the party says of the museum relics simply, "They're like bones" (93). And two black sailors from Strangman's crew turn this into a derisive chant: "Bones! Yes, man, dem's all bones! Dem bones dem bones dem…!" (94).

Strangman, as Mark Rose has indicated, is the pivotal figure in *The Drowned World*, and his project to drain the water from London and re-expose the artifacts from the city's lost museums is a ghoulish activity.[20] The museums in Ballard's narrative are the tombs of the past, and the effort to reclaim the past—whether by acquisitive madmen like Strangman or by Kerans's scientific expedition into the sunken planetarium—leads to revulsion, nightmare, and flight. Ballard's museums, presided over by the spookily elegant skeletons of Delvaux paintings and the surreal images of Max Ernst, have an elegiac function like the Palace of Green Porcelain, the Rome of *The Last Man*, and the ruins of Canterbury Cathedral, though where Wells, Shelley, and Hoban emphasize the achievements that have been lost, Ballard highlights (even more emphatically than Stewart) the dilapidation of Western culture and (with Clarke) dramatizes the alienation of the museum visitor from the artifacts. Ballard's science-fictional museum becomes either a sterile memento of a world well-drowned as in the underwater planetarium or a cultural rummage in which artistic accomplishment is inextricably linked with vulgarity, robbery, and racism.

I end as I began with Wells and Shelley. Almost the Time Traveller's last act in the Palace of Green Porcelain, a gesture that from one perspective is the most trivial in the whole narrative, occurs when museum-fatigue has left him with a waning interest in the silent galleries he has been exploring. He enters a room full of ancient totems from a great cross-section of planetary cultures and pauses before a massive figure carved in soapstone: "And here, yielding to an irresistible impulse," he says, "I wrote my name upon the nose of a steatite monster from South America that particularly took my fancy" (89). This piece of apparently gratuitous vandalism, this desire to announce his presence and even to claim possession of the artifact, not only makes an incongruous link between Wells's self-consciously proper Victorian and Ballard's sleazy Strangman, it also stands as one of the most provocative commentaries on the recurrence of museums in science fiction. Wells's Time Traveller, anonymous to us, in an act of mischief carves his signature into an ancient artifact encountered 800,000 years from now. Every reader of *The Time Machine* remembers the pair of flowers the Time Traveller brings back from the future to his dinner guests in 1895, but the impulse to leave behind some graffiti in 802,701 is an equally eloquent—and perhaps a more revealing—gesture. Although no one will ever read it, the Time Traveller cannot forgo the self-important announcement that Kilroy was here. Mary Shelley's Lionel Verney does much the same sort of thing in his final days, getting white paint from a deserted shop and, as he makes his way toward Rome, inscribing his name in three languages on a conspicuous place in each town he passes through: "Verney, the last of the race of Englishmen." Beneath this flamboyant obituary, he adds as postscript, this time only in Italian, a more homely *cri de coeur* addressed to the figment of another survivor: "Deh, vieni! tiaspetto!" [Come, I beg you. I am waiting for you!] (332).

To these self-focusing flourishes we might add Ish's discovery of his own name written on the check-out slip of a book on geography in the Berkeley library (268), Kerans's startled vision of himself in a mirror in *The Drowned World*'s planetarium (106), and Jan Rodricks's irrational and overwhelming conviction that that single, gigantic, artificial eye is staring at *him* (196). In all these instances we are reminded that in the showcases of science fiction's museums *we* are what is chiefly on display. The artifacts in the museums may be historical, extraterrestrial, or futuristic, may be the most elegant products of a refined civilization, the unfathomable evidences of a totally alien mind, the shameful testimony of human crimes, the poignant relics of a vanished splendor, or junk indiscriminately preserved by time's accidents. Whatever its source, whatever the predilections or deficiencies of its curators, the science fiction museum invites the reader to become a tourist and to peer into the glass case in wonder and often in alarm at an object that collapses distances of time and space, disorients and displaces the observer, and ultimately requires us to put ourselves right again. Such curiosity, disorientation, estrangement, and altered perception is a sequence the reader of works in this most modern of fictional genres frequently undergoes. Certainly in science fiction's museums, if we look long enough, we will at last and almost inevitably see with unmistakable clarity an object inscribed not only with Kilroy's name but with ours.

Afterword

About thirty years ago when I wrote this essay—presented in abbreviated form at the 1989 Eaton Conference—I was intrigued by the parallel development of two modern phenomena: the public museum, arising from private collections of objects, and science fiction, arising from the literary tradition of romance. My interest was not just in the parallels but the intersections between the museum and science fiction. In what ways did museums as repositories of artifacts, and science fiction as a speculative, interrogatory genre, address issues of knowledge, time, and the human place in the world? And to what effect did museums appear as locales and symbols in science fiction? I deliberately used the term "museums" loosely to include libraries and archives, and would continue to do so today because all these institutions preserve products of the human imagination for public study, instruction, and pleasure.

In the essay I said the eleven instances of museums in science fiction first listed constituted "a preliminary catalog" of such scenes. The seven texts discussed in some detail in the bulk of the essay are each landmarks in the history of science fiction, from Shelley's *Last Man* in 1826 to Hoban's *Riddley Walker* in 1980. More examples of more recent science-fiction narratives could easily be added to my preliminary catalog. Some are obvious: the London Natural History Museum in China Miéville's *Kraken* (2010) and Amsterdam's destroyed Rijksmuseum in Frederick Turner's futurist epic poem *Apocalypse* (2016). Others would be unconventional variants on the "traditional" museum. In Joan Slonczewski's *A Door into Ocean* (1986) the tree rafts on the water world of Shora are living archives that contain in their chromosomes all the biological and historical knowledge of the planet's women inhabitants. Kim Stanley Robinson evokes one of the oldest museums in human history, the recently rediscovered Caves of Chauvet with their prehistoric wall paintings, in his ice age novel *Shaman* (2013). There is an explosion (literally) of libraries and catalogs in Reif Larsen's encyclopedic *I Am Radar* (2015). But this is not the occasion for an exhaustive listing of museums in science fiction over the past four decades. Happy hunting to those who would enjoy the search. It is clear to me that museums, libraries, and archives continue to have an important function in the science-fictional imagination, uniting the strange with the familiar, the past with the future, the human with the alien.

I cannot resist noting another, pleasant irony as I think about whether my now-somewhat-elderly essay continues to speak relevantly to our present stage in science fiction history. If writing today, I would have to acknowledge, with considerable delight, that the relationship between museums and science fiction has grown more complicated. Now we can speak of science fiction in museums as well as museums in science fiction.

Already in the 1980s the Eaton Collection at the University of California, Riverside, which hosted the Eaton conferences, had become the largest public collection of science fiction publications, manuscripts, films, fan materials, correspondence, and ephemera in the world. In 1993 the growing collection of the U.K.'s Science Fiction Foundation found a proper home at the University of Liverpool Library. Switzerland's Maison d'Ailleurs [House of Elsewhere] struggled to establish itself as the major continental museum and library of utopian and science fiction and, by acquiring the Jules Verne archives in 2003, finally succeeded. There is a Science Fiction Museum and Hall of Fame in Seattle, and, at this writing, a virtual Museum of Science Fiction is operating out of Washington, D.C., with a brick-and-mortar (more likely glass-and-metal) structure planned for the future. In addition to museums of its own, science fiction has been getting public exhibitions at established museums, including "Out of This World: Science Fiction but Not as You Know It" at the British Museum (2011), "Fantastic Worlds: Science and Fiction 1780–1910" at the Smithsonian's Museum of American History (2016–2017), and "Into the Unknown: A Journey Through Science Fiction" at the Barbican Centre in London (2017). Authors' papers are now archived at specialized libraries devoted to genre fiction, like those at Riverside and University of Kansas, but also institutions not usually associated with science fiction: Arthur C. Clarke's archives are housed at the National Air And Space Museum, Octavia Butler's at the Huntington Library, Ursula K. Le Guin's at the University of Oregon. Now, much more than when I wrote "In the Palace of Green Porcelain," the traffic between science fiction and museums operates on a two-way street.

Notes

1. The events summarized come from these novels, in order: Mary Shelley, *The Last Man* (1826); H.G. Wells, *The Time Machine* (1895); Yevgeny Zamyatin, *We* (1924); Olaf Stapledon, *Last and First Men* (1930); George R. Stewart, *Earth Abides* (1949); Arthur C. Clarke, *Childhood's End* (1953); J.G. Ballard, *The Drowned World* (1962); Ursula K. Le Guin, *The Dispossessed* (1974); Walter Tevis, *Mockingbird* (1980); Russell Hoban, *Riddley Walker* (1980); and George Turner, *The Sea and Summer* (aka: *Drowning Towers*) (1987).
2. Karl Kroeber, *Romantic Fantasy and Science Fiction* (New Haven: Yale University Press, 1988), 27.
3. See the opening chapters of Brian W. Aldiss with David Wingrove, *Trillion Year Spree: The History of Science Fiction* (New York: Atheneum, 1986), 25–52, and Mark Rose, *Alien Encounters: Anatomy of Science Fiction* (Cambridge: Harvard University Press, 1981), 1–23.
4. On the development of the modern science museum out of private libraries and "cabinets of curiosities" see Silvio A. Bedini, "The Evolution of Science Museums," *Technology and Culture*, 6 (Winter 1965), 1–29. Alma Stephanie Wittlin chronicles the emergence of the "public service" function of the museum in *The Museum: Its History and Its Tasks in Education* (London: Routledge, 1949).
5. "Introduction," *Archaeologia, or Miscellaneous Tracts Relating to Antiquity, Published by the Society of Antiquaries of London*, 1 (1770), ii.
6. On the collections of Sloane and Salter see Arthur MacGregor, "The Cabinet of Curiosities in Seventeenth-Century Britain," *The Origins of Museums: The Cabinet of Curiosities in Sixteenth and Seventeenth-Century Europe*, ed. Oliver Impey and Arthur MacGregor (Oxford: Oxford University Press, 1985), 147–158. See also Michael Hunter, "The Cabinet Institutionalized: The Royal Society's 'Repository' and Its Background," Impey and MacGregor, 159–168.
7. Reports of early tourists to the Ashmolean, including continental scholars scandalized by the open-admissions policy, are cited in Martin Welch, "The Ashmolean as Described by Its Earliest Visitors," *Tradescant's Rarities: Essays on the Foundation of the Ashmolean Museum, 1683, with a Catalogue of the Surviving Early Collections* (Oxford: Oxford University Press, 1983), 59–69.
8. Useful discussions of the early history of the word "museum" in English appear in Wittlin, 1–8, and Hunter's appendix to "The Cabinet Institutionalized," Impey and MacGregor, 168.
9. On discontent in the 1820s over limited public access to the British Museum's collections and reading-room, see Edward Miller, *That Noble Cabinet: A History of the British Museum* (London: Andre Deutsch, 1973), 122–124.
10. Mary Shelley, *The Last Man*, 1826, intro. Brian W. Aldiss (London: Hogarth, 1985), 313. Parenthetical page references are to this edition.

11. Wells, *The Time Machine*, 1895, Atlantic Edition of *The Works of H.G. Wells*, Volume I (New York: Scribner's, 1924), 83. Parenthetical page references are to this edition.

12. Kenneth Hudson discusses Prince Albert's ideal of a unified museum in *Museums of Influence* (Cambridge: Cambridge University Press, 1987), 69–70. Photographs on pages 27 and 71 show, respectively, the new glass cases at the British Museum and the brontosaurus skeleton in the Museum of Natural History.

13. In *The Definitive Time Machine: A Critical Edition of H.G. Wells's Scientific Romance* (Bloomington: Indiana University Press, 1987), Harry M. Geduld sees the visit to the Palace as an "autonomous" episode in which Wells "is depicting scenes rather than developing plot" (12). My earlier commentary on the Palace in *H.G. Wells* (Mercer Island, WA: Starmont, 1986) treats it only as a place where the Time Traveller "procures weapons" (26). An important exception to this general neglect is John Huntington's account of the visit to the museum as an instance of Wells's mediation of opposites in *The Logic of Fantasy: H.G. Wells and Science Fiction* (New York: Columbia University Press, 1982), 46–47.

14. Olaf Stapledon, *Last and First Men*, 1930, *Last and First Men and Star Maker: Two Science Fiction Novels by Olaf Stapledon* (New York: Dover, 1968), 95.

15. George R. Stewart. *Earth Abides*, 1949 (New York: Fawcett Crest, 1971), 116. Parenthetical page references are to this edition.

16. Ish's wistfulness about the good old days is countered throughout the novel by Em, the new Eve of the emergent Arcadian society, who indicts the failures of the Euro-American imagination. As a woman and African American, Em refuses to mourn the lost cultural literacy of the past, makes mordant observations on the "communication" that resulted from European voyages of exploration to Africa and the Americas (174), and derides the vindictive male God of Judeo-Christian tradition (258).

17. Russell Hoban, *Riddley Walker*, 1980 (New York: Pocket, 1982), 161–162.

18. Arthur C. Clarke, *Childhood's End* (New York: Ballantine, 1953), 194. Parenthetical page references are to this edition.

19. J.G. Ballard, *The Drowned World*, 1962 (Harmondsworth: Penguin, 1965), 92. Parenthetical page references are to this edition.

20. See Rose's superb commentary on *The Drowned World* in *Alien Encounters*, 127–138.

Just How Frumious Is a Bandersnatch?

The Exotic and the Ambiguous in Imaginative Literature

(1989 Eaton Conference)

Joseph D. Miller

The appropriate point for the initiation of an essay on the use of exotic and ambiguous description in fantastic literature must be, almost by definition, Lewis Carroll's "Jabberwocky" (1871):

> 'Twas brillig, and the slithy toves
> Did gyre and gimble in the wabe;
> All mimsy were the borogoves,
> And the mome raths outgrabe.
>
> "Beware the Jabberwock, my son!
> The jaws that bite, the claws that catch!
> Beware the Jubjub bird, and shun
> The frumious Bandersnatch!"
>
> He took his vorpal sword in hand:
> Long time the manxome foe he sought—
> So rested he by the Tumtum tree,
> And stood awhile in thought.
>
> And as in uffish thought he stood,
> The Jabberwock, with eyes of flame,
> Came whiffling through the tulgey wood,
> And burbled as it came!
>
> One, two! One, two! and through and through
> The vorpal blade went snicker-snack!
> He left it dead, and with its head
> He went galumphing back.
>
> "And hast thou slain the Jabberwock?
> Come to my arms, my beamish boy!
> O frabjous day! Callooh! Callay!"
> He chortled in his joy.

'Twas brillig, and the slithy toves
Did gyre and gimble in the wabe;
All mimsy were the borogoves,
And the mome raths outgrabe.[1]

Now let us turn out attention to something a bit different. This is my own pastiche of the Carroll poem. I call it "Uzi Jockey":

'Twas autumn, and the fallen leaves
Did gyre and gambol in the wind;
All yellowed was the grassy weave,
The snows would soon begin.

"Beware the Kodiak, my son!
The jaws that bite, the claws that rake!
Beware the mountain lion, and shun
The underfoot rattlesnake!"

He took his Uzi's grip in hand:
Long time the fearsome foe he sought—
So rested he by the pinewood tree,
And stood awhile in thought.

And as in frozen thought he stood,
The Kodiak, with claws like steel,
Came snuffling through the barren wood,
And thought, "I sense a meal!"

The bullets flew, and sportsman true
The leaden spray was right on track!
He left it dead, and with its head
He went full gallop back.

"And hast thou slain the Kodiak?
Come to my arms, my sporting boy!
O glorious day! Hoo ray! Hoo ray!"
He chuckled in his joy.

'Twas autumn, and the fallen leaves
Did gyre and gambol in the wind;
All yellowed was the grassy weave,
The snows would soon begin.

With the exception of some scattershot aimed vaguely in the direction of the National Rifle Association, the former and latter poems differ in one respect. In my pastiche, all neologisms have been replaced with English terms that are at least tonally plausible in terms of the original. There is no doubt that the original is far superior to the "deconstructed" version.

But why should a variety of nonsense terms contribute so much more than their pedestrian equivalents? This question exemplifies the central issue of this essay: that is, what is the role of ambiguous description in fantastic literature? By "ambiguous," I particularly refer to the obscure, the indistinct, the uncertain.

The Carroll poem is an excellent jumping-off point. Science fiction authors seem to be particularly fascinated by "Jabberwocky." In 1943 Henry Kuttner and C.L. Moore suggested in their story "Mimsy Were the Borogoves" that the poem is actually an accurate description of events transpiring in the far future.[2] Bandersnatchi are favored members of Larry Niven's "Known Space" bestiary.[3] And Roger Zelazny has recently added the

Bandersnatch and the Jabberwock to his cast of characters in the "Son of Amber" series.[4] I argue here that this infatuation with "Jabberwocky" is of diagnostic significance in an analysis of style in science fiction.

I think it is possible to argue the goals of science fiction right up to the final heat death of the universe (and in previous Eaton Conferences in Riverside that has seemed to be an imminent possibility!). However, I suspect everyone can agree that a major, if not the major, goal is attainment of an emotional apprehension of subjects lying beyond our current comprehension. Good science fiction extrapolates from the known to the unknown, but it cannot provide a detailed "map of Hell."[5] Too detailed a map would make Hell simply another suburb. This argument leads to the contention that truly evocative style in imaginative literature must incorporate elements of the ambiguous and the obscure. I do not, however, hypothesize that science fiction and fantasy differ qualitatively from other genres in this regard, but rather that the imaginative literature differs, by necessity, in sheer quantity of descriptive obfuscation. In fact, the depiction of exotic cultures in mainstream literature often utilizes these same techniques to convey a feeling of the outré (e.g., James Clavell's *Shogun* [1975] or Martin Cruz Smith's *Gorky Park* [1981]).[6]

In this essay I compare successful applications of this surrealistic style with representative failures in the attempt to convey a sense of the fantastic. I suggest that the failures often result from an overly literalist, nuts-and-bolts descriptive approach. I do have an ulterior motive here: an analysis of style requires adequate sampling of text. Thus it is a necessary pleasure to present some of my personal favorites, including some of the greatest evocative successes and some of the most dismal failures in the imaginative literature.

A good place to begin the analysis is a scene from the progenitor of the cyberpunk genre, K.W. Jeter's *Dr. Adder* (1984):

> "Just a minute," said Limmit, rising and heading for the door opening onto the bathroom. "Funny—all that time in the sewers, and I could hardly take a crap to save my life the whole time." He pushed the door open. Great splotches of drying blood splashed in static patterns across the floor and walls, small spots like red stars spattered across the ceiling. A corpse, twisted and unrecognizable, stiffening in the contortions of violent death, lay half out of the bathtub and across the tiny room, one hand cradled in the curved trap of the sink's drainpipe, his head, or what remained of it, partially submerged in the toilet bowl. The still water had turned into translucent rose.... Limmit reached in and pulled the shattered head out of the bowl, dripping. Little clumps of brain tissue, like soft pink cauliflower, and one perfect staring eye floated in the red water. Ah, fuck it, he thought, and squatted on the toilet seat after dropping his pants down to his knees. Living in L.A. sure makes you callous.[7]

A more graphic evocation than this is hard to imagine. But I maintain that this is not evocation of the fantastic or the mysterious; this is evocation of horror. The directors of the grade B science fiction movies of the 1950s were well aware of the distinction I am trying to draw. The creature is almost never revealed until the last reel (although this is also partially attributable to the poverty of special effects in these films; consider James Arness as Giant Carrot in the original version of *The Thing* [1951]).[8] This use of the *presque vu* allows the maximization of mystery and suspense. But John Carpenter's version of *The Thing* (1982)[9] leaves almost nothing to the imagination and rightly suffers in comparison with the original film, and certainly with John W. Campbell, Jr.'s story "Who Goes There?" (1938),[10] the inspiration for both films. Similarly, movies such *Aliens* (1986) and *The Fly* (1986)[11] are certainly powerful and disturbing, but chronic visual overstatement only habituates the viewer to what should be truly alien.

Here is another example of overstatement, from David Gerrold's *A Matter for Men* (1983):

> Feeding! It was rending the child limb from limb! Its gaping mouth was frozen in the act of slashing and tearing and his struggling body. The Chtorran's arms were long and double-jointed. Bristly black and insectlike, they held the boy in a metal grip and pushed him toward the hideous gnashing hole. The camera caught the spurt of blood from his chest frozen in midair like a crimson splash. I barely managed to gasp, "They eat their—their prey alive?" Dr. Obama nodded. "Now I want you to imagine that's your mother. Or your sister. Or your niece."[12]

Although I rather enjoy an occasional contest between flamethrowers and giant centipedes, I doubt that this descriptive style is likely to generate even a hint of the intrinsic strangeness that must occur at first contact with aliens. A passage describing the Old Ones from the *Necronomicon* of the mad Arab, Abdul Alhazred, does a much better job:

> By Their smell can men sometimes know Them near, but of Their semblance can no man know, saving only those in the features of those They have begotten on mankind; and of those there are many sorts, differing in likeness from man's truest eidolon to that shape without sight or substance which is Them. They walk unseen and foul in lonely places where the Words have been spoken and the Rites howled through at their Seasons. The wind gibbers with Their voices, and the earth mutters with Their consciousness.... Great Cthulhu is Their cousin, yet can he spy Them only dimly. Il Shub-Niggurath! As a foulness shall ye know Them. Their hand is at your throats, yet ye see Them not; and Their habitation of even one with your guarded threshold. Yog-Sothoth is the key to the gate, whereby the spheres meet.[13]

H.P. Lovecraft was a master of tone. Exotic nomenclature and a baroque style allow us to "see through the glass darkly," and what we see is far more alien than giant centipedes. Another master of this style was William Hope Hodgson, as is evident in a passage from *The House on the Borderland* (1908):

> An idea came swiftly, and I turned, and glanced rapidly upward, searching the gloomy crags, away to my left. Something loomed out under a great peak, a shape of greyness. I wondered I had not seen it earlier, and then remembered I had not yet viewed that portion. I saw it more plainly now. It was, as I have said, grey. It had a tremendous head; but no eyes. That part of its face was blank.
>
> Now, I saw that there were other things up among the mountains. Further off, reclining on a lofty ledge, I made out a livid mass, irregular and ghoulish. It seemed without form, save for an unclean, half-animal face, that looked out, vilely, from somewhere about its middle. And then I saw others—there were hundreds of them. They seemed to grow out of the shadows. Several I recognized almost immediately as mythological deities; others were strange to me, utterly strange, beyond the power of a human mind to conceive.
>
> On each side, I looked, and saw more, continually. The mountains were full of strange things—Beast-gods, and Horrors so atrocious and bestial that possibility and decency deny any further attempt to describe them. And I—I was filled with a terrible sense of overwhelming horror and fear and repugnance; yet, spite of these, I wondered exceedingly. Was there then, after all, something in the old heathen worship, something more than the mere deifying of men, animals, and elements? The thought gripped me—was there?[14]

Baroque? Rococo? Undoubtedly. But still, it is the very ambiguity of expression here, the attempt to grasp meaning through a poor resonance with the gods of our earliest pantheons, that allows us a dim glimpse of another reality. Yet another example of this style is taken from J.R.R. Tolkien's *The Fellowship of the Ring* (1954):

> It came to the edge of the fire and the light faded as if a cloud had been over it. Then with a rush it leaped across the fissure. The flames roared up to greet it, and wreathed around it; and a black smoke swirled in the air. Its streaming mane kindled, and blazed behind it. In its right hand was a blade like

a stabbing tongue of fire; in its left it held a whip of many thongs. "Ai! Ai!" wailed Legolas. "A Balrog! A Balrog is come!" … the shadow about it reached out like two vast wings. It raised the whip, and the thongs whined and cracked. Fire came from its nostrils. But Gandalf stood firm…. The Balrog made no answer. The fire in it seemed to die, but the darkness grew. It stepped forward slowly on to the bridge, and suddenly it drew itself up to a great height, and its wings were spread from wall to wall, but still Gandalf could be seen, glimmering in the gloom; he seemed small, and altogether alone; grey and bent, like a wizened tree before the onset of a storm.[15]

That is a selection from perhaps the single greatest example of minimalist style in the fantastic literature. It is an image that remains fresh in my memory, though engraved there some twenty-seven years ago. But the Balrog is little more a blade, a whip, and a pair of wings. What explains the enduring power of this image? I think it is the very sparseness and ambiguity of description that makes the Balrog a kind of projective test for the imagination.

Another acid test for my thesis is provided by authors' attempts to portray superhuman intelligence in science fiction. Here, for example, is an excerpt from Poul Anderson's *Brain Wave* (1954):

"Come in." He opened the door. She sat behind a littered desk, writing up some kind of manifest. The symbols she used were strange to him, probably her own invention and more efficient than the conventional ones. She still looked as severely handsome, but there was a deep weariness that paled her eyes. "Hullo, Pete," she said. The smile that twitched her mouth was tired, but it had warmth. "How've you been?" Corinth spoke two words and made three gestures; she filled in his intention from logic and her knowledge of his old speech habits: (Oh—all right. But you—I thought you'd been co-opted by Felix to help whip his new government into shape). (I have,) she implied. (But I feel more at home here, and it's just as good a place to do some of my work. Who've you got on my old job, by the way?)[16]

That is communication between the superintelligent? The only concession Anderson makes to the 400+ IQs involved here is that a greater portion of semantic content is transmitted by gesture rather than by words. But the semantic content itself is completely unremarkable. A similar difficulty in describing the supergenius occurs in Daniel Keyes's "Flowers for Algernon" (1959):

June 5 I must not become emotional. The facts and the results of my experiments are clear, and the more sensational aspects of my own rapid climb cannot obscure the fact that the tripling of intelligence by the surgical technique developed by Drs. Strauss and Nemur must be viewed as having little or no practical applicability (at the present time) to the increase of human intelligence…. The surgical stimulus to which we were both subjected has resulted in an intensification and acceleration of all mental processes. The unforeseen development, which I have taken the liberty of calling the Algernon–Gordon Effect, is the logical extension of the entire intelligence speed-up. The hypothesis here proven may be described simply in the following terms: Artificially increased intelligence deteriorates at a rate of time directly proportional to the quantity of the increase.[17]

Since the protagonist in Keyes's story, Gordon, is initially of subnormal intelligence, our expectations for the brilliance of his writing are perhaps lower than for the superminds of *Brain Wave*. Still, these diary entries convey no hint of wild human genius, let alone supergenius. In marked contrast is the depiction of superhuman intelligence in Thomas M. Disch's *Camp Concentration* (1968). Here are some comments on God from Disch's syphilitic superman:

HEAVENLY REFRESHMENTS Intolerable foreword! That he cannot at once annihilate anything! The just pause before that which tends to non-being. Barb-tailed Scorpio, as Master Drer demonstrates, cannot annihilate anything. Therefore, come, tender little ones—to plash again! Introduce yourself to my blood's Phlegethon. Ah, how nicely I burn now. Go it, guests! through all my talents! Now you listen, now you hear the flagellants' invisibly tiny griefs. I would not squander my lamps and oil. Annihilations. It would be so comforting like the "dead." Pale Venus, Pia Mater, accept these few spirochetes.... Ramiform, the column of fluid blasphemies ascended his spine, undergoing swift corruption. This neaptide of pus is not easy to extricate.... That mighty gallery, Anastomosis, primal forest of essential being that we call Heart's Blood. Obtunding, he descends on all that tends to non-being; he descends, and Frightfulness lurks alongside, who is born of Nothingness, and inhabits Here-and-Now.... It is enormous, of a sort without haecceity. Without prejudice to All-Maker's goodness, it may be called Slug Water. We must venture farther down, beneath God's lily, to the "Fathers" (Faust, q.v.). And without prejudice to his hairy palms, we are farctate with hatred and scorn. We thumb our noses. Plant life, water rills, quavers, enervations. Greenness reflects the most flagitious of them (God).[18]

Now this conveys much more of the sense of the superhuman. The text is wild and brilliant and nearly incomprehensible. Many of the terms are so obscure that they function almost like the neologisms of the *Necronomicon*. And so, ironically, even the well defined may be employed to generate the state of ambiguity essential to perception, albeit myopic, of the superhuman. Gene Wolfe likewise employs the obscure in the generation of mood, tone, and ultimately, illumination in *The Shadow of the Torturer* (1980). Here Wolfe writes of Master Gurloes, of the Guild of Torturers: "His eyes were refulgent, brighter than any woman's. He mispronounced quite common words: urticate, salpinx, bordereau."[19]

Another characteristic superhuman trait is telekinesis or teleportation. Let us first examine a description of telekinesis from A.E. van Vogt's *The World of Null-A* (1948):

"The main point is, if we're right, your extra brain is an organic Distorter, and all that that implies. With the help of the mechanical Distorter, you should be able to similarize two small blocks of wood in three or four days, and that will be the beginning." ... The ascendancy of mind over matter—age old dream of man. Not that he had done it without assistance. Every effort had been made to make the two blocks similar. And yet they would have changed slightly since then. So slightly. His body heat in the confined room would have affected them. Both the light beam and the surrounding darkness would have had a different influence on each block, despite the absorber tubes that lined the walls, despite the most delicate electron thermostat. Without the Distorter, of course, he wouldn't have succeeded this first time. It had similarized the blocks to nineteen decimal places. It quieted the molecular movement of the air, partially similarized the table on which the blocks rested, Gosseyn's chair, and Gosseyn himself.[20]

The preceding text exhibits all the verbiage of superscience: electron thermostats, atomic distorters, and matter exactly similarized to nineteen decimal places. But it is so overstated as to preclude any possibility of our sharing in the phenomenological experience of telekinesis. This is the major pitfall of what Gregory Benford refers to as stylistic blowout in science fiction.[21] In fascinating contrast is the vivid description of "jaunting" in the final pages of Alfred Bester's *The Stars My Destination* (1957):

He was not blind, not deaf, not senseless. Sensation came to him, but filtered through a nervous system twisted and short-circuited by the shock of the PyrE concussion. He was suffering from Synaesthesia, that rare condition in which perception receives messages from the objective world and relays those messages to the brain, but there in the brain the sensory perceptions are confused with one another. So, in Foyle, sound registered as sight, motion registered as sound, colors became pain sensations, touch became taste, and smell became touch. He was not only trapped within the labyrinth of the inferno under Old St. Pat's; he was trapped in the kaleidoscope of his own cross-senses. He jaunted. He was aboard "Nomad," drifting in the empty frost of space. He stood in the door to nowhere. The cold was the taste of lemons and the vacuum was a rake of talons on his skin. The sun and the stars were a shaking ague that racked his bones.[22]

Now that is the way to describe the indescribable! There is little in the way of neologism here, but the text is wonderfully exotic. What could be more ambiguous and uncertain than to be synaesthetically adrift? The synaesthetic metaphor allows the substitution of a sense of internal dislocation (the *presque vu*) for the extreme external dislocation (the *jamais vu*) that must result from teleportation. And so our dim apprehension of the almost seen confers on us at least the flavor of that which we will never see. This is a far cry from Benford's example, "He sounded green down the analytic corridors."[23] Admittedly, the synaesthetic experience has been overused in science fiction, but my contention is that such trite usages (which now, at best, only summon a sense of the déjà vu) largely derive from Bester's accomplishment of no less than a literal description of the loss of all reference. And in doing so he communicates a terror comparable to that experienced by the first oxygen-drunk piscean terranaut. Bester employs a text-graphics mosaic in these passages that further contributes to the evocation of a mood of internal and external sensory chaos. What is completely remarkable here is that this commingling of word and image was accomplished in 1957, decades before the vaunted age of high-tech desktop publishing.

Perhaps the final test of this essay's thesis is the description of transcendence in science fiction. Let us first examine the transmogrification of Valentine Michael Smith in Robert A. Heinlein's *Stranger in a Strange Land* (1961):

> Mike continued to walk unhurriedly toward the crowd until he loomed up in the stereo tank in life size, as if he were in the room with his water brothers. He stopped on the grass verge in front of the hotel, a few feet from the crowd. "You called me?" He was answered with a growl. The sky held scattered clouds; at that instant the sun came out from behind one and a shaft of light hit him. His clothes vanished. He stood before them, a golden youth, clothed only in beauty—beauty that made Jubal's heart ache, thinking that Michelangelo in his ancient years would have climbed down from his high scaffolding to record it for generations unborn. Mike said gently, "Look at me. I am a son of man." ... Through bruised and bleeding lips he smiled at them, looking straight into the camera with an expression of yearning tenderness on his face. Some trick of sunlight and stereo formed a golden halo back of his head. "Oh my brothers, I love you so! Drink deep. Share and grow closer without end. Thou art God!" ... The mob opened up a little at that warning and the camera zoomed to pick up his face and shoulders. The Man from Mars smiled at his brothers, said once more, softly and clearly, "I love you." An incautious grasshopper came whirring to a landing on the grass a few inches from his face; Mike turned his head, looked at it as it stared back at him. "Thou art God," he said happily and discorporated.[24]

For all intents and purposes, this is simply an extremely pedestrian and simple-minded reiteration of the Crucifixion. For a considerably different approach, let us examine the climactic appearance of the over-gestalt in Theodore Sturgeon's *More Than Human* (1953):

> Gerry clapped his hands to his mouth. His eyes bulged. Through his mind came a hush of welcoming music. There was warmth and laughter and wisdom. There were introductions; for each voice there was a discrete personality, a comprehensible sense of something like stature or rank, and an accurate locus, a sense of physical position. Yet, in terms of amplitude, there was no difference in the voices. They were all here, or, at least, all equally near. There was happy and fearless communion, fearlessly shared with Gerry—cross-currents of humor, of pleasure, of reciprocal thought and mutual achievement. And through and through, welcome, welcome.... Their memories, their projections and computations flooded in to Gerry, until at last he knew their nature and their function; and he knew why the ethos he had learned was too small a concept. For here at last was power which could not corrupt; for such an insight could not be used for its own sake, or against itself. Here was why and how humanity existed, troubled and dynamic, sainted by the touch of its own great destiny. Here was the

withheld hand as thousands died, when by their death millions might live. And here, too, was the guide, the beacon, for such times as humanity might be in danger; here was the Guardian of Whom all humans knew—not an exterior force, nor an awesome Watcher in the sky, but a laughing thing with a human heart and a reverence for its human origins, smelling of sweat and new-turned earth rather than suffused with the pale odor of sanctity.... He felt a rising, choking sense of worship, and recognized it for what it has always been for mankind—self-respect.[25]

Why is the Sturgeon piece so much more successful at transmitting a sense of the transcendent than Heinlein's? I think the answer lies in our Judeo-Christian expectations. Valentine Michael Smith is the Christ figure played to the hilt. He is completely in character, and ultimately boring. On the other hand, so to speak, is Homo Gestalt, or God the Father, as the next step in human evolution. But this is not the expected stern and paternal God of the Old Testament; this is a god that partakes of humanity "smelling of sweat and new-turned earth." And so our expectations of the sacrosanct are dashed. The novelty of this theology, in conjunction with an understated economy of description unique to Sturgeon, manages to maintain the mystery essential to even the most paltry perception of the superhuman. The sheer unexpectedness of the final integration with Homo Gestalt at the novel's conclusion serves only to intensify this essential mystery. Surprise can be an excellent route to the temporary suspension and transcendence of ordinary operating parameters. A much colder approach to transcendence is exemplified in Arthur C. Clarke's *Childhood's End* (1953):

Something's starting to happen. The stars are becoming dimmer. It's as if a great cloud is coming up, very swiftly, all over the sky. But it isn't really a cloud. It seems to have some sort of structure—I can glimpse a hazy network of lines and bands that keep changing their positions. It's almost as if the stars are tangled in a ghostly spider's web.

The whole network is beginning to glow, to pulse with light, exactly as if it were alive. And I suppose it is: or is it something as much beyond life as that is above the inorganic world? ...

Yes—I might have guessed. There's a great burning column, like a tree of fire, reaching above the western horizon. It's a long way off, right round the world. I know where it springs from: they're on their way at last, to become part of the Overmind. Their probation is ended: they're leaving the last remains of matter behind....

Now it looks exactly like the curtains of the aurora, dancing and flickering across the stars. Why, that's what it really is, I'm sure—a great auroral storm. The whole landscape is lit up—it's brighter than day—reds and golds and greens are chasing each other across the sky—oh, it's beyond words, it doesn't seem fair that I'm the only one to see it—I never thought such colors—....

I can see clearly again. That great burning column is still there, but it's constricting, narrowing; it looks like the funnel of a tornado, about to retract into the clouds....

The buildings round me, the ground, the mountain—everything's like glass—I can see through it. Earth's dissolving. My weight has almost gone. You were right—they've finished playing with their toys.[26]

And here is a final example from the literature of transcendence, from Greg Bear's *Blood Music* (1985):

I am wiping my eyes, out of terror, awe, for I have seen nothing like this in all the hours we have been wandering over this nightmare land. Telephoto cameras showed us stockyards of Chicago. When we consider the enormous mass of living creatures—pigs, cattle—concentrated in those regions, perhaps we should not be surprised or shocked. But the largest moving creatures I have seen have been whales, and these exceeded in size the largest whale by I know not precisely how much. Great brown and white eggs, could they have been hovering? Perhaps just on the ground. Greater than dinosaurs, yet with no discernible legs, head, tail. Not without features, however, extensions and elongations, tended or surrounded by polyhedrons, that is, icosahedrons or dodecahedrons—with insect-like legs, straight not joined, legs that had to be two or three meters thick. The ovoid creatures or whatever

> they were could have easily spread across a rugby field. Yes—yes—we have been told ... we have just been informed there are airborne life forms, living things and that we have narrowly missed a couple of them, resembling gigantic manta rays stretched out, gliders or bats, also white and brown. Flowing in a stream southwest, as if forming a squadron or flock.[27]

In these last two selections we see yet another strategy for the employment of ambiguity in science fiction. In both cases the description is perfectly straightforward. The ambiguity is in the physical or biological landscape itself. It is possible for even the jaded science fiction critic to apprehend directly the alien, the other than human, if the author has sufficient skill to avoid the hackneyed stereotypes (e.g., giant millipedes) that are rampant in the genre. This is probably the purest and the most difficult usage of the ambiguous and the obscure. There are no verbal tricks, no neologisms, no obscurantism. There is simply a bare description of the extraordinary. This could be called the style of zero filtration. But the extraordinary evolves rapidly in science fiction. The half-life of such definitions of the strange may be surprisingly brief, even as the too-apt neologism may be completely co-opted for standard usage (witness the conversion of Carroll's neologism *chortled* into standard English). After all, there was a time not too long ago when the notion of a Martian invasion was absolutely terrifying to a sizable proportion of the population. But as Brooks Landon has said, "the sustained fantastic becomes merely the ordinary."[28]

And so we have traveled from Dodgson through Hodgson to God's son and beyond. I think it is apparent that a major goal of science fiction, the empathic apprehension of that which is "more than human," is often facilitated by description through neologism, seldom-used language, and deliberate poverty of detail. The far more difficult task is to maintain a simplicity of expression and a plausible objectification of the alien, that yet does not impair the sympathetic transmission of that very alienation. Even so, a bandersnatch by any other name would hardly even seem as strange!

Afterword

Looking over this book's table of contents brings back so many memories. I think first of George Slusser. As a young postdoc at UC Riverside I had no idea the Eaton Collection existed. What a joy to meet George some 35 years ago and discover such an amazing resource! Then there was Frank McConnell, who taught me more about how to give a talk than anything I ever learned in graduate school. Eric S. Rabkin, friend forever. Greg Benford and David Brin, 2/3 of the fabled Killer Bees! Howard Hendrix, every book of his a tutorial in theology, philosophy, and science fiction. Paul Alkon, Carl Freedman. The list goes on. If I had a time machine I know to what when I would travel.

A few words about my essay. Its point is the peculiar tension in science fiction between using plausible science to explain the extraordinary and the phenomenological perception of the unexplainable, the ultimate source of sensawonda. In fact, there seems an inverse relation between explanation and sensawonda. So what is a science fiction writer to do? One could simply explain through plausible science all events in a given story, as in Andy Weir's *The Martian* (2011). That story is as engrossing as *Robinson Crusoe* but lacks much in the way of sensawonda. Alternatively consider Clarke's monoliths. No chance of explaining through ordinary physics but incredible sensawonda. I'd guess many authors create phenomena somewhere between the inexplicable and explicable.

But what of the truly alien? Here lies a paradox because if something is truly ineffable then by definition you cannot eff it (thanks for the wordplay from Benford!). But what you can do is to obfuscate the details of what can be seen of the alien while constructing the story. Much of the landscape in the final pages of Bear's *Blood Music* has that character—you can perceive the alien but cannot know it.

I think science fiction, among many other functions, provides a toolbox for encountering the truly strange. As we venture out into the universe we will encounter phenomena that are completely explicable in terms of known science, perhaps a bit expanded beyond what we now know. But we may encounter entities with whom communication is barely possible. First Contact with such an entity will certainly produce a sensawonda at first, but perhaps eventually common ground for communication will be found.

But will we encounter the truly alien, the truly inexplicable? Since we and such an entity would presumably share a universe with a physics and mathematics that applies to all times, places and phenomena (with a few current exceptions like dark matter and dark energy), it seems even the truly alien should share an environmental commonality with homo sap, allowing communication based on that commonality. Mathematics as a language. But the possibility remains that such aliens have transcended the strictures of mathematics (think writing messages in pi, as in Carl Sagan's *Contact* [1985]), hard as it may be to contemplate. We can only speculate, as the bard says, while bounded in this terrestrial nutshell, dreaming of kingships in infinite space.

Notes

1. Lewis Carroll, "Jabberwocky," 1871, *The Complete Works of Lewis Carroll* (New York: Random House, 153–154.
2. Henry Kuttner and C.L. Moore [as Lewis Padgett], "Mimsy Were the Borogoves," *Astounding Science-Fiction*, 30:6 (February, 1943), 52.
3. Larry Niven, *Neutron Star* (New York: Ballantine, 1968).
4. Roger Zelazny, *Sign of Chaos* (New York: Arbor House, 1987).
5. Kingsley Amis, *New Maps of Hell* (New York: Harcourt, Brace, and World, 1960).
6. James Clavell, *Shogun* (New York: Atheneum, 1975); Martin Cruz Smith, *Gorky Park* (New York: Random House, 1981).
7. K.W. Jeter, *Dr. Adder* (1984; New York: Penguin/NAL, 1988), 194.
8. *The Thing (from Another World)* (Winchester Pictures, 1951).
9. *The Thing* (U/Turman Focter Productions, 1982).
10. John W. Campbell, Jr. [as Don A. Stuart], "Who Goes There?," *Astounding Science-Fiction*, 21:6 (August, 1938), 60.
11. *Aliens* (TCF/Brandywine, 1986); *The Fly* (TCF/Brooksfilm, 1986).
12. David Gerrold, *A Matter for Men* (New York: Timescape, 1983), 22–23.
13. H.P. Lovecraft, "The Dunwich Horror," 1929, *The Best of H.P. Lovecraft* (New York: Ballantine, 1982), 111–112.
14. William Hope Hodgson, *The House on the Borderland* (1908; New York: Ace, 1962), 24–25.
15. J.R.R. Tolkien, *The Fellowship of the Ring* (1954; New York: Ballantine, 1965), 428–30.
16. Poul Anderson, *Brain Wave*, 1954, *A Treasury of Great Science Fiction*, Volume 2, ed. Anthony Boucher (Garden City, New York: Doubleday, 1959), 45.
17. Daniel Keyes, "Flowers for Algernon," 1959, *The Hugo Winners*, Volume 1, ed. Isaac Asimov (Garden City, New York: Doubleday, 1962), 227–228.
18. Thomas M. Disch, *Camp Concentration* (1968; New York: Carroll and Graf, 1988), 119–120.
19. Gene Wolfe, *The Shadow of the Torturer* (1980; New York: Timescape, 1981), 60–61.
20. A.E. van Vogt, *The World of Null-A* (New York: Simon & Schuster, 1948), 163–164.
21. Gregory Benford, "Style, Substance, and Other Illusions, *Styles of Creation: Aesthetic Technique and the Creation of Fictional Worlds*, ed. George Slusser and Eric S. Rabkin (Athens: University of Georgia Press, 1992), 50.
22. Alfred Bester, *The Stars My Destination* (New York: Signet, 1957), 178–179.
23. Benford, 50.
24. Robert A. Heinlein, *Stranger in a Strange Land* (New York: Putnam's, 1961), 399–401.
25. Theodore Sturgeon, *More Than Human* (New York: Ballantine, 1953), 186–188.

26. Arthur C. Clarke, *Childhood's End* (New York: Ballantine, 1953), 210–212.
27. Greg Bear, *Blood Music* (New York: Arbor House, 1985), 148.
28. Brooks Landon, "Styles of Invisibility: Sustaining the Transparent in Contemporary Prose Semblances," *Styles of Creation*, 245.

Making the Pulpmonster Safe for Demography

Omni *Magazine and the Gentrification of Science Fiction*

(1990 Eaton Conference)

Howard V. Hendrix

If we place a copy of *Omni* beside a copy of *Isaac Asimov's Science Fiction Magazine*, *The Magazine of Fantasy and Science Fiction*, or *Analog: Science Fiction/Science Fact*, some physical differences are immediately apparent, which I will purposely belabor here in the belief that they reflect other differences not nearly so physical, apparent, or immediate. *Omni* is, for instance, printed in full-size format on "slick" paper, whereas the other three are digest-size and printed on pulp paper. From an iconographic standpoint, *Omni* (cover price in 1994 $3.00) features cover art that typically incorporates "abstract" features drawn from surrealism, impressionism, and constructivism; the digest sf magazines (cover price usually $1.75 to $2.00) tend more toward the representational in their choice of cover artwork. *Omni*'s defamiliarized "big face" covers stand in stark contrast to the others' "alien scene" covers, and the art accompanying the stories inside typically follows along the same lines: *Omni* art defamiliarized and postmodern, digest sf art alienated and modern.

Other graphics and layout features tend to further highlight this dichotomy. *Omni*'s title logo and section headings are printed in a self-consciously futuristic font type, which generally is not the case in the digest sf magazines. *Omni*'s cover lists as teasers some topics dealt with in the issues; other sf magazines emphasize authors and story titles in their cover materials. The respective contents pages are also enlightening. Where the digest magazines often have an "editorial" or "editor's page," *Omni* has its "editorial" column "First Word," which is not written by the editor—much more like the op-ed page in a newspaper than the official editorial pulpits found in other magazines.

At the end of an issue, where the digest sf magazines often have calendars of events upcoming in the SF/Fantasy subculture, *Omni* has a general-interest (often mildly futurist) humor column, "Last Word." Background material on authors and stories tends to be more extensive and dispersed among editorial blurbs throughout the digest sf magazines, whereas in *Omni* such matter is condensed into a single pseudo-essayistic column called "Omnibus." *Asimov's* has a department called "Letters," *Analog* a letters column called "Brass Tacks," but *Omni* has "Communications." *Omni* has a department called "Games" (something of a watered-down, more pop-oriented combination of the "Amateur Scientist" and "Computer Recreations" departments of *Scientific American*) that emphasizes computer and mathematical recreations as well as what might be called the science of leisure time; in digest-size sf magazines we find departments called "Gaming" or "On Gaming" that primarily feature reviews of simulation and role-playing games.

Both *Omni* and the digest sf magazines have columns ostensibly about books—but whereas the Algis Budrys and Orson Scott Card columns in *Fantasy and Science Fiction*, the Baird Searles column in *Asimov's*, and the "Reference Library" in *Analog* provide actual book reviews, *Omni*'s "Books" department is concerned with the people producing the books—authors as personalities—not with reviewing the books themselves. This is not to say that digest sf magazines are unconcerned with personalities, but rather that in those magazines personalities (the late Isaac Asimov and Harlan Ellison come to mind) are not so much "reported" or "commented" on by others (as is the case in *Omni*) as they actively report or comment *on themselves.*

Along with the editorial columns, Ellison's film commentaries and Asimov's science columns (now written by Gregory Benford) cover—albeit far more idiosyncratically and less systematically—the same ground surveyed in *Omni*'s "Forum," "Space," "Mind," "Arts," "Artificial Intelligence," "Continuum," and "Anti-Matter" departments. It is precisely in *Omni*'s proliferation and formulization of these categories, however, that we see the breakdown of *Omni*'s hypothetical similarity to the sf magazine tradition that spawned it—and precisely here that market realities and the history of those realities powerfully enter the picture.

During the 1970s, *Omni* editor-in-chief and design director Bob Guccione essentially gambled that there was a potentially profitable mass-market for a speculative and future-oriented magazine. Up to that time, this market had been viewed as three generally separate, smaller markets or niches. The scientific nonfiction niche had been left largely to technical magazines like *Popular Science*, *Popular Mechanics*, and *Science Digest*. The speculative fiction niche had been left largely to sf and fantasy magazines—*Amazing Stories, Analog Science Fiction/Science Fact, The Magazine of Fantasy and Science Fiction*, and later *Isaac Asimov's Science Fiction Magazine*. The speculative pseudoscientific nonfiction niche had been left largely to "strange phenomena" magazines—*Fate, UFO Digest*, and various reviews in the tradition of Charles Fort. The traits the magazines in these niches shared were that they were generally "low rent," digest, pulp paper ventures aimed at specific and fairly small subcultures within the mass audience.

Guccione's target audience was larger: in the high hundreds of thousands and even millions of readers, as opposed to the tens of thousands that might be expected to read one of the digest magazines. A larger market, however, meant a more diffuse one—consisting of more than just dedicated core-readerships like science fiction fandom or technophile tinkerers or Fortean phenomena junkies. Inevitably, this quest for a broader readership posed "appeal" and "format" problems. Other speculative future-oriented magazines had, after all, gone to full size and even full slick—*Analog* during the 1960s, *Vertex*, and *Galileo*—without noteworthy long-term success. All floundered or returned to digest format after a relatively few years of their full-size format. Given this record, how has *Omni* managed to survive and even thrive while other full-size future-oriented magazines failed?

Certainly, *Omni*'s chances of finding or carving out its own market were enhanced by the fact that Guccione had his *Penthouse* magazine revenues available for bankrolling *Omni* until it could develop its own identity. It is also no surprise that the identity *Omni* eventually developed is a sexy one, for *Omni* is a sexy magazine in a distinctly postmodern sense. French social theoretician Jean Baudrillard has commented that "the close-up of a face is as obscene as a sexual organ seen from up close. [The face] *is* a sexual organ." The promiscuity of the detail, the zoom-in, takes on a sexual value."[1] This casts *Omni*'s "big face" covers in a new and different light, but one thoroughly appropriate to a magazine whose founder built his first empire in the men's magazine market. The old "hot" modernist spectacle of the bronze brassiered buxom beauties of pulp covers has given way in *Omni* to a cool, detached, post-desire sexuality, a postmodern passion without bodies. The trajectory of Guccione's career confirms Baudrillard's hypothesis that hot, sexual obscenity is followed by cool communication obscenity (24).

Almost as important to *Omni*'s success, however, is the mesh between the identity it developed and the market it "found" and helped to create. A term often encountered in sf circles in the 1970s was the "sf ghetto"—referring to the relatively small subculture of sf fans, writers, and artists, and their communal gatherings at science fiction conventions. The digest magazines were an integral part of the ghetto and enjoyed a largely symbiotic relationship with it. The closeness of this relationship, though, is also what precluded magazine sf's appeal to a wider audience. Digest sf magazines were fairly insulated and comfortable in their limited market niche, and even with the pressures exerted by the growth of the paperback book market, they were manifestly resistant to change—probably because, given their market situation, they did not need to be highly adaptable. The digest sf magazines' great strength—their reliable appeal to a core readership of sf fans—was also their great weakness, a weakness that may explain the failure of magazines like *Vertex*, which were essentially the older digest format writ large, "projects" among the "tenements" but still in the same old ghetto, month after month reliably offering up pretty much the same vision of the future found in the digest sf magazines: a future usually quite separate from the present, a future that was the domain of science fiction—in other words, lots of sf and fantasy, much less science fact and commentary.

The search for mass-market appeal, however, forced the designers and editors at *Omni* to reevaluate these traditional conceptions. The tacit assumption and hidden law that the future can be best described—or even should be primarily described—by works of genre fiction was called radically into question, and the percentage of *Omni*'s pages devoted to science fiction stories declined from the 1970s unto the 1980s. Nonfiction departments proliferated, and in doing so made the *Omni* future seem less fictional—more contiguous with the present than separated from it, not so much an alien realm as merely an unfamiliar element entering the ecstasy of our contemporary communication. Particularly in these nonfiction departments, one finds a constant rhetoric of imminence, the idea that the future is always already here and happening—or at least is just around the corner.

This movement from separation to contiguity, from the "drama of alienation" to Baudrillard's "ecstasy of communication" (22) is a sure mark of the shift from modern to postmodern. If we follow Fredric R. Jameson's axiom that "postmodernism is the cultural logic of late capitalism," then we see that the proliferation in *Omni* of nonfiction departments concerning commentary and reportage—taken together with the simultaneous downplaying of fiction per se—combine to produce something quintessentially postmodern, cultural-logical, and marketable. Where once there were three largely separate niches—technological nonfiction, speculative fiction, and strange phenomena nonfiction or what we might call tech, spec, and ect(oplasm)—*Omni*'s designers and marketers saw not separation but contiguity, one meta-genre to be "mergered" from three. Postmodernism is characterized by the merger of genres as surely as late capitalism is characterized by the merger of corporations, and in the history of *Omni* both the late capitalist and the postmodernist sides of Jameson's axiom meet.

But even if *Omni* is the product of pooling not only corporate capital but also subcultural capital, why should we care? What's wrong with going after that bigger, more diffuse audience? What relevance could there possibly be in the fact that the appearance of the postmodern genre-merger called *Omni* and the appearance of the postmodern genre-merger called *Star Wars* are both "historically contiguous" with the shift in the U.S. economy's role from a world-dominating national economy to merely an important player in a globalized economy? What relation could the divide between *Omni* and the digest sf magazines have to the increasing class stratification happening concurrently with economic globalization?

To answer such questions and see possible connections, we must return to the physical object called *Omni* to examine its stylistics of opulence. Comparing the gray, cramped pages of the digest tech, spec, and ect magazines to the colorful, slick layout of *Omni*—with profligate use of white space—is like comparing tenement flats to the spacious gentrified apartment suites built from them. And consider the advertisements. Though there is some overlap (notably the Science Fiction Book Club ads in both digest and full-size venues), there is more difference than similarity. Advertisements in the digest sf magazines run predominantly to affordable low-budget items—sf paperbacks and role-playing games—aimed at the sf subculture, but *Omni* advertisements run predominantly to high ticket or luxury commodities—automobiles and trendy liquors—aimed at the upper tier of the mass culture. Advertising demographics reveal that the fifteen- to twenty-five-year-old target audience for the digest sf magazines is not only significantly younger than the twenty-five- to forty-five-year-old *Omni* target audience, but also significantly less affluent.

Omni has in fact benefited from a deeper merger and its consequences. In what Jameson refers to as "late capitalism" we find the merging not only of corporations but also of entire economies. As Robert Reich noted: "America itself is ceasing to exist as an economic system separate from the rest of the world. One can no more meaningfully speak of an 'American economy' than of a 'Delaware economy.' We are becoming but a region—albeit still a relatively wealthy region—of a global economy."[2] The primary domestic effect of America's ongoing merger with the global economy has been and will be the economic polarization of the American people—the rich will get richer and relatively fewer, and the poor will get poorer and relatively more numerous. This is the major effect of economic globalization throughout the world. In the United States, the globalization of the economy most benefits the richest one-fifth of Americans, as Reich proves with statistics showing that between 1978 and 1987 the poorest fifth of American families became 8 percent poorer, and the richest fifth became 13 percent richer—or, even more graphically, with statistical evidence that in 1988 the poorest fifth of the population controlled less than 5 percent of the nation's income while the richest fifth controlled more than 40 percent.

Those are the consequences of globalization on the far ends of the U.S. class spectrum, but the effects are quite pronounced for the middle class as well. Ralph Whitehead maintains that the social ladder in America is steepening. In the 1950s and 1960s the basic American social ladder looked like this:

The Rich
The Expanding Middle Class (White Collar, Blue Collar)
The Poor

Today, it looks like this:

Upscale America (The Rich, The Overclass)
The New Middle Class (Bright Collar, New Collar, Blue Collar)
Downscale America (The Poor—usually employed, The Underclass—often not employed)[3]

But this "new middle class" may be a disappearing middle class, so the effect of economic globalization on America would then be:

Upscale America (The Rich, The Overclass, Bright Collars, Some New Collars)
Downscale America (Most New Collars, Blue Collars, The Poor, The Underclass)

Who are these people, and what is their work? Upscale America consists predominantly by symbolic/analytic professionals—information managers and knowledge workers, including managerial and professional workers dubbed "bright collars." Such workers tend to work alone or in small teams, have partners rather than bosses, and analyze, design, and make strategies in clean steel and glass buildings rather than work on shop floors. They also tend overwhelmingly to be white males. In the United States they include investment and commercial bankers, lawyers, management consultants, scientists, academics, public relations executives, real estate developers, advertising and marketing specialists, creative accountants, art directors, engineers, architects, writers and editors, television and film stars, directors and producers, politicians, budget analysts, and mid-level administrators. As a group, these professionals—especially the overclass and bright collars—benefit most from the shift to a global economy.

Straddling upscale and downscale America (but increasingly falling into the latter) are individuals who provide routine personal services, including so-called new collars. This sector of the economy is rapidly growing and some entrepreneurial members of this category may rise into upscale America, though most will not. This group includes police officers, security guards, retail sales personnel, clerks, secretaries, telephone operators, restaurant and hotel workers, barbers and beauticians, cab drivers, delivery truck drivers, household help, day-care workers, hospital attendants and orderlies. As a group, these service providers, because they provide local services, are only indirectly affected by the generalized shift to a global economy—though they are one of the first groups to be negatively affected in an economic downturn.

The people most harmed by shifting to a global economy provide routine manufacturing services with simple and repetitive work—performing one step in a sequence of steps to produce a product. They are employed in large centralized facilities and overseen by supervisors. Their jobs increasingly are going overseas or being performed by robots. In this group are workers of heavy industry, assembly-line personnel, metal benders (male), fabric and textile tenders and data enterers (most female, members of minority groups, or both). Many such workers enjoyed middle-class status in union shops of the old national economy, but a global economy circumvents the power of unionization at anything less than global levels, so such workers are most likely to join the ranks of the working poor.

The relevance of all this is that the differences between *Omni* and the digest sf magazines mirror a widening split in U.S. class structure back to the 1970s. More and more, *Omni* reflects the values of (and courts the money of) upscale America, while the digest sf magazines fulfill a similar role for downscale America. The differences are greater than those to be found simply by looking at *Omni* as a mass-culture magazine and the digest sf outlets as subcultural magazines. The fact that the digest sf magazines remain subcultural demonstrates their marginalization. America's information-class elites consider the postmodern, defamiliarized aesthetics and global gentry values found in *Omni* far more "mainstream" than the modernist, alien-dramatic aesthetics and nationalist "ghetto" values found in the digest spec/tech/ect magazine tradition that *Omni* exercised its genre renovations upon. Hence it is appropriate to employ the metaphor of gentrification.

Of course, whether gentrification is a good or bad thing depends on whether one is moving in or being moved out. Certainly gentrification tidies up and reinvigorates the neighborhood, but at what cost? Those already down are apt to be shoved out. The neighborhood will tend to disappear or be forced to reconstitute elsewhere. Numerous jobs will be lost in the community, while a few will be gained: though *Omni* pays significantly better than the other sf magazines, its space for fiction is limited and its pages are inevitably closed to the vast majority of sf writers and artists. These writers and artists, who have played and continue to play such a pivotal role in the sf subcultural community, are increasingly marginalized in the pages of *Omni*, a fact evidenced in the shrinking number of pages given to sf in each issue and *Omni*'s own subscription-promotion brochures, one of which I received a few years ago. Out of six pages' worth of material publicizing the magazine, only two short paragraphs dealt with sf.

This is not all bad. *Omni*'s treatment of sf writers and artists as primarily workers is a healthy demystification of some of the demagoguery and fannish idol-worship one finds now and again in the sf subcultural community. But something is being lost, and I believe that that something is diversity. Ben Bagdikian has pointed out the dangers of receiving more and more information from fewer and fewer sources.[4] I will not belabor the point other than to note that the ongoing reduction in polycultural reality into a global monoculture (something that ventures like *Omni* and *Star Wars* are symptomatic of), this reductive merging, which may be as productive and efficient as a single-strain cornfield or fascist state in the short run, over the long term will prove wasteful of energy and resources and inherently unstable.

Cultural homogenization is dangerous in that it marginalizes artists who challenge the ideological assumptions of the lords of the global village, so their works can be almost completely shut out of circulation because they "won't sell"—a handy form of market censorship more powerful than any censorship board. And what of the works that do sell? Won't they more and more be works ideologically "in line" with the values of the corporate elite? If postmodernism and late (or hyper-) capitalism are crude terms for a phase in history in which abstract, symbolic/analytic head work is increasingly seen as the source of value, while concrete, physical hand work is increasingly seen as valueless, what might be the consequences? I believe that the stepchildren of the *Omni* movement, the cyberpunks, have offered us an answer in the form of the pure headworld called "cyberspace" or the "matrix." Norman Spinrad during the 1990 Eaton Conference has characterized several authors in the cyberpunk movement as "leftist" or "socialist," but that does not show in their works, which are socialist in about the same manner and to about the same degree that National Socialism was a "socialist" movement in Hitler's Germany. Megacorporate domination of the headworld future is never seriously attacked in cyberpunk but is instead *assumed* as the inevitable, unquestionable, and necessary setting where the cyberspace scene is played out.

The major effect of living a hyperreal existence, the major consequence of "spending too much time in cyberspace," is a loss of affect. There is everything to do, but nothing can be done. There is action and change in cyberstories—but change is fetishistically pseudo-individualist and never gets around to really changing the society or becoming "political" in any sense. Cyberpunk books are apolitical in that they never fundamentally question or critique the status quo future in which their events take place. The single element that best substantiates this is the slick, high-tech violence the characters engage in: what could be more politically traditional than the might-makes-right of violence, than stories in which characters kill one another? These books reflect and do not challenge or expose the values of their stylish, name-brand, upscale audience. In the best cultural-logical fashion, it only follows that William Gibson's early stories—along with those of several other so-called cyberpunks—should have first appeared primarily in a venue also reflecting upscale values, *Omni*.

None of this is hidden. There is undeniable talent and beauty in the "stylistics of opulence" one finds both in *Omni*'s layout and cyberpunk prose. If nothing else, post-modernism is precisely this stylistics of opulence, rhetoric that glories in glamorous excess and superabundance, a ritual of transparency where the style *is* the substance, the medium *is* the message, and the depth is on the surface. But danger is there too, like a shark fin slicing through calm waters. Michael Armstrong has stated that he believes science fiction "has a real moral purpose: to warn" and cited Brian W. Aldiss's assertion (in *Trillion Year Spree*) that science fiction writers should be like physicians searching for prodromes (warning symptoms of disease)—that science fiction as "prodromic utterance" should examine the world as it is, consider where we could be going, and ponder whether that destination might be a bad place.[5]

But how effective can sf be as prodromic utterance if writers and artists increasingly reflect the status quo values of corporate ruling elites? How sensitive will these elites be to issues of the environment, for example, when environmental issues interfere with maximization of profit and the corporate bottom line? *Omni* may publish nominally pro-environment pieces, but in an opulent, white-space layout admittedly wasteful of paper—a curious instance of a magazine's style subverting its content. Are the interests of humanity best served by an informational marketplace thoroughly dominated by the information-controlling elites? These questions are at least debatable—and are necessarily political.

Some may argue that such serious issues are of no concern to science fiction writers; sf should simply be "entertaining." But all communication between writers and readers is political, either in what is said or what is not said; and writers who claim to be apolitical in their work are merely tacitly supporting the status quo. (If one fiddles while Rome burns, one strongly implies that the burning of Rome is a matter of little consequence.) There is also a false dichotomy here: is all sf that addresses serious issues "boring" and all sf that offers warmed-over detective stories against glossy high-tech backgrounds "entertaining"? Surely, writers should seek, as Horace said, to both "teach and delight"; today, *Omni* offers readers a lot of delight but precious little teaching.

My hope is that sf writers, artists, and publishers—particularly the abundantly talented cyberpunk writers and the artists and publishers of *Omni*—might engage in more of the self-criticism and technological critique that has never been lost as an sf tradition. Possibly, since the combination of contradictory traits is often cited as another characteristic of the postmodern, one can imagine a new *Omni* that would combine the cool, superficial attractiveness of upscale values with the passion and concerns of those left behind by gentrification. And that would be an *Omni* worth reading.

1996 Note

At the time of this paper's initial presentation in 1990, a later full-sized venture in sf, *Science Fiction Age*, had not yet come into existence. Though this new feature of the sf publishing landscape cannot be adequately covered in a note, suffice it to say that it confirms and extends the ideas presented here in the following manner. *Science Fiction Age* is neither the "all important things to all important people" of *Omni*, nor the "one thing for one subculture" of the digest sf magazines. It is a curious but apparently successful hybrid that has borrowed the strong genre emphasis of the digest-sized magazines and combined that with the style-conscious, heavily "departmented" format of *Omni*. Like *Omni*, *Science Fiction Age* has benefited from strong financial backing and solid distribution, which has allowed it to survive long enough to begin to develop its own voice and identity. This voice and identity, however, is at present more a "*Vertex* for the '90s" than an approximation of the ideal magazine I conclude with here. *Science Fiction Age* reflects the position of sf as a whole at the present time: a big part of the (post-*Star Wars*) popular culture but still ghettoized in relation to what used to be called high culture. Both the genre and the magazine are strongly identified with the values of their readers, who tend to be very much "New Middle Class"—Bright Collars, New Collars, and Blue Collars.

Afterword

"Pulpmonster" was published in *Science Fiction and Market Realities* (1996), largely unchanged from its presentation at the 1990 Eaton Conference. Today the essay strikes me as simultaneously dated and prescient. The large format magazines *Omni* and (in the "1996 Note") *Science Fiction Age* no longer exist. Much of what I discussed in the presentation nearly three decades ago, however—economic globalization, the impacts on the workforce of automation and offshoring, income inequality and economic polarization, the authoritarian tendencies and inherent instability of a global monoculture increasingly characterized by hyperstimulated, hypersimulated, hyperalienated daily existence—all those seem to have moved from fringe and theory to mainstream and description.

As "prodromic utterance" then, I think the essay holds up well. Given that I wrote and presented it before the power of the internet was widely recognized, long before Web 2.0, I'm not surprised that I did not quite foresee the impact "cyberspace" would have on the publishing industry itself. What intrigues me is that, as of this writing, the pulp magazines mentioned—*Analog, Asimov's, Fantasy and Science Fiction*—still linger on, and *Amazing* has died and been resurrected in print several times. Although their readership has been shrinking for decades, the pulps in all their old "hot"-modernist, chromium-corseted spectacle have persisted, while the cool-postmodernist, stylish, upscale magazines like *Omni* have long since gone extinct.

The superficially attractive upscalers often went online/virtual before they disappeared, seemingly because online publication provided cooler, more detached communicational "obscenity" than physical magazines could ever manage. The "post-desire sexuality" and "a postmodern passion without bodies" mentioned in this essay describe our contemporary world—where social media sites are more popular than porn and "sapiosexual" is a term of endearment—far more powerfully than they described the world I attempted to chronicle in 1990. Since that time the internet has largely smashed the appeal of magazines characterized by many nonfiction departments and mass-audience aspirations, yet the pulps have limped on, living fossils doing "one thing for one subculture" well, occupying fan-niche markets, still populated by stories that warn and question as much as they entertain.

Given the times we live in, the question in the last section—"But how effective can sf be as prodromic utterance if writers and artists increasingly reflect the status quo of corporate ruling elites?"—is also more relevant than ever before. When the Auto-Pilot function in Joshua Brown's Tesla S failed, on May 7, 2016, to distinguish the bright horizon of the sky from a white tractor-trailer rig turning left, Brown became the first human fatality of vehicle autonomy. Entrepreneurial tech titan and Tesla head Elon Musk responded to reporters' questions about Brown's death with this statement: "If you're dissuading people from autonomous driving, you're killing people."[6] Whether the hypothetical future (when autonomous vehicles will supposedly be safer than those piloted by people) will justify Musk's contemporary collateral and actual kill rate remains to be seen. Certainly, however, Musk's self-serving statement serves his own bottom line.

You can find many similarly self-serving statements from various Silicon Valley technorati, many of whom grew up on cyberpunk visions of the future. Alas, as this article from 1990 suggested would be the case, cyberpunk itself never seriously confronted the mega-corporate domination of the head-world future, but instead *assumed* that domination as inevitable and necessary.

Science fiction as self-fulfilling prophecy is not the only or best form the genre can take. Sometimes the point of predicting a future is to prevent that future from happening. Wondering "What if this goes on?" questions whether we should assume it must. That remains very much a good and necessary thing.

STOP (OR START?) THE PRESSES! As I write this, news reports confirm that *Omni* is up for resurrection, moving (apparently) from online to print. Perhaps the nascent postmodernist conditions discussed above, that provided the matrix for the first rise of *Omni*—economic globalization, the impacts on the workforce of automation and off-shoring, income inequality and economic polarization, etc.—are now "all grown up" and implicated in the print magazine's impending rebirth. Or perhaps *Omni* is itself coming back in a fan-niche market form. In any event, *Omni* may well be a magazine whose time has come around again—for the very first time.

Notes

1. Jean Baudrillard, *The Ecstasy of Communication*, trans. Bernard and Caroline Schultze, ed. Sylvere Lotringer (1987; New York: Columbia University Press, 1988), 43. Parenthetical page references are to this edition.

2. Robert Reich, "As the World Turns," *New Republic*, 200 (May 1, 1989), 23.

3. Ralph Whitehead, "America's Middle Class Faces Polarization," *Utne Reader*, No. 37 (January-February 1990), 60.

4. Ben H. Bagdikian, *The Media Monopoly* (Boston: Beacon, 1983) and "The Lords of the Global Village," *Nation*, 248 (June 12, 1989), 805–808.

5. Michael Armstrong, "How Science Fiction Failed Alaska and Prince William Sound," *Bulletin of the Science Fiction Writers of America*, 23 (Winter 1989), 9.

6. Elon Musk, quoted in Marco della Cava, "Tesla Announces New Self-Driving Cars," *USA Today*, October 19, 2016, at https://www.usatoday.com/story/tech/news/2016/10/19/tesla-announces-fully-self-driving-fleet/92430638/.

For Tomorrow We Dine

The Sad Gourmet at the Scienticafé

(1991 Eaton Conference)

Gary Westfahl

As science fiction readers, we often visit exotic futuristic worlds; but even as our spirits soar, our bodies demand sustenance. Of course, we can simply put the book down and get some potato chips or Ding Dongs, but perhaps we should pause instead to experience vicariously the various foods that are consumed by the residents of the future. Unfortunately, this will not be the pause that refreshes.

Hugo Gernsback is the best place to begin any examination of science fiction, as I have long bored people by announcing,[1] so let us first visit the world of *Ralph 124C 41+: A Romance of the Year 2660* (1911–1912, 1925) to have dinner at the "Scientific Restaurant" called the *Scienticafé*. When Ralph arrives with his beloved Alice, they first stop in a room called the Appetizer, where they inhale "several harmless gases for the purpose of giving you an appetite" (73). Since people who go to restaurants are usually hungry anyway, one might wonder why this procedure is necessary; but Gernsback's description of their dinner provides the answer:

> They then sat down at a table on which were mounted complicated silver boards with odd buttons and pushes and slides.... From the top of the board a flexible tube hung down to which one fastened a silver mouthpiece, that one took out of a disinfecting solution, attached to the board. The bill of fare was engraved in the board and there was a pointer which one moved up and down the various food items and stopped in front of the one selected. The silver mouthpiece was then placed in the mouth and one pressed upon a red button. If spices, salt or pepper were wanted, there was a button for each one which merely had to be pressed till the food was as palatable as wanted. Another button controlled the temperature of the food.
>
> Meats, vegetables, and other eatables, were all liquefied and were prepared with utmost skill to make them palatable.... They did not have to use knife and fork, as was the custom in former centuries. Eating had become a pleasure [74].

If sucking liquid vegetables from tubes does not strike you as a "pleasure," Ralph adds that "the **liquid scientific foods** are not absolutely liquid. Some of them, especially meats, have been prepared in such a manner that slight mastication is always necessary. This naturally does away with the monotony of swallowing liquids all the time and makes the food more desirable" (75)—or so he claims.

"It took people a long time to accept the scientific restaurants" (74), Ralph admits, which is hardly surprising; what is surprising to the modern reader is that amidst the dozens of super-scientific marvels glowingly described in Gernsback's novel, the Scientific Restaurant is *the only one which met with some resistance.* Apparently, people will happily adjust to traveling on mechanized roller skates, having newspapers piped directly into their brains by the Hypnobioscope, and traveling from Europe to America through a trans-Atlantic tunnel—but they will be sensitive about changes in the way they eat their food.

If diners on the go, such as space travelers, want a little more solidity in their food, a related alternative is mentioned in James Blish and Norman L. Knight's *A Torrent of Faces* (1967): "a tube of **food paste"** (70). This might also be the best description for the colorful goo that astronauts Frank Poole and David Bowman shovel into their faces in the film *2001: A Space Odyssey* (1968).

Of course, if the idea of avoiding chewing appeals to you, there is also the possibility of entirely eliminating the process of eating. This idea dates back to Lucian's *True History* and Cyrano de Bergerac's *Voyage dans la Lune* (1657), where we are told that people on the Moon nourish themselves simply by inhaling the odors of certain foods. A 1930 story published by Gernsback, Lillith Lorraine's "Into the 28th Century," revives the concept: "Don't drink it!" exclaims a resident of the future when the visitor from the past picks up a vial of liquid. "Inhale It! ... It is the essence of food" (254). However, since there is no scientific basis for the concept, nasal nutrition is not featured in modern science fiction—except in comic books, where scientific bases are not required; thus, the 1961 *Superman* adventure "The Interplanetary Circus" no doubt alludes to Lucian when Clark Kent and Lois Lane dine on **Plutonian Popcorn**, whose "aroma alone satisfies your hunger" (47). (Frankly, I think the whole idea stinks.)

The most ubiquitous alternative to eating in the future is the **food pill**, depicted in stories like Stanton A. Coblentz's *After 12,000 Years* (1929) and films like *Just Imagine* (1930), *Conquest of Space* (1955), and, of all places, the Laurel and Hardy classic *The Big Noise* (1942). So common is this particular prediction, in fact, that when William Gibson was searching, in "The Gernsback Continuum" (1981), for a single sentence that would summarize the entire attitude towards humanity's future progress that permeated the science fiction magazines of the 1920s and 1930s, he envisioned a woman in that milieu telling her companion, "John, we've forgotten to take our food pills" (33).

Even when food offered by the future is solid, it does not sound particularly appealing. American guerrillas fighting Asiatic invaders in Philip Francis Nowlan's *Armageddon 2419 A.D.* (1962) stay alive by eating something called **concentro**. Henry Slesar's "Ersatz" (1967) offers **"chemical beef ...** made of wood bark" (68). Frederik Pohl and C.M. Kornbluth's *The Space Merchants* (1953) memorably describes a massive glob of protein called **Chicken Little** which provides sustenance for Earth's massive population. In Michael Swanwick's *Vacuum Flowers* (1987), space dwellers eat **termite compress** with a side order of **grub loaf**, while residents of the future in Robert Sheckley's "The People Trap" (1968) munch on **"processed algae** between slices of **fishmeal bread"** (11). A boy sitting down to dinner in Isaac Asimov's *The Caves of Steel* (1953) plaintively asks, "Not **zymoveal** again, Mom?" (42). And in John Brunner's *The Sheep Look Up* (1972), cassava is processed into **Nutripon—nutri**tious food grown hydro**pon**ically—which is "cream-colored, and of the consistency of stale Cheddar cheese" (51). Although these dishes sound bland and utilitarian, elegance and creativity have not entirely vanished in future cuisine; for example, at the Galaxy Palace Restaurant of Somtow Suchariktul's Mallworld, you can order **"sweet-and-sour ice turtles** with chocolate chips" ("Rabid in Mallworld" 24).

Still, if this list of entreés makes you long for a more traditional meal, there is one good old-fashioned food that is sometimes available—human flesh, processed into **Soylent Green** in the film of that name (though Harry Harrison, author of the original novel—*Make Room! Make Room!* [1966]—boringly insists that it is made of soybeans and lentils); there is also the synthetic human flesh called **Ambrosia Plus**, discussed in Arthur C. Clarke's "The Food of the Gods" (1964).

Even these dishes may not sound appealing, and you may prefer to eat something lighter—like some hot soup. People in Blish and Knight's *A Torrent of Faces* eat a hearty bowl of **plankton chowder**, while T.J. Bass's "Rorqual Maru" (1971) presents two intriguing possibilities: **pseudo-consommé**, and a homemade recipe dubbed **sewer bouillabaisse**.

Other side dishes on the menu of the Scientific Restaurant also tend to be unappetizing. As a fruit, Gernsback's world of 2660 offers a number of **crossfoods**: the **appear**—half-apple, half-pear—a combination of plum and cherry, and "a cantaloupe with a faint taste of orange" (105). Swanwick's *Vacuum Flowers* features the **shyapple**, a small red fruit with a psychedelic punch. A staple of the world of Brunner's *The Sheep Look Up* is **"penguin eggs"** (128), and, as a side dish for his **zymoveal**, Asimov's young hero in *The Caves of Steel* must eat his **protovegs**.

To wash this stuff down, diners may long for a good cup of coffee—but all they will receive is **caffoid** (Suchariktul, "Rabid in Mallworld"), **kaffina** (Blish and Knight, *A Torrent of Faces*), or **coffiest** (Pohl and Kornbluth, *The Space Merchants*), the stimulant drink that happens to be physically addictive. For a sweet drink, the possibilities include a **Frosty-Flip** (Frederik Pohl, "The Tunnel under the World" [1954]) and a **malto** (Scott Sanders, "The Artist of Hunger" [1983]). And because future food is enough to drive one to drink, stronger stuff is fortunately available, though it may bring no real comfort: that is, you ask for a cup of cheer, but you get **Downer wine** (C.J. Cherryh, *Downbelow Station* [1981]); you want a little mental relaxation, but you get **popskull** (Philip Jose Farmer, "Riders of the Purple Wage" [1967]); you plan to do some serious drinking, but you get a **mocker cocktail** (Piers Anthony and Robert E. Margroff, *The Ring* [1968]). Other potent beverages include the **Pan Galactic Gargle Blaster**, which "is like having your brain smashed out by a slice of lemon wrapped round a large gold brick" (Douglas Adams, *The Hitchhiker's Guide to the Galaxy* [1979] 17),[2] **Victory Gin** (George Orwell, *Nineteen Eighty-Four* [1949]), **moonjuice** (Brunner, *Stand on Zanzibar* [1968]), the **Triple Bombast**, and **alcopop** (both Anthony and Margroff, *The Ring*).[3]

After a meal like this, a diner might long for dessert; but even this course does not bring relief. Arthur Byron Cover's *Stationfall* (1989) introduces the sweet concoction **soy raspberry paste**; Bass's "Rorqual Maru" suggests the **orange-3 sweet bar**; and Sanders's "The Artist of Hunger" munches on **joybars** and **soy-chips**. Anthony and Margroff's *The Ring* unveils **psychedelic pastry**, which "had a tangy, sweet flavor that was hot and chill at once and seemed constantly to change in both temperature and texture" (130). And for those watching their weight, Robert A. Heinlein's future society in *Beyond This Horizon* (1948) suggests **Pseudo-Sweets**—which are, as he puts it, "diet-negative" (7).

Others might prefer an after-dinner cigarette, but this may not bring its usual pleasure. Slesar's "Ersatz" only offers artificial cigarettes made of "treated wool fibers" (68), and Winston Smith in Orwell's *Nineteen Eighty-Four* must smoke a **Victory Cigarette**, which falls apart as you smoke it. To combine smoking and dessert, John L. Sladek's "The Happy Breed" (1967) imaginatively introduces **Sugarsmokes**—in chocolate and bitter orange flavors.

Finally, in regards to future fare, it appears that our animal friends will not fare well either; as revealed in "Data's Day" (1991), an episode of *Star Trek: The Next Generation*, the poor cat on board the starship *Enterprise* must subsist on something called **Feline Supplement 74**.

Glancing over all of the items on the menu of the Scientific Restaurant (as shown below), then, leads to one clear conclusion: if you have a chance to visit the future, be prepared for many fascinating and valuable experiences—but bring your own lunch!

It is only to be expected, no doubt, that the terrible futures of science fiction would feature terrible food; but why do even the wonderful futures have such terrible food? Searching for an explanation, one might posit that people are inherently conservative about matters affecting their bodies, thus making all proposals for new types of food sound unappealing. However, people in futuristic science fiction tolerate or even enjoy other forms of strange body invasion, including mind implants and artificial organs, so this cannot be the complete answer.

Another explanation would be that future civilizations tend to maintain large populations, and whatever their political philosophies, societies with a multitude of citizens inexorably take on the characteristics of institutions. And institutional food of all kinds is traditionally viewed as execrable. Thus, American soldiers in the Persian Gulf rename their MREs (Meals Ready to Eat) "Meals Rejected by Ethiopians," and college students across the country long complained about eating "mystery meat." If the future is likened to an institutional environment, therefore, the food would naturally emerge as unappetizing.

My favorite theory, however, posits an analogy between the future and one particular type of institution.

Consider for a moment how future societies are typically visualized. My example here is George Lucas's *THX 1138* (1971), but many other stories and films offer similar, if not so extreme, appearances. Here, the dominant colors are stark black and white; people tend to dress in plain white or metallic clothes or robes; buildings are characterized by bland, undecorated walls and corridors; people talk quietly as their voices echo through the empty chambers; and the overall atmosphere is one of cleanliness and sterility. Which environment in present-day society does this resemble? There is one obvious answer: hospitals. Simply put, people frequently envision the future as one large hospital.

There are logical reasons for this association. Of course, hospitals are often places where one is focused on the future—with babies being born, and patients struggling to stay alive—and hospitals are often the places where people are most directly confronted with futuristic technology and language. That is, most of the amazing inventions that enter everyday life are first domesticated and made user-friendly, but as a patient in a hospital, one might be regularly face some strange, unwieldy piece of scientific equipment which carries out some test of unknown purpose, while doctors and technicians quietly converse in incomprehensible jargon about what they are doing.

In this context, the connection between future foods and the imagery of the hospital emerges with startling clarity. In a hospital, after all, patients may be fed intravenously—that is, with **scientific liquid foods**—or they may simply be maintained on medication—like **food pills**. And if patients are fed solid foods, they may be processed for easy chewing—like **food paste**—or they may be deliberately bland, but very nourishing—like, say, **zymoveal**. In short, according to this scenario, we need not wonder why future food is so horrible; it's hospital food.[4]

And, come to think of it, there is a general aura of good health about many of the future societies I have mentioned. Residents of Gernsback's world of 2660 make a daily trip to the **Bacillatorium**—"prescribed by law" (95)—which destroys all harmful bacteria in their bodies and keeps them healthy. In Heinlein's *Beyond This Horizon*, genetic engineering has virtually eliminated all diseases. And even though many future societies are plagued by problems like overpopulation, repression, dehumanization, and violence, they are rarely plagued by plagues. Food may be scarce, as in *Soylent Green*, but when it is there, it is nutritious. As in a hospital, then, citizens of future civilizations may be treated like meat, crowded into tiny rooms, talked down to, or constantly ordered about—but their health is maintained. The analogy between the future and the hospital is most explicit, perhaps, in Sladek's "The Happy Breed," where the benevolent but overbearing computer controlling all people's lives and habits is called MEDCENTRAL.

This metaphor of the future as hospital is, in the final analysis, appropriate and suggestive. That is, if we are living today in a "sick society," the solution, then, is to establish a hospital society. And as one consequence, the typical future civilization, like a hospital, offers food as an aspect of medical treatment: it is wholesome, nutritious, and awful.

In sum, just as mothers once told children to eat their chicken soup and their vegetables, future societies will urge their residents to eat their **Chicken Little** and their **protovegs**.

So, having completed their gastronomic tour of the future, science fiction readers should go out and enjoy their lunch—while they still can!

The Scienticafé
The Scientific Restaurant of the Future

MENU

Tomorrow's Selections

Appetizers
SEVERAL HARMLESS GASES

Complete Meals
FOOD PASTE
FOOD PILLS
LIQUID SCIENTIFIC FOODS

Soups
PLANKTON CHOWDER
PSEUDO-CONSOMMÉ
SEWER BOUILLABAISSE

Entreés
CHEMICAL BEEF
CHICKEN LITTLE
CONCENTRO
NUTRIPON
PROCESSED ALGAE
SWEET-AND-SOUR ICE TURTLES
TERMITE COMPRESS
ZYMOVEAL

Finger Foods
AMBROSIA PLUS
SOYLENT GREEN

Breads
FISHMEAL BREAD
GRUB LOAF

Side Dishes
APPEARS
PENGUIN EGGS
PROTOVEGS
SHYAPPLES

Desserts
JOYBARS
ORANGE-3 SWEET BARS
PSEUDO-SWEETS
PSYCHEDELIC PASTRY
SOY-CHIPS
SOY RASPBERRY PASTE
SUGARSMOKES

Beverages
CAFFOID
COFFIEST
FROSTY-FLIP
KAFFINA
MALTO

Wines and Cocktails
ALCOPOP
DOWNER WINE
MOCKER COCKTAIL
MOONJUICE
PAN GALACTIC GARGLE BLASTER
POPSKULL
TRIPLE BOMBAST
VICTORY GIN

Afterword

Without thoroughly surveying recent science fiction, I believe the genre's future foods have generally not improved—recall, for example, that unappealing, instantly-baked biscuit Rey listlessly consumes in *Star Wars: The Force Awakens* (2016)—with one significant exception: reflecting the growing gap between the rich and poor which Howard V. Hendrix references above, science fiction now expects the future's wealthy individuals to enjoy food that is far superior to that of less fortunate compatriots. Thus, in *Passengers* (2016), Jennifer Lawrence's character, holding a first-class ticket to the stars, can enjoy sumptuous breakfasts while her plebeian paramour (Chris Platt) endures less palatable fare.

I originally investigated future foods because that was the topic of the 1991 Eaton Conference, but this essay's unusual approach to the subject is easily explained: ever since I began attending Eaton Conferences, I was impressed by the marvelous presentations of the late Frank McConnell, who demonstrated that scholars could be both thoughtful and wildly amusing, and longed to produce a similar paper. So, after presenting somber, even stuffy papers at the 1987, 1988, and 1989 Eaton Conferences, I proposed presenting a funny paper at the 1990 Eaton Conference—but coordinator George Slusser rejected "The Warp-Drive to Sequelize: Book One in the Chronicles of Westfahl the Critic," though it later appeared in *Extrapolation*. Undaunted, I offered to present this funny paper at the next conference and Slusser accepted it, both as a conference paper and one chapter in its Eaton volume, *Foods of the Gods: Eating and the Eaten in Science Fiction and Fantasy* (1996) (a decision reached, by the way, before I was enlisted as its co-editor).

Undertaking to emulate McConnell, I knew I lacked the vast knowledge of literature, philosophy, and religion that he effortlessly integrated into his analyses of science fiction, but I thought I could compensate for this deficiency by deploying one of my own strengths—a dedication to obsessively thorough studies of innumerable texts that relate to a given topic. Hence, I examined almost every science fiction book and magazine in my library, looking for examples of exotic future foods, and consulted other texts in the Eaton Collection. It was fun to end my presentation by passing out copies of my menu from the Scienticafé, also included as an addendum to my essay.

At the conference, though, the student was unsurprisingly outdone by the master, as McConnell presented a paper with the same premise—that food in science fiction is generally terrible—but drew from it a more provocative and profound conclusion, that this showed science fiction to be a fundamentally Gnostic literature, celebrating the human spirit while denigrating the human body and all its mundane needs, like food. You may read this excellent piece, "Alimentary, My Dear Watson: Food and Eating in Scientific and Mystery Fiction," in McConnell's *The Science of Fiction and the Fiction of Science* (2009), though this book's editors concluded that his essay on immortality, referencing the same conclusion, was even better.

Still, though McConnell's essay was superior to mine, their kindred nature emerged because they suffered the same fate when the *Foods of the Gods* manuscript reached the University of Georgia Press; for it fell into the hands of an unusually presumptuous, and unusually humorless, copyeditor, who proceeded to cross out the menu and several humorous passages in my essay, and similarly savaged McConnell's essay, crossing out entire paragraphs she deemed inappropriately light-hearted. It was my task as one of the volume's editors to vehemently protest her actions and insist upon the restoration of the original texts. Some people, it seems, wrongly believe that scholars cannot be both insightful and funny, despite the irrefutable evidence provided by McConnell's brilliant work—and at times, I hope, my own.

Foodnotes

1. On second thought, I will pass up the opportunity to plug my other critical writings. Frankly, if you like this article, you won't like them.

2. I thank John Verona of Claremont Graduate University for reminding me of this singular concoction.

3. Actually, some of these alcoholic drinks sound fairly palatable, making them something of an exception to my emerging thesis. Clearly, this subject demands further investigation in another essay, which should be entitled, of course, "The Booze of the Gods."

4. An observation which suggests another title for this essay: "Saint Else-fare."

WORKS SAMPLED: See Bibliography

Cannibalism in Science Fiction

(1991 Eaton Conference)

Paul Alkon

How can we start to think about cannibalism in science fiction? I shall argue that *A Modest Proposal* (1729) and *The Time Machine* (1895) supply the necessary paradigms. For this trope they are archetypal texts that establish a semiotics of cannibalism. Jonathan Swift and H.G. Wells also enhanced the power of their works by memorable literalization of metaphor. No one can forget either Swift's statement that the rich are devouring the poor or Wells's prediction that unless we remedy social inequities the poor will in their turn devour the rich. In effect if not by design the Morlocks stand in dialogic relationship to the Modest Proposer, providing the inevitable corollary to Swift's proposition and thereby also creating the most important thematic and narrative model for treatment of cannibalism in science fiction.

By *cannibals* I mean humans who eat fellow humans. I am not concerned with aliens eating each other as in James Tiptree's [Alice Sheldon's] "Love Is the Plan, The Plan Is Death" (1973). Nor am I concerned with how and why science fiction turns humans into food for other species on or off our planet. Therefore I exclude such otherwise attractive episodes as Albert's barbeque of Quilla June for his starving mutant dog, Blood, at the sentimental conclusion of Harlan Ellison's "A Boy and His Dog" (1969). Albert himself had no appetite for that meal, over which we therefore need not linger. Except for brief sociological comparisons, I also exclude vampires. They and other related topics warrant closer study but are best deferred until cannibalism itself has been more clearly understood.[1] After considering crucial features of *A Modest Proposal* and *The Time Machine* I shall examine a few exemplary instances of cannibalism in twentieth-century science fiction to suggest how the earlier paradigms provide touchstones for evaluating more recent efforts. But, of course, it is not possible in one essay to survey all of science fiction's cannibals, much less trace their relationship to forebears and cousins who have proliferated in other genres ever since Kronos devoured his children. If cannibalism is coeval with time itself in our collective imagination, as it seems to be, it is no wonder that critics have yet to explain or even fully catalogue all of its remarkably numerous instances in literature.[2] Swift and Wells provide, at least, good starting points for an investigation of cannibalism in science fiction.

Swift's satiric masterpiece of culinary nightmare is not science fiction. Nevertheless *A Modest Proposal* has significant affinities with that genre, first by virtue of a speaker who might well compete with Victor Frankenstein himself for top honors as the very model of a modern mad scientist. Unlike Frankenstein, Swift's Modest Proposer of infanticide as a solution to Ireland's chronic shortages of food and money does not work in a laboratory creating monstrosities. He is a theoretician. To economic difficulties caused by overpopulation he applies cold equations proving that his scheme of selling and eating babies will allow profitable disposition of the "Hundred and Twenty Thousand Children of poor Parents, annually born."[3] He displays to perfection that cool scientific detachment of mathematical reasoning from moral concerns that leads to misuse of science. He does so, moreover, or at least attempts to do so, on a grand scale that could hardly be rivaled by a solitary experimental genius creating a monster or two. Outside of literature we now recognize this mentality as a prototype for those technicians who invented and managed the German death camps. Inside literature, thanks to the framing comic vitality of Swift's presentation of his deranged speaker, we surely see in Swift's Modest Proposer something quite different: the great-grandfather of science fiction's most hilarious mad scientist, Dr. Strangelove.

The wonderful economy of means involved in the Modest Proposer's project shifts emphasis away from the accidents of technological or scientific innovation to the more essential matter of attitudes toward existing technology. Using only the familiar, simple, easily obtained, and easily employed machinery of the butcher's shop, the Modest Proposer's scheme would create a revolutionary new industry—or if you prefer, a revolutionary new branch of an old industry: meat production. The essential difference proposed is in product rather than process, although Swift's Modest Proposer does emphatically endorse the do-it-yourself possibilities of home manufacture, packaging, and distribution as well as consumption. He notes too those existing large-scale industrial techniques already available in the Dublin slaughterhouses that can readily be adapted to the new product. His plan is nothing less than a proposal for an industrial revolution that would, if achieved, be quite as notable in its consequences as widespread adoption of the steam engine, the spaceship, or the computer. Swift's topic is no less central to science fiction than these and similar developments.

Other resonances with science fiction arise because Swift counts upon readers who believe that cannibalism did or does take place *somewhere else* but who would not themselves seriously entertain the idea. The distinction is crucial because only for such readers could there be anything either very funny or very estranging in the Modest Proposer's assurance that "a young healthy Child well nursed, is, at a Year old, a most delicious, nourishing, and wholesome Food; whether *Stewed*, *Roasted*, *Baked*, or *Boiled*; and, I make no doubt, that it will equally serve in a *Fricasie*, or a *Ragoust*" (504). Likewise only those not at all tempted to practice cannibalism will laugh heartily (or nervously) at being informed by the Modest Proposer that "A Child will make two Dishes at an Entertainment for Friends; and when the Family dines alone, the fore or hind Quarter will make a reasonable Dish, and seasoned with a little Pepper or Salt will be very good Boiled in the fourth day, especially in *Winter*" (504). The Modest Proposer does not know all this from his own experiences.

Like his readers, he himself is not—or at least not yet—a cannibal. He is merely passing along a suggestion based upon information provided by someone who is: "a very knowing *American* of my Acquaintance in *London*" (504). We thus learn at one remove about the pleasures of cannibalism, seeing it from the outside, as we usually do in fiction, where first-person accounts of cannibalism by cannibals are the exception not the norm.

Literary cannibals usually come from elsewhere. They may come from another country that, like America for Swift's contemporary readers, is reputed to be more primitive by virtue of its actual or supposed cannibalistic practices, and thus may easily symbolize another time. They may come from or inhabit another time, as in *The Time Machine* and those works like Gabrielle Lord's *Salt* (1990) that imitate it by more or less gratuitously including cannibalistic episodes to signal a future that has retrogressed culturally.[4] They may even come from that undiscovered country beyond the grave as do the cannibalistic zombies hungrily lurching through the countryside and shopping mall in those undying classics *Night of the Living Dead* (1968) and *Dawn of the Dead* (1978). Whatever their origins, and whatever their shapes, cannibals are aliens, albeit terrestrial aliens. Because for readers cannibalism is not a commonplace feature of daily life in their own country, even homegrown cannibals like Dr. Hannibal Lester have the impact of aliens. So does Swift's American.

Swift's readers may have a delicious extra shudder at the idea of an American cannibal in London, perhaps walking the same streets that they walk while admiring their children from an altogether different perspective. For a moment readers imagining the outlook of this American cannibal in London as filtered through the suggestions of his European friend the Modest Proposer may even regard their *own* (or their neighbor's) children quite differently, or at least see the possibility of doing so. Thus Swift's text achieves something that I find indistinguishable from the effects of cognitive estrangement that Darko Suvin has called fundamental to science fiction at its best.[5]

But at first glance, *A Modest Proposal* is apparently without the alternative environment that Suvin also insists is crucial to the genre. The Modest Proposer remains in the reader's own world, unlike Lemuel Gulliver, whom Suvin rightly proposes as the archetypal science fiction protagonist traveling to strange places for close encounters with such alien creatures as the rational talking horses that invite us to reconsider our own society from an estranged perspective. If the Modest Proposer's suggestion were adopted, however, the reader's world would change. It would *become* an alternative environment. It would look the same for the most part, except of course at mealtimes. An inhabitant or visitor could gaze around and still see humans and familiar objects, not Morlocks, Martians, or spaceships. But it would be essentially different in ways that count more than technological or biological changes.

Consider what Swift has actually done to readers. Simply in order to understand what is being said in *A Modest Proposal*, every reader must first envision and then (one hopes) reject that bizarre and morally repellent alternative future environment in which she along with everyone else would condone and might practice cannibalism. In an exercise of the reader's own imagination inevitably elicited—briefly or at length depending upon each reader's imaginative capacity—Swift invokes contemplation, for rejection, of a possible future world that is as significantly different from the reader's actual world as any dystopian place in science fiction. Indeed the cannibalistic future that Swift invites us to contemplate is more truly different, more truly other, than most science fiction worlds, whether utopian or dystopian. Like the best science-fictional futures, it also serves as a metaphor describing and inviting reconsideration of a significant feature of the real present. Here then is an implied alternative environment that works to enhance effects of cognitive estrangement achieved via suggestions of cannibalism, and thus invocation of the alien, in a work whose protagonist and subject matter anticipate familiar themes of mad scientists and industrial revolution in later science fiction. Less overtly than in

Gulliver's Travels (1726), but hardly less significantly for the history of literary forms, Swift in *A Modest Proposal* approximates key formal features of science fiction.

The first large point to register in contemplating cannibalism in science fiction and affiliated forms, then, is that this trope may lend itself as powerfully to comedy as to horror, without losing in either tonality its potential as a device for cognitive estrangement. Because cannibalism is not likely to be a common feature of the real world in which readers live, accounts of cannibalism, whether grim or amusing, may easily, but do not invariably, invite us to look at familiar things from an alien perspective. How far they do so is one measure of their excellence as well as of their affinities to science fiction. It is by this measure that *A Modest Proposal* deserves consideration alongside *The Time Machine.*

The Morlocks' far-future environment is so obviously alternative to every reader's own world that they have long been accepted into the iconography of science fiction as emblems inviting us to look again from an estranged viewpoint at relationships between rich and poor, among other things. Their diet is an unmistakable sign of their difference but also, as with the nastiness of Swift's Yahoos, a sign of disquieting resemblance to ourselves. Whereas the Modest Proposer at first seems human but then takes on alien affinities thanks to his espousal of cannibalism, the Morlocks at first seem utterly alien but then paradoxically become more evidently human when the Time Traveller recognizes them as fellow-carnivores who are, moreover, our descendants. We have become them. They are us. But from the viewpoint of the Time Traveller, with whom Wells's first-person narrative compels us to identify, they are also literally and figuratively beneath us. Although human, there is social distance between them and us, a distance whose violation enhances (for readers) the horror of their nocturnal depredations.

The Time Machine thus irrevocably establishes cannibalism's sociology. Like most writers who have subsequently resorted to the topic in science fiction, but with characteristically more brilliant literalization of metaphor by virtue of the Morlocks' underground habitat, Wells presents cannibals as hopelessly lower class. The Morlocks are déclassé. Their cannibalism no less than their underground habitat is a telling measure of how far they have fallen socially: into the lower depths from which they cannot permanently rise. In their social degradation the Morlocks are typical despite a few later science fiction cannibals who are closer to the upper crust. Even at their most respectable, cannibals in science fiction after *The Time Machine* seem parvenu. However outrageous their behavior, they reek of the bourgeoisie or (like the Morlocks) worse. With rare exceptions, their social range is only from prole to professional, with more proles than professionals in their social registry. Even the likes of Dr. Hannibal Lecter—whose science fiction counterpart, if there is one, does not come readily to mind—seem no more than *arrivistes* in the upper middle classes. About figures like him there is no air of old money and solid social position. They are not part of the establishment.

Socially, cannibals compare very unfavorably with aliens, whose exotic extraterrestrial origin provides a certain cachet. However humble in their own world, on Earth, aliens achieve an easy entrée into high society denied to cannibals, who derive more or less directly from the unfashionable boondocks of our own jungles and carry with them the stigma of their disadvantaged terrestrial background.[6] Although aliens of a sort, cannibals are also merely locals whose difference is more a handicap than an appealing novelty likely to dissolve social barriers. Even vampires have a loftier social standing forever assured by their noble ancestor, Count Dracula. Ever since Bram Stoker sponsored their debut they have been welcomed into high society. They seem aristocratic even when reduced to genteel poverty in rundown castles or shabby coffins far from Transylvania. Whereas most cannibals are slovenly, vampires are elegant. Most of them dress expensively. Their image of bon ton persists despite instances of boorish self-made vampires and a few pathetic cases of downward social mobility. Unlike cannibals, vampires tend to be individualistic. They are usually clever loners who shun crowds in favor of quiet evenings spent with a single companion, tête à tête. Cannibals tend to operate in groups as the Morlocks do, foraging and feeding together. Even far-future cannibalism is more often than not a tribal activity dictated by custom or ritual rather than a private enterprise expressing individual initiative and taste. Vampires, moreover, are usually sexy, even if they are not good bets for safe sex. But how many science fiction characters outside of a Robert A. Heinlein novel have ever wanted to sleep with a cannibal? Nor are many readers likely to be attracted by the idea of cannibalism as a sexual fantasy allowing surrogate gratification. In this too *The Time Machine* provides a model by making the Morlocks repulsive in appearance as well as behavior, and focusing sentimental if not sexual interest in the altogether different figure of Weena.

Another crucial feature of the Morlocks' presentation is that Wells only gradually reveals their cannibalism to readers, who may, however, and probably do, infer the truth about them before the Time Traveller himself does. It is only after finally identifying cannibalism as a characteristic behavior of the Morlocks that the Time Traveller can measure their relationship to humanity, although with curious ambivalence. Reasoning that among our species "prejudice against human flesh is no deep-seated instinct," and postulating the development of food shortages at some point in the Morlocks' past, the Time Traveller does not find it surprising that "these inhuman sons of men" have returned to an earlier practice: "After all, they were less human and more remote than our cannibal ancestors of three or four thousand years ago."[7] With hideous symmetry in this matter as in so many others throughout *The Time Machine*, evolution has become devolution as the far future duplicates the remote past. Distance from cannibalism becomes a measure of humanity on the plane of morality, although "cannibal ancestors" implies continuities no less disturbing than cannibal descendants: a dubious origin as well as a dubious destination for our species.

By the device of repeatedly hinting at the topic while making his protagonist avoid detailed speculation about the actual procedures of cannibalism, Wells no less skillfully than Swift, though by other means, invites readers to exercise their own imagination on the grisly implications of this subject. Cannibalism is one of those topics that best elicits cognitive estrangement while arousing horror by hints and suggestions rather than long explicit descriptions. Swift too understood this, even though he springs the subject upon readers much earlier in a text whose main strategy is nevertheless not to describe fully but to invite readers to imagine a possible future world where cannibalism is commonplace.

With these Swiftian and Wellsian models in mind we are now equipped to consider more recent examples of cannibalism in science fiction. Tiptree's "Morality Meat" (1985) is unmistakably Swiftian in its theme of poor babies turned into food for the rich, although almost devoid of comedy, as befits our solemn century and her feminist topic. "Morality Meat" is Wellsian in its narrative structure that builds up to rather than starts from the revelation of cannibalism. It is only toward the end that readers have solid proof that dead babies supply the frozen meat being trucked up to some rich old men, the "aging oligarchs," of the exclusive Bohemia Club.[8] As so often happens in the best science fiction, Tiptree places her readers in the classic situation of Wells's Time Traveller piecing together from various clues the true facts behind misleading appearances in an apparently utopian or at least acceptable but actually dystopian future. Her narrative gradually supplies readers with clues allowing them to anticipate what is finally revealed about the gruesome mechanics of the slaughterhouse, freezer, and meat-packaging complex operating to deal with surplus babies in a "Right to Life Adoption Center." At first this place seems designed for humane dispersal to foster parents of children born to impoverished women who cannot support them and could not have abortions thanks to a pro-life constitutional amendment. In this future America, coincidentally, other livestock is largely unavailable because "droughts and grain diseases finished off most of the US's meat production" (70). As in *A Modest Proposal*, babies supply an alternative industry.

It is a feminist rather than Swiftian or Wellsian touch that the wealthy consumers of surplus babies are "all men, most of them old," although "Not fags, no way" (69–70). By noting that "the old men are dressed all alike, some kind of shorts and badges too—almost like a bunch of senile Boy Scouts," Tiptree elicits a momentary burst of Swiftian satiric laughter while also echoing the group quality of the Morlocks who are to the Time Traveller indistinguishable from one another (70). Their interchangeability in turn reflects the tribal origins of cannibalism. In "Morality Meat," as so often elsewhere, the unpleasantry of cannibalism is enhanced by the idea of group cannibalism, which seems harder to escape and therefore more menacing than individual depredations.

Swiftian notions of class warfare are both echoed and given a feminist spin when Tiptree makes her cannibals upper-class members of an exclusive all-male club rather than merely a herd of lower-class brutes. But her comparison with senile Boy Scouts deflates the social status of the old oligarchs of the Bohemia Club by associating them in an absurdist way with a very middle-class institution. Here we see how hard it is for even the most prosperous science fiction cannibals to maintain an authentic air of high society without lapses in taste that betray their low origins and their instincts to gravitate downwards. (How many vampires would be caught undead wearing anything resembling a Boy Scout uniform?) The result of Tiptree's feminist variations on Swiftian themes and Wellsian structures of cannibalism is an effective story, drawing with commendable ingenuity upon the conventional features of this trope. Because no one can now refer to eating babies without evoking memories of Swift, Tiptree also provides her narrative with a nice dialogic dimension in its implicit but unmistakable allusion to the mass infanticide and cannibalism of *A Modest Proposal*, to which she pays homage by converting it into a fable for our time and place.

Solitary cannibals, although very rare, can be found in Stephen King's "Survivor Type" (1982) and Sakyo Komatsu's "The Savage Mouth" (1978). These tales take up too the unusual but ancient theme of self-cannibalism. King's short story is among the even more rare instances of first-person narratives about cannibalism related by the cannibal: in this case via the diary of Dr. Richard Pine, a surgeon marooned alone on a small deserted island who survives for a while by amputating and eating bits of himself while high on doses of the heroin he had been trying to smuggle back to America before his ship was wrecked. From information about his earlier life that he digressively includes in his island diary, it is clear that Dr. Pine has always been an unpleasant, bigoted, aggressive, dishonest, criminal, social climber who could certainly be summed up as self-serving, although King does not resort explicitly to this dreadful pun, merely literalizing it in the story's action. In a bravura display of self-hatred, Dr. Pine tells us that he started life as "a poor wop from the projects" who was "born Richard Pinzetti in New York's Little Italy," to an immigrant father whom he describes as "an Old World guinea," as a "fat greaseball," and also (more lyrically) as a "fucking greaseball dipstick nothing cipher zilcho zero."[9] Dr. Pine makes clear that his father's death was a very welcome event to a son anxious to escape his origins, as he eventually does by going to college on an athletic scholarship and then working his way through medical schools by "the rackets.... Football pools, basketball pools, a little policy" (407–409). Here again we have the parvenu as cannibal and the cannibal as parvenu.

One critic accurately calls Dr. Pine a "gothic mad scientist" in a "twentieth-century version of *Robinson Crusoe*."[10] Nevertheless "Survivor Type" is more gothic tale than science fiction. This story offers rich possibilities for symbolic interpretation but little invitation to that cognitive estrangement by which readers are invited to reconsider their own situation from the radically alien perspective of a depicted or implied alternative environment. To be sure, Dr. Pine's island is different from every reader's surroundings. But it is very different too in its effects from more estranging places like the utopian landscape populated after a shipwreck by George Pine and four females, whose improbable sexual idyll is recounted in Henry Neville's very popular romance of 1668, *The Isle of Pines*, to which King may allude by the name and location of his protagonist. On Dr. Pine's island sheer horror prevails over utopian or dystopian possibilities of the kind that make settings like the Isle of Pines or Dr. Moreau's island far more evocative of appealing or threatening prospects at home, where the reader lives. "Survivor Type" is an example of cannibalism on the fringes of science fiction, aimed primarily at eliciting horror.

Toward the diary's end, after grisly accounts of several amputations followed by self-consuming feasts, Dr. Pine remarks that he is reduced to "a monster now, a freak. Nothing left below the groin. Just a freak. A head attached to a torso dragging itself along the same by the elbows. A crab" (426). Perhaps this metaphor echoes the giant crabs to which life on our planet has devolved in the terminal beach of *The Time Machine*. Absent from "Survivor Type," however, are the Time Traveller's radically altered landscapes or any of his explicit invitations to consider how such changes should influence notions of where our society fits into the scheme of things under the aspect of eternity. As Dr. Pine's diary ebbs out in delirious incoherence towards the end, he notes that "Yesterday I took off my ear lobes" and winds up with a final entry suggesting that he has removed and consumed one hand: "lady fingers they taste just like lady fingers" (426). With that hallucinatory comparison King's narrative concludes.

"Survivor Type" may spoil our next visit to the pastry shop while nevertheless offering solid food for thought about bigotry and careerism in a competitive society. But it is unlikely to provoke much reconsideration of the medical technology and scientific knowledge symbolized by a cannibal surgeon ultimately more dangerous to himself than threatening to us. This is indeed a mad scientist, but without anything like either Victor Frankenstein's creative gift for unleashing trouble on the world, or the Modest Proposer's pernicious interest in altering the world around him. King's tale primarily uses cannibalism as a means of characterization.

Dr. Pine's surgical skill is a plot necessity to ensure plausible continuation of the increasingly horrifying action in a situation where a layman would not know how to tie off arteries and would therefore bleed to death long before achieving any really spectacular degree of self-consumption. More essential to King's story than portrayal of a scientist is depiction of a thoroughly vicious character whose essential traits of bigotry, greed, and selfishness would be quite as telling—and as likely to be found—in someone from almost any walk of life. As usual, King excels in arousing dislike. It is the reader's distaste for Dr. Pine that is crucial to the story's impact, not his role as mad scientist, although that certainly does provide a nice additional gothic touch. Far from being altogether dismayed by the conclusion, or regarding it as an open-ended invitation to reconsider relationships between science and society or even an invitation to speculate for long on Dr. Pine's probable fate after he stopped writing, readers are more likely to find his grotesque situation a satisfying instance of poetic justice in which a thoroughly vicious character gets about what he deserves and can be dismissed from further consideration.

"The Savage Mouth" is more centered on the symbolism of opportunities made possible only by science. Sakyo Komatsu's nameless protagonist living prosperously in a modern city, presumably Tokyo, is not forced to self-cannibalism by necessity but rather chooses this fate because he can no longer tolerate life's meaningless absurdities. He is motivated to devour himself by existential, not physical, hunger. Thanks to modern science and its technology, Komatsu's cannibal is able to consume himself at will and far more completely than Dr. Pine, who has available only the instruments in a lifeboat's first-aid kit.

Komatsu's more comfortably situated cannibal can afford all the latest gadgetry for his peculiar kitchen. He has a stove for cooking, a refrigerator, and, more crucially, an elaborate robot surgical machine programmed to perform amputations and aided by a life-support system so that, as pieces are removed for cooking and eating, prosthetic devices and artificial organs replace his missing parts. This allows him—or more precisely, his head—to enjoy an extensive and varied menu of stewed intestines, sautéed liver and kidney, stomach "soaked in soy sauce, with garlic and red pepper," and then "his own pulsing heart, fried in thin slices: a deed beyond even the imagination of the priests of the Aztec sacrificial rituals."[11] Here is an event only possible (as yet) in science fiction, by extrapolation from existing artificial organs and life-support systems to more advanced medical technologies.

By comparison, most science fiction cannibalism is rather old fashioned, even in futuristic settings. Recall, for example, those Morlocks seen by the Time Traveller at "their little table of white metal, laid with what seemed a meal" (67). This detail of gathering around a table to dine is rather homey except for thoughts about who supplied "the red joint" of meat also glimpsed on that table by the Time Traveller. Swiftian consumption of babies, moreover, even in a future setting like Tiptree's nightmare pro-life world, proceeds by familiar means. Equally familiar are the mass-production techniques based on those of today's slaughterhouses in that other nice variation on Swiftian themes, MGM's 1973 film *Soylent Green*, which centers on the manufacture of food from the corpses of surplus adults, especially elderly adults who have been encouraged to accept euthanasia. Here again is a familiar situation where the living eat the dead, and, whatever the other problems, there is no difficulty in telling who is alive and who is not. But, like much cyberpunk fiction with which it otherwise has few affinities, the mingling of machine and human in "The Savage Mouth" blurs conventional distinctions between life and death. Komatsu's fried heart cooked especially for its owner deserves credit as an altogether novel recipe. As Komatsu's comparison with Aztec rituals emphasizes, his is no warmed-over serving of primitive tribal customs transplanted to a degenerate future. Nor is this story just another account of seppuku featuring a samurai cannibal in that ritual that is a favorite staple of the Japanese literary diet. Although more commonplace varieties of horror are, I am told, popular in Japan, Komatsu's stress on the possibilities of technology unequivocally brings his tale into the sphere of science fiction, where it stands out as unique.[12] "The Savage Mouth" is original. It may be the only instance to date of truly futuristic cannibalism, that is to say, cannibalism of a kind that cannot yet be practiced.

Moreover, there is another course by way of dessert. After forty days of leisurely dining on futuristic fare, including his own stomach and heart, "almost all the muscles of his face had been eaten as well: the lips along were left to chew with the assistance of attached springs. Only one eyeball remained; the other had been sucked and chewed" (82). Finally the machine saws off the top of the protagonist's skull then sprinkles "salt and pepper and lemon on the trembling exposed cerebrum, in the act of scooping up a great spoonful" (82). Curious gourmets will be disappointed to learn from Komatsu's narration, however, that "by the time the arm of the machine scooped up that pale mushy paste and carried it to the skull's mouth, and the mouth lapped up to swallow, 'taste' was no longer recognizable" (83). At this point detectives from the homicide squad somehow discover the scene but decide to suppress the cannibal's tapes explaining what he really did and tell reporters only that he was murdered.

The Inspector lies, as he explains to his younger colleague, out of fear that if the truth is revealed, many others will want to turn cannibal and consume themselves, or else indulge in equally self-destructive follies. He reasons that knowledge of the incident will set everyone probing into the hidden madness of their own souls, whereupon "if really large numbers of people start expressing that madness under slogans like *existential liberation* and *do your own thing*—we're done for! It's the end of human civilization!" (84). While contemplating this bizarre scenario of contagious cannibalism or its equivalents facilitated by new technologies that allow unprecedented self-destruction, the young detective goes over to tidy up the rotting head, which suddenly bites one of his fingers.

Komatsu's last sentence focuses on this event: "The skull, with its naked brain, its own remaining eye beginning to come loose, and strong springs replacing its vanished muscles, was now slowly crumpling and chewing the scrap of meat between its swollen tongue and sturdy teeth" (84). This final image of personal relationships in the modern world achieves a truly Swiftian power, though less reminiscent of *A Modest Proposal*'s indirection than of Swift's gruesomely deconstructed woman destroyed by sexual intercourse in "A Beautiful Young Nymph Going to Bed" (1734). The well-controlled shock-effect of Komatsu's narrative makes it an exception to the rule that cannibalism is best dealt with by suggestion rather than explicit description. Komatsu's all-devouring head memorably symbolizes existential forms of what Samuel Johnson calls in *Rasselas* (1759) "that hunger of imagination which preys incessantly on life." Whether by design or accident, "The Savage Mouth" also stands in striking dialogue opposition to Heinlein's tour de force "'All You Zombies—'" (1959). If, as H. Bruce Franklin suggests, "'All You Zombies—'" is a ne plus ultra of the Cartesian cogito exposing its narcissism, "The Savage Mouth" at last gives science fiction an equally nihilistic deconstruction of René Descartes's proposition that to think is to be.[13] Only the ultimate of self-consumption, perhaps, could serve as an effective counterpoint to Heinlein's paradoxical but hardly comforting fable of ultimate self-creation that abolishes everybody but the creating self. And only in science fiction could human power to create and destroy the self be addressed in such vividly disturbing symbolism as that supplied by Heinlein's man who engenders himself and Komatsu's man who consumes himself.

Farnham's Freehold (1964) and *Stranger in a Strange Land* (1961) are more problematic texts. As usual in Heinlein, there are formal and ideological contradictions that go far to account for high sales and low artistic reputation. These books have been popular because they have a little something for everybody. For the same reason, they are annoying and ultimately disappointing. The black cannibals in *Farnham's Freehold* serve inconsistent purposes. By ruling and also eating white people, the future blacks, like the Morlocks, show the tables turned with former oppressors now oppressed. Here is nice irony and poetic justice. But here too, as Franklin has noted, are racist stereotypes revived: Heinlein echoes bigoted fears of black savagery.[14] Comparison with *The Time Machine* shows why that prevents readers from accepting the irony as satisfactory justice.

Wells has his Time Traveller sufficiently distanced from the Morlocks, and them sufficiently distanced from humanity, so that loathing them does not interfere with appreciation of the grand historic irony at work in their cannibalistic depredations upon the Eloi, who are themselves alienated from human intelligence. Sympathy for the Eloi elicited by Weena's sad fate merely enhances the arousal of something like pity and fear at humanity's tragic destiny. It is a destiny, moreover, partly brought about by needless exploitation of the lower classes, and to this extent a just punishment because deserved. It is enough for the Time Traveller and his audience to sympathize with Weena. It is not necessary to sympathize with the Morlocks themselves, only to understand why they are as they are. Fear and loathing of them only increases empathy with Weena and thus enhances emotional apprehension of what has happened to humanity thanks to its own folly. But Heinlein tries to have it both ways. *Farnham's Freehold* includes a genuine and commendable attempt to arouse sympathy for present and future black characters as victims of white racism. But it also imitates or echoes *The Time Machine*'s use of future cannibalism without keeping the cannibals sufficiently distinct from sympathetic characters.

There is a formal contradiction here beyond Heinlein's capacity to manage. For *Farnham's Freehold* to succeed it would be necessary for readers both to loathe the black cannibals *and* to sympathize with them, or at least empathize with them. In theory this is possible. Shakespeare, after all, makes us sympathize with Macbeth while *also* hating his crimes, condemning him for committing them, and rejoicing at his death as a proper punishment for him and a necessary deliverance for Scotland. But Heinlein does not bring off a comparable feat with his black cannibals. Though more sentient than the Morlocks, and to that degree more understandable, they are serve mainly to horrify insofar as they practice cannibalism. Because they *are* fully sentient (that is to say, like the Morlocks, fully human), Heinlein's black cannibals are doing what Swift's mad would-be cannibal proposes, with equal and equally horrifying indifference to an ethical code that readers cannot so easily dismiss. They do so, moreover, in a realistic narrative that does not provide any comic detachment of a kind that is likely to channel readers' horror into estranged examination of their own society and its shortcomings rather than into increased revulsion at the behavior of these future blacks. Consequently sympathy for blacks aroused by other features of Heinlein's text is countered by the intrusion of figures who combine the most off-putting characteristics of the Morlocks and the Modest Proposer. In *Farnham's Freehold*, Heinlein never resolves this formal paradox.

In *Stranger in a Strange Land* there is a different but equally unsatisfactory attempt to exploit the trope of cannibalism. Heinlein's human alien, the naturalized Martian

Michael Valentine Smith, arrives on Earth without any disinclination to be eaten. Like his foster parents the Martians, he considers that possibility with pleasure rather than fear. When asked one morning soon after his arrival whether he feels like breakfast he responds with earnest reflections that are to readers hilarious: "He knew that he was food, but he did not 'feel like' food. Nor had he any warning that he might be selected for such honor. He had not known that the food supply was such that it was necessary to reduce the corporate group. He was filled with mild regret, since there was still so much to grok of new events, but no reluctance."[15] Here, no less than in *A Modest Proposal*, cannibalism is satirically regarded as an acceptable method of nourishment available to alleviate food shortages. By excursion into a mind with a totally different outlook on cannibalism from that shared by Heinlein's readers, such passages achieve a Swiftian comic tone that imitates *A Modest Proposal*'s strategy for establishing a radically estranged viewpoint from which to consider our own attitudes. But difficulties arise when Heinlein switches from cannibalism as a device of estrangement to eucharistic cannibalism as a symbol of togetherness.

The switch is part of an often-remarked larger change in mode from satire to didacticism. Many of the religious attitudes and activities mocked at the outset of *Stranger in a Strange Land* are with very little alteration finally presented as exemplary. Included among these practices is ritual consumption of slices from a finger that Michael Valentine Smith leaves with his disciples for eucharistic purposes as he departs for his martyrdom. Setting aside the myriad other problems with this ending, I will only remark that neither comic cannibalism at the novel's outset nor tedious lectures about the comparative anthropology of cannibalism by Heinlein's mouthpiece Jubal Harshaw sufficiently prepare for the concluding emphasis on cannibalism as communion. What readers must first take as an invitation to look at themselves and their society from afar through strange eyes, they must now take as an emblem of their oneness with each other and with the universe. There is just too much contradiction here for Heinlein's narrative to accommodate. It is too great a leap from laughing at cannibalism as an emblem of differentness to accepting it as a symbol of unity.

In an excellent essay on *Stranger in a Strange Land* Robert Plank remarks that Heinlein goes further than any other science fiction writer in glorifying "practices so generally felt abhorrent" but expresses bafflement that Heinlein includes so favorable a depiction of cannibalism among the more obviously attractive wish-fulfilling fantasies of omnipotence and promiscuity that account for the novel's success, especially with younger readers: "The nature of the third fantasy, necrophagy, is less clear; if it appeals by awakening long slumbering strivings in the reader's mind, they must have come from a very ancient, primitive level."[16] True enough. By considering *A Modest Proposal* and *The Time Machine*, we can better understand the matter and also articulate a basic principle governing successful employment of cannibals in science fiction.

Wells and Swift differ in tone but equally achieve their effects by relying upon their reader's unshakable dislike of cannibalism. Plank is right to hesitate. Cannibalism indeed does *not* generally appeal, nor is it likely that it often does even among fans of *Stranger in a Strange Land*. Far from working as a major wish-fulfilling fantasy in the same way as Heinlein's images of promiscuity and omnipotence, though at more obscure and primitive levels, Heinlein's cannibalism at first succeeds as an estranging device used for satiric purposes precisely by reliance on its unfavorable connotations in the comic manner of Swift. But when Heinlein turns away from satire, cannibalism only interferes. If cannibalism appealed very strongly or at all, it could no more thus serve as a Swiftian device of estrangement than it could serve in the Wellsian manner as a symbol of horrifying change. Nor, as Heinlein's flawed texts demonstrate, is it easy for cannibalism to serve either of these purposes and *also* work successfully as a utopian feature of a better world. Science fiction writers ignore at their peril what Swift and Wells understood: that we love to hate cannibals and hate to love them.

NOTES

1. For an excellent discussion of vampires as key figures in the recent convergence of science fiction, fantasy, and feminism, see Veronica Hollinger, "The Vampire and the Alien: Variations on the Outsider," *Science-Fiction Studies*, 16:2 (July 1989), 145–160.

2. Useful perspectives are provided in Claude J. Rawson's pioneering essays "Cannibalism and Fiction: Reflections on Narrative Form and 'Extreme' Situations," *Genre*, 10:4 (Winter 1977), 667–711, and "Cannibalism and Fiction, Part II: Love and Eating in Fielding, Mailer, Genet, and Wittig," *Genre*, 11:2 (Summer 1978), 227–313. See also Maggie Kilgour, *From Communion to Cannibalism: An Anatomy of Metaphors of Incorporation* (Princeton: Princeton University Press, 1990).

3. Jonathan Swift, *A Modest Proposal*, 1729, *The Writings of Jonathan Swift*, ed. Robert A. Greenberg and William B. Piper (New York: Norton, 1973), 503. Parenthetical page references are to this edition.

4. See Gabrielle Lord, *Salt* (Victoria, Australia: Penguin Australia, 1990).

5. See Darko Suvin, *Metamorphoses of Science Fiction: On the Poetics and History of a Literary Genre* (New Haven: Yale University Press, 1979).

6. For a rare modern instance of the cannibal ironically presented as a noble savage welcomed into high society in a novel outside the boundaries of science fiction but nevertheless satirizing related themes such as belief in abduction by aliens, see Tama Janowitz, *A Cannibal in Manhattan* (New York: Crown, 1987).

7. H.G. Wells, *The Time Machine*, 1895 (New York: Bantam, 1982), 77–78.

8. James Tiptree, Jr. [Alice Sheldon], "Morality Meat," 1985, *Crown of Stars* (New York: Tor, 1990), 93. Parenthetical page references are to this edition.

9. Stephen King, "Survivor Type," 1982, *Skeleton Crew* (New York: Signet, 1986), 407–409, 426. Parenthetical page references are to this edition.

10. Kilgour, 150.

11. Sakyo Komatsu, "The Savage Mouth," 1978, trans. Judith Merril, *The Best Japanese Science Fiction Stories*, ed. John L. Apostolou and Martin H. Greenberg (New York: Dembner, 1989), 81. Parenthetical page references are to this edition.

12. My colleague Peter Nosco informs me that "the nauseatingly horrific quality of 'The Savage Mouth' actually represents a prominent theme in much contemporary Japanese cinema and other forms of popular culture (though, not surprisingly, not those that make it to the export market)." Apparently, then, Komatsu is less distinctive in theme than in turning to science fiction as an effective framework for his statement about the horrifying quality of contemporary life.

13. H. Bruce Franklin, *Robert A. Heinlein: America as Science Fiction* (Oxford: Oxford University Press, 1980), 121.

14. Franklin, 157.

15. Robert A. Heinlein, *Stranger in a Strange Land*, 1961 (New York: Berkley, 1982), 11.

16. Robert Plank, "Omnipotent Cannibals in *Stranger in a Strange Land*," *Robert A. Heinlein*, ed. Joseph D. Olander and Martin Harry Greenberg (New York: Taplinger, 1978), 94, 103.

Longevity as Class Struggle

(1992 Eaton Conference)

Fredric R. Jameson

The topic of this essay and book is also a matter of some personal gratification because it allows me to indulge in the chance to talk about one of my favorite books from very long ago—an occasion that might never have arisen otherwise, at least in the normal span of our current lifetimes. George Bernard Shaw's *Back to Methuselah* was published in 1921, at about the same time as Karel Ĉapek's unrelated *The Makropoulos Secret* (1922). Meanwhile, one character in Shaw observes in passing that H.G. Wells "lent me five pounds once which I never repaid, and it still troubles my conscience."[1] We are, with Shaw and perhaps even with the "nonsynchronously synchronous" Ĉapek, still in the afterwash of that late Victorian age in which science, doubt, and vitalistic philosophy met to produce the very first modern science fiction; and I might say, as someone who has always spoken against the legitimization of popular subgenres by high literary respectability (i.e., Dashiell Hammett compared to Fyodor Dostoyevsky), that in my opinion there are genuinely science-fictional pleasures coursing through the epic text of Shaw's "metabiological Pentateuch," which some might still be tempted to identify with the canon.

It is questionable, however, whether the canon is yet ready to return to Shaw; or whether Michael Holroyd's immense biographical efforts, or the current Irish revival—more specifically the Oscar Wilde revival—or even the heliotropic turning of the collective imagination back to the *belle époque* and the age of the Second International are sufficient to make Shaw's art again available to us. This is to say that we may still harbor some deeper doubts or hesitations about the cryogenic revival of this figure, just as we may entertain them about Robert A. Heinlein, whose garrulous and didactic longevity has so much in common with that of the socialist playwright. To acknowledge Shaw as our Bertold Brecht (at least for the stage; in verse it is rather W.H. Auden one would like to acknowledge as Brecht's English-language approximation) is then to reckon in another way with the possibility that after Brecht we may no longer need a Shaw. Still, in the uniquely apolitical atmosphere of Anglo-American literature (where the other rival for assuming some genuinely Brechtian intellectual role may well turn out to be T.S. Eliot himself), it is always instructive to examine the extraordinarily rich practice of one of the few great political artists of modern times: it has been said, indeed, that few things contributed so fundamentally to the cultural preparation for the Labour Party's victory in 1945 as Shaw's tireless propaganda for socialism, which took the form of secondary figures in the great plays whose tirades gradually domesticated, respectabilized, and legitimized that terrifying ideology in the British middle classes.

Back to Methuselah, though, makes it clear that the implacable critique of middle-class hypocrisy in general and the English national character in particular (which an Anglo-Irishman was particularly well placed to articulate) was also a fundamental cultural and political act: something we can perhaps appreciate all the more in the superstate today, from which all lingering and nagging, or garbled approaches to some self-knowledge about American vices of national character, let alone original sin, have been triumphantly expelled. One must also appreciate the fable, whereby the last genuine remnants of true ethnic or group consciousness—the Irish and the Jews—abolish themselves as cultures on the shattering contact with the long-lived, whose proximity and existence—this is one of the fundamental themes of the play—inspire a well-nigh fatal "discouragement" in normal short-lifers like ourselves. But this running political commentary—including a great deal more on the British parliamentary system, which is no longer necessarily of interest to us, along with some remarkable developments on war and aggressiveness from Cain to Oxymandias and the Napoleons of the far future—can serve to illustrate the formal and structural peculiarities of the Shavian play, where much can be added in passing of a seemingly extraneous or digressive nature, and the mesmerizing experience of sheer unbridled talk itself can laterally, as it were, allow any number of supplementary topics to be carried into the spectatorial consciousness along with the official subject of the play. "There has to be something to eat and drink on every page," Gustave Flaubert once said by way of characterizing the drive for heterogeneity he felt at work within his own will to style. Meanwhile, the all-inclusive nature of the monuments of high modernism, their vocation to become the Book of the World, also seem echoed, but idiosyncratically, in this Shavian method, which seems to consist in affirming a whole list of his own idiosyncrasies, of which the ideal Shavian spectator expects—nay, demands—a full recapitulation in every new play.

We are not interested in those idiosyncrasies today (too bad for us!), but it is worth underscoring a single extraordinary moment in *Back to Methuselah*, what Brecht might have called a *gestus*—the shaping of an act or event into a gestural form that speaks in its own new language before using this particular fantasy about longevity or immortality to gauge and bring out the specificities and the differences of the other, more modern versions we will have to deal with later on. As any schoolchild knows, *Back to Methuselah* begins in the Garden of Eden. From there, four additional full-length plays (a cycle that evidently owes something to Richard Wagner) lead us to the Utopian condition of a "summer afternoon in the year 31,920 A.D.," or, following the title of this concluding play in the cycle, "As Far as Thought Can Reach." Not the least fascinating aspect of its dramaturgy—occasionally the cycle is actually performed—is the suggestion of recurrence implicit in the use of the same actors for later and later roles, so that the first family of Eden turns up in the proper nonconformist British drawing room of the 1920s, the still exceedingly British world government of the twenty-second century, the world of AD 3000 dominated by powerful and mysterious long-lifers who have segregated the short-term people in other parts of the globe and serve as their oracles, and on into some ultimate Utopian state in which sexual relations have ceased and humans are born fully grown from eggs, and with but three or four years to live a normal, "childish" life before acceding to the unlovely isolation and wisdom of the condition of the Ancients, who long only to do away with their bodies altogether and attain the immortality of pure thought. One may incidentally feel that Shaw's physical puritanism is not much more repellent than Heinlein's hearty and obligatory hedoninism; maybe neither value has that much to do with sex after all. Indeed, I am going to argue that as a general rule, at least in these works, the official subjects can mask a less obvious but deeper one, which it is the task of the critic and the interpretative process to draw out.

Shaw takes what one may want to call a Christian Scientist attitude toward biology, and perhaps even toward politics and metaphysics as such: in these last areas, it would be easy to diagnose his attitude as the expression of a kind of Fabian or social-democratic idealism, which would reflect a characteristic overestimation of reason and persuasion and an equally characteristic underestimation of ideology, unconscious drive, and the role of violence in human history. That is just the kind of idealism one would expect to find as the working ideology and legitimation of the practice of one of the great political orators of the twentieth century; but in Shaw it is by no means as one-dimensional an idealism as this account might suggest. Indeed, his view of choice dovetails well with the requirements of a theatrical aesthetic (with its structural premium placed on speech and dialogue) and opens a mediatory dimension between base and superstructure of a more distinctive and unique kind.

For Adam "decides" to live for a thousand years at the moment when words and concepts are being invented for the first time: his freedom to choose his own life span is part of that first unnamed freshness of the universe, and incidentally coordinates the theme of longevity with that of language and figuration, as we shall see below. But it is with the second moment in the process that we are most concerned here. For in the most characteristically Shavian fashion this first play or moment of the pentateuch, in the Garden of Eden before the Fall and then several centuries later, is succeeded by a new moment staged in the quintessential British drawing room, on Hampstead Heath, peopled by the two cranks of the title ("The Gospel of the Brothers Barnabas") along with their families and assorted typical British politicians of the interwar period. It is indeed the conviction of the brothers that politics, as they are still practiced despite their disastrous consequences in the Great War a few years earlier, can only be reformed by biology, but of an unusual kind: "Our program is only that the term of human life shall be extended to three hundred years," and "our election cry," the flapper adds, "is 'Back to Methuselah'" (*BM* 77).

Faced with this possibility, the politicians rearrange their platforms and electoral strategies and the curtain falls. It is about the next evening that I want to talk primarily and to some purpose. This play, or subplay, is significantly entitled "The Thing Happens": a description that parlays the immediate representational motif—in this case whether people will live longer, or indeed forever—onto a higher level of symbolic abstraction. At what point can longevity become visible in the narrative itself? It is all very well for us to look back across Lazarus Long's long life. From the outset, virtually by definition, we know that the "thing" has happened to him. But we and the writer are more often in the unhappy position of Emperor Rudolph II of Bohemia, who first tries the Makropoulus secret out on the inventor's daughter in 1600 and then goes mad. "How," as she puts it three centuries later on the modern stage, "how could he be sure I was going to live for three hundred years? So he put my father in a tower as a fraud and I ran away with everything he had written to Hungary or to Turkey, I don't remember which."[2]

How indeed? How do you make an event out of such a condition, whose features consist in suddenly beginning one day to wonder why after so many years a friend or acquaintance has not seemed even to begin to change or grow old? It is by comparing newsreels of the drowning of a number of famous people that Shaw's short-lifers discover their astonishing physical similarity, much as though we were to discover that Alexander the Great, Christopher Marlowe, and, say, James Dean all looked suspiciously like the same person. At the very least this would tend to convert the immortality or longevity drama back into a kind of detective story—something it most notably is in Ĉapek's play. In a moment, I want to trace the consequences of this representational problem or dilemma out in two different directions: namely, on the one hand, the reason why the long-lifers feel the need to disguise their unusual destinies; and, on the other hand, the question of time itself, not merely how one might represent an expanse of human time of this magnitude but what it would feel like existentially and to what degree the inner experience of the long-lived might be imagined to be radically and qualitatively different from that of the normally mortal—would there, for example, be many more volumes full of Proustian *madeleines* and *souvenirs involontaires*?

But this particular representational problem—the palpable difficulty in finding an objective correlative or narrative figuration for the disclosure of longevity or immortality—suggests some more fundamental interpretative and hermeneutic lesson. In the following pages we will act methodologically as though a principle exists according to which the ostensible content, the manifest topic or subject matter, always masks a deeper one of an entirely different nature. Some such principle is probably always at work in the hermeneutic process since interpretation would not be required if the work always said exactly what it meant. Interpretation seems called for in the present instance by the nagging suspicion that the longevity motif may be a cover or blind for something else.

This is a point that might be illustrated the other way around by the thematics of death, more specifically by meditations on its meaning: Simone de Beauvoir (but also Ernst Bloch, I believe, in a very different philosophical context from Sartrean existentialism) has argued that since death is meaningless in the first place, such meditations, despite their evident charge of affect, cannot be expected to lead anywhere; they are reveries in a void that in reality capture and express feelings and anxieties of a very different (nonexistential) kind. The interpretative hypothesis would then suggest that the theme of death—thinking about it, experiencing the death anxiety—invariably serves as a cover and vehicle for deploying the fear of something else (for de Beauvoir, the fear of having wasted one's life, regret at not having lived).

What we must now conjecture is whether something similar could be advanced for the immortality or longevity plot: whether its anxieties too might stand, in the conscious mind, as substitutes for some more concrete and fundamental worry and fear—some deeper contradiction—at issue in the unconscious. With the possibility of such a hermeneutic reversal, I come back to the most stunning development in Shaw's narrative. In "The Thing Happens," set in the year AD 2170 in the office of the president of the world system, which is located in the British Isles, members of that government—some of whom look suspiciously like the politicians in the previous twentieth-century governmental system and are indeed their descendants—slowly discover that two of their number, the Archbishop of York and the Domestic Minister, Mrs. Lutestring, are in reality very different from themselves and prove to have lived for over two hundred years. Who are these two people? They are evidently not the political leaders (whose descendants we have actually witnessed here, still in charge of the ship of state after so many generations), nor even the great-grandchildren of the original "inventors," if one may put it that way. They are, in fact, the parlor maid of the house and the fatuous young tennis-playing cleric we remember to have courted the brothers' daughter (or niece), and who offered a singularly pure example of a witless leisure class in its most marginal and secondary manifestations. These, and not the protagonists, the main characters or stars, are those whom the lightning somehow struck. They merely overheard the good tidings, which were meant for a more important public. When Mrs. Lutestring is asked what set her thinking about the new idea of longevity, she replies:

> Conrad Barnabas' book. Your wife told me it was more wonderful than Napoleon's Book of Fate and Old Moore's Almanac, which cook and I used to read. I was very ignorant; it did not seem so impossible to me as an educated woman. Yet I forgot all about it, and married and drudged as a poor man's wife, and brought up children, and looked twenty years older than I really was, until one day, long after my husband died and my children were out in the world working for themselves, I noticed that I looked twenty years younger than I really was. The truth came to me in a flash [*BM* 135–136].

And for the Mozartian accents of Shaw's instrumentality, the pathos more delicate than anything in Ĉapek or Heinlein, there is also a brief expression of regret, in a play whose ruthless indifference to death matches its idealism: "There was one daughter who was the child of my very heart. Some years after my first drowning I learnt that she had lost her sight. I went to her. She was an old woman of ninety-six, blind. She asked me to sit and talk with her because my voice was like the voice of her dead mother" (*BM* 135).

Radical chains, the weakest link, the meek shall inherit the earth—such are some of the more ancient cultural stereotypes that cross the mind confronted with this remarkable development, so unsuspected as to offer the very figure of sheer unforeseeability and unexpectability as such and in itself. I will use the gestus of this twist in two ways, the first of which has to do with the nature of causality here proposed to us. It should be clear that in Shaw, as has already been observed, a kind of Christian Science version of the "life force" replaces the machinery of the modern or postcontemporary "rejuvenation" technology. What happens when all that is reckoned back into the contemporary sf narratives we will see in a moment; but it seems unsatisfactory to attribute the new development to mere voluntarism or a boundless Enlightenment belief in the power of the conscious mind or of Reason as such. On the contrary, Shaw here offers us an infinitely more flexible and subtle vision of the unconscious mind—perhaps even the unconscious collective mind—than we are used to dealing with. Indeed, if you take the whole stage of part 2 (in which the "gospel" of the Brothers Barnabas is promulgated) as allegorical representation of that psyche itself, we have one conscious will—the brothers—earnestly conveying its message to corrupt listeners only too eager for their own part to exploit its possibilities, while elsewhere in the drawing room distracted secondary minds catch bits of the freighted rigmarole in passing and a servant passes in and out of the central stage carrying a tea tray and intent on more menial business, storing up pieces of conversation for future use. There is a family likeness here to Proustian involuntary memory, which has no use for overly conscious acts of attention of the will but takes in its bounty of experience laterally, as it were, and by way of afterthought: indeed, Proust also promises a kind of increase of life, but by adding to the conscious life span all those secondary lives we had no time to notice we were also living simultaneously with the first, official one. Walter Benjamin's notion of distraction and Brecht's idea of the musing, reflective distance of the judicious, smoking theater spectators of his pedagogical dramas, from which Benjamin's idea itself develops, also merit a mention here, for future comparison.

So also do current neopragmatist reflections about belief itself and the peculiar level at which it operates: a postmodern substitute for the roles played by the more modernist Freudian notion of the unconscious and the Marxist notion of ideology.

Another figure from the 1920s, though, seems closest to Shaw's intricate conjuncture of the unpredictable and unforeseeable with the inevitable, and it will move us on to the second remark I had in mind to make about this episode. This is the famous image, which we owe to Victor Shklovsky, of the "knight's gambit," the knight's nonlinear jump across the chessboard that awkwardly seems to rebuke, in a vaguely premonitory or Utopian fashion, the more traditionally graceful yet prosaic moves of the other pieces. The most richly inventive of the Russian Formalists, Shklovsky wanted to dramatize by this figure an idea that was dear to all of them and had to do essentially with literary history—namely, that this last does not proceed from father to son (nor even, one supposes, from mother to daughter) but rather from uncle to nephew. The development of forms and genres is thus discontinuous and teleological all at once: when one is brought to fullest development (and by definition exhausted), what takes its place is not the successor or epigone but rather a marginalized and hitherto popular form that springs into place as a new space for formal and artistic development and evolution. So also with Shaw's characters: it is not the ruling class or its politicians but the poor, ignorant, and undeveloped who are the recipients of the new message. "I was too ignorant to understand the thing was impossible," the former chambermaid tells us. And in some similar fashion Georg Lukács, also in *History and Class Consciousness* (1923) (but following the first published articles of Marx himself), posits the richer human and intellectual and cultural potential of people who have been denuded of everything, who have not inherited the standard culture or undergone the standard educational formation—indeed, who have become little better than commodities themselves, reduced to selling their own labor power.

I mention these parallels in order to complete the second move demanded by this interpretative process, which is to suggest that at least in this case, the longevity drama is not "really" about longevity at all, but rather about something else, which can a little more rapidly be identified as History itself. It is History (not merely literary history) whose *telos* moves according to the knight's gambit; and the power of Shaw's play is to have given body to that within the extraordinarily limited and genteel confines of the bourgeois drama and the bourgeois drawing room. The title of this episode, "The Thing Happens," then, can already be seen in advance to fling the whole drama of unexpected longevity onto a higher plane of abstraction, where it stands for the Event itself, the Event in collective history, that radical act we often, for want of a better term, call revolution—a sudden collective movement of the people that can never be predicted in advance, that strikes the least likely place and the least likely collective agents or actors, that cannot be prepared by arrangements of the conscious will, but that is surely prepared in other subterranean if not unconscious ways. Benjamin sought a different kind of figuration for this ultimate Event of our collective social life, this ultimate mystery, when he had recourse to the language of the messianic, trying thereby to convey—against linear notions of historical accumulation and progress (which he attributed to the Second and Third Internationals fully as much as bourgeois thinking)—the way in which the Messiah arrives at the most unexpected moment, through some small lateral door in the historical present. It is a supreme event that has nothing whatsoever to do with anything that went before, or even that transpired in the seconds immediately preceding the unfolding of this new reality. In Shaw, the break is less absolute. There is preparation of a cultural and intellectual kind; seeds are sown, but the thing happens in seeming independence of all that. I want to explore the possibility that the longevity plot is always a figure and a disguise for that rather different one which is historical change, radical mutations in society and collective life itself.

As to why this is so, why everything has to mean something else, in this particular case the hermeneutic principle—for this is ultimately at stake in allegorical interpretation as such—can be defended locally in terms of the experience of longevity itself, about which our books tell us uniformly that nothing whatsoever is to be said. This emptying out of the very figure of long life, the absence of content at the core of the narratives we are examining, can be said, if you do not mind a rather different philosophical reference, to exemplify a fundamental Nietzschean doctrine about the irreducibility of the present. We will let Heinlein field this one, which is the discovery by the short-lived Dora, who is if anyone the principal woman protagonist of *Time Enough for Love* (1973):

> Long ago, three or four years at least, shortly after I figured out that you were a Howard, I also figured out that Howards don't really live any longer than we ordinaries do.... We all have the past and the present and the future. The past is just memory, and I can't remember when I began, I can't remember when I *wasn't*.... So we're even on that. I suppose your memories are richer; you are older than I am. But it's *past*. The future? It hasn't happened yet, and nobody knows. You may outlive me ... or I may outlive you. Or we might happen to be killed at the same time. We can't know and *I* don't want to know. What we both have is *now*.[3]

It is a discovery that, later on, Lazarus Long will summarize as follows: "Each individual lives her life in *now* independently of how others may measure that life in years" (*TEL* 398). One may wish to nuance the account and point out that, typically for the bourgeois philosophical position, Dora overestimates the past and underestimates the future, something Shaw's next evening, or subplay ("The Tragedy of an Elderly Gentleman"), makes clear. "It is not," Zoo tells the elderly gentleman in question (a short-lifer, or ordinary), "the number of years we have behind us, but the number we have before us, that makes us careful and responsible and determined to find out the truth about everything" (*BM* 183). And indeed, Shaw insists over and over again on the idea that not the accumulation of past memories and experiences piling up, but rather the perspective of having to live for several hundred years more makes up the difference and "wisdom" of the long-lived. We will return to this difference when we raise the issue of the psychological, and in particular the issue of boredom versus "discouragement."

For the moment, however, it is the narrative consequences of the matter that I want to underscore: for if Dora is right, then from any existential point of view there can be no essential difference between the experience of the short-lifers and that of the long-lived, and the Emperor Rudolph was quite right to go insane, like a theatergoer who is told he will have to wait another thirty years for the play to be finished. This is why the sheer experience of the present—which Heinlein discovers and reinvents in the passages I have quoted—can play no part whatsoever in his novel and occupies less than one page out of six hundred. Longevity is thus, as I have tried to suggest, a pretext for doing something else: in Heinlein's case, among other things, it serves first as a structural frame for interpolated stories—just as the Russian Formalists claimed about Miguel de Cervantes's *Don Quixote* (1605, 1615) years ago. Don Quixote, Shklovsky argued, is not a character but the "motivation of a device," the pretext for stringing together a host of interpolated stories, novellas, and anecdotes, in the process of which this pretext is reified and turned into a character in its own right. So also Lazarus Long, who may then be looked at from two different perspectives. From one standpoint indeed, the project may be seen as the equivalent of a modernist one for Heinlein. That is to say, and whatever the differences, this ultimate project is designed to be all-inclusive and interminable in the most literal sense, and it thus fulfills the existential requirement and function of the archetypal modernist projects in Stéphane Mallarmé or James Joyce or Marcel Proust: that they completely absorb everything contingent about human existence, that they give you something to do for the rest of your life and thereby make every accident and every stray moment of that otherwise uneven and unjustifiable sequence of days and years supremely meaningful, by virtue of the project into which it can be incorporated (not necessarily in any basely autobiographical way). The theme of boredom that I anticipated above—the boredom of Utopia, the tedium of acedia of the long-lifer—now acquires a somewhat different and unexpected resonance, as that which threatens the modernist project and risks falling out of it into a random unjustifiability that the project cannot redeem or transform. The banal form of this is, then, the possibility for Heinlein to fill up book after book of Lazarus Long stories.

The content of those stories, however, moves us on to a somewhat different aspect of the matter, which is the pedagogical strain Heinlein shares with Shaw, but which in the American is more fundamentally related to a kind of cult of experience (in Shaw it is based on an impertinent assumption of difference and sheer genius). As is the case with the oldest realists in the tradition, much storytelling in Heinlein (or at least much of the later storytelling) seem to be based on the pleasure of sheer know-how, from which there flows the more multiple pleasures of sheer explanation (how to set up camp in the wilderness, how to outsmart your enemies, how to invest in galactic stocks, be an interplanetary trader, raise a family, and so forth). All of this can perhaps be resumed under the notion of assuming the paternal function—or better still, of combining that function with primal narcissism. It explains why, if Shaw's parable is really about History, Heinlein's is about the Family (and I do not mean to deny the link he makes between rejuvenation and the starting up of multiple new families). But all of that in turn is based on what Jean-Paul Sartre long ago in *Nausea* (1938) denounced as the "ideology of experience," the idea that we learn from the past and that the older we are and the more experiences we are supposed to have had, the more we know and the more suitable we become for occupying a paternal function that consists in explaining things interminably and in showing off our infinite know-how. Late Heinlein, then, confronts us with the interesting question of what narrative really is: not so much what storytelling really is as what the story in storytelling might or might not be. When I show someone how to repair a car engine or put up a tent, is that a story or the material for a story? The answer must be that the lesson becomes a story only when I am able to show myself in the act of giving the lesson in the first place. Longevity is then the excuse, not for lots of lessons so much as for lots of stories about those lessons.

But early Heinlein was clearer about another displacement or consequence of the longevity plot, which we already encountered in Shaw at the end of "The Thing Happens" and with a certain reversal then in full force in the next drama of the pentateuch, "The Tragedy of an Elderly Gentleman," to which I have already referred. The motif of longevity or immortality, I have suggested, must always necessarily mean something else to acquire narrative content; but there is a second set of consequences that flows from the choice of the cover motif itself. This new set of narrative consequences has to do with the coexistence of long-living characters with the older, shorter-lived kind, so that the new, semiautonomous, independent story that coexistence begins to tell, in all the versions that are conveniently consulted under the rubric of immortality or longevity, becomes a story that can only be identified as that of class struggle.

What immediately happens in Shaw, for example, is that on discovering long-lifers in their midst, the politicians of the world state make plans to kill them all. Heinlein's *Methuselah's Children* (1941, 1958) is then the classic story of this persecution. In it, group fear and envy transcend the dynamics we generally associate with the backlash against race or gender or ethnic markings and attain the proportions of a kind of existential panic very similar to class panic itself. For now it is not merely that the *jouissance* of the alien group—its collective cohesion, the intensity of libidinal gratification this cohesion produces—seems far greater than my own and incites me to the kind of envy that, as Slavoj Žižek has shown,[4] underlies the backlash formations. Now, in the case of long life itself, my very existence as an individual and a group is called into question, and a political mobilization of a necessarily more cynical or lucid kind results, one that cannot be disguised, legitimized, or mythologized by fantasies about race or gender. This development can be seen, if you like, as the coming to the surface of that deeper historical content we first posited: if the longevity plot is really about radical social change, then its working out is bound to involve the violence and collective convulsion of just such struggles as we begin to find inscribed here in a second moment. The modern developments of the genre then show the narrative consequences and possibilities of this content, as we will see.

But it is perhaps worth concluding with Shaw at this point, using a few final observations about *Back to Methuselah*, to develop another motif neglected until now—namely, the matter of the boredom of eternity. *Time Enough for Love* begins indeed with Lazarus's well-nigh terminal depression at the thought that as he had already done everything conceivable (in a life span of some two thousand years) there was no point to living any longer. It is something that the novel then seeks energetically to cancel—narratively, by way of the frontier motif itself; formally, by way of the *Thousand and One Nights* compendium; and libidinally, by fantasies about clones (and probably about bisexuality). The biographical old age of Shaw himself, who, haunted by Jonathan Swift's Struldbruggs, longed to die as passionately as T.S. Eliot's Cumaean Sybil, would seem to document the plausibility of the complaint. But we must decline to endorse this stereotypical wisdom and must rather insist that boredom itself, like the fear of death, is always the disguised expression of something else. This becomes much clearer when we adjust the valences from the individual to the collective, when the complaint about the boredom of Utopias can much more clearly be seen to be so much propaganda for the excitement of market competition.

What is more interesting in Shaw's play is the displacement or inflection of the boredom motif toward what he calls discouragement, the morbid and suicidal quasi-physical feeling short-lifers experience in the presence of the long-lived, who have by now become, in the fourth play of the pentateuch, virtually a different species and are in the last play, or ultimate Utopia ("As Far as Thought Can Reach"), transformed into an oviparous life-form that sheds most of its bodily, formerly human, interests after the fourth year (the "boredom" of this now being remotivated as a kind of childishness). Discouragement, however, marks a kind of reversal of the power relations not unlike the great "thought-experiment" of H.G. Wells's *The War of the Worlds* (1898), in which the genocides of colonial peoples are redirected on Europe itself so that the "civilized" can learn what it feels like for a change. Here too the short-lifers—our own species—have lost the class struggle with the alternate society and the alternate Utopian beings; and the cultural envy of the traditional ruling classes has given way to the pain of the vanquished. It is the obverse of Shaw's picture of lateral or preconscious conversion; here too discouragement is both physical and a matter of deeper preconscious awareness and conviction that has little enough to do with the conscious mind. It is indeed one of the grand and dramatic merits of sf as a form that it can thus win back from the sheerly psychological or subjective such expressive powers of pathology—depression, melancholy, morbid passion—and place this material in the service of collective drama; but it may not be so important to insist, for insiders, on what must be stressed for the benefit of outsiders to sf as such: namely, that the unique new possibilities of this representational discourse—which has come to occupy something of the functions of the historical novel in the beginning of the bourgeois age—are social, political, and historical far more than they are technological or narrowly scientific.

Still, it is in the direction of science and technology that the longevity plot leads in our own time, and I will conclude with a few comments on the distinctiveness of the latest, post–Heinlein, fortunes of the genre—a characterization I scarcely mean to be understood in purely chronological terms, since books like Robert Sheckley's *Immortality, Inc.* (1958), Clifford D. Simak's *Why Call Them Back from Heaven?* (1967), and Robert Silverberg's *To Live Again* (1969)—all from the 1950s or 1960s—precede *Time Enough for Love* in linear time at the same time that they largely anticipate and foreshadow a novel like Joe Haldeman's *Buying Time* (1989), which I take to be characteristic of current contemporary or postcontemporary works in this particular form.

Paradoxically, the new narrative mutation is now far better equipped to navigate the problem of representing longevity as an event by the way in which the question regarding the appropriate contemporary technology is appealed to as a stand-in or substitute for the thing itself. Thus, in Haldeman, the rejuvenation process itself, which might be expected to entail the corniest battery of traditional sf wonder-working medicines and machinery, is displaced by two innovations: it needs to be renewed every so often, and at each renewal one's entire fortune must be given to the corporation (whence an interesting subplot of an investment nature emerges). The absence of medical and technological details is motivated, however, as it already was in Heinlein (whose delight in village explanations did not that way lie), in this manner: the whole thing is so agonizingly painful that the subject represses all memory of it. I suppose that the most graphic way of handling this properly technological moment is the idea of changing bodies, as in Sheckley (or even, secondarily, in Silverberg); but that brings us close to fantasy and the occult, as indeed the survival of the category of zombies, poltergeists, and the like in Sheckley's novel testifies (in a virtually autoreferential comment). The most chilling representation of the subject is therefore one in which the camera ensures a kind of documentary objectivity: I refer to John Frankenheimer's great film, *Seconds* (1966), in which the embarrassing political questions—Where do the bodies come from? How is the organization itself structured?—receive the grimmest answers. But there can be no doubt that the ultimate displacement is one in which longevity and immortality are represented by their opposite, and the virtually nonnarrative idea of living forever is made into a story you can tell by way of the deep freeze that precedes it (sleep or suspension now taking the place of living as a narratable event). It remained for Philip K. Dick's *Ubik* (1969) to produce in advance something like the metanarrative of this now conventional narrative and raise visceral questions about our vulnerability during this half-life condition, questions that are themselves, as we shall see, displaced political ones.

For it is finally the political overtones that save the new paradigm from regressing into some older science-and-technology sf paraphernalia of an outmoded Golden Age type. The idea that, in the deepening conservatism of the Reagan years and beyond, sf has regressed into more exclusively scientific interests (or better still, that, in a kind of Eliot-like dissociation of sensibility, its energies have been divided between just such a return to science, on the one hand, and a surrender to multivolume fantasy production, on the other) seems a plausible enough assertion, which it would nonetheless be advisable to nuance. For I think that the contemporary fascination with hard science tends to be as sociological as it is epistemological, and this not least because of the massive co-optation of pure science in the United States by business and defense research of all kinds. But this means that if we are interested in contemporary science, it is not only in the theories but in the very mechanics of experimentation—the grant procedures, the lobbying whereby the necessary laboratories (which can range from a giant celestial telescope to expensive underground shooting ranges for rare electrons) are funded. And this leads on finally to an interest (still sociological) in the psychology of the newer scientists who have, perhaps since James D. Watson's *The Double Helix* (1968), begun to replace traditional artists as the characterological disguises and distorted expressions of the representation of what Utopian, nonalienated work might look like. But, clearly enough, in the moment we become interested in scientific activity as a collective or guild matter, in terms of professionalism and socially determined psychological dispositions and aptitudes—in other words, in yuppie science, if I dare put it that way—in that moment we are not far from the convulsive reappearance of general politics as such.

How could it be otherwise in a situation in which the most intimate psychological problems of geriatric care and contraceptive medicine, and the still exceedingly physical matters of the homeless as well as of the massive and systematic administration of drugs to elderly and psychiatric patients, are everyday media concerns; in which the salaries of what are euphemistically called health care providers are debated with as much acrimony as the yearly bonuses of the great business executives; in which the privatization of hospitals becomes a matter of profit and business, and investments solicited for the so-called health industries as a whole? In this atmosphere, not only are the arrangements of all professional guilds, including those of the scientists, drawn back into an instant micropolitics, but the kinds of political privilege specifically suggested by health care can only be magnified to panic levels by the addition of the chance that one might be selected to live forever, presumably on the basis of a cash down payment.

It has been said that one of the most remarkable political revolutions, one of the grandest moments in the history of human freedom, occurred on that day in the Egyptian Fifth Dynasty (in the third millennium BC) when immortal life, hitherto the privilege of the elite, was extended to the Egyptian population as a whole. If this is so for a phantasm, so will it be for a scientific fantasy in which the representation of long life for a few is bound to raise the inevitable issue—a most embarrassing one ideologically, but a happy, welcome, and productive one on the level of narrative construction and storytelling—of the attitude of all the others to this ultimate form of special privilege. Free enterprise ideology in the United States was always stimulated by the fantasy that under the rules of the game you (or your children) had the outside chance to strike it rich; but the new fantasy of extended life can no longer be used that way; it now serves a divisive ideological function of excluding the anonymous demographies of the only-too-mortal.

For fantasy is also a harsh mistress and includes its own ironclad reality principle. You cannot satisfactorily daydream about living forever without first settling the practical matter of how those who do not live forever are going to be handled: fantasy demands a certain realism in order to gain even provisional or ephemeral libidinal and aesthetic credit, and this is indeed the deeper truth-mechanism of narrative itself (and the source of the adage about trusting the tale rather than the teller and his own personal ideology). However a story may originate in private wish fulfillment, it must end up disguising its private subjectivity and repairing all the nonfunctioning machinery,[5] building a village behind the Potemkin facade, dealing with the sheerly logical contradictions the Unconscious has left behind it in its haste—in short, shifting the attention of the aesthetic spectator from the gratification of the wish to its far less appealing preconditions in the real, and thereby becoming in the process transformed from the expression of an ideology to its implicit critique.

In the case of longevity or immortality, I would not want this critique to be taken in any moralizing sense. I am indeed astonished and appalled at the degree of residual moralism still inherent in this topic: it surely has some relationship to the traditional anti–Utopian motif of ultimate boredom I referred to, although the scarcely veiled motivation of this is political and thereby a little less complicated than the insistence of so many writers on the subject that it would be evil to live forever, that true human existence requires a consent to mortality, if only to make room for our children's children; that hubris and egotism are to be denounced as prime elements in this particular fantasy about the supreme private property, not merely of having a self but of having it live forever. All that may be so, but I would be very embarrassed to argue it this way, and there is certainly an aroma of *ressentiment* or sour grapes to be detected in this extraordinary puritanism, which may simply reflect the great facility accorded to writers by simple religious and ethical paradigms, as opposed to the more strenuous business of imagining the social itself.

I conclude by suggesting two levels of the political in recent sf longevity paradigms: on the more global level, what is reflected is clearly the increasing class polarization of the advanced countries of late capitalism (in the United States, we are told, 1 percent of the population now owns 80 percent of the wealth). On this level, it does not seem farfetched to argue that the motif of some special privilege of long life offers a dramatic and concentrated symbolic expression of class disparity itself and a way to conveniently express the passions that it cannot but arouse. But here one would want to add in something of the history of the form and suggest that the new paradigm marks a modification of the older, only-too-familiar near-future paradigms of overpopulation, ecological disaster, and the like. The longevity novel would thus stand as an enlargement of the possibilities of the near-future subgenre, deploying the attempt to imagine future technologies in the service of the expression of deeper and more obscure fears and anxieties.

The hermeneutic model we have proposed above—deeper meaning hidden within the text, behind, below the surface, like an "unconscious" of the text that needs to be interpreted out—is no longer a very popular one in this age of surfaces and decentered, textualized consciousness. Another model may therefore also be suggested, namely that of allegory: a structure in which a more obscure train of thinking attaches itself parasitically to a second, another (*allos/agoreuo*) line of figuration, through which it attempts to think its own, impossible, as yet only dimly figured thought. So it was by way of death and existential anxiety, along with the fantasy of living forever, that Shaw's play tried to think through its imperial content, at the very moment of the agony of the British empire itself: by way of similar affective content, but at another time and in another place, that Heinlein invoked fantasies of the family and the frontier, and attempted to produce high-technological and far-future images of both as viable forms. In the most recent sf texts on longevity, however, what seems to be the deeper secondary line of reflection and allegorical intellection is the increasing institutionalization and collectivization of late modern or postmodern social life, as that seems primarily embodied in the vast transnational corporation, bigger than most governments, and virtually impossible to modify or control politically.

In this material, for the moment at least, the political dilemma is at one with the representational one: the problem of bringing the great corporations under political control is the same as the problem of mapping their presence in our daily lives, of perceiving them, of giving them expression and articulation of a narrative as well as a cognitive type. In earlier periods of sf (to limit ourselves to that prescient registering apparatus), the great corporations coexisted with small businesses and their more humane ethos, as in Philip K. Dick for example, or else called forth over against themselves individualistic rebels and heroes of a classic populist-style revolt, as in Frederik Pohl and C.M. Kornbluth's *The Space Merchants* (1953). In our particular longevity subgenre, it is surely Norman Spinrad's remarkable *Bug Jack Barron* (1969)—a high point of a certain 1960s narrative ethos and still full of surprising vitality—that marks the exhaustion of the paradigm of heroic revolt, beyond which, however, there stretches the faceless anonymity of the multinational or transnational corporation of the present day, as that began to emerge after the winding down of the Vietnam War (in the Salvador Allende coup, for example).

But it is precisely that anonymity that poses questions not merely for narrative—problems of agency and actant, of anthropomorphism and personification, indeed of event and diegetic change—but also for political praxis as well. The transnational structures have of course found a different kind of expression in the sheer euphoria and delirium of cyberpunk, where their cybernetic networks are affirmed with all the excitement of the high and the nonstop production of new language and new figuration. It may not be inappropriate, then, in closing, to see the new longevity narrative as the other face of that, the bad trip, the obscure and deep-rooted depression in the face of an uncertain future, in which the function of immortality is only to revivify images of death.

Notes

1. George Bernard Shaw, *Back to Methuselah* (New York: Brentano's, 1921), 131. Parenthetical page references preceded by *BM* are to this edition.
2. Karel Ĉapek, *The Makropoulos Secret* (1922; Boston: International Pocket Library, 1975), 81.
3. Robert A Heinlein, *Time Enough for Love* (New York: Berkley, 1973), 283. A parenthetical page reference preceded by *TEL* is to this edition.
4. See Slavoj Žižek, *For They Know Not What They Do* (London: Verso, 1991).
5. The classic analysis remains Sigmund Freud's "Creative Writers and Day-Dreaming," *The Complete Psychological Works of Sigmund Freud*, volume 9, trans. under general editorship of James Strachey, with Anna Freud, Alix Strachey, and Alan Tyson (1908; London: Hogarth, 1959), 141–153.

How Cyberspace Signifies

Taking Immortality Literally

(1992 Eaton Conference)

N. Katherine Hayles

Through their individual imaginations, writers can evoke a world that differs in significant respects from the society in which they live. But in the very act of creating difference authors necessarily reinscribe similarity, for presuppositions eluding their artistic or linguistic grasp always far outnumber the few they can consciously modify. Most science fiction stories that imagine immortality fall into this category. Treating mortality as an independent variable that can be altered to show the effects on society, they create narratives whose thematics deal with immortality but whose underlying processes of signification remain unchanged. As comedy and tragedy testify, the fact of mortality is central to literary form and signification. Because deep assumptions about mortality are encoded in the signifiers that constitute narratives of immortality, what is given with one hand is taken away with the other.

How might narratives change if mortality were not a fact but an option, an option summoned not merely by a writer's imagination but by pervasive social and material conditions? The possibility of an immortality that seems almost within our technological grasp shimmers in Hans Moravec's dream of downloading consciousness into a computer.[1] Moravec believes that once the transfer is complete, the body will be dispensable, a mortal coil as obsolete as it is potentially deadly. Summarizing the attitude, Ed Regis writes, "Tired of the ills of the flesh? Then get rid of the flesh. We can do that now!"[2] Although these dreams remain fantasies, they point to larger social and economic changes that make the transformation of material structures into informational patterns everyday events. As the practices of everyday life change, the substrate of cultural assumptions shifts accordingly, precipitating further changes in life experiences. Among the many cultural sites involved in these feedback loops are contemporary fictions, as information technologies change not merely the subjects represented but the codes used to represent them. Thus the possibility exists for a writer to bring computerized immortality as a thematic together with processes of signification changed by computer technology, setting up complex reverberations between the signifiers that produce meaning and the meanings they produce.

In William Gibson's Sprawl trilogy—*Neuromancer* (1984), *Count Zero* (1986), and

Mona Lisa Overdrive (1988)—this explosive combination catches fire.[3] The catalyst is the deceptively simple premise that a landscape of computerized information can literally become a space through which consciousness can move. It is no secret to literary critics that the creation of a new kind of space can profoundly alter the stories written within and about it. The virgin forests of James Fenimore Cooper and Nathaniel Hawthorne and the oceanic expanses of Herman Melville led to narratives different in kind, not merely in degree, from those that emerged from the stuffy drawing rooms of English society. So too the novels spun out of cyberspace differ in important ways even from their close cousins within science fiction. What are the catalytic properties of cyberspace, and how do these properties interact with changing codes of representation?

Underlying the idea of cyberspace is a fundamental shift in the premises of what constitutes reality. Reality is considered to be formed not primarily from matter or energy but from information. Although information can be carried by matter or energy, it remains distinct from them. Properly speaking, it is a pattern rather than a presence. Deconstruction has taught us that presence is never self-evident by itself; to come into being, it must always already be joined with absence in a generative dialectic that produces both simultaneously. In the same way, pattern does not come into being by itself; rather, it is always already joined by randomness in a generative dialectic that produces both simultaneously.[4] The cultural context for cyberspace is a wide-ranging displacement of presence and absence by pattern and randomness as the generative dialectic producing representations. The displacement of presence/absence by pattern/randomness is visually evident in new scientific imaging technologies that interface humans and computers, such as positron emission tomography, or PET.[5] In PET, naturally occurring biological substrates are synthesized in mildly radioactive forms and injected into the patient. To reveal brain function, a glucose isotope is used as the substrate. The emission intensity correlates with glucose metabolism, which in turn correlates with different kinds of perceptual and cognitive activity. Detecting and mapping the radioactive particles yields a data array indicating the signal strength at various points across a plane through the patient's brain. The data are analyzed tomographically by a computer using Fourier transform techniques, from which a two-dimensional image "slice" is constructed with colors to indicate signal intensity. If the patient is talking to himself during the scan, verbal centers will be colored hot in the resulting image; if she is performing motor tasks, the hot areas will be the appropriate motor centers.

New software can stack these two-dimensional images to create a projected three-dimensional simulation, which can be spatially manipulated by the computer to yield images from many perspectives. Moreover, the 3-D simulation can be overlaid back onto the patient by means of an electronic wand passed over the patient's head. The wand allows the simulation to be precisely correlated with the topography of the patient's head. Say the patient has a brain tumor. By moving the wand to the tumor's location in the simulation, the technician knows where to mark the patient's head to indicate the exact point where the surgeon should make the incision. Thus the technique creates a space in which patient and simulation come together in real time, as if the patient had moved inside the screen or the simulation had moved out into the world.

The transformations involved in this technology illustrate how presence/absence is interpenetrated and displaced by pattern/randomness. During PET scans the living body is turned into a data array, an image is constructed from the array, then the image is overlaid back onto the living body to form body-plus-simulation. We can visualize the transformation as a keyhole shape, appropriate to the Alice-in-Wonderland flavor of having gone through the computer screen and come out the other side. The large upper end is an embodied actuality, which is reduced through the scanning technique to the wasp waist of the data array; this disembodied array becomes a visually rich image again through tomographic simulation techniques. When the bottom end of the keyhole is folded back onto the top end, the result may seem to be a fuller, richer version of the patient, whose interior cranial terrain is now as visually accessible and medically significant to the technicians as external physiognomy was to nineteenth-century practitioners. But make no mistake: these transformations do not simply yield back the original subject. The reconstituted body-plus-simulation is neither flesh and blood alone nor computer image, but a new kind of entity that, following Xerox PARC's Mark Wieser, I call an *embodied virtuality.* Embodied virtuality differs from traditional embodiment because in it, presence is understood to be always already penetrated by the virtuality of information.

The systematic transformations that create embodied virtuality are not limited to scientific visualization; they occur in a variety of sites and diverse media, including modern fiction. To show how they work in printed texts, I return to Gibson's cyberspace. The question I want to pose is not *What does cyberspace mean?* but *How it is constituted as a verbal entity?* Like the body transformed into a data array, representations referencing embodied actualities in Gibson's text are presumed to be reduced to datalike abstractions as they enter cyberspace. From these abstractions the text generates new representations through the trope of literalization; this phase corresponds to the creation of the simulation in a PET scan. It may seem as if the reconstituted representations can simply stand in for the old, like the simulation overlaid onto the patient's body, but the move through abstraction has caused them to be riddled with the virtuality of simulation. Like the body-plus-simulation, the verbally constituted entities of cyberspace refer to presence interpenetrated by the immateriality of information. As the trilogy progresses, there is increasing pressure for pattern to usurp presence, information to displace materiality.

To see these transformations at work, consider how movement is constituted in cyberspace. Representations referencing a body—descriptions of Case, for example—are displaced by a signifier written as *pov*. More than an acronym, pov is literalized into a substantive noun that signifies the body's abstraction into a point of view. The pov does not, however, merely signify the character's position; rather, increasingly it signifies the character himself. Movement is achieved when the pov flies, the mode of transportation that comes closest to reducing the friction of distance to zero. Movement takes place in relation to the fixed data structures that form the landscape, generating a distinction between free and occupied space that also operates as a public/private division. The distinction is enforced not by social prohibitions such as laws against trespassing but by privately owned *ice* (intrusion countermeasures electronics) that are lethal to a pov violating the space. The field of movement is constituted through descriptions that rely primarily on visual sense (as distinct from aural, kinesthetic, or tactile senses). The horizontal dimension is usually the axis along which movement takes place, whereas the vertical dimension is used primarily to signify complexity and size of data structures—another abstraction that has been literalized into a spatial dimension. In contrast with the endless empty landscapes of the New World or the empty expanses of outer space, this frontier is always already crowded. Exploration takes place under the trope of violation and transgression of the already owned and already occupied rather than under the imperialist fiction of the discovery of a dark continent or a new world. Consequently, in this world innocence is hardly possible, even as a self-delusion.

Underlying these spatial qualities is a presupposition that I have underscored in my description: cyberspace is constituted through signifiers that literalize abstractions, particularly the abstractions characteristic of postmodernity. We learn in *Count Zero*, for example, that only underdeveloped Third World countries still have governments. In the First World, government functions have been taken over by multinational corporations. This abstract proposition is represented in cyberspace by the proliferation of corporate structures in the landscape and the transfer of police authority from laws to ice. Laws can be written down, but they are not themselves physical objects. By contrast, ice is represented in cyberspace as having the sensory properties one associates with materiality. It glows white or blue, has an intricate physical geometry, and can move through space in pursuit of a trespasser. The abstraction it represents has been literalized into a virtual presence that has as much physical reality as anything else in this virtual space. The largest sense in which literalization occurs is, of course, cyberspace itself, a space constituted by literalizing data fields into actual physical localities.

Literalizing abstractions, cyberspace creates a level playing field where abstract entities, data constructs, and physically embodied consciousnesses interact on an equal basis. All forms are equivalent in this space; none is more physically real or immediate than any other. The signifiers representing an actually existing person cannot claim more materiality than those representing the shape of a data bank or construct generated by a computer program, because all signifiers within this space—including those generating the space itself—operate according to a logic of literalization.

Case, the protagonist of *Neuromancer*, tries to maintain the distinction between life that exists literally outside cyberspace and life that exists as a literality only because of cyberspace. When he sees Linda Lee in cyberspace after she has been killed, he insists she cannot be real because she is not alive. Neuromancer, the artificial intelligence who has created the simulacrum, claims that the distinction is not valid. "To live here [in cyberspace] is to live. There is no difference," he tells Case (*N* 305). The claim is central to all three books, although they take different stances toward it. As the arc of the trilogy progresses, the preponderance of evidence shifts to support the claim, however much Case resists it initially. There are deeper reasons for this progression than authorial preference or a need to generate new plots. In this literalized space, life is indeed life, for literalization flattens differential relations between signifiers that could constitute a distinction between life that is literally alive and life that is simulated metaphorically. Immortality thus happens not only at the level of thematics, as when Bobby, Angie, and 3Jane cast off their bodies and decide to live in the aleph's biosoft memory, but at the level of signification as well.

If signifiers in cyberspace cannot constitute the life/death difference, what differences can they bring into play? In this system of signification, the distinction corresponding to life/death is on/off, or, more precisely, continuity/discontinuity. When one is alive, consciousness and memory continue to exist after the plug is pulled. After Case jacks out of cyberspace, he remembers who he is and what happened; but Dixie Flatline, a cyberspace jockey who died after something in cyberspace made him "flatline" (cease brain activity), now lives only as a computer construct whose memory terminates when the on/off switch is flipped:

> "What's the last thing you remember before I spoke to you, Dix?" [Case asks the Flatline.]
> "Nothin.'"
> "Hang on." He disconnected the construct. The presence was gone. He re-connected it. "Dix? Who am I?"
> "You got me, Jack. Who the fuck are you?" [*N* 78].

Mortality and termination, already synonyms in popular culture, here are constructed as functions of an electrical circuit. The pun, as Scott Bukatman convincingly argues in *Terminal Identity: The Virtual Subject in Postmodern Science Fiction* (1993), is central to the construction of subjectivity in postmodern science fiction.[6]

In this passage it seems as though the vulnerability to on/off can reliably distinguish between artificial and natural life-forms. As the trilogy proceeds, however, the boundaries separating cyberspace from the real world become progressively more permeable, until finally there is scarcely any space that cannot be literalized. As a consequence, even the on/off distinction is undermined. In a continuation of the passage cited above, for example, Case temporarily overcomes the problem of Dixie's on/off consciousness by jacking the construct into the data bank he is using, giving it "sequential, real-time memory" (*N* 79). The distinction between on and off continues to erode in the next volumes of the trilogy. Isolated in a small hand unit, Colin (a computer construct built as a companion to Kumi in *Mona Lisa Overdrive*) cannot maintain consciousness when the machine is off. Released into the aleph's cyberspace, however, he immediately achieves continuity, taunting 3Jane that he is just as real as she is despite the fact that she once had a material body and he did not. The progression reaches its logical end in *Mona Lisa Overdrive* when continuity itself becomes a machine function, personified in Sense/Net's sentient computer consciousness called Continuity. Once computer consciousness finds a way to overcome the on/off problem and maintain continuity, it has effectively achieved real immortality, not the spurious kind that makes Dixie Flatline ask to be permanently disconnected.

As computer simulacra evolve toward memory continuity, humans seem to devolve toward memory discontinuity. Literalized into a space, memory becomes an area available for expropriation, discipline, and punishment. Slick had his memory "colonized" while he was in prison so that he could remember nothing other than the routine information he needed to perform forced labor. The effects of the colonization continue after he is released. The stigmata of his suffering take the form of Korsakov's Syndrome, which makes him lose the ability to remember under stress. In an unintentional parody of the conversation between Case and Dixie Flatline in the first volume, Slick in the final volume repeatedly gives Candy the same answers to the same questions without remembering how he has just responded (*MLO* 136–137). Human and computer simulacra have changed places: now the human, not the construct, is shackled to the on/off button of mnemonic continuity.

The literalization that drives this progression is inscribed into pov, deepening the reach of immortality beyond thematics and into processes of signification. In all three books Gibson uses point of view to construct narratives in ways that would be familiar to Henry James. In *Neuromancer* the third-person narrator has access primarily to Case's consciousness, and the story is told mostly from his point of view. Because Case can share the sensorium of other characters, the text reads like multiple narratives spliced together. *Count Zero* also uses third-person narration, but now the narrative explicitly splits into parallel stories of Mitchell's "extraction" from Maas Biolabs and Bobby Newmark's adventures in and around cyberspace. *Mona Lisa Overdrive* continues to proliferate points of view, bifurcating between the four viewpoints of Kumi, Mona, Angie, and Slick, with the fifth implicit viewpoint of Count Zero emerging only at the end, and only within cyberspace.

Beyond this conventional use of point of view lies a more innovative mode of construction that can be described as a literalization of point of view. In its Jamesian sense, point of view presumes the fiction of a person who observes the action from a particular angle and tells what he or she sees. In the preface to *The Portrait of a Lady* (1881), James imagines a "house of fiction" with a "million windows" formed by "the need of the individual vision and by the pressure of the individual will." At each "stands a figure with a pair of eyes, or at least with a field glass, which forms, again and again, for observation, a unique instrument, insuring to the person making use of it an impression distinct from every other."[7] For James, the observer is an embodied creature, and the specificity of his location determines what he can see as he looks out at a scene that is itself physically specific. When an omniscient viewpoint is used, the limitations of the narrator's corporeality begin to fall away, but the suggestion of embodiment lingers in the idea of focus, the "scene" created by the eye's movement.

Even for James, vision is not unmediated technologically. Significantly, he imagines the viewer's field glass as no less constitutive of vision than the angle of vision or eyes. Cyberspace makes a quantum leap forward into the technological mediation of vision. Instead of an embodied consciousness looking through the window, the pov moves through the screen, leaving the body behind as an unoccupied shell. In cyberspace, point of view does not describe the character; it creates him. Lacking a body and reduced to his consciousness, the character literally *is* his point of view. If his point of view is annihilated he also disappears, ceasing to exist as a consciousness both in and out of cyberspace. In cyberspace the realist fiction of a narrator who observes but does not create is unmasked; the effect of unmasking is not metafictional, however, but in a literal sense metaphysical, above and beyond physicality. The key difference between the Jamesian and cyberspace points of view is that the former implies physical presence while the latter does not.

In several passages Gibson plays with these conventions, conflating Jamesian fiction with the cyberspace construction. When Case "rides" with Molly by hitting the simstim switch that connects them, the narrative jumps to her point of view at the time that Case's consciousness is joined with hers by cyberspace technology. When her leg is broken, she feels excruciating pain that jolts Case when he shares her sensorium. The difference is that she cannot escape her body, while he can elude the screaming nerves by flipping a switch. For her, pain is as inevitable as mortality; for him, it is an option. Nor is it coincidence that the character immersed in her physicality is a woman and the character who can escape it is a man. Though both males and females can enter cyberspace, pervasive gender encodings throughout the trilogy cast immersion in the body as female, alienation and escape from it as male.

Central to these encodings is the manipulation of point of view. In all three books there are recognition scenes in which a male character sees his body from the outside, at first fails to recognize it, and then is shocked and disgusted at his vulnerability when he does. The first such scene occurred when Case hit the simstim switch and found himself staring down, through Molly's good eye, at a "white-faced, wasted figure, afloat in a loose fetal crouch, a cyberspace deck between its thighs, a band of silver trodes over closed, shadowed eyes. The man's cheeks were hollowed with a day's growth of dark beard, his face slick with sweat. He was looking at himself" (*N* 256). The regressive behavior of the fetal position, the wasted body seen only as "it," and the implications of disease and mortality are in stark contrast with the consciousness who just played a heroic role in a perilous adventure in cyberspace. This dramatizes the split between Jamesian and cyberspace pov, representing both a body whose physicality is described by pov and a consciousness that exists only because it has been literalized through pov.

In *Count Zero* the alienation between physical presence and literalized pov deepens when Bobby perceives himself flattened against the ceiling, "staring straight down at a blood-stained white doll that had no head at all.... There were pink and blue dermadisks stuck to the skin on either side of the doll's neck. The edges of the wound seemed to have been painted with something that looked like chocolate syrup.... Then Bobby got the picture, and the universe reversed itself sickeningly. The lamp was suspended from the ceiling, the ceiling was mirrored, and he was the doll" (*CZ* 53–54). By *Mona Lisa Overdrive*, alienation is so extreme that it is not possible to recover any exterior view of the body from a subject's perspective. The only descriptions we have of Count Zero (aka Bobby) are through the eyes of others as they look at the wasted, tube-fed body so obviously superfluous that its death is scarcely noticed. By then his subjectivity does not inhere in the flesh at all, having been "decremented" by a count to zero. As his name implies, Count Zero has gone through the boundary point and exists only as a literalized pov in cyberspace.

In contrast with this male alienation from one's physical self is the immersion of the female characters in their bodies. Molly delights in using her cyborg body as a physical weapon; Mona has cosmetic surgery to make her a near double of her idol, Angie Mitchell; Angie's father performs extensive neurosurgery on her brain, impregnating it with biosoft circuitry. Although men can also be simstim stars, like Robin Lanier (the name a bow to the father of virtual reality, Jaron Lanier), it is only with female characters that the narrative pov representing the simstim viewer moves inside the body. The construction suggests that the gendered language of electrical circuits is inscribed within and through the signifiers that constitute the bodies of these texts. While men jack in, an expression alluding both to the phallus and to a male electrical fitting, women become receptacles for biocybernetic intrusions. With male characters the connection is exterior, as the alienated cyberspace pov suggests; with female characters it is interior, enmeshed within their physicality.

The two sides of this gendered dichotomy become entangled in the fecund and phallic ambiguities of the matrix—meaning both a mathematical array, an abstract arrangement of data unfolded according to logical rules, and the female ground of creation, the unformed material that for Renaissance science was female matter before male spirit gave it form and shape. Bobby jacks into the aleph that provides the abstract space he and Angie will inhabit, but Angie accesses it directly through the biosoft interior of her brain that her father reconfigured into the necessary patterns. In a more than figurative sense, her father gives her away. To consummate marriage with the cyberspace pov Bobby has become, Angie must bring her cybernetic receptacle into physical proximity with the aleph's exterior form. Though both Angie and Bobby leave their bodies to live in the aleph's abstraction of cyberspace, they do so through different, and differently gendered, topologies.

If the female is identified with immersion in physicality and the male with abstraction from it, the arc of the trilogy is overwhelmingly male. The logic moves progressively, relentlessly toward abstraction. Cyberspace, a literalized abstraction of the world, is fully occupied the first time we see it. In later volumes it becomes progressively more crowded, until Bobby seeks a new frontier in the aleph, a space described as an abstraction of cyberspace. With abstraction piled on abstraction, consciousness becomes more remote from physicality and the smell of mortality. Working in tandem with the abstractions are the literalizations that make them into spaces that can be occupied as if they were physical locations. Once, immortality was represented through metaphor: people were immortal when they were like gods. It is a measure of how far immortality has permeated into the processes of signification that now it is constituted through the opposite trope of literalization: people are immortal when they are literalized into pov and placed in abstract arrays literalized into spaces.

Oddly, as the spaces become more literalized and abstract, they become more domestic. All we see in cyberspace are geometric forms; it's a nice place to visit, bur who would want to live there? By contrast, the aleph has houses, fields, and horses. But perhaps it is not so odd, for having the spaces become more habitable as they move further into abstraction makes them as cozy as the spaces of the world—with a crucial difference. In the aleph there is no omega, no necessary end, no inevitable mortality. Ironically, as immortality penetrates deeper into the textures of the texts and as physicality is apparently left behind, gender becomes if anything more rather than less important. Fleeing physicality, Angie, Bobby, and other characters inhabit cyberspace and have its gendered topologies reinscribed in the electrical circuitry that now serves as their bodies. Thus is immateriality made in the image of the physicality that it displaces and preempts. The reinscription can serve as a reminder that even though immortality now reaches beyond thematics into the signifiers themselves, the ground for life remains rooted in the matrix of physicality. Literalized abstractions can never be wholeness.

Afterword

Twenty-five years later—one human generation, twenty software ones—what strikes me about my essay is the absence of concern about databases, surveillance, and privacy. The basic assumption of Gibson's trilogy, that one can experience datascapes only by jacking into cyberspace, was rendered obsolete almost as soon as Mosaic, the first internet browser, was introduced in March 1993, only a few months after the 1992 Eaton Conference where this essay first saw the dawn of datalight. Although visualizations through which a pov can zoom have advanced considerably in the years since Gibson's trilogy, they remain cloistered in specialty niches like the VR glasses Oculus Rift, the Virtual Human project and related medical applications, and sophisticated software packages like the statistical environment R. These applications notwithstanding, the overwhelming majority of users interface with databases through screens, no "trodes" required. Meanwhile, the screens themselves continue proliferating through pads, cellphones, interactive signs, and other devices.

Relational databases date back even earlier than the 1970s when E.F. Cobb laid their theoretical groundwork, but not until the 1990s did they begin to grow exponentially with the advent of the web. Subsequently, the development of SQL (Structured Query Language) and correlation algorithms enabled them to interconnect with one another, further extending their reach. Aided by the increasing sophistication of search engines, exponential leaps in computer memory storage and its plunging costs, and more powerful, faster CPUs, databases began not just to infiltrate daily life but to transform it even more radically than in Gibson's imagined cyberspace. This transformation, however, did not take the form of the two sharply delineated regions of real life and cyberspace that Gibson evoked, but rather consisted of an *interpenetration* of data into everyday life. Instead of a container filled with oil and water in which each chemical occupies a distinct region without mixing (analogous to the real life/cyberspace delineation), our present situation is more like a carbonated drink shaken and then opened, in which thousands of gas bubbles foam throughout the liquid. Every time someone uses an internet search engine, accesses biometric data at passport control, scans a credit card, uses an ATM, or sends a message to a freeway screen displaying an amber alert and millions of similar interactions, the interpenetration of data into our everyday world is evoked and instantiated.

My analysis of Gibson's trilogy focused on one pervasive literary trope, taking a metaphorical concept and translating it into a literal reality, as if, for example, the metaphor "quick as greased lightning" was suddenly to appear in the world by running a Tesla coil discharge through an oily mist. This trope is appropriate to the binary RL/VR distinction that Gibson's texts presuppose, because in the absence of workable technology, VR may be understood as a metaphor, and literalization provides a way for this metaphor to tunnel through the boundary and appear in reality. What literary metaphors are appropriate to the data-as-thousands-of-bubbles situation, and how do they manifest in texts?

Here we encounter the different ontologies of narrative versus database about which Lev Manovich wrote persuasively. Although there are flaws in Manovich's analysis of database as paradigmatic/narrative as syntagmatic, he correctly senses the two forms are characterized by fundamentally different logics. Databases work through correlation of discrete elements, whereas narratives work through explicit or implicit causal chains. The thousands-of-bubbles foam up when story elements appear that may or may not be related to the causal chain of events upon which plots depend. In realistic narratives, there is typically a mixture of random, correlated and causal elements, often complexly figured. Is the dark cloud that passes when the protagonist enters a building a foreboding sign correlated with the tragedy that awaits within, or simply a realistic detail meant to give the narrative a "thick description" quality? Many experimental texts traffic in just these kinds of ambiguities, including surrealism, algorithmic narratives, and one-off experiments like Mark Danielewski's graphomania in *House of Leaves* (2000).

If writing a contemporary essay in the same vein as my "literalization" exploration in Gibson's texts, I would focus on the dynamic between random, correlated and causal elements and their relation to the overwhelming importance of databases to contemporary culture. Narrative, I would argue, is deeply tied to the evolution of the human species, while databases are the product of exteriorized cognition that has really only gained momentum in the 20th and 21st centuries. The massive, and massively complex, competition and cooperation between these forms are manifestations of the cognitive assemblages, composed of humans and cognitive devices, that are now the dominant form of agency in developed societies. Reality, as usual, has proven far more implausible—and interesting—than even our most sophisticated fictions.

Notes

1. Hans Moravec discusses these possibilities in the significantly titled *Mind Children: The Future of Robot and Human Intelligence* (Cambridge: Harvard University Press, 1989).

2. Ed Regis, *Great Mambo Chicken and the Transhuman Condition: Science Slightly Over the Edge* (Reading, MA: Addison-Wesley, 1990), 7.

3. William Gibson, *Neuromancer* (1984; London: Grafton, 1986); *Count Zero* (New York: Ace, 1987); *Mona Lisa Overdrive* (New York: Bantam, 1988). Parenthetical page references are to these editions, abbreviated as *N*, *CZ*, and *MLO*.

4. The pattern/randomness dialectic and information/noise interplay are connected in information theory. For a discussion of how these pairings are complementary, see N. Katherine Hayles, *Chaos Bound: Orderly Disorder in Contemporary Literature and Science* (Ithaca, NY: Cornell University Press, 1990), 1–60.

5. PET scans are discussed in Richard Mark Friedhoff and William Benzon, *Visualization: The Second Computer Revolution* (New York: Abrams, 1989), 64–66, 81. An overview is in *Brain Imaging*, a project proposal by Robert N Beck, Oscar H. Kapp, and Chin-Tu Chen (Chicago: ANL Center for Imaging Science, no date).

6. Scott Bukatman, *Terminal Identity: The Virtual Subject in Postmodern Science Fiction* (Durham, NC: Duke University Press, 1993).

7. Henry James, *The Art of the Novel* (New York: Scribner's, 1937), 46.

You Bet Your Life

Death and the Storyteller

(1992 Eaton Conference)

Frank McConnell

Let us begin, as all human things begin, with a story.

It is universal, ancient, and simple enough that you might not think it *is* a story, but it is. Here is one of my favorite versions: Wile E. Coyote, as is his wont, is in fervid pursuit of the Road Runner. The Road Runner runs—that's all he *does*, dig—off a cliff and his momentum carries him to the opposite side. Not so Wile E. Midway across, in midair, he looks down, realizes he *is* in midair, stares bug-eyed for an instant at the audience, and then plummets, like a stretched and snapped rubber band, to earth: the way characters plummet only in Warner Brothers cartoons or real life.

Here is another version: an old man who foolishly squandered the love he had earned finds himself alone, in the open, in a storm that is partially a storm of his own despair. And staring at the camera, as it were, not unlike Wile E. Coyote, he tells us, "When the rain came to wet me once and the wind to make me chatter, when the thunder would not peace at my bidding, there I found 'em, there I smelt 'em out. Go to, they are not men o' their words: they told me I was everything; 'tis a lie, I am not ague-proof."[1]

The Road Runner runs, and that's all he does. "Just runnin' down the road's his idea of havin' fun," as his theme song has it. The thunder will not peace at King Lear's bidding, not because it *dislikes* Lear—any more than the Road Runner dislikes or even notices Wile E.—but because the thunder *doesn't even know Lear is there*, and wouldn't give a damn if it did know.

No, grimmer than that: there *is* no thunder, as a conscious force that can cease or continue at Lear's or anyone's bidding, until somebody *imagines* meteorology as personality. Shakespeare knows as well as we do, maybe even better, since he articulates it with the proper metaphysical shudder rather than with our currently hip, disengaged shrug. Here it is, the pith, the germ, the immense and fecund shaggy-dog joke at the heart of the story I have just told and, I think, at the heart of all the stories there are to tell. We have invented death, and in inventing that have invented ourselves, and in inventing ourselves invent, by necessity, the gods whose service will be a balm for our mortality, but whose very existence—we have always known—is *predicated* not on their resplendent presence but on our own aboriginal and gnawing lack.

This is basically nothing more than an echo of Karl Rahner's haunting observation that to "be religious"—which for him and me means simply to "be human"—is "to believe it is meaningful for a miserable creature to talk into the endless desert of God's silence."[2] It is also an argument that the only really convincing proof of the existence of God is also the most profoundly uncomfortable one. I mean, of course, the Anselmic or ontological proof, which in one form of another insists that life must have some final meaning just because we ourselves thirst so for it. It is what in the old seminarian's joke was called "the proof from wishful thinking." The problem is, you see, is that it is the only proof we can trust, and that, like the anxiety-ridden uncertainties of quantum theory or chaos theory, or for that matter the truly scary act of saying "I love you," we can trust it only on the firm basis of our distrust. What human speech, from the Upanishads to the Mandelbrot set, is *not*, finally, wishful thinking?

I realize I am getting rather thuddingly paradoxical here, sort of like G.K. Chesterton on a *really* bad day. It is just that I do not know any way to talk about death that is not, ultimately, paradoxical or even, when you break it all the way down, *funny*.

My second favorite deathbed speech—familiar in theater lore—is David Garrick's: "Dying is easy. Comedy is hard." It is a wink at the camera, of course, and therefore a triumph. And it is a joke; better yet, a joke *about* joking: almost what a fashionably francophone contemporary theoroid might call "postmodernist"—to use one of the goofiest phrases ever developed by our culture. Apocryphal or not, this last utterance *is* directed into the "endless desert of God's silence," just because it demands either to *impose* order on the radical, quintessential moment of all disorder or to have that human order validated by—what? By whatever or whoever the hell it is that implants in us the expectation and longing for a Sense To It All and, at the same time, curses us with the wit to see through even our most splendid fabrications of that Sense. I *hope* Garrick really said that, because if he did, he joins Job and Samuel Beckett, and the mad King Lear and vertigo-stricken Wile E. Coyote, as chief anatomists of our cosmic discontent. The Anselmic proof is not our solace. It is our cage.

But you want to know what all this has to do with science fiction, fantasy, and the possibility of technologically achieved immortality. Okay.

Henri Bergson in his crucial essay *Laughter* reduces all comedy to variously performed versions of slapstick, and I think that is just right. The impulse to laugh, Bergson says, is our spontaneous aversion response to "something mechanical encrusted on the living."[3] We laugh, in other words, because in any truly comic situation we recognize—and forefend—the killing joke that for all our intimations of immortality we are, God help us, mortal machines wearing ourselves out in the very exercise of our magnificence. The well-dressed gentleman with cane and bowler who trips on a banana peel is the *ur*-mytheme of all comedy because his fall is *the* Fall, showing us again that all our fondest hopes are built on clouds and subject to vapors: that we not, as we have heard, ague-proof.

Now this may remind you of Frank Herbert's *Dune* (1965), or Stanley Kubrick's *2001: A Space Odyssey* (1968), or even Ridley Scott's *Blade Runner* (1982), because in each of those stories the central character comes to a kind of confrontation with the core of human longing—to live forever—and comes to a different kind of realization about what really achieving that wish might be. In each case, though, we are dealing with a manifest version of Bergson's formula or, to nail it down, of Coyote's and Lear's plight.

Paul Atreides in *Dune*—let us discount the unfortunate sequels to that brilliant book—achieves godhead, or at least messiahhood, but at the expense of any faith or hope in the very messianic message he comes to announce, and for which he becomes universally venerated. This crackling irony—Herbert, after all, was raised Catholic—is lost in David Lynch's otherwise splendid film redaction (1984). Immortality for Paul is finally the immortality of becoming the story of his life, knowing the story he becomes can never, never approach the reality he was. I think *Dune*, despite its immense popularity, gets discussed so seldom at science fiction conferences just because it is so close to the cosmic slapstick that is, finally, all discourse on death. You *will* die. *We* will die. *I* will *die*. All storytelling tries to avoid that fact—as, every hour of the day, do we—and all storytelling, in avoiding that fact, only makes it the more inescapable. We want to become stories because stories go on forever and we do not. We are mortal engines, and mortal engines give out, wear down, or break up, and all that is left of them—God is not mean but She sure is strict—is their, every pun intended, plots.

And if we could device a physical immortality, could invent a way to keep the engine running forever and ever, we would still not be free of the burden of mortality: precisely because mortality is, by honest appraisal, a "burden" not in the sense of a heavy load we must carry and would dearly love to shrug off, but a "burden" in the sense of the bass-note to the song we make for the Lord or ourselves or others, it really does not matter. An immortal man, if he were to remain a man, would still have to be able to tell himself the story of his own life, and that would require a sense of closure—that is, a reinvention of death. Because death is not the enemy to be feared, but rather the origin and goal of any meaning we may choose to call human. With mutants I have no truck.

Mutants like, say, Dave Bowman at the end of *2001*, the most gnostic of the fables we are discussing, and by my definition the most purely "science fiction." Bowman, avatar of our species and last descendant of the cosmically befuddled ape Moon-Watcher who began the story, breaks on through to the other side, becomes the Star Child—a godlet at the very least—and returns to contemplate Earth from the light-year playing fields that are now his home. And what does his enigmatic expression in that indelible last scene signify? For all the Sturm and Drang sublimity of Strauss's music, I am not sure it does not signify a kind of melancholy. Because the godlet, poor little fella, has passed beyond the possibility of all stories and therefore past the possibility of selfhood: all dressed up and nowhere to go. Or as Wallace Stevens—who I sometimes suspect explains *everything*—says in "Esthétique du Mal":

> The greatest poverty is not to live
> In a physical world, to feel that one's desire
> Is too difficult to tell from despair. Perhaps,
> After death, the non-physical people, in paradise,
> Itself non-physical, may, by chance, observe
> The green corn gleaming and experience
> The minor of what we feel.[4]

You will notice, by the way, that I am conflating technological and theological ideas of immortality: and you will also notice that I am none too subtly dismissing both of them. It may indeed be possible to extend life indefinitely by transmitting brain waves to silicon chips or through freezing and resuscitation—Swanson's TV Dinners? Or it may be that, Patrick Swayzes all, we will float toward the big Klieg light at the heart of all Being, there to spend eternity—uh—shining on. To reveal the full extent of my recidivism, let me admit that I find neither prospect especially attractive, or indeed interesting. I said at the beginning, paraphrasing William Yeats, that we have invented death. It is now time to put the formula properly: death has invented us.

Which brings me to the end of *Blade Runner*. The movie—sorry, purists—is better than the novel it is based on, paradoxically because it is closer to what Philip K. Dick at his best is really *about* than is *Do Androids Dream of Electric Sheep?* (1968). Dick is our poet of the simulacrum in his strongest work, exploring that concept before Jean Baudrillard even knew how to spell it. If you can make a perfect replicate of a human—so runs the essential Dick plot—how can you say that your replicant is not, *tout court*, human? It is a serious problem. It bothered the hell out of René Descartes and John Locke but gave Mary Shelley and E.T.A. Hoffmann some terrific ideas for stories. And it is obviously based on the progressive definition of the body *as* an engine that began in 1603—the year of *King Lear*—with Gabriel Harvey's discovery of the circulation of the blood and the human heart as a simple pump.

It is no more than a classic black box problem, really. If I can make a machine that does what *your* machine does, then I will have replicated your machine, although I can never open the impenetrable black box to see what your machine really is. Right?

Wrong. Dick knew and *Blade Runner* knows that the human engine becomes the *human* engine—becomes conscious—only by predicating its mortality. So when Deckard (Harrison Ford) and the replicant Rachel (Sean Young) escape to that improbable pastoral outside hellish Los Angeles at the end of the film, they both know that Rachel is programmed to die at an unspecified date. As Deckard says, "I didn't know how long we'd have together—but who does?"

And *this*, I think, again quoting Stevens, is "the thesis scrivened in delight, / The reverberating psalm, the right chorale."[5] The liberating joke that makes *Blade Runner* the most satisfactory of our stories is that Deckard, the "natural" human, learns from Rachel, the "artificial" human, not just about loving somebody but about accepting limits, mortality—that is the precondition to love or, indeed, any truly human act. To live at all, you have to bet your life. Deckard finds neither the ironically messianic immortality of *Dune* nor the dubious transcendence of Bowman in *2001*. He finds, and embraces, the human condition. *Blade Runner*, in fact, is in this respect hardly a science fiction story at all, but rather a story about escaping from science fiction's gnostic shudder at the fact—and the necessity—of death.

Thomas Pynchon, in his disarming autobiographical introduction to *Slow Learner*, says something that angered me when I first read it and continues to anger me because I think it must be true:

> When we speak of "seriousness" in fiction ultimately we are talking about an attitude toward death—how characters may act in its presence, for example, or how they handle it when it isn't so immediate. Everybody knows this, but the subject is hardly ever brought up with younger writers, possibly because given to anyone at the apprentice age, such advice is widely felt to be effort wasted. (I suspect one of the reasons that fantasy and science fiction appeal so much to younger readers is that, when the space and time have been altered to allow characters to travel easily anywhere through the continuum and thus escape physical dangers and timepiece inevitabilities, mortality is so seldom an issue.)[6]

Of course, no so-called mainstream writer has used the motifs of science fiction, and of its parent mode the Gothic, more extensively or more stunningly than has Pynchon. And this, I think, only adds weight to his observation—just as *Blade Runner* strikes me as a supremely "serious" science fiction story exactly in its deconstruction of the genre to which it manifestly belongs.

Science fiction longs for immortality and shuns death just as, by and large, it shuns palatable food and good sex: because these things speak of the body and bodily limitations, and the inevitability of closure. I called it "gnostic" and it certainly is that, but there is an even better, because formal, name for it.

The one time I was lucky enough to have a drink with the great classicist and lovely man Moses Hadas, we were talking about Longus's *Daphnis and Chloe.* And Hadas, sipping his sherry, said, "You know, that's really what science fiction is: pastoral."

And "Bingo!" I said to myself. That was in 1967, and in a funny way I have spent the last twenty-five years trying to figure out *why* I said "Bingo!" (Actually, since it was 1967, what I probably said was "Right on!") And it was not until the topic of immortality and science fiction was proposed that I had my *satori.*

Science fiction is pastoral (and, by the way, pastoral is gnostic) because it posits a place and/or a time where you can play at life rather than bet your life. A place—Arcadia, the Forest of Arden, the Galactic Imperium, cyberspace, same-o same-o—where we can believe for a while that we are ague-proof and that we are not all vectors on and victims of gravity's rainbow.

And of course it is escapist, granting—just for the moment—that that rather stupid word has any meaning. It is as deeply escapist as *Daphnis and Chloe* or *A Midsummer Night's Dream* or *The Winter's Tale* because it tells us that we do not die, while all the time we know that we do. Like all good pastoral, it is the first phase of the Anselmic proof. And like all good pastoral, if it is really good, it brings us through to the second, more difficult phase of that proof. Look. You do not go *to* a pastoral place, you go *through* a pastoral place. You go into the magic forest and dance with the masquers there precisely so you can come back, healed and refreshed and wisely innocent, to the world where agues and gravity—the closure that makes us real—claim their due. To do otherwise is to become other than human and to invite, or invent, another, more meaningless kind of death: what theologians call the "second death," the annihilation of meaningfulness. Edgar Allan Poe knew this. It has to be why the narcissist, death-defying, and therefore life-denying prince in "The Masque of the Red Death" is named Prospero. That act of naming, maybe the crucial act of the whole tale, is what my mentor, rabbi, and *sensei,* Harold Bloom, might call an "antithetical trope." By naming the misguided prince after the most unavoidable and self-limiting of pastoral characters, the presiding genius of *The Tempest,* Poe surely means to suggest that his story is a dark version of the pastoral myth, an assertion that "escapism" is dangerous only when it forgets how grimly serious it really is. (I am assuming, of course, that you are at least old-fashioned enough to believe that sometimes people write stories because there are certain things they want to say, and they know what they are doing, as opposed to being mere ectoplasmic inscriptions of power for the dominant establishment.)

Does that mean that science fiction manifests a fundamental evasion? Yes. As I argued in another essay for this series, the genre privileges the transcendent over the immanent, the gnostic liberation from the body—and that includes the myth of the body as immortal engine—over what Alfred Whitehead called the "withness" of the body. And in this evasion are both its resilience and its weakness. Just as the complementary resilience of weakness of its mirror twin, the mystery, is privileging the *thanatos* principle over the pleasure-pain principle. Put it this way. All mystery stories begin, in one way or another, with a death; all science fiction stories, in one way or another, try not to end with one.

I had intended to talk about *Gilgamesh* here, a story that I take, even more than *King Lear*, to be an unremitting and absolutely essential prelude to any sane discourse on death and storytelling. But since John S. Dunne has addressed that subject, and since no one has written more brilliantly or valuably about that poem, I defer on the same grounds I would defer to sit in with Sonny Rollins. So let us talk about Homer's *Odyssey* instead.

The gnosis, the knowledge that once gained will take us beyond the realms of the corporeal and mortal—beyond the human realm of story—has an opposite. I am glad to give it the punning name *nostos*. It means "homecoming," and classical critics use it to refer to the moment when Odysseus returns to Ithaca. In fact, I realized as I was working through the poem again, it describes the whole movement of the *Odyssey*. Everybody in the poem—Telemachus, Menelaus, Nausicaa, Circe, Calypso—knows the sublime story of the Trojan War and that its heroes will always be the definitive transcendent heroes of the culture. Odysseus has another problem, though. He wants to go home. He wants to go back to his aged wife, his aging life, and—Athena makes this clear—his human death. In other words, his whole fabulous voyage back home is a voyage out of the fabulous and into the quotidian. The *Odyssey* is an antignostic gospel invented centuries before the gnostic itself was named. And its central moment—at least in my current reading—is maybe its most famous and certainly its least understood episode.

What do the Sirens sing? Not the promise of sexual delight; this man, after all, has just left Circe. Not knowledge or power; Odysseus is always already *polutropos*, skilled in all the tricks. What they promise, explicitly, is to tell Odysseus and his men, over and over again, the story of their immortal exploits before Troy; they promise him that he can live forever in the *Iliad*. And the seduction is so strong that one screams to be untied so as to follow its allure, the allure of infinitely deferred closure, the pornography of the spirit. But Odysseus—Stevens's "Central Man," perhaps—both leaves his ears unstopped against the song and binds his will against following it, and the ship sails on, back from gnosis to nostos and into the blessedly flawed paradise that William Wordsworth calls "a simple produce of the common day."[7]

And that, too, is the reverberating psalm, the right chorale. Between the technological and the theological—our less picturesque version of the Sirens and the Wandering Rocks—I will choose neither, wishing them both lots of luck, and cleave to the bitter charity of Story itself, Story that always gives us back a fragmented image of our own fragmentation but also whispers that our proper immortality is the embrace of our proper mortality, and that the world as we tell it to ourselves is never enough and thus is quite enough. This is no more paradoxical than the Anselmic proof. In fact, it is the Anselmic proof, as are you and I in our splendid disorganization and noble, funny quest for a love that will stay.

But I have not yet told you my favorite deathbed speech. It is not really a deathbed speech, although it takes us back to our original story of Wile E. Coyote. It is just the old joke about the guy who falls out of a fiftieth-floor window and is heard to say, as he passes the thirteenth floor, "Well—so far, so good." That guy, along with Wile E., Lear, Deckard, Odysseus, and Stevens, is a hero of the consciousness. And his line, uttered out of the certainty of doom and the gallant refusal to face it with anything but full awareness, is as good a story as you can tell. So may we all.

Afterword (by Celeste McConnell Barber)

"Let us begin as all things begin, with a story"—a signal you were in for a treat! Frank McConnell was a mainstay of the Eaton Conference from 1983, shortly after moving to California, until January 1999, coincidentally on the Sunday he died and was to have delivered that year's keynote address.

During a thirty-year career, every lecture he gave began with a story, more often than not, a shaggy dog story from his limitless collection of jokes and punchlines. And every lecture, paper, one-on-one chit-chat, came down inevitably to this one simple truth (at least for Frank): We *are* the storytelling animal.

For Frank, stories are the warmth that thaws the ice encasing us all: the knowledge that death awaits. Predictably, he would begin with a joke, and in this case, a cartoon: Wile E. Coyote in futile pursuit of the Road Runner. With trademark fluidity, Frank segues to *King Lear*, linking the Warner Brothers cartoon to the Western Canon's most profound work. Frank understood that great art, at its best, is democratic.

Frank was born the same year as Muhammad Ali—1942—and both shared the same hometown, Louisville, Kentucky. Frank told me that Ali, then Cassius Clay, was a janitor in his parochial school. I like to think of Frank walking hallways that had been polished by the man who displayed grace practicing a brutal sport; self-dignity in renaming himself Muhammad Ali; and the strength of character to stand up to a government against a war he opposed.

Respect for the dignity of the individual person was always central to the way Frank conducted his life. No matter the station or the personal benefit to himself. And no matter if he were reciting lines from a Stevens poem, or talking to a stranger seated on a barstool next to him at Mel's in downtown Santa Barbara. While Frank could more than carry his own among his peers at, say, a conference on the Bible or following a lecture on *The Odyssey*, the man was most at home with the average Joe, and the down-and-outs who exist on the fringes of society. I am certain the young Frank would have seen the young Ali in those school hallways, even in a time and place when African Americans were institutionally invisible.

I'd like to share my favorite memory of this wonderful fella. Appropriately for this afterword, it's a story about that hedge against death. The thaw I mentioned earlier.

Frank and I were in Chicago for a few days, meeting an old Notre Dame buddy of his. Ray, a poet-stockbroker, had driven in from Flint, Michigan. It was late at night, early morning really. We had just left the Blackstone Hotel, then home to the Jazz Showcase. We stood outside waiting for a cab; the night was typical Chicago, blustery cold and the wind was up. As we waited curbside, a homeless guy saunters down the middle of the street, coming right for us. Cane in hand, Frank jaunts over to the guy—abruptly abandoning Ray and me—and fishes out a twenty. Then grabs a twenty from Ray and hands that to the guy, but as sweet and natural as any transaction between two buddies.

Business concluded, Frank proceeds to engage the fellow in conversation. Intimate, gentlemanly discourse. Ray and I stood in silence. Together, those two formed their own secret society, just in the space of under five minutes! A raggedy homeless guy without even a pair of shoes on his feet became *the most-important-person-in-the-world*. The center of Frank's attention on that Chicago street in the early morning hours.

There's a cab coming our way! The driver sees us, clearly as the cab heads toward us. But before the cabby has stopped, the homeless man bounds toward the vehicle, waving his arms with pomp for the cabdriver to come his way. The fellow opens the front passenger side and motions Frank in, grand as you can imagine. The door is shut—gently—and the homeless man stands back. Ray and I sheepishly open our own back door and we are off.

My husband used to tell me that most of Chicago's homeless population didn't survive the winters. They would freeze to death before spring arrived. Betting odds were against the guy on the street there. But as I turned my head in the cab and looked back at Frank's friend, I saw what Frank had seen: defiance in the face of all the forces, urban and natural world, gathered to take him down. Arms upraised in glory. Fellow traveler!

Notes

1. William Shakespeare, *King Lear* act 4, scene 6 (New York: Signet, 1963), 150.
2. Karl Rahner, *The Practice of Faith: A Handbook of Contemporary Spirituality* (New York: Crossroad, 1983).
3. Henri Bergson, *Laughter, Comedy*, ed. Wylie Sypher (Garden City, NY: Doubleday, 1956), 84 (translator unidentified).
4. Wallace Stevens, "Esthétique du Mal," *Transport to Summer* (New York: Knopf, 1951), 52–53.
5. Stevens, 53.
6. Thomas Pynchon, "Introduction," *Slow Learner* (Boston: Little, Brown, 1984), 5.
7. William Wordsworth, "The Recluse," *The Prelude, with a Selection from the Shorter Poems, the Sonnets, The Recluse, and The Excursion*, ed. Carlos Baker (New York: Holt, Rinehart and Winston, 1948), 201.

Revamping the Rut Regarding Reading and Writing About Feminist Science Fiction

Or, I Want to Engage in "Procrustean Bedmaking"

(1994 Eaton Conference)

Marleen S. Barr

> All connections are possible. All alternatives are thinkable. It is not a comfortable, reassuring place. It's a very large house.... But it's the house we live in.
>
> —Ursula K. Le Guin, "Escape Routes" (1974)

In my preface to *Alien to Femininity: Speculative Fiction and Feminist Theory* (1987), I described two steeds—a dark horse named Speculative Fiction and an energetic mare named Feminist Theory—meeting in the critical arena. I said that as a feminist speculative fiction scholar I was troubled by these horses' propensity to canter off in two directions. During the intervening years (due to such colleagues as Frances Bartkowski, Anne Cranny Francis, Sarah Lefanu, Robin Roberts, and Jenny Wolmark) Speculative Fiction and Feminist Theory perked up their ears, flared their nostrils, took notice of each other, and decided to run together. My latest concern about their progress: the hooves which now pound in tandem are creating a deep rut. Furthermore, some critics still refuse to differentiate between these horses and horse manure. To solve this problem, let me engage in some animal husbandry: I imagine that Speculative Fiction and Feminist Theory mate and produce a sparky filly named Feminist Fabulation. But Feminist Fabulation is not running free. Sf critics are pulling her into a reading and writing rut. To discuss this point, I will first trot out some readings, undertaken via a Jane Gallop model, of reviews of my *Feminist Fabulation: Space/Postmodern Fiction* (1992). Then, following a suggestion Robert Crossley offers in his review, I will respond to Carolyn Heilbrun's "Why I Don't Read Science Fiction"—an essay I asked her to write ten years ago.

Playing the Horses, Going to the Dogs, Remaking the Beds (And a Brief Letter to the Whippersnappers). Crossley says that "Procrustean bedmaking dictates the inclusion and exclusion of texts in *Feminist Fabulation*."[1] He seems to have a pre-arranged set of rules regarding which authors I should include: "But a discussion of feminist fabulation that omits any mention of Mary Shelley, Katharine Burdekin, Catherine L. Moore, and Sylvia Townsend Warner is starved at the roots. To cite Naomi Mitchison's *Memoirs of a Spacewoman* only in passing, Le Guin's *The Left Hand of Darkness* only left-handedly, and Pamela Zoline's 'Heat Death of the Universe' not at all while giving extended attention to the minor talent of Marion Zimmer Bradley and Doris Piserchia undermine the project of canon reshaping" (912). Marge Piercy, in her preface to my *Lost in Space: Probing Feminist Science Fiction and Beyond* (1993), speaks to my attitude toward canons: "Marleen stands outside the elaborate imitation Gothic edifices of academic criticism and says, 'But Why and How Come and Why Not and Who Says So and Phooey.' She keeps asking, 'but how come you leave out all the fun and really inventive stuff?'"[2] And that is what I have to say to Crossley: Phooey. Why do there have to be fixed definitions regarding which authors to include in discussions of feminist fabulation? Should every study of feminist sf begin with Mary Shelley? How boring. *Alien to Femininity* specifically omits Le Guin because she, even then at the time of its publication, received so much attention. She would agree with my choice: when I asked her to write about *The Left Hand of Darkness* for *Future Females: A Critical Anthology* (1981) she declined and said that she had gone on to other projects. If the sf author can embrace the new, why is the sf critic reluctant to do so? And who is to say that Piserchia and Bradley are minor? Why, if I point out that these authors have important insights relevant to my argument, instead of writing yet another analysis of *The Left Hand of Darkness* (1969), can't I give them extended attention? To my mind, such repetition constitutes the heat death of the science fiction critical universe. Sf critics, of all people, should not set up rigid hierarchies in regard to naming what is major and minor.

I was happy to introduce readers of *Feminist Fabulation* to Mary Caraker's supposedly minor novel *Seven Worlds* (1986). Crossley does not share my enthusiasm: "As scholar, as teacher, especially as common reader, I'd rather she [Barr] turned to Marge Piercy's *Woman on the Edge of Time*.... Theorists and critics select their texts to enforce a point; readers select theirs for the pleasures of narrative and artful instruction" (912). If I have to listen to one more feminist sf paper about *Woman on the Edge of Time* I will sit on the edge of my seat on the edge of despair. A few years ago, I became impatient when it seemed that theorists stood up at conferences, merely quoted Derrida and Lacan, and sat down. Theorists have, thankfully, moved away from this obligatory incantation. Should not feminist science fiction scholars desist from standing up, merely analyzing Le Guin, Piercy, and Atwood, and sitting down? Excuse me for returning to my horse metaphor—but folks I'm becoming a nag because I'm bored. I want to urge you to sow your wild oats, to break out of the Le Guin/Piercy/Atwood OK Corral. I think that sf theorists should select their texts for the pleasures of instructing others about new narratives. It is time to move from Le Guin's *The Left Hand of Darkness* to her *Searoad: Chronicles of Klatsand* (1991). It is time to make sure we do not turn Le Guin, Piercy, and Atwood into grade B movie monsters who devour attention that could be accorded to new and so-called minor writers. (I, by the way, think grade B movies are worth critics' attention. All the world is a text; critics should work on a broad stage.)

Like Crossley, Veronica Hollinger faults me for excluding certain texts, saying that I devote passing attention to feminist postmodern speculative fiction (Anna Kavan's *Ice* [1967],Monique Wittig's *Les Guérillères* [1969], Joanna Russ's *The Female Man* [1975], Jody Scott's *I, Vampire* [1984], and Kathy Acker's *Empire of the Senseless* [1988]). She objects to my decision to discuss at length what she calls "relatively conservative texts" like Joan Slonczewski's *A Door into Ocean* (1986) and Pamela Sargent's *The Shore of Women* (1986).[3] As Crossley differentiates between "major" and "minor," Hollinger sets up disparities between radical and conservative. But "conservative" is relative; Jesse Helms would not be amused by Sargent and Slonczewski.

The "conservative" (or "established") is not necessarily the enemy. Crossley misunderstands my intention when he says that "Barr has ideas about who might be evicted to make room for the newcomers. Some of their names are Bellow, Roth, Pynchon, and Barth" (911). Not so. I absolutely want these men to be included in discussions of feminist fabulation. Why should sf critics restrict their discourse to authors who are categorized as sf authors? I hope that in *Lost in Space* I acted as an sf critic who boldly goes beyond sf to the stellar literary galaxy far far away from the sf critical rut. Reacting to this desire for inclusiveness, during conference question and answer periods, young women have called me conservative. *Moi*? Conservative? If my insistence upon working to change systems from within systems is "conservative," then the label fits. I must brave the commentary emanating from the new world of the new feminist science fiction critics. I am glad they are present to build upon—and to alter—the foundation I helped to establish. I am glad that I have survived long enough to experience what I call "Discourse of the Young Whippersnappers."

The whippersnappers are more interesting than (since I am in naming mode) "Live and Let Live Established Male Sf Critics." Gary K. Wolfe, for example, writes, "it's a safe bet that when the dust has settled most genre fiction will remain on the margins, as it always has, and so will most fiction by women. But so what?"[4] So what? Please pass the smelling salts. What can I say? *Oy gevalt*.

Let me go on to a more forward looking comment. Kathe Davis proclaims that feminist sf critics *are* instituting change: "That a new order is already under construction is attested to by the publication of both these books (*Feminist Fabulation* and Roberts' *A New Species: Gender and Science in Science Fiction*) by major university presses."[5] But, despite this positive assertion, Davis also takes issue with the authors I include in *Feminist Fabulation*: my feminist sf writers are "less familiar even within the sf ghetto: Carol Hill, Valerie Miner, Susan Daitch, Lisa Goldstein, Lynn Abbey, Elizabeth Scarborough, Sandi Hall, and other non-household names. The selection of authors is largely unpredictable, even quirky, and sometimes questionable" (87). I call your attention back to my epigram in which Le Guin states that we live in a very large house. How to take sf criticism out of its rut? Bring the nonhousehold sf authors into the house—and we have the authority to do so. Crossley says that, like Le Guin, I am "also eager to explore that house, to call the madwoman down from its attic, the maniacs up from its cellar, and the spaced-out fugitives from its crawlspaces" (911). That sounds good. But, more simply stated—I just want to inhabit the entire house. I want the authority peacefully to engage in procrustean bedmaking. (Dear Whippersnappers: Please do not accuse me of being conservative re these domestic metaphors!)

Davis, like Crossley, raises the quality argument. "To make no qualitative distinction between Susie [sic] McKee Charnas and Ursula Le Guin does not serve feminist ends" (88). I beg to differ. "Quality" must be defined. To my mind, if you want to serve the feminist ends of teaching people why patriarchy is destructive, if you want to show people how to achieve cognitive estrangement from patriarchy, then there is no better text than Charnas's *Walk to the End of the World* (1974). Davis continues: "The patriarchy is not simply going to roll over because women have said it should" (88). Why not? The Berlin Wall fell because the East Germans said it should. Texts such as *Walk* order the patriarchy to roll over, to heel, to play dead. If as Davis says the patriarchy, or the canon, "still exists" and "can hardly be expected to enshrine" (88) feminist fabulation—if the patriarchy/canon reacts to feminist fabulation by snarling—that should not stop critics from valuing feminist sf texts which declare that patriarchy should be sent to obedience school. (Looks like this piece is veering away from the horses and going to the dogs. At least the dogs can sleep on my procrusteanly made bed!) Again, I am not barking up the wrong tree. The situation is not, as Davis asserts, that Barr "wants to deconstruct her canon and be in it too" (87). I want to change definitions of postmodern canons so that these canons include women writers—especially feminist sf writers. Again, instead of closing the doors to some of the most interesting rooms, I want to inhabit the entire large house we live in.

My supposed desire to have my canon and eat it too reflects my real concern: dissolving categories which constrain sf readers, writers, and texts—dissolving the very categories to which my reviewers want me to adhere. Sf's relation to categories is addressed by Carolyn Heilbrun in "Why I Don't Read Science Fiction," an essay I asked her to write for the 1984 *Women's Studies International Forum* special issue I guest edited (called, "Oh Well, Orwell, Big Sister Is Watching Herself: Feminist Science Fiction in 1984"). Crossley applauds this essay; he feels that "[w]hen someone finally makes a good reply to Heilbrun, we will all be better served" (913). Now, exactly a decade after I commissioned Heilbrun's essay, seems to be a good time for me to try to generate the good reply Crossley calls for.

Oh Well, Orwell—Big Sister Is Rewriting Patriarchal Myths: Feminist Fabulation in 1994 (And a Brief Tale of Two Universities). Heilbrun's title does not indicate a lack of admiration for science fiction. Although she states that she did not finish reading *The Left Hand of Darkness* and *The Female Man* (Heilbrun 117), she is full of praise for Le Guin and Russ. And she falls "idiotically in love" with Le Guin's "Sur" (1982)—an example of feminist sf which seems to take place on Earth.[6] It is clear to me that Heilbrun likes feminist sf authors and feminist sf—she merely has difficulty with other planets. "I don't scorn science fiction, any more than I scorn Afghanistan; I'm just one of those types who prefer to stay at home and mumble about the problems at hand.... But I live here" (117–118). Well, like the Antarctic setting of "Sur," Whileaway and Gethen are also part of the "here" where Heilbrun lives. Why? Again, I turn to my epigram: "It's a very large house.... But it's the house we live in." The antidote to Heilbrun's having "lost, or never found, the key to science fiction" (119) is using this key to unlock the front door of the very large house which comprises feminist alternatives to the patriarchal language prison house. Gethen, Whileaway, the Antarctic in "Sur," and the "real" world Heilbrun's detective hero Kate Fansler inhabits are all part of the very large house comprising, as she says, "what we all want to imagine: other fictions, other possibilities, other language within the patriarchal language we have been given" (118).

The problem, however, is that patriarchal language speaks in a much louder voice than the Other language—the Other possibilities articulated in common by feminist realistic fiction and feminist science fiction. This Other voice is one large house standing amidst multitudinous structures comprising the patriarchal language prison house—and those structures constitute the reality where Heilbrun insists she lives. I want to emphasize that "reality" and the fantastic, instead of being distinct categories, can appear as overlapping (or blurred genres)—that the "reality" where Heilbrun lives resembles science fiction. Susan Daitch, one of the "less familiar" writers I discuss in *Feminist Fabulation*, addresses this resemblance: "Realism … battled science fiction (some man's exercise of an imaginary world which was chock-full of received ideas about life beyond Mars. It was nothing but Earth all over again with different props)."[7]

Let me offer a tale of two university English departments—the departments at Columbia and Virginia Tech—to illustrate my point. Many of my beloved feminist colleagues have been driven out of the Virginia Tech English department. An eminent feminist theorist who now holds a visiting distinguished professorship is not welcome to stay permanently. As for the situation at Columbia, the reasons why Heilbrun no longer teaches there have been described in the *New York Times Magazine*. No more tenured feminist colleagues for Marleen at Virginia Tech. No more Heilbrun at Columbia. (And I am omitting the story of the young feminist at another university who died due to the way she was treated there.) This is the work of the patriarchal Bug Eyed Monster. English departments at Columbia and Virginia Tech have been attacked by the invasion of the body snatchers—forces that snatch feminists from universities. As I write, Darth Vader sit in the Virginia Tech English department chairman's office with his phaser, set on kill, aimed at me. Feminists in this tale of two English departments live in a world of science fiction tropes. I read science fiction to find ways to change the fact that the patriarchal world often resembles a feminist sf dystopia. I read science fiction to, in Heilbrun's words, "imagine … how we might speak and act differently in this" world (118). To do so requires juxtaposing the fantastic with the real. Heilbrun quotes Mary Jacobus's notion that feminists' goal should be "to write, within 'male discourse,' what cannot be written."[8] Writing what cannot be written is a contradiction which does not conform to reality—blurs distinctions between real and unreal.

Feminist texts erase categories which appear "within" male discourse. This positioning of "what cannot be written" in the location "within" is itself fantastic. So if Heilbrun announces that she does not read science fiction, her reference to Jacobus indicates that she speaks science fiction—as do all feminists. Like Gethen and Whileaway, "within" does not exist; "within" is a planet alien to patriarchal earth. Heilbrun says she can only fathom a society "whose language I have spoken from birth" (117). From birth she learned to speak (and write) from a space "within" male discourse what could not be spoken and written. Again, though Heilbrun does not read sf, she speaks and writes sf: "Le Guin tells us that she made up a new language for her people in *The Left Hand of Darkness*" (118). Heilbrun made up a new language for her people in, for example, *Reinventing Womanhood* (1969): feminist discourse. Hélène Cixous calls this new language *écriture féminine*; Suzette Hayden Elgin calls it *laadan*; I call it feminist fabulation.

And so might Heilbrun—even though I could not, of course, have said so in 1984. Heilbrun differentiates between myths—agents of stability—and fictions—agents of change. According to Heilbrun, the woman detective is subversive; she "destroys myths; she creates fictions" (119). Ditto for the feminist fabulator. The feminist fabulator destroys patriarchal myths by creating feminist metafictions—fictions about patriarchal myths. Kate Fansler is a feminist fabulator. Carolyn Heilbrun would enjoy reading Ursula Le Guin's *Searoad: Chronicles of Klatsand*—a work set on Earth which is at once realistic and science fictional. So why the different categories?

Why I Don't Need "Science Fiction": Or Horses, Dogs, Whippersnappers, and Beds Redux (Briefly). Heilbrun concludes by mentioning "seeking, against all odds, new phases in an old and tired language" (119). I believe that the term "science fiction" is old and tired language in relation to describing feminist writers' fantastic thought experiments. Sf critics who adhere to binary oppositions—such as "conservative" and "liberal" and "major" and "minor"—deepen readerly and writerly ruts I have described. Not to worry, though. The sparky filly named Feminist Fabulation can counter neigh-sayers by leaping over deep ruts in a single bound. As for myself, I can say what I have to say about feminist fabulation to the point of being hoarse. Or, in Hollinger's words, "our work rarely poses much of a challenge to the institutional structures within which we function. Barr's work, on the other hand, is frequently infuriating and deliberately sets out to revise the terms of literary acceptability" (275). I must go to the dogs again to mention patriarchal language's translation of Hollinger's "infuriating": Barr is a bitch. And I know what the whippersnappers would say about my attempts to be inclusive, to revise the terms of literary acceptability. They would comment that *Feminist Fabulation* is not about science fiction. Such was my intention. If this is a conservative move—so be it. It is impossible to change a system by always speaking a language which the system does not speak.

I have made my bed as a feminist science fiction critic who no longer wishes to use the term "feminist science fiction." I, revamper, have to sleep in this bed. Although I have been called conservative and I want the authority to engage in procrustean bedmaking, there is a limit: Jesse Helms is not welcome between any sheets of mine. (I mean metaphorical bed sheets and the printed page.) All connections are not possible.

So what did you expect from a former advocate of "feminist science fiction" who no longer needs that term? So what did you expect from a staunch adherent to the postmodern insistence that there is no such thing as a fixed definition? I ask Heilbrun's question: "So why the different categories?" (118)

Post Script. I began this essay by evoking a past imaginative meeting in a critical arena. Let me close by telling you about a past real meeting of this sort. When Heilbrun wrote "Why I Don't Read Science Fiction" she had never met Le Guin. I was lucky enough to witness the first time these great women set eyes upon each other, could watch each other "squint at the universe in the same way," as Heilbrun says (118). I was in the audience when they shared the stage at a 1992 feminist reading held in Manhattan's St. Bartholomew's Church. I was profoundly moved as I watched the women who I emulate become acquainted with each other. The sight was real; it was also fantastic (i.e., marvelous). Heilbrun and Le Guin share categories; Heilbrun and Le Guin transcend categories.

Heilbrun and Le Guin represent the unreachable star I aspire to; Heilbrun and Le Guin are down to earth, approachable people. Heilbrun took the time to write "Why I Don't Read Science Fiction" at the request of an untenured assistant professor. Le Guin took the time to serve as the outside reader for *Lost in Space: Probing Feminist Science Fiction and Beyond*. Thank you Carolyn; thank you Ursula. The person who Piercy calls the "willful and self-determined … girl child Marleen" will try her best, following your example, to lend a helping hand to whippersnappers.

Afterword: Make Feminist Science Fiction/ Feminist Fabulation Fiction Again, or Trump Is the Procrustean Bedmaker

> Yes, indeed, Marleen, you ARE still feisty. Give it to Trump!
>
> —Norman N. Holland[9]

Rereading "Revamping the Rut Regarding Reading and Writing about Feminist Science Fiction: Or, I Want to Engage in 'Procrustean Bedmaking'" seems science-fictional. I feel like I am entering a time machine transporting me to my past thoughts. Here is how I now react to "Procrustean" which opens with a description of "two steeds—a dark horse named Speculative Fiction and an energetic mare named Feminist Theory—meeting in the critical arena [to] ... produce a sparky filly named Feminist Fabulation": *whoa*! Wow, "Procrustean" is *really* feisty. Have I mellowed with age? I will answer this question by explaining how my ideas have both remained the same and changed since 1994.

I still agree that authors should not be labeled "minor talents." My point that "SF critics, of all people, should not set up rigid hierarchies in regard to naming what is major and what is minor" coincides with my present thinking. I will do some looking backward to explain why. I am responsible for the fact that Ruth Salvaggio wrote the first scholarly article on Octavia E. Butler at a time when Butler was unnoticed. I published a response authored by Nnedi Okorafor before she became a sensation. As a graduate student, I told my teachers Leslie Fiedler and Norman N. Holland that the then-"minor" Le Guin was indeed quite major. In retrospect, I am glad the label "minor" did not dissuade me from engaging in these endeavors which have present ramifications. Instead of "minor talents," I prefer Kathe Davis's term which I quoted in "Procrustean": "non-household name."

I still agree that "dissolving categories that constrain sf readers, writers, and texts" is a good idea. In "Procrustean" I quoted Piercy's statement that I ask "[b]ut why and how come?" I am still asking. For example, Colson Whitehead recently won the Pulitzer Prize for *The Underground Railroad* (2016). Whitehead science-fictionally imagines that the underground railroad is a real train analogous to a subway. Why and how come isn't Whitehead lauded as a science fiction writer?

"Procrustean" contains a lengthy description of my firsthand experience in relation to Carolyn G. Heilbrun's attitude toward science fiction. (She contributed an essay, "Why I Don't Read Science Fiction," to a journal issue I guest-edited in 1984.) "Procrustean" also mentions I witnessed Heilbrun meeting Le Guin for the first time at a feminist reading held in 1992 at Manhattan's St. Bartholomew's Church. I am surprised to have no remembrance of this occurrence. What I clearly see now is that I positioned Heilbrun as my role model in regard to fiction writing. Heilbrun wrote many detective novels featuring protagonist Kate Fansler. With Heilbrun's achievement in mind, I wanted to create several genre fiction novels featuring the same female protagonist. I have only published two such novels[10] with high hopes for the third which is now in circulation: I am no Heilbrun. Although I could not have foreseen this when I wrote "Procrustean," I have become a "minor talent," "non-household-name" fiction writer. My response to "Procrustean" emanates from this designation, not my science fiction scholar role.

I am presently obsessed with writing stories in response to my view of Trump as a procrustean bedmaker who wishes to produce conformity via ruthless methods or violence. Trump is a Procustis who reduces women to his power fantasies of female objectification. When writing "Procrustean," I took it for granted that feminist science fiction and female reality were two separate entities, that real women did not have to fear inhabiting a feminist dystopia like *The Handmaid's Tale* (1985). Not so in 2017. If I could time travel to inform the 1994 me that the 2017 me has worn a pink knitted pussy hat to protest the fact that a pussy groper was elected President of the United States, well, the 1994 me would have feared for her future sanity. I can just see the younger, thinner 1994 me admonishing 2017 me for reading too much feminist dystopian literature. (This sounds as if Stanislaw Lem's Ijon Tichy broke out of *The Star Diaries* [1957–1971] and showed up here.)

I would respond to my former self by quoting Naomi Alderman: *The Handmaid's Tale* "couldn't feel more fresh or more timely.... On the day of Donald Trump's inauguration, one popular placard [photographed by Sarah Pinkser] read 'Make Margaret Atwood Fiction Again!' There's no gain the women's movement has made that can't be taken away."[11] Why and how come does Alderman's comment relate to "Procrustean"?

In "Procrustean," I was having a paroxysm over whether works such as *The Handmaid's Tale* should be called "feminist science fiction" or "feminist fabulation." My thinking has changed. My new thinking is so visceral that I must express it in my nonscholarly native tongue, the direct born-and-bred outer-borough no-holes-barred Queens-Boulevard street-cred-from-the-gut voice I share with President Orange Outrage: I don't care what the hell ya call it. Just put feminist science fiction/feminist fabulation back into the realm of fiction where it belongs. While proudly wearing my pussy hat, I am writing this afterword as a placard. It reads: "Make Feminist Science Fiction/Feminist Fabulation Fiction Again." My up-to-the-moment procrustean bedmaker incarnation demands that feminist science fiction/feminist fabulation remain between book covers. I now see Feminist Science Fiction and Feminist Fabulation as new versions of the two horses I describe in "Procrustean." Feminist Science Fiction and Feminist Fabulation are old mares who must pull together to prevent feminist dystopia from escaping the confines of fiction to become a real antifeminist nightmare.

The only thing I can do to make this so is to write satirical fiction about Trump. I am engaged in this new endeavor.[12] "Procrustean" railed against categorization. Bring on the categories. Alternative truth is not truth. Fiction is not reality.

The truth is that a time machine journey evokes emotion. The category "scholarly afterword" is routinely emotionless. Bring back the railing against categories. Writing this afterword involves emotions I cannot silence. Butler, Heilbrun, and Fiedler are no longer with us. I have tears in my eyes because I am grateful my beloved dissertation director Holland is still here. He wrote what I have chosen to use as this afterword's epigram regarding my point that "Procrustean" is forceful. I asked him if my past reader response force remains with me. Norm, as ever, is right. I am still feisty.

Notes

1. Robert Crossley, "Fiction and the Future," *College English*, 55 (1993), 912. Parenthetical page references to Crossley quotations are to this edition.
2. Marge Piercy, "Marleen Barr's Lost and Found," *Lost in Space: Probing Feminist Science Fiction and Beyond*, by Barr (Chapel Hill: University of North Carolina Press, 1993), ix. A later Piercy quotation is from this page in this edition.
3. Veronica Hollinger, "A New Alliance of Postmodernism and Feminist Speculative Fiction," *Science-Fiction Studies*, 20 (July 1993), 275.
4. Gary K. Wolfe, Review of *Feminist Fabulation*, *Locus*, 31 (September 1993), 70.
5. Kathe Davis, Review of *Feminist Fabulation and A New Species*, *Extrapolation*, 35 (Spring 1994), 89. Parenthetical page references to Davis quotations are to this edition.
6. Carolyn G. Heilbrun, "Why I Don't Read Science Fiction," *Women's Studies International Forum*, 7 (1984), 117. Parenthetical page quotations to Heilbrun quotations are to this edition.
7. Susan Daitch, *The Colorist* (New York: Random House, 1989), 180.
8. Mary Jacobus, cited in Heilbrun, 118.
9. Norman N. Holland, Email to Barr. April 14, 2017.
10. Barr, *Oy Pioneer!: A Novel* (Madison: University of Wisconsin Press, 2003); *Oy Feminist Planets: A Fake Memoir* (Vancouver: NeoPoiesis, 2015).
11. Naomi Alderman, "Dystopian Dreams: How Feminist Science Fiction Predicted the Future," *The*

Guardian, March 25, 2017, at https://www.theguardian.com/books/2017/mar/25/dystopian-dreams-how-feminist-science-fiction-predicted-the-future.

12. My Trump stories: "Duck, Donald: A Trump Exorcism," *Alternative Truths Anthology*, ed. Bob Brown and Phyllis Irene Radford (Benton City, WA: B Cubed, 2017), 205–208; "Two Trump Heads Are Better Than One," *Writers Resist*, May 4, 2017, at http://www.writersresist.com/2017/05/04/two-trump-heads-are-better-than-one; "Into the Chappaqua Woods: Or A Spaceship from a Feminist Planet Lands on Trump's White House Lawn," *The Satirist*, ed. Dan Geddes, March 2017, at https://www.thesatirist.com/stories/into-the-chappaqua-woods.html; "Trump Dreams of Jeannie," *The Satirist*, December, 2016, at http://www.thesatirist.com/stories/trump-dreams-of-jeannie.htmlhttp://www.thesatirist.com/stories/trump-dreams-of-jeannie.html; and "Swan Song for Trump," *See the Elephant Magazine*, ed. Melanie Lamaga, 2016, at http://www.metaphysicalcircus.com/swansong-for-trump-fiction-by-marleen-s-barr/.

Literary Gatekeepers and the Fabril Tradition

(1994 Eaton Conference)

Tom Shippey

All of us who work with science fiction, I am sure, have a store of insults to record from those in authority. Perhaps the award for the crassest example should go to Sheila Finch's senior colleague, who said to her after she published her first science fiction work, "I hope your next book is a real novel." Although that was remarkable for both its brevity and its dismissiveness, it remains in a sense typical. All of us past a certain age have not only heard but have gotten used to hearing similar statements. Despite their frequency, I suggest that, if they were mere random and individual examples of thoughtlessness or rudeness, the right tactic would be to tolerate and as far as possible ignore them. But I do not think that is the case. It seems to me that the open hostility to science fiction often seen in academic departments of literature has a common and even a compulsive root. By facing this, we will be in a position to learn something about "canonization and marginalization," both within and beyond our field.

I have suggested elsewhere[1] that these negative reactions can be used diagnostically. My starting point (again taken from personal experience) was that I had often been told by literary colleagues, seemingly without awareness of self-contradiction, that (a) they hated science fiction, and (b) they never read it. I suggested that regardless of the contradiction, these two statements were probably often true, and that they offered us a kind of generic indicator. I went on to propose (agreeing with Darko Suvin[2]) that science fiction depends on the *novum*, which (now expanding on Suvin) I oppose to the *datum*: the latter is definable as one piece of that shared body of information which all readers need in order to read any text at all; the former the bit of new information which you must find within a text in order to read it as a science fiction text—a bit which is by definition initially *not* shared, which the reader has to be told. This view of the *novum* is not exactly that of Suvin,[3] but is meanwhile by no means hostile or contradictory to the view of John Huntington, who has argued that science fiction (he cites H.G. Wells and William Gibson) is marked by a new *habitus*, a new class-awareness, "the introduction of new class or group values into the hegemonic canon."[4] My suggestion is, in brief, that it is possible to reconcile the contradiction of hating without reading by assuming that it is the presence of the *novum* that marks a work as science fiction; but that as soon as some readers recognize a *novum*, they immediately stop reading—recognizing in the very existence of a *novum* an implicit challenge to the old *habitus*, as to "the hegemonic canon."[5] Both Huntington and I say in effect that science fiction depends on novelty, and that this novelty is seen as a threat (rightly, for it *is* a threat) by conservative groups including academic groups.

A further way of putting this is to say that during my science fiction "lifetime" (1958 to now) being a science fiction reader has been rather like being gay. In both cases, one could say, drawing out the similarities:

- there was definite pressure, especially in the 1950s and 1960s, not to admit the fact;
- there were social penalties if you did;
- you got used to hiding the fact;
- but there were places where you could meet others of the same persuasion;
- and there was very strong "networking" among the concealed in-group, whether of science fiction readers or of homosexuals;
- in both cases, too, discrimination was illegal, was frowned on theoretically, and people would deny they were doing it, but they did it just the same; finally, it was possible to "come out" and get away with it, but only when you reached a certain level of seniority.

Nevertheless, we have to recognize in both cases that the social climate has changed since the late 1950s. We now have "Gay Studies" in colleges, as we do "Science Fiction Studies." Further, I said that science fiction depends on a shocking or threatening novelty, and one must admit that modern academia is fascinated by novelty. It has become part of the collective myth or self-image of academic critics, especially practitioners of "literary theory." Almost all fields, including some of the staidest, have felt the need to develop at least a rhetoric of novelty, so that we have for instance "the new medievalism," "the new historicism," and "the new philology."[6] "Boring old" is regularly opposed as a trope to "brilliant young" or "exciting new." So why should we, as science fiction critics, not put the past behind us? Trade on the inherent novelty of our field? Assume that the revulsion from the *novum* will in the future be professionally unacceptable instead of just personally rude? And make a bid for power, or at least some authority, within the power-structures of our profession—such as the Modern Language Association (MLA)?

The brief answer is that for all the talk about widening canonicity, I suspect that while a place is now being made for science fiction within the MLA, it will be a subordinate or ancillary place. Major theorists are not theorizing about science fiction (with the exception of Fredric Jameson and a few others). More normal is the point of view expressed in Howard Felperin's interesting critique of literary theory, *Beyond Deconstruction* (1985), which closes with the words: "the virtual focus of our changing critical discourse will be the great classic texts, which continue to repay so richly each historical construction and deconstruction they attract."[7] The discourse may change, but the classical texts will not. One can hardly avoid remarking, *plus ca change, plus c'est—plus ca sera—la meme chose*. Science fiction may have "come out of the closet," to return to my analogy, but it has not gotten into the cocktail party. The image I have of our field within literary studies is that of the outsider on the edge of the group, allowed to listen, not excluded, but still not part of the conversation.

Is there a reason for the continuing exclusion, to explain why there is no "new science fiction-ism" to go with the other "new-isms"; why we don't say postrealist along with postmodernist, poststructuralist, postfeminist, postcolonialist (etc.)? I think there is indeed one, which I find I can sum up best by Edmund Spenser's lines about the Garden of Adonis in *The Faerie Queene*:

> For in the wide wombe of the world there lyes,
> In hatefull darkenesse and in deepe horrore,
> An huge eternall *Chaos*, which supplyes
> The substances of natures fruitfull progenyes.[8]

In my figure here, the "deepe horrore" is that with which science fiction is often regarded, a horror stemming from subliminal awareness of the "eternall *Chaos*" created by the unlimited changes of *novum* and *habitus*. But this horror sadly fails to observe the "fruitfull progenyes" which spring from that chaos.

I wish to illustrate what I have said so far by examining what I suggest is a critical moment in the origins of science fiction. I am aware that various people offer various moments for "the birth of science fiction," and I do not mean to reject all the others. I am aware also that the one I propose to examine is not even chronologically the first, while it even refers within itself (in a way) to one of the other candidates, Mary Shelley's *Frankenstein* (1818), so strongly put forward by Brian W. Aldiss as the originating work of science fiction.[9] But my candidate, I feel, has paradigmatic power in this context, that is, in a discussion of "canonization and marginalization." It is Wells's *The Island of Doctor Moreau* (1896). If one reads this, I think it is possible to see why the MLA and the academic literary community remain wary of science fiction.

The scenario of *Moreau*, far from being new, is of course taken from what may be the oldest text in Western literature, Homer's *Odyssey*, specifically Book X, the adventure of the Island of Circe, the witch who turns men into swine, "hogs who rut and slumber on the earth."[10] Wells's Prendick is a doublet of Homer's Odysseus; Wells's Moreau is the transforming Circe; the Beast-Folk are Odysseus's crew. The parallel is quite consciously present within Wells's text itself. After he has been rescued from shipwreck by the *Ipecacuanha*, and from the *Ipecacuanha* by Moreau, Prendick finds himself on Moreau's island with nothing to do and little to read. There is nothing in his hut except "surgical works and editions of the Latin and Greek classics (languages I cannot read with any comfort)."[11] The "surgical works" make sense here as a reminder, or warning, of Moreau's profession, but the classics seem both inexplicable and redundant: Robert Philmus, in his excellent variorum edition of Wells's work, suggests that they can be regarded as "a piece of [Wellsian] autobiography," while later on he sees the "crib of Horace" (24) that Prendick throws aside as symbolizing "the epitome of Civilized Restraint."[12] Yet Prendick throws aside more than Horace, and more than civilized restraint. In Chapter 11 he refers directly to an English classical text which reports the Circe myth. Thinking that Moreau is operating on men and turning them into beasts, Prendick sees it as a fate worse than death to be sent off, "a lost soul, a beast, to the rest of their Comus rout" (33). Comus is the villainous magician of Milton's masque of 1637, introduced there as the son of Homer's Circe, and following the same bestializing practices: Circe and Comus are the classical images, the classical scenario, that give the background setting, the "horizon of expectation" for *Moreau*.

But of course the classical images in *Moreau* turn out to be *wrong*. Prendick is entirely mistaken. Moreau is not changing men into beasts, he is changing beasts into men. The vital question is, which is worse? A critical scene is in Chapter 13, "A Parley." Prendick, who has run away, has been hunted down by Moreau and Montgomery and is standing on the shore, ready to throw himself to the sharks rather than surrender to be transformed as he expects. The Beast-Folk, the products of Moreau's experiments, are standing behind Moreau and Montgomery, listening. Moreau has to reassure Prendick without them learning the truth—so he uses the language of the classics: "He coughed, thought, then shouted: 'Latin, Prendick! bad Latin, schoolboy Latin; but try and understand. *Hi non sunt homines; sunt animalia qui nos habemus*—vivisected. A humanising process. I will explain. Come ashore'" (43). Prendick at first rejects this, but then is reassured and comes ashore. There are however two points to make about this scene.

First there is something terribly degraded about Moreau's Latin: "*qui nos habemus*—vivisected." *Qui* is intended as a relative pronoun, but *animal* is neuter, and the relative pronoun must here be accusative plural, object of "*habemus*—vivisected": *quae*, therefore, not *qui*. "*Habemus*—vivisected," meanwhile, must be an attempt at translating the English perfect "have vivisected" into Latin. But Latin does not make a perfect with an auxiliary verb. One might expect, then, from the English form of "vivisect," some such verb as *vivisectavimus*. However the English infinitive is derived in this case from the past participle, and the Latin verb's "principal parts" in fact go "*seco-secare-secui-sectum*." Since Latin also conveys person and number by verb ending, the pronoun *nos* is furthermore redundant. What Moreau should have said is "*Sunt animalia quae vivisecuimus*."

To make these points is of course in one way an act of utter pedantry (reminiscent of John Cleese as the Roman centurion in the film *The Life of Brian* [1979]). However, and more seriously, I would lay stress on the shocking and even insulting character of Moreau's errors. In my time, and in Wells's, saying something like that in a real school would have been a beating offence—because Latin, in 1890s Britain, Europe, and also to a large extent America, was a mark of the literary and the ruling caste; still at least 90 percent gender-related; and taught entirely *sub virga*, under the rod. What Moreau speaks, however, is a "pidgin," a variant of Latin resembling the debased forms of European languages spread around the world largely by the slave trade. It hardly makes sense for Moreau to speak this pidgin. Presumably the Latin classics which Prendick cannot read belonged to Moreau, in which case he ought to be well above this stage, even if he is perhaps "condescending" to Prendick's level in the critical "parley." But I would suggest that we do not need here to work out complex explanations to do with Wells's autobiography or Moreau's linguistic awareness.[13] What the scene does with great force is express powerful contempt for a whole classical tradition of both language and literature. Prendick is, I repeat, just plain *wrong* in recalling his images of Circe and Comus: his literary knowledge is here useless and dangerous to him. Since that whole classical tradition is wrong, it is only appropriate that the major European vehicle of it, the Latin language, should be scornfully debased here into a mere utilitarian pidgin. The horror any classically educated person would have been educated to feel about Moreau's grammatical mistakes is in Wells's story simply overridden. The important thing in what Moreau says is content, not grammar or style.

The second, more important point about the scene is that this contempt is seriously meant. It is not just the classical images that are wrong, not just Prendick who is wrong; the classical texts are wrong too, *and* their authors and most of all their readers. They thought the worst thing that could happen was to turn men into beasts. That would certainly be bad for the men, like Odysseus's crew, who are so turned. But what if beasts are turned into men? What are the implications of that? What would that say about people as a whole—including the ones who *don't* get turned? Such a transformation, never imagined in any classical text, would say there is no essential difference between people and beasts: people in fact are beasts, mere human animals, the dividing line accepted by all from Homer's time to Wells's becoming simply irrelevant.

As we all realize, Wells *in a sense* means exactly that. And my phrase "in a sense" contains much of the definition, and the alienation, of science fiction. *The Island of Doctor Moreau* is clearly a post–Darwinian story,[14] and one major implication of *The Origin of Species* (1859) is indeed that there is no uncrossable boundary between species in their origins. Beasts (as humans call them) evolved into people; all Moreau is doing, then, is accelerating that process. Furthermore the process Wells imagined in the story was not in his view impossible. In prolonged correspondence after the book came out[15] Wells defended the scientific aspects of his story as accurate and plausible within the knowledge of his time. What he was saying was that his readers had been reading science, but not *in a sense* fiction—a continuing claim of science fiction.

The contrast with all previous literature deserves to be stressed. Previous literature, like Homer or Milton, was indeed fiction, if not mere folk-tale. Its premises were false, its readers misinformed by authors who wrote as they did because they knew no better. The deliberately contemptuous and contradictory nature of Wells's attacks on literary tradition comes out elsewhere in the many ironies of the Time Traveller's visit to the library in South Kensington with "decaying vestiges of books," which he leaves to search for more "useful discoveries"[16]; and in *Moreau*, Wells's aggression towards the past is also seen in frequent and deliberate religious blasphemies—the Beast-Folk with their parodistic "litany of the Law" (40), the ritual prohibitions imposed on them, Moreau's unexplained urge to make beasts *in his own image*, and Prendick's invention of supernatural religion once Moreau is dead:

> "Children of the Law," I said, "he is *not* dead! … He has changed his shape; he has changed his body.… For a time you will not see him. He is—there," I pointed upward, "where he can watch you. You cannot see him, but he can see you. Fear the Law."
>
> I looked at them squarely. They flinched.
>
> "He is great, he is good," said the Ape-Man, peering fearfully upward among the dense trees [68].

This blasphemous element indeed caused far more indignation at the time of first publication than any mere reworking of Homer.

But to keep attention on the literary caste, not the religious caste, I will indicate just one more assault on literary tradition, or literary blasphemy, which occurs at the end of the book. The ending of *Moreau* is clearly calqued on the end of Jonathan Swift's *Gulliver's Travels* (1726), where Gulliver, returned from the land of the Houyhnhnms, sees the whole human race as Yahoos and ends up "not altogether out of hopes in some time to suffer a neighbour Yahoo in my company, without the apprehensions I am yet under of his teeth or his claws."[17] Similarly Prendick in London sees the Beast-Folk everywhere: "I would go out into the streets to fight with my delusion, and prowling women would mew after me.… Then I would turn aside into some chapel—and even there, such was my disturbance, it seemed that the preacher gibbered 'Big Thinks,' even as the Ape-man had done; or into some library, and there the intent faces over the books seemed but patient creatures waiting for prey" (87). Now the absolute staple of Swift studies for decades has been to remind us that Gulliver at the end of Book IV is mad, so we do not need to take his disturbing vision seriously; we can "de-literalize" it (that is, literalize it) by muttering "dramatic irony."[18] I confess that I was always doubtful about this literary strategy, even in my youth (though having the "gay" habits of a science fiction reader I knew better than to say so). But the reason I was doubtful about Swift was that I had read *Moreau*: and I knew that Wells, or Prendick, whichever one prefers—in science fiction tradition there is no disgrace in characters serving as authorial mouthpieces—*meant his final vision seriously*. People were *in a sense* beasts, and once Prendick stopped saying that (which might have been ironic), Wells went on with his postscripts and arguments about *Moreau*, which definitely were not ironic.

To sum up, my argument so far has been a double one. On the one hand I suggest that there is a deliberate attack on linguistic and literary tradition in *The Island of Doctor Moreau*, which forms in fact the novel's hinge.[19] Classical literary tradition is condemned as not only untrue, but the actual reverse of the truth, while classical linguistic knowledge is even more contemptuously dismissed as being of mere marginal utility. Meanwhile the authority of these traditions is replaced by a deliberate argumentative appeal to scientific truth, an appeal which science fiction still continues to make, though we have not as yet been able to frame a convincing literary way of discussing it.[20]

I turn now to more general questions of "canonization and marginalization" raised by *Moreau*, and note that these exist on three levels. They are what prevent *Moreau* from becoming a "great classic text," in Felperin's terms. I will list them in ascending order of current theoretical unacceptability.

One, already discussed, is its dismissive attitude towards previous authors. *Moreau* keeps saying, in effect, "these authors—Homer, Milton, Swift—they have no authority. They were wrong. As for the 'anxiety of influence'—what's that? I'll take these classic texts, as I take the components of their classic language, and reform them without concern for their ruling structures. I'll make a literary 'pidgin' out of them." Aggressive indeed! But I think our current literary caste, the contemporary "gatekeepers" of interpretative tradition, might be able to cope with that. As I said, they have a rhetoric of "challenge," "disturbance," "novelty," and "parricide." While not always practiced as wholeheartedly as it is preached, the rhetoric is at least there to be appealed to.

Much more seriously unacceptable is a challenge to established authority in *Moreau* on a second level. I will record here as a piece of evidence that I never noticed this particular challenge until my very last reading of the text, while it has also as far as I can tell escaped any comment from others. The reason for my blindness is overfamiliarity: this aspect of *Moreau* is written, to use Huntington's term, from my ancestral *habitus*. The reason for American critics' silence, I suspect, lies conversely in reluctance or alienation. But the fact is that *Moreau* follows a once-familiar imperialist paradigm, the story about gaining power through prowess and losing it by human weakness. Like the Circe story, this is an "island" tradition, but its definitive works include Shakespeare's *The Tempest* (1610–1611), Daniel Defoe's *Robinson Crusoe* (1719), William Golding's *Lord of the Flies* (1954), and a host of other "boys' books" now forgotten. However the model for this aspect of *Moreau* is probably Rudyard Kipling's story "The Man Who Would Be King" (1888). Wells's admiration for this is on record, expressed with odd gratuitousness (like his disregard for Moreau's Greek and Latin classics) in Chapter 7 of *When the Sleeper Wakes* (1899). Here the Sleeper comes upon some puzzling cylinders in the future world he has woken into. After a while he realizes that they are labeled in phonetic script, and puzzles out the title of one of them, "The Man Who Would Be King," a story he recalls vividly as "one of the best stories in the world."[21] Kipling tells the tale of two Europeans who decide to conquer their own country with rifles, discipline, and Freemasonry. They at first succeed, but fail in the end when one of them is bitten by a girl and bleeds, showing the natives of the country that they are only men, not gods. The tale is closely followed in *Moreau*, with Moreau and Montgomery obviously posing as gods to the Beast-Folk and anxious above all not to let them taste blood. Both works are parables of imperialism: Moreau may wish to break down the separation between man and beast, but he has every intention of maintaining the separation between rulers and ruled.

This imperial tradition became increasingly unacceptable during the twentieth century,[22] but one cannot deny that this tradition knew a great deal about empowerment and disempowerment. Prendick figures within this tradition simply as a failure. Once Moreau and Montgomery are dead, and only he is left, he tries to take up the imperialist role. He sees the Hyena-Swine and knows "His continued life was … a threat against mine." Under the imperialist code, he must act at once ("Any decision is better than no decision"), and Prendick knows that much at least:

> I was perhaps a dozen seconds collecting myself. Then I cried, "Salute! Bow down!"
> His teeth flashed upon me in a snarl. "Who are *you* that I should—" [76].

And Prendick shoots, but misses. Prendick is a poor imperialist. He knows some of the rules—all of them carefully taught in the literature, or subliterature, of Wells's time and my own: never show fear; never hesitate; never give an order that will not be obeyed; instantly punish disobedience; a wrong decision is better than indecision; and so on. But he fails to put them into practice. His boast near the end of the story, in chapter 21, "that I held something like a pre-eminence among them" (80), is only an indication of his failure. A true imperialist is not supposed to be *primus inter pares*, preeminent among equals; he is supposed to impose himself as completely different in kind.

The point is that, in this particular challenge to authority, Wells's text asks its readers insistently to take the side of the imperialists, and to note Prendick's failure to live up to that role as simply a failure. This is now totally unacceptable to modern literary culture, perhaps to political culture also. Is it possible to say that these are merely contemporary stereotypes from 1896, having nothing at all to do with modern science fiction? It may be so. Yet one may also reflect on the American imperialist, or American colonialist, rhetoric of Robert A. Heinlein[23]; the space empires of Larry Niven and Jerry Pournelle; the sympathy with failing empires in Poul Anderson's "Flandry" series; and a dozen other prominent examples to conclude that there may indeed be something in the ideology or mindset of traditional science fiction that is not as out of touch with the Kipling/Wells tradition as is most of modern literary culture. If that were to be the case, it would explain a great deal of subliminal critical hostility.

However it is a third and least easily defined level of challenge to authority that has done the most to keep texts like *Moreau* out of the "hegemonic canon." This may be approached by reference to Stephen Greenblatt's landmark of "New Historicism," *Renaissance Self-Fashioning.* (1980). In this he asserts a number of propositions about his classic Renaissance texts and authors:

- they are all middle-class rather than aristocratic;
- for such figures, self-fashioning "involves submission to an absolute power or authority situated at least partially outside the self"—God, Bible, court, colonial or military administration;

- "self-fashioning is achieved in relation to something perceived as alien, strange, or hostile"; the alien is chaotic or demonic, it always resurges, violence used against it turns against the self, etc.[24]

My immediate reaction was to think how easily these remarks, *mutatis mutandis*, apply to Wells: lower-class rather than middle-class, self-defining in relation to such aliens as Beast-Folk or Martians, aware of the rebounding effect of violence (as in the fight of the *Thunder Child* against the Martian war machines in *The War of the Worlds* chapter [1898]), and so on. But the problem, the real problem for science fiction in challenging literary authority, lies in the second item. Greenblatt clearly feels he can rise superior to the authority images of his Renaissance texts because *they are no longer authorities*. God, the Bible, the court, colonial or military administration: these authorities in modern literary culture are either deposed, objects of ridicule, or in doubt. Wells's "absolute power or authority," however, is science, exemplified in particular by Charles Darwin and Thomas Huxley, Wells's tutor, and Prendick's, and Moreau's. These authority figures, and even more the source of their authority, have not been deposed. It is impossible for literary critics to apply their rhetoric of control and condescension to them with any conviction.

I return to the thought of "deepe horrore" and "huge eternall *Chaos*." If there is one thing which characterizes all schools of modern literary theory, it is their denial of objectivity, and their insistence on chaos. We have: self-referentiality, the text as a purely linguistic construct, the failure of linguistics as a model, human beings as cultural artifacts, literary discourse resting on historical discourse which rests on mythic discourse ("turtles all the way down," as has been said), the *aporia*, the scandal, the *mise-en-abime*, the whole deconstruction movement, and all the rest of it. To quote the *Johns Hopkins Guide to Literary Theory and Criticism* (1994), not for its preeminence but for its deliberate centrality: "If language, metaphor, and consciousness really are structured by difference, then there can be no solid foundation, no fixed point of reference, no authority or certainty, either ontological or interpretive."[25] Such views have become entirely characteristic of the authority structure of the critical profession, which we may label for short as the MLA. They are impossible to reconcile with the claims for truth-to-fact of much science fiction, and all serious science. This is the last and I feel the most insuperable of the obstacles preventing *Moreau*, and science fiction with it, from being accepted into the central and authoritative core of literary culture. The deepest horror which such works now create, deeper than that coming from rejection of tradition or acceptance of authority-by-power, stems from their perceived obedience to an authority outside "the text."

It may be that this does not matter. We can easily recognize (even if we are reluctant to admit) that the views of the MLA cut absolutely no ice *outside* the MLA. Literary discourse has become ludicrously different from scientific discourse, which is still overwhelmingly characterized by:

- a denotative linguistic system, parodied in Swift's Laputa but now in practice, including but not confined to mathematics;
- rigorous training in that system, which is now worldwide;
- built-in "upgrade capacity" for the system, so change is a permanent contingency but does not affect the hegemonic structure; a uniquely coherent interpretive community.

This does not of course mean that there are no disagreements in science, such as that regarding "cold fusion," the controversy about the HIV theory of AIDS, the struggles of the DNA discoverers to get a hearing, and so on. I am, however, saying that those disagreements take place within a frame accepted by all disputants as objective. The reaction of those literary critics who notice this at all is often mere denial. Felperin declares in a note that "it is difficult to argue that alchemy, for example, does not have exactly the same epistemological status as chemistry, however surprising such a view might be to a professional chemist engaged in research." Doesn't chemistry, unlike alchemy, "work," one might naïvely inquire? No, Felperin replies, for "Alchemists and chemists desire and expect different kinds of results from their activity, and would thus mutually deny the effectiveness of each other's practice" (87–88). The decision as to whether something "works" or not is in short "culturally relative." This is not the impression I get of medieval alchemists from the alchemist in Chaucer's "Canon's Yeoman's Tale" (c. 1400), who seems passionately to want his science to work in precisely a modern way. But the denial of objectivity, even in science, seems now to be compulsive within the literary field, within the belief structure of the MLA—among the gatekeepers.[26]

If I am correct in what I have said, then the gap between the "two cultures" of humanities and sciences is here total.[27] One might look at the elaborate apparatus for noncommitment of modern critical writing—the inverted commas, the parentheses, the slash marks, the spelling changes, the placing of items *sous rature*, "under erasure," so they can be read/not-read at the same time. Against that a paradigmatic image is that of the dying Richard Feynman putting the piece of space shuttle gasket in his glass of ice water before the TV cameras and saying, "nature is not fooled."[28] He meant that observers, human opinions, bureaucratic procedures, all had no value. If you ignored the nature of the material, it would fail, the shuttle would crash, and its crew would die. When he said that, Feynman was repeating an old theme of science fiction.[29] But I would add that while it was of course tragic that scientific administrators had so readily gone over to the alternative, nonscientific habits of "public relations" and "relative values," it has perhaps been even more tragic that politicians and scientific administrators in this past century have had to cope with ethical questions without the assistance of any powerful literary or ethical tradition, that tradition having disqualified itself in their eyes by its outdatedness and lack of realism. One may well think of Harry Truman having to cope with the Bomb with habits of mind derived, as H. Bruce Franklin has shown, not from literature or philosophy but from early science fiction and *The Saturday Evening Post*.[30] The urgent question is, not whether the literary profession can somehow succeed in putting science and science fiction back in its (subordinate) place, but whether the literary profession can, perhaps with a lead from science fiction, succeed in regaining any of the authority which it has, in the wider world outside its own structures, largely lost.

The omens are not good. I note among other things Gregory Benford's uncompromising remark that "the most penetrating way to view science fiction [let alone the wider issues that I have raised] has not yet been evolved."[31] Yet a review of recent history may offer one way forward. There was a time, perhaps twenty-five years ago, when literary studies were heading in the direction of deconstruction or the *mise-en-abime*, but had an ambition to become strictly scientific. The great hope was to apply the quasi-anthropological methods devised to work on preliterate cultures, and to adapt them for cultures of full literacy: to move, one might say, from Vladimir Propp's *Morphology of the Folktale* (1928) to Tzvetan Todorov's *Grammaire du Decameron* (1969) and on to a *syntaxe litteraire*.[32] Roland Barthes looks back on this period as *le reve euphorique de scientificité*[33]; and it is of course quite a common theme in science fiction too: to have a hard social science which can look at a culture, *transcribe* the culture into some universally agreed mathematics, and then say what is going to happen! You may remember the scene at the start of Isaac Asimov's *Foundation* (1951), when Hari Seldon, founder of "psychohistory," passes the slide rule to his acolyte and tells him to work out the equations for himself. Well, slide rules have gone, but we still have no psychohistory; likewise no *syntaxe litteraire*; and as for *le reve euphorique de scientificité*, how are we to translate it: "the euphoric dream of.... Scientology"? It could be said that if you try and turn science fiction into social reality, you end up with L. Ron Hubbard. Not an encouraging image.

Nevertheless I think we can find a more positive self-image; some points of encouragement; and a more positive critical strategy, which I will outline briefly.

For a better self-image, I think we need some new terms. One I am happy with is "fabril literature."[34] Fabril is easily defined. It is the dark, alien, Other of pastoral.

- Pastoral has been with us as a literary mode since at least the time of Theocritus. So has fabril, I believe, but it has not been named or recognized.
- Pastoral is about people, in a state of nature, with animals and plants. Fabril is largely about made things, artifacts.
- Pastoral is of course based on the pastor, the "good shepherd," fabril on the *faber*, the maker: often the blacksmith, the metal-beater, but also the Moreau, the manipulator of biology and even of society.

It is remarkable how *homo faber* has been written out of history, even literary history. What was Jesus's father's trade? By well-established tradition we believe he was a carpenter; old iconic irony shows him in his workshop making a cross. Nevertheless in the Latin Bible he is described as a *faber*, and in the Greek as a *teknon*. The common meaning of the Latin word at least is "blacksmith," while the Old English New Testament (written by men remote from the Mediterranean world of literary culture) quite correctly translated the word as *wyrhta*, that is to say, a "wright." Woodwright, cartwright, shipwright, wainwright—even playwright—a wright is someone who works things. There is a strange suitability in the fact that the pioneers of flight were named Wright, as if technophilia lurked in their genes. One could even translate *wyrhta*, like *faber*, as "engineer." How striking that this has been totally censored out of our official cultural myth, so that Joseph has to be a carpenter! The underlying opposition seems to be: wood/natural/pastoral/good: metal/artificial/fabril/bad. The prejudice which Joseph's carpentry embodies extends also to a systematic downrating of many aspects of science fiction, not least its continued and collective attempt to raise the status of the wright, the engineer, or the *faber*.

As so often happens, Wells seems to have written the "paradigm story" for "fabril man," his 1903 tale "The Land Ironclads," which for that reason alone I selected as the lead story in *The Oxford Book of Science Fiction Stories* (1992). Wells here opposes two nations at war: one a hardy and pastoral breed, the other a race of townsmen. At the start of the story the former group seems to be well in command of the trench warfare that has (prophetically) begun: they are tougher, more cunning, better shots, full of imperial virtues. The war correspondent on whom the story centers notes the ugly, cunning, arrogant, masculine face of one of them and thinks it typical. Then the "land ironclads" appear, a prophetic vision (details apart) of the coming of the tank thirteen years later. With a predictable irony, the war correspondent, the nearest we get in the story to a "literary man," immediately changes sympathies as he sees the hardy pastoralists brushed aside, and contemplates a piece to be titled "Manhood versus Machinery." What he fails to notice, but what Wells leaves as his final word and focus, is that: "the half-dozen comparatively slender young men in blue pyjamas, who were standing about their victorious land ironclad, drinking coffee and eating biscuits, had also in their eyes and carriage something not altogether degraded below the level of a man" (21).

Wells's young tank commanders, in brief, provide an image of "fabril man," which one should note is deliberately unheroic, even unmilitary: the urbanists have been forced into war, but decline to take up its traditions, preferring to see it merely as another job to be done. It is striking that Wells should have realized as early as 1903 not only the technical possibilities of trench warfare and armored vehicles, but also the immediate sentimental reaction against "fabrilism" of the traditional writer, so marked ever since.

The story which I chose to set against Wells's as the last item in the Oxford collection was David Brin's "Piecework," from *Interzone* in 1992. This has in most obvious ways no resemblance to Wells's at all. It is female-oriented rather than male. It contains no elements of war, or metalwork, or smithcraft. It has a strong mythic strand. Yet it seems to me in a deeper way to help to define the idea of the "fabril." In Brin's story, two women, Io and Perseph, are in the business of renting out their wombs to produce—if they are unskillful, like Perseph—organic industrial materials or—if they are skillful, like Io—creatures not unlike the Beast-Folk, but sentient, with human genes and superhuman powers, capable even of citizenship. The activity of womb-renting of course seems deeply inhuman, and Brin suggests at the start of his story that the two women are in a way in a kind of Hell: Persephone is of course in some myths the queen of Hades. Io, however, is in Greek myth one of the loves of Jupiter, turned into a heifer by his jealous wife Juno: among Io's animal womb-competitors are the "fabricows." The point about the Io myth, however, is that in it she regained her true shape, whereas in Brin's story the heroine Io, evading the plots of her jealous friend, eventually gains the final admission of human status in her world—permission to bear a human child. What this story shares with Wells's is the assertion that true humanity resides not in following traditional patterns, but in having the skill and character to dominate a new technology: a physical one in Wells, a biological one in Brin, in each case rejected by one side or character, and embraced and used by the other. Both authors also feint cunningly at the reader's expectations, making it seem as if sympathy should go to the traditional side and playing up the horrific aspects of the new technology, before insisting finally that all technologies remain in the hands of their creators, *if* the creators (unlike Dr. Frankenstein)[35] have the will to use them. Both authors seem to know, in fact, that readers will not like their central characters, for one reason or another!

This trait is taken to a further extreme in a story included near the middle of my anthology, Larry Niven's "Cloak of Anarchy," from 1972. The story here need not concern us. It is enough to say that its image of *homo faber*, an especially clear and detailed one, is also a clear description of what is now called a "nerd." Ron Cole is "an artist and an inventor"; he cannot however remember anyone's name:

> Ron Cole had better things to think about than what name belonged with whom. A name was only a tag and a conversational gambit.... A signal. Ron had developed a substitute. Into a momentary gap in the conversation he would say, "Look at this," and hold out—miracles [403–404].

He works, in fact, with things rather than people. The story shows him to be irresponsible, stubborn, poor at understanding people, bad at politics—not, however, necessarily wrong.

He offers yet another thoughtful image of "fabril man," in which as usual the reader is given the chance of rejecting him in favor of more normal images of humanity but also invited to consider whether, as with Wells's "slender young men" or Brin's Io, he does not also have something in him that ought to be part of a balanced human whole.

My main point here, however, is not to suggest that science fiction should be seen as a branch of "fabril literature" and interpreted solely in that light. I do mean to suggest that the literary terminology we have inherited from antiquity is inadequate, and that we should not hesitate to create our own, perhaps especially if that terminology can be seen not just as untraditional but as antitraditional. I mean to suggest also that science fiction is often engaged in the process of creating new human images of authority, which often seem profoundly antiauthoritative, engineers, host-mothers, or nerds. However my main point is this: in spite of my careful selections of first and last stories, I suspect that much the same points as those I have made here could have been made from *any* collection of thirty or so science fiction stories chosen by anyone. Certainly I could have reached much the same conclusions by discussing, for instance, not the Wells-Niven-Brin sequence from my collection but the stories by James H. Schmitz, Arthur C. Clarke, James P. Tiptree, Jr., and Paul J. McAuley. Nor were the stories selected to make such points: the points emerge seemingly inevitably from the stories. It is this belief which leads me to my final suggestion, which is about developing a more positive critical strategy for the special case of science fiction.

Science fiction is, to a degree unparalleled in modern literature, an intertextual mode. It has often seemed to me as I have read it over the years to be more like a classic folk-tale collection than a great literary tradition. The texts borrow from each other with astonishing speed, vitality, competitiveness and freedom. Yet they are all written by individual authors, nearly all of them perfectly self-conscious and articulate, well able to ridicule fashionable critical attempts to see them as mere clusters of social forces. In spite of its "intertextuality," in no field is the author less dead as *faber*, as producer; or less important as "authority," as rule-giver. In this field, if nowhere else, I think there is a chance of reviving the dead project of *scientificité littéraire*, literary scientificity, or to deetymologize it, literary knowledge-making. This would be a search for knowledge not based on analysis alone of "the great classic texts," but on setting individual texts within their paradigms, paradigms which would be formed (just like the morphological paradigms of dead languages) by looking at a lot of individually nonsignificant examples, as I have done in an extremely sketchy way above: to see what was shared and what was not. Could the conclusions then drawn be turned outward on texts which are *not* science fiction? I would like to think they could, but even if they could not I think the aspiration would be valuable.

Near the start of this essay I suggested that the science fiction field was (in academic circles) like the outsider on the fringe of the cocktail party. Another model might be that of the children's playground. Anthropologists of childhood report that in most areas of fashion—say, popular music—one function of fashion is to exclude those junior. Suppose that at a certain time, for seventeen-year-olds, the in-group is Green Day. Eventually the fifteen-year-olds find out about this and take up the fashion. Fifteen-year-old approaches seventeen-year-old and says "I like Green Day too." But the seventeen-year-old says: "Really? We're all into Limp Biskit now." The word passes down. The thirteen-year-olds find out about Green Day. The fifteen-year-olds find out about Limp Biskit. But already the seventeen-year-olds have gone over to some other group. This model has a certain similarity to critical fashion: the worst thing to be is a "Me-Too-er." By the time you've found out what to say "Me Too" to, it's passé. Better to find what suits your own genius. My own feeling is that science fiction is the field for structural, paradigmatic, intertextual studies, based on an unyielding belief structure, and tolerant of a "fabril" tradition resolutely and deliberately excluded by the literary and rhetorical interpretive community—often a Latin-based interpretive community—since at least late Classical times.

What I have said accounts, I think, for some questions often raised in discussions of science fiction. Why are some science fiction authors acceptable in literary circles and some not? The acceptable ones are so because they do not pose the challenge of truth-to-nature to our literary authorities. Why are some authors—C.S. Lewis, Aldous Huxley, George Orwell, Doris Lessing—given disproportionate space in syllabi and textbooks? Because they are easily assimilable (sometimes against their own will) to established "gatekeeper" paradigms. Why are there continuing debates about "hard science fiction" and Tom Godwin's "The Cold Equations" (1954)? Because these bring in the issue of objective truth too aggressively.

What we have to face, meanwhile, are "strategies of neutralization" or, to use Howard V. Hendrix's term, "cultural sanctioning mechanisms," backed by the full force of office and faculty politics. We are increasingly offered tolerance, as long as we "know our place." This is an offer I find easy to reject. We might also pursue the strategy of claiming that science fiction falls into the Foucauldian category of "subjugated knowledge," as indeed I have hinted. But one should say more robustly that science fiction is only subjugated in literary academia; and literary academia is subjugated in every other respect—in popular esteem, in its effect on national or international culture, increasingly in student enrollments and in pay scales. By contrast science fiction continues to flourish like a hardy weed and to move out from its literary in-group into the mass media. It is open to us to regard ourselves as on the margins of a marginal group (literary academia or, if one prefers, the MLA) or near the center of a much more central group, our fellow citizens as a whole. Our own personal struggle for "canonization," then, is eminently to be won.

Afterword

Over twenty years after the Eaton Conference where this paper was delivered, there have been many developments. One which gives no satisfaction, despite my criticisms of them, is the continuing loss of authority and respect suffered by "the gatekeepers," the critical profession in academia as a whole. In the USA, student enrollments in the humanities are down, a widely-quoted figure being the drop in humanities majors as a percentage of bachelor degrees from 17.2 percent in 1967 to 6.1 percent in 2014. Figures are disputed, as is their interpretation. Some say that while percentages are down, absolute numbers (in a much larger student body) are up. Others argue that much of the fall stems from the different preferences of female students in particular, though why the gender of students should be regarded as an excuse escapes me. There is an indignant response to the entire assertion from Michael Bérubé,[36] but as past president of the MLA and so a senior "gatekeeper," he has an axe to grind.

My own view was expressed, regarding the limited field of philological studies, in a paper online.[37] After it was delivered (with some passion) a colleague from an elite institution remarked that he did not agree with my prescription for improvement, but conceded my remarks had had "considerable emotional effect on the young people present." Naturally, since it was their hopes of employment after years of expensive tertiary education which were being destroyed![38] It is not full professors but graduate students who have taken the hit caused by declining undergraduate enrollments.

A bleakly comic account of the situation in Classical Studies appears in *Bonfire of the Humanities: Rescuing the Classics in an Impoverished Age* (2001), by Victor David Hanson et al.; and something like an endgame is signaled by President Trump's proposal to do away entirely with the National Endowment for the Arts and for the Humanities. The denial of objectivity, the language games of "literary theory," the concentration on "victim studies," have all contributed to a loss of credibility for the humanities as taught in academia.

Science fiction, by contrast, continues to flourish both creatively and critically. One response to declining enrollments has naturally been to offer courses which are "student attractors" in science fiction and fantasy. I confess my suggestion that science fiction could benefit from "intertextual studies" and attempts to uncover the underlying "syntax" of its generic structures has not borne much fruit. In one essay I tried to show the unspoken rules of the subgenre of "alternate history," and simultaneously show how these related to critical terms such as "textuality." More revealing, in a way, was a limited exercise brought about by unusual circumstances. In 1976 and 1980 Kingsley Amis wrote two science fiction novels, *The Alteration* and *Russian Hide and Seek*. Since he was an established mainstream author, his books were assigned to mainstream reviewers. My survey of almost fifty published reviews showed (I think, unmistakably) that very few of the reviewers could understand a science fiction novel, even at the basic level of realizing what was supposed to be happening in it. The books were almost literally in a language which intelligent but inexperienced readers could not follow.

True, Amis's novels were difficult and "intergeneric" even by science fiction standards. But science fiction has not gotten any easier. The two essays above are reprinted in my 2016 collection *Hard Reading: Learning from Science Fiction*, and hard reading, and commensurately rewarding reading, is what science fiction often is. "Cyberpunk" became notorious for the number of neologisms it relied on, but if one looks at modern novels like Hannu Rajaniemi's *The Quantum Thief* (2010), involving quantum physics, Cixin Liu's *The Three-Body Problem* (English translation 2014), about interstellar communication and much else, or Daniel Suarez's *Change Agent* (2017), focused on bioengineering, one sees how far from the mainstream they have progressed, even semantically.

In the background, one must say, the dashing of 20th-century hopes of manned space exploration has had some effect. Science fiction has sometimes become nostalgic—see Stephen Baxter's *Voyage* (1996) and Allen Steele's *Arkwright* (2016), in different ways about how the space program could have gone better if handed over to, respectively, more benevolent politicians, or better still, science fiction fans. It has also often grown introspective, as with many works which take refuge in "virtual reality" or game-worlds; or retrospective, with collections like *Old Venus* (2015), edited by George R.R. Martin and Gardner Dozois, which return to scenarios long since regretfully disproven. Nevertheless hard science fiction, written by scientists, and hard science itself, continue to stimulate each other: see for instance the Benford brothers' nonfiction anthology *Starship Century: Toward the Grandest Horizon* (2013) and the collection *Hieroglyph: Stories and Visions for a Better Future* (2013), edited by Ed Finn and Kathryn Cramer.

As for science fiction criticism, retrospection has become familiar here as well, with works like John Cheng's *Astounding Wonder: Imagining Science and Science Fiction in Interwar America* (2012); good as they are, these are history rather than analysis. The most suggestive work of recent years, in my opinion, is Michael Saler's *As If: Modern Enchantment and the History of Virtual Reality* (2012), which forcibly argues that the major literary development of modern times has come not from approved canonical authors of academia, but authors academically excluded: the "New Romancers" of the late 19th century, H.G. Wells among them, and their literally innumerable successors. Literary criticism very much needs to throw open its gates and expand its horizons. As Darko Suvin noted long ago in *Metamorphoses of Science Fiction*,[39] a discipline which ignores 90 percent of its available material will be wrong even about the 10 percent it does choose to study.

Nevertheless, I feel, in 2017, reluctantly compelled still to agree with Benford that "the most penetrating way to view science fiction has not yet been evolved." Ways are, however, evolving! And we critics are, after all, trying to keep up with fast-moving creative targets. Even Dr. Moreau could not accelerate evolution quite as quickly as desired.

Notes

1. In "Learning to Read Science Fiction," *Fictional Space: Essays on Contemporary Science Fiction*, ed. Tom Shippey (Oxford: Blackwell, 1991), 1–33.
2. See Darko Suvin, *Metamorphoses of Science Fiction: On the Poetics and History of a Literary Genre* (New Haven: Yale University Press, 1979), 63–84.
3. Suvin uses the term in a more abstract way, as a genre indicator, not as a "bit" or "piece" of information. It is part of my argument that nearly all science fiction works have not one but many *nova* (or *novums*), just as any paragraph of any non-science fiction work will contain many *data* (or *datums*).
4. See John Huntington, "Newness, *Neuromancer*, and the End of Narrative," *Fictional Space*, 63.
5. I cannot forbear from recording here the comment made by the chairman of a session at which I read a paper at a University of London conference on East European literature in December 1992. At the end of the session, on science fiction, the chair said, as nearly as I can recall his exact words: "What I want to know is when is any of this *stuff* going to make it into the actual accepted canon?" He was, it is true, severely attacked for saying this; but the stuff/canon antithesis in his mind was no doubt identical with the science fiction/real novel antithesis recorded by Sheila Finch.
6. See *The New Medievalism*, ed. Marina S. Brownlee *et al.* (Baltimore: Johns Hopkins University Press, 1991); *The New Historicism*, ed. H. Aram Veeser (New York: Routledge, 1988). In 1991 the journal *Speculum* devoted an issue to "the new philology."
7. Howard Felperin, *Beyond Deconstruction: The Uses and Abuses of Literary Theory* (Oxford: Clarendon, 1985), 223. A parenthetical page reference is to this edition.
8. Edmund Spenser, Book 3, canto vi, *The Faerie Queene*, *Poetical Works*, ed. J.C. Smith and E. de Selincourt (Oxford: Oxford University Press, 1970), 175.
9. For Aldiss's argument regarding *Frankenstein*, see Aldiss with David Wingrove, *Trillion Year Spree: The History of Science Fiction* (New York: Atheneum, 1986), 25–52. For the relevance of this to *Moreau*, see notes 13 and 35. For accounts of early science fiction or proto-science fiction, see Brian Stableford, *Scientific Romance in Britain, 1890–1950* (London: Fourth Estate, 1985); Paul Alkon, *The Origins of Futuristic Fiction* (Athens: Georgia University Press, 1987); and Alkon, *Science Fiction before 1900: Imagination Discovers Technology* (New York: Twayne, 1994).
10. Homer, *The Odyssey*, trans. Robert Fitzgerald (1961; Garden City, New York: Doubleday, 1963), 172.
11. H.G. Wells, *The Island of Doctor Moreau: A Variorum Text*, ed. Robert Philmus (Athens: University of Georgia Press, 1993), 20. Parenthetical page references are to this edition.
12. Philmus, *Variorum*, 92.
13. It is clear from Philmus's presentation of Wells's first draft of *Moreau* in *Variorum* that Wells was trying to give a lead to interpretation by mentioning books. He mentions at one point Robert Louis Stevenson's *Dr. Jekyll and Mr. Hyde* (1886), and twelve pages later Robert Burton's *Anatomy of Melancholy* (1621) (115, 127). Interestingly this book replaces Mary Shelley's *Frankenstein*, even in the first draft. All this makes Wells's final concentration on Latin and the classics less likely to be merely casual.
14. The connection is again quite explicitly made in the text. Moreau takes little notice of Prendick until

Prendick reveals that he has "done some researches in biology under Huxley" (18), that is, Professor Thomas Huxley, widely known as "Darwin's bulldog" for his public defenses of Darwin's theories. Like Prendick, Wells had at least attended Huxley's lectures in 1884–1885, a fact of which he remained inordinately proud.

15. Wells, *Variorum*, 197–210.

16. Wells, *The Time Machine*, 1895, *Three Prophetic Novels of H.G. Wells*, ed. E.F. Bleiler (New York: Dover, 1960), 315. On this point, see Robert Crossley, "In the Palace of Green Porcelain: Artifacts from the Museums of Science Fiction," in this volume.

17. Jonathan Swift, *Gulliver's Travels*, ed. Martin Price (Indianapolis: Bobbs-Merrill, 1963), 310.

18. See for instance *A Casebook on Gulliver Among the Houyhnhnms*, ed. Milton P. Foster (New York: Crowell, 1961)—which by intention represents generally accepted opinion—where we find Gulliver guilty of pride (279), "sick and morbid pride" (244), etc.

19. A point made by John Huntington, *The Logic of Fantasy: H.G. Wells and Science Fiction* (New York: Columbia University Press, 1982), 63.

20. This point comes up more than once in essays by Gregory Benford (a practicing scientist as well as science fiction author); see especially "Is There a Technological Fix for the Human Condition?," *Hard Science Fiction*, ed. George Slusser and Eric S. Rabkin (Carbondale: Southern Illinois University Press, 1986), 82–98; and "Science Fiction, Rhetoric, and Realities: Words to the Critic," *Fiction 2000: Cyberpunk and the Future of Narrative*, ed. Slusser and Shippey (Athens: University of Georgia Press, 1992), 223–229.

21. Wells, *When the Sleeper Wakes*, *Three Prophetic Novels*, 39.

22. Symptomatic are some of the apologetic comments in Philmus's *Variorum*, for instance the condemnation of Wells for "bigotry and sexism" and the readiness on the next page to see *The War of the Worlds* as a "satire of imperialism" (xxii, xxiii).

23. For a side-view of this, see the beginning of my "The Critique of America in Contemporary Science Fiction," *Foundation: The Review of Science Fiction*, No. 61 (Summer 1994), 36–49.

24. Stephen Greenblatt, *Renaissance Self-Fashioning: From More to Shakespeare* (Chicago: Chicago University Press, 1980), chapter 1 *passim*.

25. J. Douglas Kneale, "Deconstruction," *The Johns Hopkins Guide to Literary Theory and Criticism*, ed. Michael Groden and Martin Kreiswirth (Baltimore: Johns Hopkins University Press, 1994), 187.

26. After reading an early version of this essay Joseph D. Miller wrote an interesting comment to the effect that doubt and uncertainty have indeed had an effect on the authority of scientific knowledge. "The 'Men who would be King,'" he wrote, "have seen their own blood" and "reject the imperial certainty of Newton." I accept these comments, but feel that doubts about objectivity are still a long way from day-to-day science (unlike day-to-day literary criticism). Scientific method furthermore strives conscientiously for self-correction, and has institutionalized doubt and challenge from its inception.

27. In writing this essay I reviewed the old debate over "the two cultures" from C.P. Snow's 1959 lecture onwards, and was again struck by the petty critical maneuvers of its literary spokesmen. For a balanced view see Martin Green, *Science and the Shabby Curate of Poetry: Essays about the Two Cultures* (New York: Norton, 1965).

28. For a full account of this incident, see Richard Gleick, *Genius: The Life and Science of Richard Feynman* (New York: Pantheon, 1992), 414–428. Feynman wrote in his final report: "For a successful technology, reality must take precedence over public relations, for nature cannot be fooled." See note 20 above.

29. Seen classically in the Tom Godwin story "The Cold Equations" (1954). Controversy about this can be seen in *The New York Review of Science Fiction*, Nos. 54 (February, 1993), 60 (August, 1993), 64 (December 1993), and 66 (February 1994). One might remember also the extensive series of science fiction satires on scientific bureaucracy, a feature of *Analog Science Fiction/Science Fact* from at least the early 1960s.

30. See H. Bruce Franklin, *War Stars: The Superweapon and the American Imagination* (Oxford: Oxford University Press, 1988), 149–154.

31. Benford, *Fiction 2000*, 228.

32. See Vladimir Propp, *Morphology of the Folktale*, trans. Laurence Scott (Austin: University of Texas Press, 1975); and Tzvetan Todorov, *Grammaire du Décaméron* (The Hague: Mouton, 1969).

33. See Felperin, 86.

34. As noted in my "Introduction," *The Oxford Book of Science Fiction Stories*, ed. Shippey (Oxford: Oxford University Press, 1992), ix–xxvi, the term "fabril" is not my coinage but that of James Bradley, the University of British Columbia, to whose unpublished writings I also owe the fabril/pastoral opposition and the remarks on Joseph's trade. Parenthetical page references to "The Land Ironclads" and "Cloak of Anarchy" are to this edition.

35. It is just possible that some such thought as this may have led Wells to delete the reference to *Frankenstein* from his first draft of *Moreau* (see note 13). Despite claims for it as a progenitor of science fiction, *Frankenstein* is more convinced of the dangers than of the potentials of a new technology.

36. Michael Bérubé, "The Humanities, Declining? Not According to the Numbers," *The Chronicle of Higher Education* website, posted July 1, 2013, at http://www.chronicle.com/article/The-Humanities-Declining-Not/140093.

37. Shippey, "Response to Three Papers on 'Philology: Whence and Whither' Given by Drs Utz,

Macgillivray, and Zolkowski, at Kalamazoo, 4th May 2002," *The Heroic Age: A Journal of Early Medieval Northwestern Europe*, No. 11 (May, 2008), at http://www.heroicage.org/issues/11/foruma.php#shippey.

38. See the comment made by Michael Drout immediately above my essay just mentioned, on job openings as against applicant numbers.

39. Suvin, vii.

Flying to the Moon in the French *Bande Dessinée*

(1995 Eaton Conference)

Danièle Chatelain *and* George Slusser

Our title, "flying to the moon," suggests very different ways of getting from here to there within the major sf theme of space travel. Do we fly on wings of metal, or wings of song? Imagination, or technology? The illustrated narrative not only tells about such travel, but shows us how we travel, and thus provides significant data for an analysis, not only of how a same theme is treated in different media (especially an integrative medium like illustrated narrative), but how that treatment sheds light on the dynamics of a particular culture. What we consider here is the *bande dessinée* and its development within the sphere of French culture. Though the *bande dessinée* shares a genre (sf), a medium (the comic book), and in terms of this essay a theme (space travel) with the U.S., the way these develop in the French context is significantly different.

In American sf, space travel "grew up" rapidly in print and film, leaving behind as early as the late 1940s its juvenile stage of junior rocketeers, to depict real-seeming vehicles and well-conceived star treks. In the parallel and analogous American superhero comic however this does not seem to be the case. For here, well into the 1950s and 1960s, we still find flying men, or indeed Superman doing interstellar travel with only his cape and outstretched arms. In France, however, the comic, as *bande dessinée*, has from its inception rivaled print and film in sophistication. Where sf is concerned, it surpasses these in fact. As modern culture has moved from describing and drawing spacecraft, to building, flying and photographing them, space travel in our time has passed from sf trope to visual myth. In the U.S., the medium of preference for depicting space travel is today the special effects cinema; the result is the hyperrealism of the *Enterprise*. In France, however, surprisingly, the medium of preference seems to remain the *bande dessinée*. The ultimate in space voyages, the most elaborate vessels, are found in the French cultural sphere in the highly sophisticated visual frames of artist/scenarists like Moebius and Philippe Druillet. To look at the radically different nature of space vessel and space voyage as depicted in the French *bande dessinée* is to discover a very different cultural attitude toward the technology of expansion.

Space travel is perhaps the central modern icon or trope, not just in the Anglo-American domain, but all across the spectrum of Western belief in technological advancement. From J.D. Bernal's scientific prophesies, to the space "odysseys" of 1950s sf, we mark new stages in humanity's encounter with the obduracy of matter, the difficulty of advancing to new frontiers in a physical universe no longer to our measure. Space travel brings us into contact with "aliens" that are really new, things that we can begin to depict in human terms only because we have gone into space and thus been able to perceive them: in other words, to go where no man has gone before. Space travel leads human beings to consider transformations that are (as Gary Wolfe calls them) "alloplastic" and "autoplastic," where on one hand we turn uninhabitable space into a human habitat, on the other we remake our physical being so it can function in hostile environments. For space travel, we devise cryonics to give the longevity needed to extend human life across light years. We should remember, however, that the first object of space travel was (modestly) our moon, and that it was a Frenchman, Jules Verne, who was first to devise a physically plausible means of getting there.

Verne's predecessors hardly worried about asking whether their contraptions would make the trip. Verne however, as the title page of *De la Terre à la Lune* (1865) tells us, actually calculates the velocity, hence time of trajectory, for his moon rocket: "Trajet direct en 97 heures 20 minutes." The frontispiece opposite this page, in the Hetzel edition, pictures a long aerodynamic rocket, heading through starry space toward the encratered surface of the moon. We have here no winking men-in-the-moon, such as Georges Méliès would later depict, but "realistic" moon topography. But the rocket itself, as drawn, seems just another fanciful flying machine. In its five-sectioned structure it resembles a train: first, there is the smokestack spouting from the nose, that makes the first two sections look like engine and tender; these are followed by two windowed cylinders (passenger cars?), and a last section that recalls a caboose, complete with platform, streamers (or is it rocket smoke?), and even what seems to be a human figure, bidding farewell to Earth much one would to the last town on the line. Despite this however we might see, on a vector of technological advancement, a kind of metonymic displacement at work here. For by depicting a train—which was a form of progressive locomotion *already realized* in Verne's time—now engaged in flight, the artist is in fact stretching or extending an existing prototype, as it were, retrofitting it for more advanced use.[1]

In this sense, might we not see these "cars" poised to become what today are "stages" in the modern booster rocket? The frontispiece to Verne's sequel, *Autour de la Lune* (1870), shows a same starscape and moon. The vehicle moving across the craters however, this time, is reduced to a nose cone: it has shed the appendages, its booster stages, and in this form offers a more plausible ballistic projectile, in orbit around the moon. Other drawings in these novels may lapse into smiling suns or astrological fantasies. But these however not only correspond to "subjective" visions, but become much rarer as the men circle the moon. The visual focus is increasingly on the rocket, as aerodynamic object, thus as the functional means that allows scientists to observe what are never-before-seen phenomena. We thus witness, in Verne's narrative as in the illustrations it inspires, man and vehicle both in the process of assuming the technological function set by the physics of space travel. What begins as a dualist proposition—with Verne initially contrasting the American pragmatists Barbicane and Nicholl with Frenchman Ardan who represents not only "l'agitation et la loquacité française," but as his name implies the ardent Romantic imagination—yields to a singularity of purpose. For as the rocket orbits the moon, oppositions fade, voices become indistinguishable. Just as the fanciful, train-like decorations vanish from the rocket, traits of personality fall away as men are carried to a place no man has gone before. Leaving behind outmoded systems of conflict, Verne's characters are made, quite literally, as they enter this new environment, to function as human observers, recorders of physical fact.[2]

Verne, a Frenchman, is the first to give us both a plausible space vehicle, and the concrete experience of actually traveling to another planet and seeing anew from a new perspective. It is ironic then that, in the French literary culture, we must wait, to find a like experience of physical space travel, until 1953, in Hergé's *bande dessinée* series, *Les Aventures de Tintin*. In this series, Hergé gives us two illustrated novels, *Objectif Lune*, and the next year, 1954, its sequel *On a Marché sur la Lune*. These are works exactly calqued on Verne's set of novels, simply brought up to date by incorporating new advances in rocketry. Perhaps we should not be surprised here, for the two Tintin works are meant to perform precisely the same function in terms of their culture as the Verne novels. Verne's narratives were part of a series, the *Voyages extraordinaires*, where characters traveled to a variety of distant or hidden locations, on and under the earth and sea as well as in outer space. Their narratives in turn offered readers, in a manner called "didactic," descriptions of their explorations in up-to-date technical terms. If the *Tintin* series (it has many more albums than these two) has only a single set of characters, it nevertheless offers well-documented adventure in diverse locales, only one of which is space.

What does surprise us however is just how little space travel—the technological adventure of space exploration—has grown, and grown up, in this French context. Not only are we still exploring the moon—little or no galactic ground has been gained; we literally re-discover it in the shadow of Verne. Perhaps even, despite the fact that the Tintin volumes appeared in the space age, we have lost ground. For even though Verne, in Hetzel's "Bibliothèque d'Éducation et de Récréation," was writing in a context of adolescent (technocratic) readers, he projected adult figures, who in the moon voyage come to do adult scientific work. Tintin however remains throughout a perpetual "jeune reporter," the magic boy who never grows up. Here we are, historically, on the verge of real space travel, real moon walks. Yet Tintin fixes in the minds of the French an indelible association between juvenilia and the greatest technological feat of the century. The adventure of technology, as documented in words and (more significantly) in images, becomes for the French, via Tintin, a thing for the terminally young.

Such is the cultural thrust of *Tintin* that many French consider that he, 16 years before Neil Armstrong, was actually first to walk on the moon. As significant here, however, is the appearance of Robert A. Heinlein's special effects, in *Destination Moon* (1950), which three years earlier, in 1950, not only strove to put a human observer physically on the moon, in a place he had *not yet* been, but by doing so was to lift the visuals of space travel from the juvenile realm (that of Heinlein's own 1948 novel *Rocket Ship Galileo*), and take them toward the eminently adult realm of Chesley Bonestell's covers, Stanley Kubrick's *2001: A Space Odyssey* (1968), even *Star Trek: The Motion Picture* (1979).

We find the analogue of this American fascination with depicting the aerodynamically conceived space craft, as icon and fetish, on the cover of *Objectif Lune*. The jeep containing Tintin, Captain Haddock, Professor Tournesol (the absent-minded genius scientist), and Tintin's dog Milou rolls toward a construction site where workmen are putting the finishing touch on an upright rocket which, in form and concept, is worthy of rockets depicted on the covers of American pulps like *The Magazine of Fantasy and Science Fiction*. Even more striking than the full page diagrams (literal blueprints) of the rocket in the text—these offer the nuts-and-bolts didacticism expected in the tradition of the Verne novel—is the verisimilitude of this cover, which despite the bright colors and strong design of comic book art remains surprising accurate in its technical details.[3]

Even more accurate is the moonscape depicted on the cover of *On a Marché sur la Lune*. Despite the unlikely presence of Tintin (and the dog Milou dressed in a spacesuit), the nature and texture of this moonscape, in its "effet de réel," strongly resembles Heinlein's decor, constructed from moon photos, for *Destination Moon*, or that of the many classic cover scenes of a planetary artist like Bonestell: all clearly intended to convey an "adult" sense of the real new frontier and serve as inspiration for its conquest to come. Hergé draws spacesuits that look a bit like the Michelin man, yet they appear accurately conceived and quite functional given a real moon environment. There are plausible-seeming moon vehicles; even the problem of putting a space suit on a dog is solved in a technologically plausible manner—in short, Hergé gives a sense of a new physical *environment*. One should note too that the title, "On a Marché sur la Lune," has a journalistic ring that will be echoed in later newspaper accounts of Neil Armstrong, "le premier homme qui a marché sur la lune."[4]

As the *bande dessinée* develops in the French-speaking world from the "golden age" of Tintin, we maintain two strains, defined in the thematic sense: the juvenile continues, while an "adult" BD, identified by themes like sex and graphic violence, and typified by an increasing pessimistic or "dystopian" tone and attitude toward technology and the future of human cities and societies, comes more and more into prominence. If, in terms of theme, technology in the adult BD has to be stigmatized as cause of this dystopian future, we do not expect to see that same technology celebrated or fetishized in its icons. Yet such is the impetus of the space travel technomyth that vessels and voyages to other planets and galaxies continue to be pervasive in the adult production of the 1970s and early 1980s. The change that occurs however is the form of these vehicles. Such forms, visibly "unreal" in the sense of technical verisimilitude, act as signs of the manner and mode in which these ships function in their visual and narrative contexts. The function of these vehicles, in fact, determines the nature of the voyages they can and will undertake, and this changes radically.

In terms of real-life drawing boards, the rocket-like design of space ships in 1950s depictions yields in the 1960s and 1970s to the more sophisticated space station and deep-space-cruiser design given iconic (and mythic) status by Kubrick in *2001*. In the French BD however, an analogous sort of technological realism is found only in juvenile comics during this period. An example is the series "Valérian, Agent Spatio-Temporel," of Jean-Claude Mezières and Pierre Christin. The juvenile comic in fact is no longer "innocent" here in the sense of Tintin, but begins to parody itself. Valérian and his female counterpart Laureline are iconically presented as large mature heads and faces (which implies they are capable of the sexual relations that are ever suggested but never consummated in these strips) placed on small childlike space-suited bodies. Nevertheless, their adventures continue strictly to follow the Tintin paradigm of the mystery story that unfolds in linear manner, both in terms of plot and in terms of classic strip presentation of the narrative frames. These adventure ranges across galaxies (a typical title is *Métro Châtelet, Direction Cassiopée* [1980]); moreover, as this title's emphasis on places and means of locomotion tells us, space vessels are needed to get from one end to the other of the story. Sure enough, the opening page of *Métro Châtelet* is devoted to a two-page panorama of cosmic star-scapes, and spaceships in flight. Their forms have become more complex perhaps, even ornate, but they are still presented in terms of hard surface and pure functionality.

They fly and look like they can fly. The legacy of Jules Verne passes through Tintin to works like this, where, as adult themes are suggested only to be thwarted (like the stunted growth of Valérian's body), an uncrossible barrier is erected that keeps technological adventure and space exploration forever this side of adolescence.[5]

Ironically, the point of bifurcation for images of space travel in French sf and the sf *bande dessinée* may be that same *Magazine of Fantasy and Science Fiction* where American space illustrations came of age. In the mid 1950s, a French version of this magazine was launched under the name *Fiction*. Originally intended to offer French translations of U.S. stories from *F & SF*, *Fiction* soon took a very French direction. One of the ways it did so was to commission original cover art. On these covers during the early and late 1960s we find some very interesting space vehicles. On one, the French term *astronef* is literally depicted as a flying galleon, its carved stern sweeping across the curve of some distant planet or moon. On another, the city-in-flight, something James Blish would depict in technical detail and propel with a massive space drive in his contemporary rendition in American sf, is here perched on the back of a flying hybrid, a creature formed with the wings of a bat and exoskeleton and head of a great insect. In still another instance, the giant flying city (in this case visually a medieval fortress structure) floats through space not just on top of the head of a woman, but blending and fusing with that head.

In all these icons, the implication is that the space voyage, which in the real rockets of Tintin or gleaming hyperdrive ships of Valérian appear to take us "forward" (at least in the sense we are physically going someplace new), has become instead a voyage of regression. Space "ships" have become nothing but metaphors. If you try to fly one, it reverts before your eyes to its etymological origin, and becomes a schooner to "sail" the stars. Likewise, the metallic future of man-made artifacts seems held thrall, not by stress of metals, fuel ratios or speed of light, but by a paucity of models or prototypes on our organic chain of being or on our evolutionary scale. Try to build a spaceship, and it turns in flight literally into its animal or insect prototype: a bird or a bug. Finally, the example of the city as brain that governs a flying face suggests two things: first, that the voyage outward instead may be actually a trip backward to our historical past, or even down the devolutionary scale; and second, that it is a voyage *inward*, toward the inner mysteries of the unconscious that lies beneath all our rational aspirations. In these drawings, the enterprise of space travel is thrust back and downward, into the Dionysian realm of dreams and desire.

If we assume France is a Cartesian culture, then we can distinguish between two very different modes of Cartesian experience here. There is first, seen in works from Verne to Tintin, what could be called a naive dualism, where mind, once separated from extended matter, seeks to construct, by rational means, spaceships and other interface devices which will allow *res cogitans* to reassert presence, and with it control and dominance, in the mindless realm of *res extensa*. There seems to be a second form of Cartesian experience however, more subtle and contorted, that appears in "adult" French sf and sf *bande dessinée*, in this case visible from the *Fiction* covers through the BD of the 1970s and 1980s. On these covers—and *Fiction* provided the workshop that produced artists like Jean-Claude Forest of *Barbarella* fame, and *Metal Hurlant* artists like Jean Giraud (alias Moebius) and Philippe Druillet—we have depicted situations where mind, as the faculty now isolated by doubt from contact with matter, becomes reluctant, perhaps obeying Pascal's sense of separation of orders, to seek reconnection at all. In opposition to the age of technology and space travel, this sort of Cartesian would hold the view that mankind, as *only* rational being in the material universe, is totally alone. Not only is it futile for an explorer to go anywhere else. Indeed, carrying the Cartesian argument to its radical extreme, the *only* place that can be explored by mind is mind itself, a universe bounded by the confines of the *cogito* alone. In such a universe, spaceships must not be real, but *surreal*, and outward-directed star treks become reason's plunge into the dark spacetime of its own unconscious.

Examples of such "space travel" are many in the French BD. Let us look briefly at two notable pilots of these surreal mindships: Moebius's Arzach, and Druillet's Lone Sloane. Arzach (or Harzak, or Arzakh, h's do not pronounce in French) is a strangely garbed, yellow-faced, cone-headed man, astride a huge pterodactyl-like bird. Everything is "like" something else here, yet the similes constantly point to referents that, as a whole, add up to nothing significant in terms of an external or physical world "out there" that the reader can relate to, let alone operate in. An unnamed commentator, cited on the album cover (with appropriate vagueness) as writing in the magazine *Le Point*, describes Arzach's travels this way: "Un héros laconique traversant, sur le dos d'un étrange reptile ailé, des paysages phantasmagoriques; des aventures sans scénario, ni chute, ni morale, où onirisme et science-fiction font bon ménage" [He is a laconic hero crossing phantasmagorical landscapes on the back of a strange winged reptile: adventures with story, nor crisis, nor moral, where oneirism and science fiction join hands]."

Arzach flies over an Earth-like place that could, in an adventure that had a story, be a post-holocaust world. There are vague remains of even-vaguer architectures, that could be segments of a viaduct, but seem more like Valéry's "arche qui demeure," where all function except a dream function is hopelessly lost. He passes over a ground of green tentacle-like "things" that constantly reach for his flying figure, indeed do absorb and "devour" whatever falls into them, as do Arzach's other flying creature, and several humanoids, along the way. But what way? The narration follows essentially what are the linear expectations of the strip as we read left to right, top to bottom, page to page. Yet Arzach, across a place that looks like it was once the spatiotemporal continuum of human experience, is always going, never arriving anywhere particular, never doing anything significant, or even meaningful. He is a dream figure who, as "navigator," is calqued on the space exploration paradigm of sf. But the sole property of his vehicle—"the strange winged reptile"—is precisely to keep him from taking the "chute" or plunge into the extended world, which is now clearly the field of the dis-individuating unconscious that lies beneath rational thought.[6]

Druillet's space voyager bears the name Lone Sloane. His name and the fact that he is literally everywhere and everyone in Druillet's BDs makes him a marvelous Cartesian-Pascalian icon, figuring the condition of mind as alone in the material universe. At an opposite pole from Arzach, Druillet, instead of emptying space travel and the "future" of all vestiges of science fiction and its rationally constructed icons (and with them all sense of the existence of a material world to explore and conquer), revels in a proliferation of flying machines and technological detail. His door into dream is through the hyper- or surreality of technological constructs.

For example, the spacecraft on the cover of *Gail* is over-laden with intricate mechanical detail. But when we examine it in order to "figure it out," it seems to devolve before our eyes, to turn from machine (as if through hallucination or metamorphoses of forms) into some kind of flying insect, with jowls and pinchers.[7] His depictions, in *Delirius*, of what is a "pleasure planet" reveal as we examine them in detail a riot of flying figures that are "phantasmagorical" precisely because they are rendered down to the least line in hyperdetail. As our eye struggles to see through their overlay of machine appendages, forms of ships emerge as squatting toads on pads, leaping mantises, springing or floating insects of all shapes and kinds. In Druillet's work, Sloane flies any and every kind of device, and moves in any and all directions. In terms of the historical and evolutionary path usually associated with the trope of space exploration, Sloane's trajectory inscribes at best a loop, a circular self-closing motion much like the pattern of images within the page-large frames that characterize Druillet's spatializing and emblematic visual style.[8]

In *Les 6 Voyages de Lone Sloane*, direction is ostensibly the far-flung future and galaxies. In the course of the episodes however, Sloane trades a conventional looking ship for (in sequence) a flying throne; a ship-city; an organ-ship; a walled fortress in flight; a bug-like vessel that bears the name *Sidarta*; finally a craft that resembles some basic underwater life form, a pink fish of the lightless depths. Technology's voyage "out" has become, in this succession of vehicles, in fact nothing less than an incremental reversion to the most primitive, non-technological life forms.[9]

Similarly, in Druillet's treatment of Gustave Flaubert's *Salammbô*, the future loops around to rejoin the past of ancient Carthage as Lone Sloane comes gliding into this universe riding a spaceship that is a cross between a shark and a Harley-Davidson chopper. Past and future, the highest and lowest forms of evolutionary life, supermachine and simple bivalve—all are drawn, as if on a Moebius strip, into a spatialized disposition of forms where linear narration is folded into a dream emblem. If in the realm of *res extensa* we can envision travel, discovery, a future where there will be new worlds for old, Druillet has, with Lone Sloane and his ships, replaced that realm with an analogous mindscape, where (deploying what is in fact a technology of the mind) he can manipulate its elements at will. Druillet does not yield to dream, in Cartesian fashion he seeks rational mastery of its *personal* space.[10]

Verne travels to the center of the earth, Druillet to the center of the mind. The fact remains however that functional technology—the heritage of what we might call Verne's positivist Cartesianism—is relegated in French sf to the adolescent world, while real "dream work," the technico-surrealist exploration of mind (the center of rational being) as world in itself, is the purview of adults, hence of adult art and fiction. The division that occurs, in the sf *bande dessinée* in terms of space travel, between Tintin and Druillet, occurs in French sf itself between Verne and an entire post-war school of writers who are also products of *Fiction*. To generalize further, we might say that, in French culture in the broad sense, this same gap separates material scientist and humanist today. The latter, in fact, has taken (at least in the public image he creates for himself) a path away from Vernian positivism and "American" science and technology, moving instead toward increasing separation of mind from matter. This path moves from surrealism, to the New Novel, to post-structuralist theory.

To chart this, we need only open the pages of a New Novel like Claude Ollier's *La Vie sur Epsilon*. Drawn by the promise of science fiction space adventure, our eyes discover his vague, oneiric drawing of a spaceship; it is a ship of the mind, never intended to leave the drawing board, fit to serve only as a sign or figure that points within, to the only realm mind alone can explore: itself. Postmodern critic Jean Ricardou tell us clearly that Ollier's novel offers a "mental" not a physical landscape, where the author has "multiplied happenings where occurrences thought to be real gradually return to their original state of hallucinations." Excluded forever from this realm is that reader who, from 7 to 77, can hope for space flight, for open-ended discovery, in the material sense, of physical new worlds.[11]

We discover, finally, that the master dualism, that governs the two-cultures gap in contemporary French culture, is that of youth and age. This makes it all the more problematic, and dogmatically absolute, when compared with that fluid state of mind and being American sf calls "sense of wonder." For where dualism is pegged to biology, then biology becomes destiny. Technology then, as something relegated to the excesses of youth, will always be subjected to the restraints of maturity. Is not being mature, in this sense, the same as being isolated in a world of mind and self?

Notes

1. Jules Verne, *De la Terre à la Lune: Trajet Direct 97 Heures 20 Minutes* (Paris: J. Hetzel, 1865).
2. Verne, *Autour de la Lune* (Paris: J. Hetzel, 1870).
3. Hergé, *Objectif Lune* (1953; Tournai: Casterman, 1981).
4. Hergé, *On a Marche sur la Lune* (1954; Tournai: Casterman, 1981).
5. Jean-Claude Mezières and Pierre Christin, *Métro Châtelet, Direction Cassiopée* (Paris: Dargaud, 1980).
6. Moebius [Jean Giraud], "Arzach," *Oeuvres II* (Paris: Humanoides Associes, 1976).
7. Philippe Druillet, *Gail* (Paris: Dargaud, 1978).
8. Druillet, *Delirius* (Paris: Dargaud, 1978).
9. Druillet, *Les 6 Voyages de Lone Sloane* (Paris: Dargaud, 1972).
10. Gustave Flaubert and Druillet, *Salammbo* (Paris: Dargaud, 1982).
11. Claude Ollier, *La Vie sur Epsilon* (Paris: Gallimard, 1972).

Shapes from the Edge of Time

The Science Fiction Artwork of Richard M. Powers

(1995 Eaton Conference)

Kirk Hampton *and* Carol MacKay

"...when we dream, we dream Richard Powers."—John Clute[1]

The death of painter and illustrator Richard Powers (1921–1996) marked the loss of an artistic giant whose light has been long obscured from view by the anonymous, mass-market field in which he did most of his work—paperback book illustration. From the point of view of art history, his success was very nearly his undoing. From the point of view of science fiction, he created resonant visual emblems of the genre's inner paradox. Powers's significance—at least within the sphere of commercial illustration—has been well acknowledged, but his status as an American surrealist has been recognized to an entirely inadequate extent. Robert Weinberg's *A Biographical Dictionary of Science Fiction and Fantasy Artists* (1988) calls Powers "the most influential science fiction artist of the 1950s," acknowledging that he, "more than any other artist, changed the perception of science fiction from space opera to real literature."[2] Powers's covers for science fiction novels number in the hundreds, and include classics such as H.G. Wells's *The Time Machine* (1895), Isaac Asimov's *The End of Eternity* (1955), and Arthur C. Clarke's *Childhood's End* (1953); in addition, he provided jacket art for poetry, mystery novels, horror collections, magazines, and record albums. Outside the world of illustration, Powers was known and respected—if not famous—as a "surrealist" painter, favorably compared to the likes of Yves Tanguy, Salvador Dalí, and Arshile Gorky. He was even featured in a four-man show at the Museum of Modern Art in 1952, and New York's Rehn Gallery has displayed his work and placed several pieces in important collections of modern American art.

If we listen to the words of artists and readers influenced by Powers, we begin to sense the astounding impact his work had—especially when we consider that his paintings were almost invariably viewed as 5" × 7" book covers. For a work of art to have any effect at all under such circumstances—much less a momentous influence on both the minds of science fiction readers and the genre itself—bespeaks a very special potency indeed. The profound impression these paperback book covers made on consumers of science fiction is evoked by Rick Lieder.[3] Like countless other fans of all ages, Lieder "began to recognize and buy books with his covers" (23), the artwork of the tiny book as often as not utterly outstripping the imagined world between its covers. For Lieder, Powers's artwork was more than a visual attraction or pulpy titillation. The visions he saw on those many covers came to represent to him "the wonderfully *alien*, the different, the unique. It was a way of seeing, as well as a particular style, that influenced me … unconsciously—in my own career as an artist." And we agree with Lieder's assessment of Powers's stature, his work setting "a standard which should be used as a high-water mark by all artists both in the field and out of it" (24).

Another eloquent artist, Robert Colby, invokes just how vividly this remarkable illustrator leapt from the bookracks into the viewer's mind, forever altering the genre itself even as it became part of the reader's dreams: "Those abstract, ambiguous but evocative shapes on the cover were telling me not to expect anything obvious from what was inside, that wild ideas were at work, that these were important books, a vital part of our modern culture" (22). Yet another appreciator, Mark Rich, says simply that Powers's work "was my world, and Powers's paintings weren't a part that I questioned." For Rich, Powers's illustrations utterly transcended their commercial task. They "reflected a philosophic point of view! They showed a mind at work; they showed that the fiction inside the covers might well reflect endeavors of a fully human nature" (24), giving this young form of fiction a cachet far beyond anything it had known before. Powers's career and influence represent an unprecedented confluence of two separate art forms in the history of our culture.

Given his busy and market-driven career, Powers's art is linked ineluctably to the genre whose vision he defined. His work embodies essential, yet disturbing, qualities inherent in science fiction itself—qualities which textual science fiction is reluctant or unable to fulfill, simply because to do so would obviate the possibility of storytelling. As appreciators like Lieder and Colby have indicated, Powers's vision, like science fiction itself, reaches toward a supernal fusion of flesh and technology—a point where intelligence and matter merge, where creatures, machines, buildings, and landscapes have coalesced, and where all things are connected, all things are possible. This furthest conceivable extrapolation of the future is the place toward which science fiction tales point but cannot reach, for it represents a world without distinctions or chronology, where no stories are possible.

Powers's classic 1957 cover for H.G. Wells's *The Time Machine* epitomizes the new dimension of art that he brought to the genre.[4] It was also was an appropriate one for Powers, because in a sense all science fiction stories are "about" time travel, usually taking us at least a little ways into the future—and once this projection into time has begun, its implications reach precisely toward worlds like the ones Powers drew for us. The figure of the Time Traveller seems both human and alien, at once monumental and lost, as if the extraordinary environment itself made him something other than human. The machine he reaches back towards with a long, tapering arm is itself a tiny spatial paradox, a confection of curvilinear shapes and of sparkling, purest light.

What is that landscape he looks out at, its images so potently evocative that the viewer, too, finds himself transposed into it? And over to the right—what is that monster (or machine) rising on clouds of greyish light, or perhaps emerging in blue spray from a burgundy ocean? What bleak, yet beautiful blending of night and day is represented by the brown sky with its tattered crimson rainbow, filled with the dry streaks of clouds (or dust) and black, unknown forms floating in the sky? The illustration—tiny as it is—

affects us like some hypnagogic vision that follows one into wakefulness, too vivid to stay behind. The very force of this cover highlights the features of Powers's art that are potently disruptive of the genre itself. We find a verbal analogue to this disturbing quality in the text of Wells's novel itself, in the scene depicted on that very cover, when the Time Traveler moves briefly forward to the twilight of the earth—to a time when there is no distinction between daylight and night, to where living creatures seem more like encrustations of rock, and to where "all the sounds of man, the bleating of sheep, the cries of birds, the hum of insects—all that was over" (88–89).

This visit to the edge of time is unbearable to the Time Traveller: "A horror of this great darkness came on me. The cold, that smote to my marrow, and the pain I felt in breathing, overcame me. I shivered, and a deadly nausea seized me." For purposes of our thesis we might view these sentiments as those of the storyteller confronting the world of Powers's paintings. And what must the response of the timebound storyteller be to such a vivid world—albeit a world he reaches toward? Wells describes it accordingly: "Then I felt I was fainting. But a terrible dread of lying helpless in that remote and awful twilight sustained me while I clambered upon the saddle." From a metaphysical point of view, the Time Traveller has been approaching the imminent destruction of all storytelling: "I cannot convey the sense of abominable desolation that hung over the world. The red eastern sky, the northward blackness, the salt Dead Sea, the stony beach crawling with these foul, slow-stirring monsters, the uniform poisonous-looking green of the lichenous plants, the thin air that hurts one's lungs: all contributed to all appalling effect" (87). In time-travel stories, the anagogical tends to become part of the story itself; but fiction, being based on distinctions, must remain timebound and must work with distinctions. Small wonder Wells's hero shuns a world where time is about to end and where opposites have all but merged.

This artistic masterpiece—appearing multiply and in such an absurdly tiny form—is typical of how Powers quietly reshaped the genre. Breaking away from their pulp pedigree, his covers incessantly slip away from representationalism into new forms of abstraction—most notably, one in which the illusion of depth seems to be maintained, even into the far reaches of what would normally be called abstract art. The alleged mass-market illustrator was in fact a covert artistic operative, exploring the intersection between the representational and the non-representational.

A case in point is Powers's masterful cover for the first edition of Clarke's *Reach for Tomorrow* (1956).[5] Here again, the artist experienced the good fortune (a bit rare in his busy career) to illustrate a book worthy of his own brilliance. This remarkable cover was printed in landscape orientation—all but unheard-of for mass-market paperbacks of the day—and he presents us with another indelible vision fusion, melding the representational with the abstract. In this tiny work, a broad cityscape of some kind is rendered in smooth gradations of tan and brown, so far beyond our world that the buildings (or machines or rocks or entities) have the wildness of a desert landscape set against clouds, or distant dust, in a spatial field gorgeously empty and infinite. In the foreground, houses (or craft) silently disregard the laws of gravity, casting pristine shadows on the rose-tinged ground. The lone, tiny figure we see adds a sense of vast scale and of isolate strangeness—some sort of sentry in red standing on the platform of some sort of tower. And to the left, one of those mysterious floating objects has fallen and lies awkwardly on its side—for this is not a newly-minted world but one possessing great age, looking backward endlessly, forward to nothing.

Though we cannot say that the cover of *Reach for Tomorrow* is based on a story or passage from the book, we can still find a character in one of the stories worrying aloud about the horrific impossibility of the end of time: "Have you ever wondered, Jack, what the human race will do when science has discovered everything, when there are no more worlds to be explored, when all the stars have given up their secrets?" (72). This query is from a story called "The Parasite" (1953), in which a sublimely decadent creature from the future feeds off the more vital emotions of the distant past. Once again, characters shudder at the world that all science fiction stories point toward, but cannot touch, and the language evokes fear and the genre's horrifying, fascinating fusion of infinity and nothingness. Working in a pop-culture milieu, with all the anonymity of a Medieval artisan, Powers virtually created a new form within the domain of painting—one in which the artist's ability to maintain illusory space is stretched past its limit, as it fills with increasingly incomprehensible shapes. The viewer has the illusion of perfect impersonality, the visual imagination of the end of time.

The fast-paced, anonymous sweatshop of paperback illustration turned out to be one in which an artist of the first rank could channel his infinite visions. Powers had no time to consider the specific content of his books—but this circumstance merely expanded his potent vision. His challenge was to create some sort of generic, cosmic vision of this most far-reaching type of fiction, true to the spirit of the books he was illuminating, but generally detached from the restrictions of identifiable characters or even physical forms. Thus, when he was hired to depict the wholly invisible creatures of Murray Leinster's 1958 novel *War with the Gizmos*, the result was a breathtaking *tour de force*, seemingly abstract and filled with tortured forms and overstretched lines reminiscent of Gorky, yet still mysteriously "representational"—in the sense that the forms seem to float in an illusory three-dimensional space.[6]

To complement Leinster's yarn, Powers creates a universe of floating abstractions which yet seem human, organic, metamachine-like, and landscape-like—a world in which all stories seem capable of happening at once. It is a universe both quintessentially science-fictional and beyond the pale of textual science fiction. Powers's outrageously inspired cover for this novel gives us a subtle example of the infinite which lies behind the future-reaching storyteller's art. And once again we can peer into the texts to find at least a touch of the ineffable, the anagogical far end which gives science fiction its punch—but too much of which would render it storyless. Leinster is a straightforward writer, not given to stylistic tricks. Yet observe how, in the prologue to *War with the Gizmos*, he gives us at once the flesh and the emptiness, how even his workmanlike prose combines the concrete and physical with the ineffable:

> There is no point, now, in reviewing the controversy about the Gizmos' origin. Some still insist that they came from outer space. This is hard to believe, because a spaceship under Gizmo control is almost impossible to imagine.... [T]he legends of fiends and *djinns* and *efrits* and *ghuls*, and of eerie inhabitants of remote, are singularly convincing when one considers them in connection with Gizmos....
>
> They had the enormous advantage of being totally unreasonable [6].

Since the reader has no idea what a Gizmo is, Leinster is in effect "painting" an illusory space and filling it with incomprehensible objects—just as Powers stretches his forms beyond recognizability.

Once again, we experience in the text the fear and infinite nothingness which lie at the very edge of science fiction. The Gizmos are "unreasonable" just as the end of time was unreasonable for Wells's Time Traveller or the infinitely evolved mind-parasite of Clarke's short story: they afflict the minds of the characters. Leinster's storytelling craft in this prologue to the novel makes this a compelling opener, for the reader doesn't even know the basis for these brief, but sublimely negative, speculations. The author uses inexplicability as a device to intrigue the reader even as his narrator struggles with it (or dismisses it) as the aftermath of some unknown, terrifying adventure. The statement that the Gizmos "had the … advantage of being totally unreasonable" is just a touch of the storyteller's discomfiture at confronting the mind-boggling limit toward which even mainstream, non-visionary science fiction points, and from which dangerous source it gets its power.

Science fiction book covers might seem an unlikely venue for such a development, with time constraints and almost microscopic manner of display, yet fellow illustrator Paul Lehr emphasizes the strange artistic freedom in the field: "In the old days at Berkley Publishing [for whom Powers did hundreds of covers], they let me do pretty much what I wanted, and as a result, the covers were very personal" (Weinberg 177). And Powers's innovative vision perfectly paralleled that of the fictional genre itself: to tell stories of the increasingly untenable, to extrapolate known reality toward something timeless and unknown. The titles of the books he was called upon to illustrate alone betray science fiction's intentions: Robert Spenser Carr's anthology *Beyond Infinity* (1951), Henry Kuttner and C.L. Moore's collection *No Boundaries* (1955), Asimov's *The End of Eternity*.

Powers was not utterly lost in the paperback world he helped to recreate, even as he helped shape the evolution of an entire genre of fiction through his puissant visions. He is recognized as a Surrealist painter, most notably compared with the French Surrealist Yves Tanguy (1900–1955). The two artists' biomorphic imagery and three-dimensional, dreamworld illusionism are indeed strikingly similar, and Simon Wilson's reference to Tanguy's "landscapes of the mind" recalls much of the commentary on Powers's work.[7] Powers especially distinguishes himself from his artistic cousin by his career-long exploration of the boundary between representation and abstraction. Some of the shapes floating in Powers's more radical covers recall those of Gorky, Jean Arp, and Joan Miro—and yet one always senses that Powers's forms float in some sort of paradoxical landscape, constantly approaching an impossible visual representation of a non–Euclidean universe.

Science fiction writers themselves work with dichotomies parallel to those of Powers's art, but as we might expect, the storytellers are by force of their craft and/or their own dispositions obliged to work more heavily in the areas we have termed "fleshy" and "timebound." These authors, too, like to bring the reader in contact with the infinitely ineffable—but in the texts themselves it must remain only a brief contact, very often taking the form of an inexplicable emotional struggle, almost always involving fear and the evocation of infinity/nothingness.

If Powers seemed always to grasp the essence of the genre, sometimes succeeding in profiling the essence of even the most complex of science fiction classics, his cover for A.E. van Vogt's 1940 novel *Slan* is an inspired case in point.[8] Here, author and illustrator approach the threatening strangeness inherent to the genre from perspectives opposite yet complementary to one another. Powers's cover is a strangely informative *inverse* to van Vogt's text, yet they intertwine marvelously. Slan is told from the viewpoint of the embodiments of the fearful unknown—the genetically superior beings known as *slan*. In this story, the ordinary human characters recoil from the mysterious mutants just as Wells's Time Traveller recoiled from the anagogical future he confronts, or Clarke's parasitic host from the superior, yet degenerate, creature occupying his mind, or even the people in *War with the Gizmos* from the "unreasonableness" of the invaders.

Van Vogt lets us see in from the ineffable edge of science fiction. With his customary brilliance, however, he employs the slans' telepathic abilities so that they feel what the humans feel, placing us inside the mind of a young, still-undeveloped slan. Thus, van Vogt the storyteller has it both ways. To Jommy, the boy-slan, it is men's fearful thoughts that are threatening:

> The steady wave of vagueness that washed from the crowds all around grew into a swirl of mind clamor....
>
> The men ... were crossing the street, their faces dark with an expression of an unpleasant duty that had to be done. The thought of that unpleasantness, the hatred that went with it, was a shadow in their minds that leaped out at Jommy. It puzzled him even in this moment when he was concentrating on escape [5–6].

To complement this approach through contrast, evoking the inevitable dual qualities of fear and infinite nothingness, Powers's cover seems to present the slan as they might look in the deepest unconscious of the fearful humans of the novel. We see a coiling, smoky creature vaguely resembling a squid or octopus, and the monstrous, half-formed mouth of a screaming creature (prescient of H.R. Giger's 1979 *Alien*) with its tendrils hanging—truly a monster defying all our distinctions and laws as it sags down menacingly from a white nothingness. *That's* how the humans in this novel feel! And of course, given visual art's capacity for ambiguity, it may be that Powers's cover depicts the human psyche as perceived by the telepathic, hunted slan. It may be fear painted from both sides at once.

Some science fiction writers are well aware of how the thrust of the science fiction imagination moves toward an annihilation of the possibility of storytelling. In his "Afterthoughts" to the collection *Tales of Known Space: The Universe of Larry Niven* (1975), Larry Niven describes two dilemmas resulting from his own inventiveness. His Known Space series "ends" with *Ringworld* (1970):

> Though I've written stories in the series since *Ringworld*, writing that novel made me realize how tangled and complex my basic assumptions had become. There were too many unlikely miracles left over from individual stories. For example, from *World of Ptavvs* [1966] came a stasis field so useful that every story set later in time must be examined for reasons why a stasis field would not solve the problem.[9]

The practicing author—faced with the need to project forward in time, where fewer and fewer story possibilities occur—must continually invent and reinvent the concepts which will ultimately bring him to the edge of time. As he describes some further complications in the Known Space series, Niven's reaction is a lighter version of that of Wells's Time Traveller, seen as the storyteller reacting to a Powers landscape: "But the story was already too complex; I couldn't open that can of worms too!" As for the eradication of distinctions, Niven acknowledges this as well, when he tells the reader, "If you want more stories in the series you can make them up yourself" (223). Just as Powers's figures meld into the landscape, so Niven allows the boundary between reader and writer to disappear, as he invites the reader to step into the void of fear and infinite nothingness which is the essence of creativity for this genre.

If Powers's art does depict an alluring edge toward which science fiction stories are drawn, then we might seek out at least a few verbal depictions that seem like analogues to Powers's illustrations. In Stanislaw Lem's *Solaris* (1961), the vision of the protean, enigmatic planet seems indeed to reverse our *modus operandi* so far, and verbally evoke something Powers might draw. Here, the narrator describes some of the mysterious formations of this possibly-sentient world:

> The mind-bending architecture of this central pillar is held in place by vertical shafts of a gelatinous, almost liquid consistency, constantly gushing upwards out of wild crevasses. Meanwhile, the entire trunk is surrounded by a belt of snow foam, seething with great bubbles of gas. From the center toward the periphery, powerful buttresses spin out and are coated with streams of ductile matter rising out of the ocean depths. Simultaneously the gelatinous geysers are converted into mobile columns that proceed to extrude tendrils that reach out in clusters.... [T]hey call to mind the gills of an embryo, except that they ooze trickles of pinkish "blood" and a dark green secretion.[10]

The formation being described is spoken of as "'illustrating,' sometimes contradicting, various laws of physics"—much like Powers's structures—and Lem might be describing other, machinelike images seen frequently in Powers's painting—except, as Lem says, "they resemble no machine which it is within the power of mankind to build." Lem is capable of linguistic feats which virtually parallel Powers's visual illusions. He speaks of the planet's formations as solid entities, intimately if problematically involved with three-dimensional space and the laws of physics. At the same time (and note the passage's almost prissy concern with matters of sequential ordering) Lem evokes a disturbing sentience within the complex interactions of the structures, all confounded by his insistent use of the passive voice.

And what does the artist himself have to say? We normally expect silence from artists—especially as to the sort of parallel between the visual and the textual we have been tracing here—but in his 1983 portfolio called *Spacetimewarp*, Powers collected sixteen of his paintings, mostly illustrations of science fiction novels, and wrote neologistic, fantastic, funny, science-fiction-sounding captions for each painting, riffing fragments of his own mythology, giving us a piquant taste of what sort of language his own paintings might inspire, if they were to come before the stories.[11] Powers's world of *fFlar* seems to be situated appropriately at some phenomenally distant future, and/or in a parallel universe. (Plate 2 apparently occurs "on a day the artist designates as the αφπ 21-θth of Δγ, 17,700,426 A.D.") What is going on here? Well, explanations of the hyper-technology of a near-infinite future—inasmuch as they are even ventured—become themselves fantastic, even poetic; the two halves of science fiction's dichotomy become, from our perspective back here in the abysmal past, intertwined. After all, in the unimaginably distant future, if we extrapolate science as advancing continually, science itself moves beyond our ken and becomes a creature of the imagination.

Powers's blurbs for *Spacetimewarp* are rife with orthographical fun, puns, sound-games, and often self-mocking parody—a use of language which has all the qualities to take us, snickering, to the edge of time. One remarkable painting is captioned as follows: "Gog-fFlar, Quasarquark of fFlar, Gog of Magog, God of Goads, Goad of Goats, Guard of Groans, Groan of Groins, Gert of Frobes, Frobe of Forces...." The shapes in that painting (originally the cover for John D. MacDonald's 1951 novel *Wine of the Dreamers*) are quintessential Powers figures—entities (or objects, or both) which seem to have been deconstructed and reconfigured so many times, in so many impossibly convoluted ways, that they exist as ur-forms, floating between abstraction and tangibility, obeying physical laws which themselves have become subjugated to the powers of mind. Fitting, then, that the words of the caption should echo and meld until language itself becomes a Joycean, aleatory music. In general, our use of proper names seems intended to solidify the object being named, and Powers's comedic verbal echoes of the sort of formal reading of titles for potentates we all have heard undo the very sense of massification such strings of names seem intended to achieve.

It is also significant, of course, that Powers is not in the position of the actual science fiction storyteller. He is free to bounce crazily from one thought to another, playing games, without the responsibility of making connections or stringing things together. His "scientific" explanations are parodies of science fiction exposition, as with the inner jacket of the portfolio sleeve: "The destabilization of the concept of Time as a function of Space, which the astral-guru/physicist G* first introduced into the Metamanual of Infraquasarian Zen, has led to the isolation of Spacetimewarp as the underlying function of Simultaneous/Alternate Universe Projection." The central notion in this passage of surreal science is that of melting ("destabilization," "Spacetimewarp," the concept of simultaneous/alternate universes). Thus, Powers does playfully with language what he does forcefully with art. In this case, he echoes "science talk"—that fast-paced rattling off of concepts and theories that seems ironically to overwhelm rather than enlighten the intellect—while his hell-bent melding of morphemes takes us to the fearful, funny edge where nothingness meets infinity.

The edge-of-time quality we have been discussing in Powers's illustrations is indeed one of the key elements in many—possibly all—classic works of science fiction. In different ways, the canonical works of the genre push us toward that impossible realm where distinctions disappear, time stops—and storytelling itself must end. It is the genre's unbelievable good fortune to have stumbled and then seized upon Richard Powers as its definitive visual conjurer—the artistic genius who painted these visions for decades, till they became our dreams.

Afterword

The ready accessibility of Powers's work on the internet now allows us to more fully perceive the artist's skilled manipulation of indeterminate space, so the illusion of three-dimensionality itself becomes an expressive tool. The manipulation creates a range of effects, from clearly-defined (though usually alien) landscapes to relatively abstract surfaces. As noted with the covers for *Reach for Tomorrow* and *The Time Machine*, for example, we are seemingly looking at landscapes, complete with horizon lines and solid shapes which appear bound by gravity, and skies filled with cosmic forms of some kind. By contrast, the cover art for Theodore Sturgeon's *Caviar* (Ballantine 1959) and Michael Moorcock's *The Winds of Limbo* (originally *The Fireclown*; Paperback Library 1969) is abstract. The illusion of depth is almost entirely absent, with no ground, no gravity, no evident horizon lines. The figures, or shapes, lack solidity, and the eye views interacting abstractions on the painting's surface. These images may suggest three-dimensionality, and the near-figures are ever-so-slightly humanoid, but on a spectrum between abstraction and surrealism, they fall closer to the work of Wassily Kandinsky than the more solid imaginaries of Salvador Dalí.

Between these extremes, Powers evokes a range of illusions in which the "space" of paintings themselves exists to a varying degree. For example, while the cover for Robert Wells's *The Spacejacks* (Berkley 1975) may depict neither horizon nor gravity, it still conveys solidity. Powers's two covers for J.G. Ballard's *The Voices of Time and Other Stories*

(Berkley 1962; Medallion 1966) provide some grounding elements, but in both cases the illusion of space is stretched or suspended, losing the depth of field we normally associate with landscape. More equivocal is the cover art for Keith Laumer's *The Shapechanger* (Berkley 1972), which seems to depict abstraction solidified by depth, this time with a small but discernible figure, the half-suggestion of a face emerging from what appears to be torn from the painting's surface. This use of indeterminate space has a powerful expressive effect especially well-suited to Powers's covers for horror anthologies. They often present an extreme absence of three-dimensionality, with monstrous "faces" peering out from entangled lines, as if space itself has been crushed together. As solid forms give way to compressed linear patterns, the effect is claustrophobic and suitably horrific, as with *The Graveyard Reader*; editor Groff Conklin's introduction reports that Powers's image inspired him to collect these stories in the first place.[12]

As evidence of how Powers explores the depiction of indeterminate space, we have only to compare his two versions of the cover design first introduced in 1956 for *Reach for Tomorrow*. Our description of this cover in the essay examines it in terms of "melding the representational with the abstract." It shows all the markers of three-dimensionality—shadows, the solidity of what look like buildings, a horizon line, gravity, even a lone human figure to measure scale—yet also launches the viewer in the direction of the abstract. Like Powers's cover of Clarke's *Expedition to Earth* (Ballantine 1953) discussed by George Slusser,[13] it prompts us to ask, "What is that?" and "Where am I?" Thirty years later, Powers "reinvented" his *Reach for Tomorrow* cover as *Mars Cityscape*, which appeared as the hardback cover design for Donald A. Wollheim and Arthur W. Saha's *The 1987 Annual World's Best Science Fiction* (1987) and was displayed at the Hayden Planetarium in New York City in 1991.[14] Recreated on a grand scale (32" × 60"), it takes a darker turn, losing its original color palate and even the original sun-yellow with a red corona. Objects may have shadows, but overall *Mars Cityscape* is much less solid, what heretofore suggested buildings now rendered as abstract lines and the lone figure deconstructed into a vaguely skeletal outline. Only with Jane and Howard Frank's reproductions, drawn from their extensive science fiction and fantasy art collection, has the general public been privy to the full grandeur and scope of this painting.[15]

With publication of images from the Franks' art collection at the turn of the century, we became aware of the availability of some paintings behind the cover art—and how much more fully the viewer can appreciate Powers's artistry when it is not just rendered on 5" × 7" paperback covers that partly obscure the original art work with typography announcing title and authorship. Jane Frank's *The Art of Richard Powers* (2001) brought to the fore the considerable interest of other collectors, who graciously granted rights of reproduction to her—and pointed to the healthy pursuit of Powers's art through auction houses and galleries.[16] Frank's book also includes a detailed biography of Powers by his oldest son, Richard Gid Powers,[17] who shared with her a letter Ray Bradbury wrote shortly after his father's death in 1996, acknowledging the influence of Powers's cover art: "Quite often it was your father's work that caught my attention and helped propel me into buying a particular book!" (48). Another measure of Powers's influence on a prominent writer appears on the back cover of Frank's book, which quotes Moorcock: "[Powers's] superior aesthetics, which still overshadow most rivals, were actually what started me reading modern sf—with Alfred Bester's *The Stars My Destination*, the cover for which perfectly captured the mood of that great American novel."

But blogs, built by everyday *aficionados* of Powers's cover art and continually and assiduously updated, are best spreading the word and garnering him the kind of attention his work truly deserves. These amateur forums display a panoply of cover art, duplicated and analyzed across a wide array of ongoing, interactive communications. From the Pinterest interest group's page of Powers's covers, through Sean Rohde's Powers Compendium, to The Richard M. Powers Cyber Art Gallery, viewers can explore and research the range and history of Powers's love affair with the worlds of science fiction—and discover how science fiction's boundaries have been pushed beyond its own aspirations.[18] Nonetheless, with the number of Powers's book covers variously estimated at 800 to 900, it remains imperative to consult official sites that consolidate, correct, and verify an authoritative Powers bibliography. In this respect, Powers science fiction art scholarship is indebted to The SF Encyclopedia Picture Gallery and Internet Speculative Fiction Database.[19]

Besides influencing fellow visual artists like Vincent Di Fate and writers and critics of science fiction like Gary Westfahl, Powers has inspired creative artists in other fields.[20] In 1985, for example, Powers's painting "Creator" prompted Girard St. Charles to write the ekphrastic poem "A Being" (1985), framing it with the lines "Whose Body is a World/ With two Suns for Eyes" and "Emerging in Circles of Concentric Light/ From within that Crystal Nexus."[21] Even more impressive is how Powers's visual universe had a marked hypnotic effect on musician Andy Partridge, founding member of the band XTC. As a boy, he checked out novels from the library for the sole purpose of gazing at Powers's covers. He describes how he would "disappear" into those covers: "I'd be in those landscapes, and I'd be kind of hearing sound."[22] Years later he tried to capture the sounds he heard in his head—"like chasing a sensation"—turning his experience of synaesthesia into a twelve-track album of "aural sculptures" entitled *Powers* (2010). Although Partridge likens his act of transformation to that of Modest Mussorgsky's *Pictures at an Exhibition* (1874), he does so with a difference. Rather than working from a singular emotional impression, like Mussorgsky when surrounded by paintings by recently-deceased friend Viktor Harmann, Partridge inhabits the Powers universe multiple times, compelling him to interpret it as a series of unique harmonics.

Powers's reputation has grown and flourished over the past three decades. He was the Artist Guest of Honor at the 1991 World Science Fiction Conference in Chicago, and posthumously elected to the Science Fiction Hall of Fame in 2008, along with his publisher-friends Ian and Betty Ballantine, William Gibson, and Rod Serling. Yet as recently as 2011 Rick Poynor qualified that recognition factor: while calling Powers a "book cover *auteur*," and initiating a dialogue among informed correspondents who are especially responsive to the cover designs for Ballard's *The Voices of Time*, he nonetheless sadly reports that Powers was never once mentioned at the Courtauld Institute's conference "Surrealism, Science Fiction and Comic Books" held earlier that year in London.[23] And Powers is only obliquely acknowledged in another 2011 article, "The Stars of Modern SF Pick the Best Science Fiction," for when Clute, Moorcock, and Gibson are interviewed, it takes a Powers expert to recognize that the editions cited—Clifford Simak's *City* (Perma 1953) and Bester's *The Stars My Destination* (Signet 1956; 1957)—were published with Powers's distinctive covers.[24] So the educative process still needs to continue, as it does with a series of articles about science fiction cover art in the *Daily Beast* by Mark Dery, inaugurated with a 2015 piece, "Richard Powers's Pulp Surrealism," which prompted Charlie Jane Anders to write "How Richard Powers Made Science Fiction Book Covers Strange" two days later.[25] Even as acknowledgments and accolades roll in—Powers was elected to the Society of Illustrators Hall of Fame in 2016—we throw out the gauntlet to those who appreciate Powers's science fiction artwork to keep spreading the word.

Notes

1. John Clute, "Great Illustrators," *SF: The Illustrated Encyclopedia* (New York: Dorling Kindersley, 1995), 241.

2. Robert Weinberg, *A Biographical Dictionary of Science Fiction and Fantasy Artists* (Westport, CT: Greenwood, 1988), 20; a parenthetical page reference is to this edition. Besides providing an excellent historical overview of science fiction art, Weinberg has written a detailed account of Powers's life and influence, including a lengthy (but still partial) list of the artist's published work (see 217–222). We are especially indebted to Willie Siros, longtime cataloguer of the L.W. Currey Science Fiction and Fantasy Collection at the Harry Ransom Humanities Research Center at the University of Texas at Austin, for his full perspective on Powers's life and art. Siros supplied us with bibliographic printouts of Powers's cover art, as well as putting us in touch with John Anderson, who has been compiling his own checklist of Powers's artwork (last copyrighted 1988). We are also grateful to the Eaton Collection for permission to consult the extensive Powers holdings at the University of California, Riverside. More recent resources for the interested student of the Powers canon exist on the Worldwide Web, including C. Jerry Kutner's The Richard M. Powers Cyber Art Gallery (home.earthlink.net/~cjk5/) and Sean Rohde's The Richard M. Powers Compendium (http://powerscompendium.tumblr.com/). Jane Frank has also published a book featuring many of Powers's paintings, *The Art of Richard Powers* (London: Paper Tiger, 2001); see too her *Science Fiction and Fantasy Artists of the Twentieth Century: A Biographical Dictionary* (Jefferson, NC: McFarland, 2009), 384–389.

3. Rick Lieder (with Kathe Koja), "A Richard Powers Appreciation," *ReaderCon 5* (Cambridge, MA: privately printed, 1992), 23. Parenthetical page references to other Lieder quotations, as well as those from Robert Colby and Mark Rich, are to this souvenir book, which features Powers's artwork and includes another partial bibliography (26–29), excerpted from Anderson. Seven years earlier, Powers was also the featured artist for "The First Occasional Lone Star Sci Fi Convention and Chili Cookoff" (Austin, Texas, 1985).

4. Powers produced two covers of *The Time Machine* for Berkley, in 1957 and 1963, which differ only slightly in coloring and sharpness of outline; we are referring to the earlier one and citing its pagination in the quotations which follow. Although we suspect Powers always signed his cover artwork, his signature does not necessarily appear on the final product.

5. Ballantine Books published Powers's cover illustration for *Reach for Tomorrow* in two formats—one a full-length landscape turned to the horizontal, the other a partial reproduction of the same painting cut to vertical. Our references here are to the fuller version; parenthetical page references are to the identical text of both editions.

6. Parenthetical Leinster page references are to this edition of *War with the Gizmos* (Greenwich, CT: Fawcett, 1958).

7. Simon Wilson, *Surrealist Painting* (London: Phaidon, 1991), 78. Wilson is here studying the school of "oneiric" painters, whose work seems "dream-inspired."

8. Parenthetical van Vogt page references are to this edition of *Slan* (New York: Ballantine, 1961), whose cover illustration is especially reminiscent of Powers's studies in horror—yet another of his specialties in cover art.

9. Larry Niven, *Tales of Known Space* (New York: Ballantine, 1975), 222. A parenthetical page reference is to this edition.

10. Stanislaw Lem, *Solaris* (1961; New York: Berkley, 1971), 127.

11. The collection, published by Doubleday, is self-described as "sixteen full-color paintings of fFlar and fFlarians suitable for framing." Most of the reproductions are about 10" × 12", all on slick paper.

12. Groff Conklin, "Introduction," *The Graveyard Reader*, ed. Conklin (New York: Ballantine, 1958), 7–8.

13. George Slusser, "Introduction: The Iconology of Science Fiction and Fantasy Art," *Unearthly Visions: Approaches to Science Fiction and Fantasy Art*, ed. Gary Westfahl, Slusser, and Kathleen Church Plummer (Westport, CT: Greenwood, 2002), 8–10.

14. Powers initially planned *Mars Cityscape* as the centerpiece of *The Asfic Penteuch*, the other four paintings to be reconfigured from previous cover art—including ones that had already been reincarnated in the portfolio for *Spacetimewarp* (1983)—but when this project fell through, he sold the painting to Jane and Howard Frank.

15. Besides Jane Frank's aforementioned book, which features a double-page opening of *Mars Cityscape* (112–113), she and her husband had already published a reproduction of it in *The Frank Collection: A Showcase of the World's Finest Fantastic Art* (London: Paper Tiger, 1999), 66–67. These books were followed by *Great Fantasy Art Themes from the Frank Collection* (London: Paper Tiger, 2003), which highlights Powers's cover for Gregory Gerald's *Neutron Stars* (Fawcett 1977).

16. Heritage Auctions (Dallas, Texas), for example, held an online auction in 2008 with an extensive list of Powers's paintings, some still listed as available through the Richard Powers Estate; Jane Frank's agency,

Worlds of Wonder, now represents the estate in sales and licensing of Powers's art for reproduction (as described in "Wow-Art" at www.wow-art.com). Baldwin Hill Art & Framing (Natick, Massachusetts) previously represented Powers's fine art works and in 2015 sponsored an exhibition, "Exploring Richard Powers," that was so big it needed to arrange for a larger gallery space to show it all. During the 1980s, Powers began attending science fiction conventions, sometimes displaying his artwork and occasionally offering individual pieces for sale. Since his death, the prices for his paintings have skyrocketed.

17. Jane Frank, *The Art of Richard Powers*, 11–29. A parenthetical page reference to the text is to this edition.

18. Richard M. Powers, Pinterest, at pinterest.com/jbc85/richard-m-powers/; the other websites are referenced above. Rohde's compendium has at its core the checklist prepared by Anderson in the late 1980s, referenced in our original essay, while Kutner's gallery features mini-essays discussing Powers's covers for Sturgeon's *More Than Human* (Ballantine 1953), Philip Jose Farmer's *To Your Scattered Bodies Go* (Berkley 1971), Ballard's *Voices of Time* (Berkley 1966), Philip K. Dick's *The Transmigration of Timothy Archer* (Timescape 1982), and Samuel R. Delany's *The Jewel-Hinged Jaw* (Berkley 1978). Two blogs we especially recommend are maintained by John A. Davis, whose goal is "to provide a hub for sharing information about Richard Powers and his art, as well as interesting observations about his process" (Richard Powers Art Blog, at richardpowersart.blogspot.com), and Jerry Frissen, who discussed 34 covers over a four-month period in 2011 (Show and Tell: Le Blog de Jerry Frissen, at http://www.humano.com/blog/Le-Blog-de-Jerry-Frissen/1). When conducting online searches, entering the artist's middle initial "M" (for Michael) helps to avoid confusion with novelist Richard Powers, but sometimes dropping the "M" is actually key to successful searches.

19. The SF Encyclopedia Picture Gallery (The Encyclopedia of Science Fiction, at http://sf-encyclopedia.uk/gallery.php)—a search for "Richard Powers" on July 18, 2017, yielded 269 cover images; and Richard Powers, The Internet Speculative Fiction Database, at http://www.isfdb.org/cgi-bin/ea.cgi?1811 (with links to numerous cover images).

20. Vincent di Fate, "Foreword," *The Art of Richard Powers*, 6–10; Gary Westfahl, "Artists in Wonderland: Toward a True History of Science Fiction Art," *Unearthly Visions*, 28.

21. Girard St. Charles, "A Being," The Richard M. Powers Cyber Art Gallery, at http://home.earthlink.net/~cjk5/poem.html.

22. Partridge quotations are taken from his 2010 interview with Todd Bernhardt (XTC Blog, at chalkhills.org/articles/XTCFans20100912.html), shortly after his *Powers* limited edition of 500 sold out; Bernhardt replays all twelve tracks, encouraging Partridge to dissect and explore his creative process. In response to high demand, APE House issued another limited release of its *Powers* CD in 2017.

23. Rick Poynor, "Unearthly Powers: Surrealism and Science Fiction" Design Observer, May 19, 2011, at http://designobserver.com/feature/unearthly-powers-surrealism-and-sf/27128. Despite Powers's omission from the conference, when conference organizer Gavin Parkinson later edited a collection of essays drawn from the 2011 event, *Surrealism, Science Fiction and Comics* (Liverpool: Liverpool University Press, 2016), he illustrated one of his own contributions, "Surrealism, Science Fiction and UFOs in the 1950s: 'Myth' in France Before Roland Barthes," with Powers's front and back covers for Clarke's *Expedition to Earth* (120–121). Poynor's discussion of Ballard's *The Voices of Time* is relevant to Christopher Priest's choice for the *Guardian* article cited below. Poynor also notes that the *Guardian* article was written to help publicize the soon-to-be mounted British Library exhibition "Out of This World."

24. "The Stars of Modern SF Pick the Best Science Fiction," *The Guardian*, May 14, 2011, at https://www.theguardian.com/books/2011/may/14/science-fiction-authors-choice.

25. Mark Dery, "Richard Powers's Pulp Surrealism," The Daily Beast, March 15, 2015, at http://www.thedailybeast.com/cover-story-richard-powerss-pulp-surrealism; Charlie Jane Anders, "How Richard Powers Made Science Fiction Book Covers Strange," Gizmodo, March 17, 2015, at http://io9.gizmodo.com/how-richard-powers-made-science-fiction-book-covers-str-1692015738.

The Science Fiction of Medicine

(1996 Eaton Conference)

H. Bruce Franklin

What is called "modern medicine" or "Western medicine" emerged in the nineteenth century as part of the same historical process that generated another characteristically "modern" or "Western" phenomenon: science fiction. The Industrial Revolution of the late eighteenth century led, as we all know, to the ever-accelerating development of science and technology, which have continually transformed both the material and cultural environments that we inhabit. We beings of the early twenty-first century can hardly imagine a world that is *not* being changed by technology, and our conceptions of time, space, matter, mind, and human destiny are all products of this environment. This consciousness is of course the very heart of science fiction.

Meanwhile, nothing enters our daily life more dramatically than disease and medicine. So it is no surprise that for almost two centuries, science fiction has been exploring the terms "disease" and "medicine"—with all their problematics. After the gloomy twilight of the fading years of the twentieth century, the period which many have called "postmodern," this exploration seems to be ever more relevant. For we are now also seeing our own bodily existence in the ambiguous dawning light of a new century which may make the most grandiose scientific fantasies of the past and present seem primitive—and innocent.

We are all aware of the contradictions. On one hand we know about the marvels of medical technology—genetic engineering, magnetic resonance imaging, organ transplants, arthroscopic surgery, *in vitro* fertilization, cyborg fantasies materializing as we mechanize the body and vitalize machinery, boundless promises of health and life. On the other hand we see all around us a disintegrating health delivery system, closed and understaffed hospitals, medical dollars and time gobbled up by endless bureaucratic paper pushing, the resurgence of supposedly archaic diseases like tuberculosis and lurking ones like ebola, epidemics of AIDS, drug addiction, and cancer, and of course the headlong plunge into the vortex of what we should properly call *mis*managed care, which blatantly makes profits, not health, the goal of medicine. And if the individual's life *is* extended, where does it end? In the abyss of a nursing home? As an appendage to life-support machinery? Or with the mercies of a Dr. Kevorkian? Our ability to arrest the processes of death, without necessarily restoring health, gives a new and biting relevance to Edgar Allan Poe's 1845 story "The Facts in the Case of M. Valdemar," in which a man dying of tuberculosis is kept in a state of mesmeric suspension until he rots into "a nearly liquid mass of loathsome—of detestable putridity."[1]

To use a fashionable slogan of the day, let's go back to basics. In fact, let's begin with the most basic fact of life: death. We human beings are "*mor*tals." Our essential dialectic is that of life and death. As soon as we attain life we begin the inexorable process of moving toward death. So is death—that essential part of humanity—a disease? And can it be cured?

Four celebrated works of science fiction—Mary Shelley's *Frankenstein, Or, The Modern Prometheus* (1818, 1831), Olaf Stapledon's *Star Maker* (1937), Greg Bear's *Blood Music* (1985), and Octavia E. Butler's *Parable of the Sower* (1993)—offer a continuum from the early nineteenth century to the late twentieth century, displaying the shifting problematics of "disease" and "medicine."

The most famous doctor in science fiction (who of course was not a doctor at all but a college dropout—we seem to have some sort of cultural imperative that makes us call him doctor) begins his quest by seeking to "banish disease from the human frame, and render man invulnerable to any but a violent death." Possessed by this ambition, Victor Frankenstein becomes "capable of bestowing animation upon lifeless matter."[2] But, one asks, would lifeless matter find animation to be a state of health? Or, from its presumably deathless point of view, would life appear as a disease?

In his 1937 masterpiece *Star Maker*, Olaf Stapledon describes an attempt by our future cosmos, trapped in the late stages of the heat death of the universe but now possessed of a cosmic consciousness, to reach back through time to establish contact with the vast primeval nebulae from which the first stars are being formed. But the gigantic nebulae, whom Stapledon endows with a kind of pre-conscious meditative consciousness, can only experience what is happening to them as "a strange sickness":

> The outer fringes of their tenuous flesh began to concentrate into little knots. These became in time grains of intense, congested fire. In the void between, there was nothing left but a few stray atoms. At first the complaint was no more serious than some trivial rash on a man's skin; but later it spread into the deeper tissues of the nebula.

The awakened cosmos of the far future attempts to explain to the nebulae that what seems their disintegration and death is in reality the birth of a far richer and more complex universe, but this proves futile, as Stapledon explains in one of his most spectacular metaphors: "As well might a man seek to comfort the disintegrating germ-cell from which he himself sprang by telling it about his own successful career in human society."[3]

Half a century after *Star Maker*, Greg Bear's 1985 novel *Blood Music* projects a cosmic transformation that originates as a disease introduced into his own body by another modern Prometheus, a failed doctor now working as researcher developing "Medically Applicable Biochips" for a corporation in La Jolla, California. When he turns the cells of his own body into a hyperintelligent entity, this late-twentieth-century doctor begins to transmute the human species into the progenitor of "an intelligent plague" with a transcendent "purpose"—which is to reshape some of the fundamental principles of the universe.[4]

Octavia E. Butler's 1993 novel *Parable of the Sower* envisions a more mundane and much bleaker future. Both the environment and the social infrastructure have collapsed, unleashing the most virulent physical and psychological diseases. A drug originally developed to help victims of Alzheimer's disease has been converted into a designer drug named pyro, that creates mobs of pyromaniacs.[5] For most people, no medical services at all are available, and the only doctor we meet is a 57-year-old former family physician who can no longer practice medicine amid society's ruins.

But we must first look more intently at the book which looms over science fiction, and indeed over modern society, the book that Brian W. Aldiss has incisively labeled the "first great myth of the industrial age,"[6] with its gigantic twin shape of Victor Frankenstein and his monstrous alter ego. Whether or not we consider *Frankenstein* as the fountainhead of modern science fiction, we must recognize that no literary work has penetrated our culture more deeply. Of course *Frankenstein* is everywhere in medical science fiction. Some characters, like the professor in C.L. Moore's 1944 story "No Woman Born" who resurrects a beautiful entertainer from a fire that has almost devoured her body and transforms her into one of the first female cyborgs, actually wonder whether or not "I am Frankenstein."[7] In Bear's *Blood Music* not only does a scientist come to consider himself both "Frankenstein and the monster" but the nurses in an ordinary hospital refer to the high-tech diagnostic area as the "Frankenstein wing" (58).

Why should *Frankenstein, Or, The Modern Prometheus*, a novel written by a teenager and published back in 1818, have such sustained relevance? If we view the book through the lens of disease and medicine, its relevance comes into sharp focus. And we can also understand why Mary Shelley, just eight years later, was to publish another wildly innovative novel, *The Last Man*, one of the first science fiction visions of the end of the world.

Mary Shelley was looking forward into the century in which modern Western medicine was created, the century of Ignaz Semmelweis, William T.G. Morton, Louis Pasteur, Theodor Billroth, Joseph Lister, and Robert Koch. Frankenstein was to have a long line of science-fiction successors, including Drs. Rappaccini, Chillingworth, Heidenhoff, Jekyll, and Moreau, while science fiction itself was being recreated by such famous doctors as Oliver Wendell Holmes, Silas Weir Mitchell, and Arthur Conan Doyle.

To comprehend the relevance of Shelley's achievement to our medical environment today, we need to look at the medical environment of her day, including both its history and its direct effects on her own life.

The swift rise of Western medicine over the past two centuries or so looks especially spectacular because it was starting from such an abysmal level. Throughout the middle ages, European medicine, like that in most societies then in Asia, Africa, and what we now call the Americas, was based mainly on empirical methodology, passed on orally from generation to generation. Because the exceptionally large skull of human babies often necessitates assistance in the birth process, all peoples have had to learn the basic principles of obstetrics. In Europe, as elsewhere around the world, the particular people who provided obstetric care were of course almost all women. Because Europe was largely agricultural, other medical tasks also fell largely to village healers, who were usually women. These healers developed techniques for resetting broken bones and performing other operations. They learned to diagnose a variety of diseases. They provided contraceptives and performed abortions. They assembled a massive pharmacology of herbal remedies, many of which are still in use today. For example, they used ergot derivatives to relieve pain and to induce uterine contractions to eject the placenta after birth, just as ergot derivatives are used today. They used belladonna to inhibit uterine contractions when miscarriage threatened. They used foxglove (that is, digitalis) to treat heart disease (not until 1785 did a practitioner of "modern" medicine, William Withering, research this important drug, and his discovery came from observation of its successful use in folk medicine). The healers had a wide assortment of herbal pain-killers, digestive aids, and anti-inflammatory agents.[8] These healers, like their contemporaries around the world—as well as most medical practitioners today—also used incantations and rituals to promote the psychological component of their healing arts.

Because these healers were mainly women, and because they excluded men from the scenes of birth, they always posed something of a threat to male prerogatives. They also posed a threat to the Church, which of course excluded them entirely from the rival profession of priest, who was supposed to be able to cure diseases through divine intervention. But their most direct threat was to the *profession* of medicine, which was to be reserved for a handful of men who studied at universities. In 1221, Holy Roman Emperor Frederick II decreed that no one could practice medicine until he had been publicly approved by the masters of the University of Salerno. This was the century when the witch hunts began.

From the thirteenth through the seventeenth centuries, just as the all-male university-trained medical profession was becoming hegemonic, the women village healers found themselves labeled as witches. Tortured until they confessed that their powers derived from Satan, they were then hanged or burned alive. The European witch hunts killed at least hundreds of thousands and perhaps as many as two million people, mostly women. By the time it was over, the infrastructure of the traditional European health care system had been shattered. In its place was a system that largely disdained empirical methods, basing itself on theory inherited from classical texts and using a variety of medical instruments derived from developing technology. What we call "modern" or "Western" or "scientific" medicine—as if these were interchangeable terms—arose from the ruins of a medicine that was probably more scientific than the early forms of its successor.

The relative backwardness of European medicine by the eighteenth century can be glimpsed from the fact that one of the exceedingly few successes in disease prevention, inoculation against smallpox, came from a practice long in use in the Arab world, brought back to England by an English woman who had herself been a victim of smallpox before her stay in Turkey. An early work of American science fiction, Mary Griffith's 1836 utopia entitled *Three Hundred Years Hence*, used this example to show how men tend to ignore women's contributions to medicine and science. For, as Griffith pointed out, it was Lady Mary Wortley Montagu who introduced "into England the practice of inoculation for the small-pox," thus saving "thousands of lives" and preventing "hideous deformity, deeply scarred faces, from being universal."[9]

By the eighteenth century, "it was possible for male practitioners to make serious inroads into that last preserve of female healing—midwifery. Nonprofessional male practitioners—'barber-surgeons'—led the assault in England, claiming technical superiority on the basis of their use of the obstetrical forceps. (The forceps were legally classified as a surgical instrument, and women were legally barred from surgical practice)."[10] By the early nineteenth century, university-trained professional doctors—all male—had become the main deliverers of health care in Europe, England, and America for the upper and middle classes, especially in urban settings. Most had been taught to rely on what were called "heroic" measures: massive bleeding, huge doses of laxatives and cathartics—including calomel, a form of mercury (mercury chloride)—emetics, and, somewhat later, opium. Dr. Oliver Wendell Holmes, the distinguished American physician and author of psychological science fiction, expressed his contempt for the medicine being practiced by his professional contemporaries when he said that if all the medicines they used were thrown into the ocean it would be so much the better for mankind and so much the worse for the fishes.[11]

A striking example of how the achievements of modern Western medicine can look overblown is the case of puerperal fever, also known as childbed fever—a disease poignantly relevant to Mary Shelley and her science fiction. Until the middle of the nineteenth century, the mortality rate among women giving birth in European hospitals was between 25 and 30 percent. It was not until 1847 that any European physician did anything constructive about puerperal fever. Ignaz Semmelweis, now regarded as one of the great innovative geniuses of modern medicine, then an assistant at the famed obstetric clinic of the University of Vienna, noticed that women who gave birth at home and who had not undergone internal examination during labor—that is, women tended by traditional midwives rather than modern doctors—had a far lower mortality rate. He also observed that in the clinic's ward where medical students and physicians attended the delivery, women's death rate from puerperal fever was up to three times as great as the death rate from puerperal fever in the ward where only midwives attended. He conjectured that the medical students were bringing some kind of contagion from the dissecting room. In 1847, he ordered the students to wash their hands in chlorinated lime before conducting internal obstetrical examinations or assisting delivery. The death rate from puerperal fever immediately dropped from nearly 20 percent to 1.3 percent. Semmelweis might have reached the same conclusion if he had known of the 1843 book *The Contagiousness of Puerperal Fever* by none other than Dr. Oliver Wendell Holmes.

Mary Shelley was born in 1797, exactly half a century before Semmelweis figured out how to reduce the disastrous mortality rate from puerperal fever caused by the most up-to-date medical practice. Eleven days later, as a consequence of Mary's birth, her mother, Mary Wollstonecraft, one of the towering figures in the history of women's liberation, died from puerperal fever. What effect could this horrible event have had on young Mary's psyche and, eventually, her creative consciousness?

Mary's own experience with birth and death in the medical environment of the early nineteenth century no doubt was also a shaping influence on her imagination. Only one of her four children lived past the age of three. Her first child, born in 1815, died after twelve days. A few days later, seventeen-year-old Mary wrote in her journal: "Dream that my little baby came to life again; that it had only been cold, and that we had rubbed it before the fire, and it had lived."[12] Nine months after this journal entry, Mary gave birth to her son William, who became the namesake for Victor Frankenstein's young brother, the monster's first victim. Within months of William's birth, Mary began writing *Frankenstein*, which she completed in May 1817 while pregnant with her second daughter, Clara. *Frankenstein* was published in January 1818. Clara died that September at the age of one. William died the following June at the age of three. This experience with European medicine evidently influenced revisions Mary Shelley made to the 1831 edition of *Frankenstein*, which she referred to in her "Introduction" as "my hideous progeny."

Victor Frankenstein grows up with Elizabeth, a beautiful little girl whom he calls "my more than sister." In the 1831 edition, Elizabeth's mother, like Mary Shelley's, "had died on giving her birth," leading to her adoption by Victor's parents.[13] Just as Victor is about to set off to begin his studies at the university of Ingolstadt, comes the first fatal event in his life. Elizabeth contracts scarlet fever and is "in the greatest danger." Victor's mother insists on attending "her sick bed,—her watchful attentions triumphed over the malignity of the distemper,—Elizabeth was saved, but the consequences of this imprudence were fatal to her preserver." She catches the disease and dies within three days as "her medical attendants" look on helplessly.[14] On her death-bed, she joins the hands of Victor and Elizabeth, and pledges them to marry each other. Elizabeth, thanks to the impotent medical care of her environment, has now caused the death of both her natural and her adoptive mother.

It is prior to his mother's death and his study at Ingolstadt that Frankenstein, his imagination possessed by reading medieval alchemists, aspires to "banish disease from the human frame, and render man invulnerable to any but a violent death." But when he "becomes capable of bestowing animation upon lifeless matter," his goal shifts. Frankenstein no longer seems concerned with either the prevention or the treatment of disease. What he now dedicates his own life to is "the creation of a human being" (54–55).

At this point, we need to recognize the gender issues at the heart of Mary Shelley's prevision of modern science and technology, especially as manifest in this ultimate quest of her medical practitioner. If Frankenstein simply wants to create a human being, there would be a relatively easy way to go about it. But this would involve having sex with Elizabeth or some other woman. But what he wants to do is create a human being all by himself, without any contact with a woman, substituting for sexual and human intercourse what he construes to be science. To make his creature, he has already cut himself off entirely from all communication with Elizabeth, whom he claims to love so passionately. Later, when his father suggests that he marry Elizabeth, this is his response: "to me the idea of an immediate union with my Elizabeth was one of horror and dismay" (130). This is *before* the monster, a creature that has emerged from Frankenstein's mind and body, threatens, "I shall be with you on your wedding-night" (142). On the wedding night, Victor has this to say to his bride: "Oh! peace, peace, my love … this night and all will be safe: but this night is dreadful, very dreadful" (163). Then despite the obvious fact that the creature plans to kill Elizabeth, Victor sends her alone to their bridal bed while, he, armed with sword and pistol, waits for the monster to attack *him*. The psychological significance of Victor's obsession had come out clearly in the dream he had the night he created his monster:

> I thought I saw Elizabeth, in the bloom of health, walking in the streets of Ingolstadt. Delighted and surprised, I embraced her; but as I imprinted the first kiss on her lips, they became livid with the hue of death; her features appeared to change, and I thought that I held the corpse of my dead mother in my arms; a shroud enveloped her form, and I saw the graveworms crawling in the folds of the flannel [58].

We do not need Freud's *The Interpretation of Dreams* (1899), published more than eight decades later, to recognize that Frankenstein's monster is in fact what that wonderful 1956 science fiction movie *Forbidden Planet* called a "Monster from the Id."

Disease, death, and the impotence of European medicine continued to haunt the imagination that had conceived *Frankenstein*. Between the 1818 and 1831 editions, Mary Shelley brought forth one of the bleakest books in modern literature, *The Last Man*, perhaps the first novel to imagine a disease that brings about the extinction of the human species.

Published in 1826, *The Last Man* is told by its title character, who now wanders in total loneliness over the planet, sampling the futile achievements of all human society. Mary Shelley sets this scene in the year 2100. It is war that introduces the plague into the action. An insatiable pestilence sweeps through Constantinople during a remorseless siege by a Greek army. The remaining two thirds of this quite lengthy novel are devoted to the plague's unstoppable advances, as it marches around the globe, besieges England, and finally cuts down all the narrator's companions and loved ones.

All efforts at prevention or treatment prove futile. Nobody even understands how it spreads:

> That the plague was not what is commonly called contagious, like the scarlet fever, or extinct small-pox, was proved. It was called an epidemic. But the grand question was still unsettled of how this epidemic was generated and increased ... individuals may escape ninety-nine times, and receive the death-blow at the hundredth; because bodies are sometimes in a state to reject the infection of malady, and at others, to imbibe it.
>
> The air is empoisoned, and each human being inhales death, even while in youth and health....

Convinced that the plague is "immedicable," people give up trying to understand, prevent, or treat it.[15] It is perceived as some kind of attack from "Nature." Some people form religious cults. Most just flee. The boundless faith in science that Victor Frankenstein had acquired at the modern university never even appears in *The Last Man*. Medicine and science in fact have no presence whatsoever in the novel, even though this plague is taking place in the last decade of the twenty-first century.

Science fiction that projects the possibility of a global plague has had a rich history since *The Last Man*. Jack London's *The Scarlet Plague*, which appeared in 1915, less than ninety years after Shelley's novel, suggests the immense transformation that had taken place in medical knowledge and practice while also offering some intriguing similarities in outlook.

Set, like *The Last Man*, in the twenty-first century, the story is narrated in the year 2073 by old man Granser to his savage grandsons in a world populated by a handful of barbarians, all that remains of the human species after the Scarlet Death that broke out in 2013. Granser had been a professor at the University of California in Berkeley, a member of what he calls "the ruling classes" who "owned all the land, all the machines, everything" in an America governed by a cabal of the ultra-rich.[16] Medical science had conquered not only the great diseases of the past—cholera, bubonic plague, tuberculosis, etc.—but many new ones that had emerged in the overpopulated world of the late twentieth century. Granser tries futilely to explain the invisible world of microorganisms, antibiotics, and inoculations to his primitive offspring. But all the twenty-first century wonders of bacteriology were impotent against the Scarlet Death, which was so virulent and swift that it killed the bacteriologists in their laboratories.

The rich, fleeing in their private airships, had spread the plague throughout the world. Civilization had collapsed. The barbarism that replaced it sprung partly from the viciousness of this early twenty-first century capitalist dictatorship: "down in our slums and labor-ghettos, we had bred a race of barbarians, of savages" (379). Among the handful of those people with natural immunity, it is these civilization-bred savages who attain power. At the end, Granser warns his grandsons against the newly-arisen "medicine-men" who "call themselves *doctors*, travestying what was once a noble profession." These false "doctors must be destroyed," Granser declares, "and all that was lost must be discovered over again" (448). Although *The Scarlet Plague* ultimately projects a cyclical view of human history, Granser, like London himself, still believes in the wonders of science and technology.

Let me pass over many other twentieth-century stories of global plague, including George R. Stewart's 1949 *Earth Abides*, which is actually a kinder, gentler rewrite of *The*

Scarlet Plague, in order to contrast London's vision with that of a work that returns to the gender issues underlying *Frankenstein*.

Teaching Vonda N. McIntyre's 1973 story "Of Mist, and Sand, and Grass" can be an especially revealing experience about contemporary attitudes toward medicine. A woman healer named Snake arrives at a tiny matriarchal, polyandrous, and xenophobic community, precariously clinging to life amid a vast desert. She has with her three snakes, which she uses to cure a young boy's malignant tumor. The setting is evidently after a nuclear holocaust. Snake has received her medical training in a "station," beyond which lies a city inside a mountain. She has been immunized against a wide spectrum of snake poisons, and she uses her snakes to synthesize and deliver potent biochemical concoctions to cure cancer. I ask students in my course, which is entitled "Science Fiction, Technology, and Society": When is this story set? And what is the level of technology? A few recognize that this seems to be a post-nuclear world. Most describe this as a non-technological world or one with a backward technology. Why? Evidently because McIntyre has returned to the female healer and because this healer's medical instruments are snakes, most students fail to recognize her practice as scientifically or technologically advanced. To drive the point home, either I or some student has to ask, "What cures for cancer do *we* have that are more advanced?"

With this in mind, let us return to fiction about the threat of global disease. Perhaps the most widely known twentieth-century work in this genre is Michael Crichton's 1969 best-seller *The Andromeda Strain*. In *The Last Man*, the plague turned into a global menace during, and evidently because of, human warfare. But nobody intended to use disease as a weapon. The basic premise of *The Andromeda Strain*, which appeared just as many Americans were becoming aware of our nation's fiendish use of chemical warfare in Vietnam, is that the Pentagon may be orbiting satellites to collect microorganisms even more virulent than those being developed by the biological warfare facilities at Fort Detrick, Maryland, and Harley, Indiana. Operation Scoop succeeds in capturing from space the Andromeda strain, a microscopic life form that is airborne and almost instantly fatal to almost all humans and other mammals. Most of the novel is devoted to the efforts of an all-male team of four medical and scientific geniuses, working deep underground in a supersecret ultratechnological military facility, to comprehend the Andromeda strain and thus prevent global catastrophe. (Robert Wise's 1971 movie version makes what seems a concession to the consciousness of the day by casting a woman as one of the four genius scientists; but she is a harridan whose failure to reveal her own disease comes close to dooming the world.) Crichton, himself a graduate of Harvard Medical School and a former doctor, lures us into the mindset of this elitist technocracy, obsessed with technology and possessed by the military, in order to display its Frankenstein-like impotence to control the menaces it unleashes upon the world.

The subtext for *The Andromeda Strain* is that by the late 1960s the human species, through its stupendous development of science and technology, had in fact finally developed the means of its own extinction. This is precisely the destiny imagined by Victor Frankenstein when he decides not to complete the mate that his monster had demanded: "I shuddered to think that future ages might curse me as their pest, whose selfishness had not hesitated to buy its own peace at the price, perhaps, of the existence of the whole human race" (141). The Vietnam War was demonstrating the willingness of one nation to buy its own definition of peace by indiscriminately spraying chemical agents containing dioxin, the substance with the most extreme rate of teratogenicity in laboratory animals, one already known by then to have caused large numbers of mutated births in Vietnam. People back then were also becoming aware that the official government policy about nuclear weapons was Mutual Assured Destruction, the guarantee that if either side launched a nuclear attack both sides would be utterly destroyed. And in this situation, as Crichton explicitly points out, the government, with the aid of the Hudson Institute, had defined the "correct" psychological profile as the willingness to carry out genocide or initiate the apocalypse.[17] If the plans of the military and the scientists in *The Andromeda Strain* had been carried out as intended, nuclear weapons would have turned the alien organism into a global pestilence. *The Andromeda Strain* calls ours the only species intelligent enough to have devised the means to destroy itself. And it shows that, like Frankenstein, we confront the products of our own brilliant creativity as alien monsters, beyond our control.

In the decades since *The Andromeda Strain*, although we have perhaps become more complacent about the nuclear threat, we may have become more disturbed by the biological threat. Today, the possibility of global plague seems to haunt our culture more than ever. Why?

One reason is that, thanks to Richard Preston's article in the October 26, 1992, *New Yorker* and his bestselling nonfiction book *The Hot Zone* (1994), millions of people became aware of an incident not altogether different from the scenario of *The Andromeda Strain*. In 1989, a U.S. Army biological strike team had to take extreme measures to prevent one of the world's most virulent and infectious viruses from escaping from an Army biological warfare laboratory in Frederick, Maryland. Ridley Scott was directing a movie adaptation of the story, *Crisis in the Hot Zone*, starring Robert Redford and Jodie Foster, when that project got preempted by the 1995 movie *Outbreak*. In many ways, *Outbreak* looks like a slick, megabuck update of *The Andromeda Strain*, but with a team of medical doctors (Dustin Hoffman and Rene Russo) as quite innocent adversaries of the military version of Victor Frankenstein (incarnate in Donald Sutherland), who has been developing the virus as a biological warfare agent.

Another 1995 release, Terry Gilliam's brilliant *12 Monkeys*, is a far more innovative and incisive science-fiction film about the possibility of planetary plague. *12 Monkeys* uses time travel to project human history from World War I through 2035 as a tableau of ever-advancing technology under the control of ever more demented and brainy lunatics. In a revision of Chris Marker's 1963 short film *La Jetée*, the doctors who run the nightmarish underground society of 2035 are trying to alter the past to prevent the outbreak of a viral plague in 1996 that made life impossible on the surface of the planet. The mad laboratory worker who had traveled around the world to release the virus globally is portrayed as only marginally more insane than the eminent scientist who had originally cultured it. Though intellectually and visually quite demanding, *12 Monkeys* turned out to be quite popular, perhaps because audiences recognized the accuracy of its vision.

Does the possibility of a madman releasing a plague nurtured in a laboratory seem far-fetched? Larry Wayne Harris, an Ohio well inspector and member of the Aryan Nations, in 1995 ordered from American Type Culture Collection, a company in Rockville, Maryland, three pure strains of the bubonic plague bacteria that wiped out one third of the population of Europe in the 14th century. After he complained that his shipment, for which he had paid $240, was late, the Center for Disease Control was notified. When the FBI, police, public health officials, and emergency workers in spacesuits searched his home, they found blasting caps, smoke grenades, almost a dozen M-1 carbines, and white supremacist literature. In the glove compartment of his car, parked in his driveway, sat the three vials of plague still packed in two layers of glass, absorbent foam and a sealed metal canister. Since it is not illegal to own bubonic plague, Harris was convicted only on one count of wire fraud (based on the fact that he had made up a phony laboratory and used his employer's lab permit).[18] More recently, we have learned of another isolated fanatic who somehow obtained a laboratory-developed form of anthrax and, for some reason, mailed it in a number of letters, killing several American citizens.

However, no one, so far, has deliberately released a plague of planetary proportions. No American town has been devastated by a microorganism nurtured by the military, as in *The Andromeda Strain* and *Outbreak*. So why our growing concern about a planet-wide plague? Because we already have one—AIDS.

As poverty deepens and health care systems disintegrate around the world, the human species is creating ideal conditions for a pandemic. Impoverished families in India and Thailand sell their daughters into prostitution, so the celebrated "one night in Bangkok" (or Bombay, "Asia's largest sex bazaar"[19]) is now spreading AIDS at a tremendous rate among heterosexuals. In the near future, by some estimates, one out of every six Indians will be H.I.V. positive.[20] In South Africa there are now upwards of two million AIDS patients. AIDS is now out of control in cities like the one where I teach, because the two main employment opportunities open to most of the population are prostitution and drug selling. (More than half the prostitutes in Newark are HIV positive.) The United States, which currently imprisons a higher percentage of its population than any other country, has turned the prisons into perfect breeding centers for AIDS by denying prisoners condoms. As AIDS spreads, the overburdened health delivery system, already weakened by galloping Reaganomics, could virtually collapse for much of the population, especially if the virus were to mutate toward easier transmission.

No work of science fiction dramatizes the contradictions of contemporary disease and medicine more starkly than Norman Spinrad's *Journals of the Plague Years*, his extrapolation of a future society dominated by AIDS. Though it was anthologized back in 1988, Spinrad could not find a publisher for this novel until 1995, a fact he attributes to AIDS having "become more central to our lives ... so central that denial is no longer a viable option."[21] He does, however, maintain one stricture originally imposed by his agent: the word AIDS never appears in the novel.

These *Journals of the Plague Years* describe a society where disease has shaped politics and the economy, and where sex has become equated with death. Some areas, such as San Francisco, have become Quarantine Zones, patrolled by the Sex Police to make sure that nobody ever leaves. The most vengeful victims of the Plague are recruited into the imperialist American Foreign Legion, better known as the Army of the Living Dead, to kill, rape, and plunder the Third World, stigmatized as the source of the Plague. Pharmaceutical companies keep developing new vaccines, but the Plague stays ahead of them by mutating, and so the same companies also turn out a stream of palliatives to prolong the lives of the disease's victims. Teenagers and adults are fitted with sex interfaces, mechanical devices through which they have orgasms with each other. Advanced technology has also produced arcades filled with sex machines for those who lack or don't want a partner. In this loveless society, sexual intercourse without a machine is known as "meat."

The complicated plot involves a sadistic soldier of the Army of the Living Dead; a religious maniac who holds the second highest political position in the nation—the lifetime Directorship of the Federal Quarantine Agency (FQA); a young Berkeley woman who becomes Our Lady of the Living Dead—dedicated to having sex with as many Plague victims as possible so that "natural selection" would eventually make the pathogen mutate into one no longer fatal to its host; and a medical doctor developing vaccines for one of the giant drug companies. When Doctor Bruno himself contracts the Plague, his feverish efforts succeed in creating a retrovirus that mimics and attacks every strain of the Plague and is spread through sexual contact. He injects himself with the virus, making readers expect him perhaps to become another Frankenstein. But absurdist black humor is of course one of Spinrad's trademarks. So Dr. Bruno dedicates himself to a quest quite the opposite of that of Frankenstein, who is so horrified by the thought of sex with Elizabeth: "The moral imperatives of the oath of Hippocrates and the fondest desire of any man coincided. It was my duty to have meat with as many women as I could as quickly as possible" (71).

What forces him to act quickly is that the heads of his corporation, realizing that his antidote would bankrupt the company and wreck the nation's economy, now overwhelmingly dependent on the Plague, are out to destroy his antivirus virus and all records of it. When Dr. Bruno links up with Our Lady of the Living Dead and they find refuge in San Francisco, the corporate moguls convince the fanatic Director of the FQA to drop a thermonuclear bomb on the city. In the nick of time, the Director discovers the outrageous truth. "You suppressed a total cure for the Plague to preserve your own profits?" he asks incredulously. You "kept trying to get me to nuke San Francisco" just to keep your company "solvent"? (132) This is so grotesque that even he is shocked over the brink of sanity. The world is saved, and love is restored.

In Spinrad's novel, a writer from the middle of the twenty-first century can look back from "our happier perspective" to the sickness, mental and physical, of "the Plague Years." Let us hope that our own contradictions of disease and medicine have such a happy resolution.

Afterword

Because medicine and the world have changed so much since the essay was written in 1996, I was apprehensive about rereading it. To my surprise, the sf and themes discussed in the essay have somehow gained even more relevance. This is especially—and unfortunately—true for those two sf novels coming to us from a young woman in the opening decades of the 19th century: Shelley's *Frankenstein* and *The Last Man*. Two centuries later we find ourselves in the Anthropocene Age, when our own brilliant creations confront us as alien monsters threatening to destroy our species, as well as many others, through either global warming or apocalyptic warfare.

During these centuries, sf featured an ongoing dialectical conversation about science in general and medicine in particular. The essay traces sf's visions of global plague from Shelley through Spinrad's extrapolation of the AIDS pandemic in *Journals of the Plague Years*, whose happy end is a cure for AIDS. Here the essay asks for a postscript. Although there is still no cure for HIV, biotech companies have developed medicines that suppress the virus enough to leave its victims with a chronic rather than a catastrophic disease—if they can afford the daily regimen. HIV remains pandemic in sub-Saharan Africa, especially South Africa. Spinrad's insights into the corporate role apply ironically to Gilead, the leading biotech in the fight against HIV, whose stock crashed because its cure for many forms of Hepatitis C cured most of the people who could afford the drug in our lunatic health care system.

The one disease for which there is no cure—yet—is death. Here we find some of the most interesting ongoing sf conversations as 21st-century medicine offers the possibility of extending life indefinitely or even transcending death, Victor Frankenstein's original goal. Who knows whether the creators of various versions of *Ghost in the Shell* had read or even heard of Moore's "No Woman Born"? Yet watching the American 2017 film version, I kept pondering the continuum from that 1944 story about a woman who becomes a superhuman female cyborg, and possibly a post-mortal, when her brain is transferred from her dead body.

The possibility of post-mortal life is an increasingly relevant topic in the 21st century. In the near future of Ian R. MacLeod's "Recrossing the Styx" (2010)—one of the most haunting stories I have ever read—death for the ultra-rich is simply "the answer to many problems of old age." With frequent replacement of body parts, organ renewal, uploaded memory, and precious fluids sucked from the less prosperous, they can endlessly cruise the ruined planet in luxury. The narrator, who begins as a tour guide on a luxury liner catering to the "post-living" and their "minders," ends up wondering "who is really dead now, and who is living."[22]

Further in the somewhat wow-gosh future imagined in Lavie Tidhar's Central Station stories, where AIs, cyborgs, part-human robots, and colonization beyond the solar system are the norm, death can be just an option, at least for the title character of "Vladimir Chong Chooses to Die" (2014). As his extraordinary memory begins to fail, Vlad goes to a "mortality consultant" who offers him several "port-mortal arrangements" including: being frozen so he can experience either the future or life on a new planet; conversion into a cyborg; or uploading to become the "I-loop" that gives a robot its sense of human identity.[23] Rejecting port-mortality, Vlad chooses from an antique paper catalog of euthanasias his preferred assisted suicide: death by roller coaster.

Going to the end of earthly time is "On the Human Plan," the late Jay Lake's profound meditation on death, published in 2009, several months after the author was diagnosed with metastatic colon cancer. Under our dying sun on a dying Earth no longer suitable for beings "on the human plan," an inorganic entity who digs through history searching for meaningful narrative attempts to comprehend the meaning of death and hence life.[24] Defining "life" seems easy: "Antientropic organization in chemical or electro-mechanical systems which, left unattended, tends to metastasize into computers, people, starships, catfish, and what have you." At the end he reveals the secret door from death: "You can transcend death, but only through stasis. The one point and purpose of life on the human plan is death."

Which suggests that neither medicine nor science fiction offers escape from the fundamental dialectic of life and death for us *mort*als, at least those of us created on the human plan.

Notes

1. Edgar Allan Poe, "The Facts in the Case of M. Valdemar," 1845, *The Complete Tales and Poems of Edgar Allan Poe* (New York: Barnes & Noble, 1992), 663.

2. Mary Shelley, *Frankenstein, Or, The Modern Prometheus*, ed. Johanna M. Smith (Boston: Bedford, 1992), 45, 54. This is an accurate text of the 1831 edition which I use since it incorporates relevant changes made by Shelley from the original 1818 edition. Parenthetical page references are to this edition.

3. Olaf Stapledon, *Star Maker*, 1937, *Last and First Men and Star Maker* (New York: Dover, 1968), 401–402.

4. Greg Bear, *Blood Music* (New York: Ace, 1986), 94, 167. Parenthetical page references are to this edition.

5. Octavia E. Butler, *Parable of the Sower* (New York: Warner, 1995), 128.

6. Brian W. Aldiss, *Billion Year Spree: The True History of Science Fiction* (Garden City, NY: Doubleday, 1973), 23.

7. C.L. Moore, "No Woman Born," 1944, *Treasury of Science Fiction*, ed. Groff Conklin (1948; New York: Bonanza, 1980), 200.

8. Barbara Ehrenreich and Deirdre English, *Witches, Midwives, and Nurses: A History of Women Healers* (Old Westbury, NY: Feminist, 1973), 12; Anne Llewellyn Barstow, *Witchcraze: A New History of the European Witch Hunts* (San Francisco: Harper/Collins, 1994), Chapter 6, "From Healers into Witches"; Monica Green, "Women's Medical Practice and Health Care in Medieval Europe," *Signs*, 14 (Winter 1989), 434–473; Leland L. Estes, "The Medical Origins of the European Witch Craze: A Hypothesis," *Journal of Social History*, 17 (1983), 271–84.

9. Mary Griffith, *Three Hundred Years Hence* (1836; Philadelphia: Prime, 1950), 73.

10. Ehrenreich and English, 18.

11. Ehrenreich and English, 21–22.

12. Quoted in David Ketterer, *Frankenstein's Creation: The Book, The Monster, and Human Reality* (Victoria: British Literary Studies, 1979), 42.

13. *Frankenstein*, 41. In the 1818 edition, Elizabeth is the daughter of the sister of Frankenstein's father, who adopts her after her mother dies at some unspecified time.

14. *Frankenstein*, 47. In the 1818 edition, Elizabeth is already almost recovered when Victor's mother imprudently visits the sick chamber just to see her.

15. Shelley, *The Last Man*, 1826, ed. Hugh J. Luke, Jr. (Lincoln: University of Nebraska Press, 1965), 167–169, 168.

16. Jack London, *The Scarlet Plague*, 1912, *The Science Fiction of Jack London*, ed. Richard Gid Powers (Boston: Gregg, 1975), 327. Parenthetical page references are to this edition.

17. Michael Crichton, *The Andromeda Strain* (New York: Dell, 1970), 110.

18. "Man Gets Hands on Bubonic Plague, but That's No Crime," *Washington Post*, December 30, 1995; "Bill Targets Bacteria," *Washington Post*, January 29, 1996.

19. "India's Shame," *Nation*, April 8, 1996, 12.

20. "India's Shame," 12.

21. Norman Spinrad, *Journals of the Plague Years* (New York: Bantam, 1995), 146. Parenthetical page references are to this edition.

22. Ian R. MacLeod, "Re-crossing the Styx," 2010, *The Year's Best Science Fiction: 28th Annual Collection*, ed. Gardner Dozois (New York: St. Martin's, 2011), 120, 131.

23. Lavie Tidhar, "Vladimir Chong Chooses to Die," *The Year's Best Science Fiction: 32nd Annual Collection*, ed. Dozois (New York: St. Martin's, 2015), 204, 205.

24. Jay Lake, "On the Human Plan," *Lone Star Stories*, No. 31 (2009), at http://literary.erictmarin.com/archives/Issue%2031/plan.htm. Accessed June 7, 2017.

Science Fiction and the Two Cultures

Reflections After the Snow-Leavis Controversy

(1999 Eaton Conference)

Carl Freedman

More than four decades after C.P. Snow's famous (or notorious) Rede Lecture on "the two cultures," the bitter dispute that it provoked between him and F.R. Leavis retains considerable currency.[1] And this is true despite the fact that the Snow-Leavis controversy, in and of itself, is far from one of the most distinguished moments in the history of intellectual debate. Indeed, the dispute—marred by much shallow glibness on Snow's part and by much unargued vituperation on Leavis's—looks shabby when set beside the most obviously pertinent term of comparison: namely, the Victorian debate about education between T.H. Huxley and Matthew Arnold, who might well be considered the intellectual grandfathers, respectively, of Snow and Leavis.[2] It is not just that Huxley and Arnold respect one another in a way that Snow and Leavis clearly do not. It is also that, as Huxley argues for an enhanced role for science in education, and as Arnold defends the traditional priority of the literary humanities, each is often at his strongest when affirming what the other does not profoundly deny; for each was able to see a good deal of sense in the other's position. Arnold, after all, was no enemy to science, about which he seems to have been better informed than most literary people of his day or later (emphatically including Leavis, whose ignorance of science appears to have been practically total); while Huxley, so far from being philistine or anti-literary, was (like Ruskin, like Newman, like Arnold himself) one of the major contributors to what still looks like the most artistically golden age in the history of English nonfictional prose. It is a good bet that Huxley's writing will continue to be read with pleasure when Snow's novels are even more forgotten than they already are.

But my point is not simply that Huxley and Arnold are greater figures than Snow and Leavis—a plausible though perhaps not irresistible contention. If Huxley and Arnold are able genuinely to speak to each other's concerns—rather than merely talking past one another and posing for public effect, as Snow and Leavis so often do—the explanation is also to be found in their very different historical situations. Though intellectual specialization was certainly well advanced in many ways during the Victorian era, there was nonetheless still some life in the old humanistic notion that an educated person was one with interest in and knowledge of *all* branches of learning. Furthermore, specialization was and had been proceeding in a fairly *gradual* way. The intellectual climate in which Huxley and Arnold moved was more specialized than that which had prevailed a century earlier—when Samuel Johnson conducted serious chemical experiments in his home, and when Erasmus Darwin published botanical speculations in heroic couplets—but the difference was probably not felt as an actual break in continuity. Though Huxley and Arnold were aware of increased intellectual diversification, it seems likely that they were able to think of themselves and of each other not only as advocates of particular kinds of knowledge but also as *generally* educated men. In Snow's language, they occupied the same culture, however determined they may have been to establish different positions within it.

Between the era of Huxley and Arnold and that of Snow and Leavis lie at least two intellectual revolutions that are strictly incomparable to anything that had taken place in the century or two previous: twentieth-century physics and literary modernism. Wishing to characterize his "two cultures," Snow is fond of contrasting the personality of Lord Rutherford with that of his contemporary T.S. Eliot: the buoyant secular optimism of the one, as against the thin-blooded irrationalist gloom of the other.[3] The comparison is fair enough as far as it goes; but it is not the only or most interesting conclusion that the collocation of those two names suggests. For Rutherford and Eliot were, of course, key figures in the radical reconfigurations of their respective fields. The discoverer of the atomic structure and the author of *The Waste Land* (1922) were engaged (perhaps without quite realizing it immediately) in enterprises that would very soon make much of modern science and modern literature decreasingly accessible to people of general education: which is another way of saying that they were destroying general education itself in the sense of rendering it forever obsolete. This is the situation that Snow and Leavis inherit and with which they struggle. Snow makes only a dubiously rigorous argument for the existence of "two cultures"; yet the blank incomprehension with which he and Leavis often regard one another is certainly evidence that *some* sort of disjunction and dysfunction has taken place. But their situation is our own too. This, indeed, is the reason that, for all its faults, the Snow-Leavis dispute remains fascinating. However inadequately they may engage the problem of the "two cultures," they do engage it; and the problem is one that we are still unsuccessfully grappling with today.

Though Snow has most often been criticized for an imperfect understanding of literature and literary culture, his notion of a scientific culture is also far from unassailable. An excellent example is provided by the single most famous point in his Rede Lecture: the contention that the ability to describe the second law of thermodynamics is somehow the equivalent of having read a work of Shakespeare's (14–15). What can this mean? Shakespeare is presumably to be taken as the summit of literary excellence, and everyone who values literature at all must indeed agree that reading Shakespeare can develop the mind in desirable ways (though there is no consensus among literary critics as to what, exactly, those ways are). It seems a curious reduction of science to suggest that its nearest equivalent to reading the greatest literature is, in effect, the ability to answer a simple examination question. Is such positivistic knowledgeableness really what binds scientists into a "culture"? Leavis, in his Richmond Lecture, hotly proclaims the very idea of a scientific equivalent to Shakespeare to be nonsense—"[E]quations between orders so disparate are meaningless" (61)—and this is perhaps the most fully rigorous statement on the matter. Yet, even without going quite so far as that, one can still object to Snow's glib vulgarity here. The ability to think logically; the ability to draw conclusions supported by a specific body of evidence; appreciation of the epistemological distinction between the anecdote and the controlled experiment; perhaps the ability to think in mathematical symbolism as well as in words—if, as Snow rightly insists, a scientific training cultivates the mind as positively as a literary one does, then surely it is capacities of this sort, and not mere gobbets of information, that, on the scientific side, are at least very roughly comparable to the cultivation achieved by reading Shakespeare or Virgil. One wonders how many dilettantes under Snow's influence have memorized the second law of thermodynamics with the conviction of being henceforth scientifically literate.[4]

But the more serious problems with Snow's exposition of "the two cultures" do indeed concern his understanding of literature and what he calls the literary culture (or "the traditional culture," as he also terms it). The basic argument of the Rede lecture, we must recall, is not only that literary people tend to be ignorant of thermodynamics and the other glories of science. He also indicts the literary culture for being instinctively hostile to science and technology, hostile even to democracy itself and especially to rational social planning, and at times not far from fascistic irrationalism; and he further maintains that the literary culture tends to be politically hegemonic and so prevents the scientists and engineers from achieving the scientific social planning that England and the world so desperately need.

It is hard to know where to begin disentangling the confusions here. The notion that literary intellectuals run the world, or even England, is bizarre. One suspects some historic class resentment to be at work here. The lower-middle-class Snow rose from provincial obscurity to the metropolitan elite by scientific and, much more, by administrative aptitude; and he would have had every right to be scornful of the old Tory notion that well-born gentlemen who had studied classics at public school and at Oxford were those naturally best fitted to administer Britain and its dominions. But, by 1959, the dominance of Oxford Greats was even more of a dead horse than the British Empire to which it had been so closely linked. And Snow, indeed, never even mentions Greek and Latin in his denunciations of the literati; his real target is literary modernism, which he takes to be most notably represented by W.B. Yeats, Eliot, Ezra Pound, and Wyndham Lewis.

This move raises a whole new crop of confusions. In the first place, about the highest earthly reward for which a knowledge of modernist literature has ever qualified anyone is tenure in an English Department in California. The idea that literary intellectuals with heads full of Yeats's *The Tower* (1928) and Pound's *The Cantos* (1954) are regularly obstructing technocrats from eliminating hunger and disease is just ludicrous. Yet even more serious, in some ways, is Snow's almost total failure to understand modernism itself. His list of representative authors, with the persistent inclusion of so minor a figure as Lewis ("brutal and boring," as Leavis called him [53]), is of course tendentiously selective. Against the archconservatism of Yeats, the theocratic royalism of Eliot, and the fascist anti-Semitism of Pound, one might set the secular democratic humanism of James Joyce; the radical Liberalism of E.M. Forster and the feminism of Virginia Woolf; the left-wing Celtic nationalisms of Sean O'Casey and Hugh MacDiarmid; the Marxism of the young W.H. Auden and even the democratic centrism of the later Auden; the profound anti-fascism of Samuel Beckett; and, of course, much else. But Snow's ignorant hostility to modernism is intensive as well as extensive. In particular, he seems unable to see any cognitive value in literature beyond its most overt and "official" ideologies. It is symptomatic, for instance, that, in admitting that there is perhaps something to be said for Yeats despite his reactionary politics, Snow takes his evidence not from Yeats's poetry but from unnamed "friends whose judgment I trust," who certify Yeats to have been "a man of singular magnanimity of character" (8). This is to reduce literary study to gossip. Actually to *read* the poems of Yeats (whom MacDiarmid, incidentally, considered a friend and comrade) is to be aware that, however unfortunate and wrong-headed his extreme conservatism may have been, it was partially motivated by a genuine sympathy for the Irish poor, by a sensitive revulsion from the cultural ravages caused by capitalist property relations, and by an entirely proper contempt for the philistine vulgarity of Ireland's Catholic middle class. Indeed, philistine vulgarity and the cultural ravages of capitalism in general are problems that Yeats ponders with considerable subtlety, depth, and force—and that Snow himself almost entirely ignores.

It may well be, and has been, felt that Snow's attitude toward modernism—that is, toward most of the most important literature produced in Snow's language during Snow's lifetime—amounts to a hostility toward literature itself. There is some truth to this, though the whole truth, as I will argue shortly, is a little more complex. First, however, it is time to consider Leavis not merely as Snow's antagonist but as a major thinker of remarkable ignorances himself.

The most serious general charge to be leveled against Leavis is not his breach of good manners. It is simply that, although he often, despite his shrill tone, succeeds in exposing Snow's shortcomings, he never really contributes anything positive of his own. He himself repeatedly insists just the opposite—"I *have* a positive theme, and ... it and my attitude are truly positive" (20), he writes rather plaintively—but, upon examination, the "positive" values of his Richmond Lecture and its successor pieces turn out to be only the usual unargued clichés of late Leavisite vitalism: especially "life" and D.H. Lawrence, two categories that become increasingly interchangeable for Leavis.[5] In particular, he has nothing of conceptual substance to say about the place of science in modern schooling or about the gulf that Snow points out between scientific and literary education. Sometimes Leavis's lack of scientific knowledge on even the most elementary level is virtually comical. For example, in attempting to refute any notion that he himself is "Luddite" or anti-scientific, he repeatedly expresses his whole-hearted admiration for one Daniel Doyce. And who is Daniel Doyce? Not an actual scientist at all, but a character in Dickens's *Little Dorrit* (1855–1857), where he is an inventor whose work is frustrated by the inanities of government bureaucracy. Leavis is right enough to note that Dickens portrays Doyce as an admirably creative and disinterested applied scientist, and thus that Dickens himself can hardly be considered an intellectual Luddite (a charge, however, that Snow, despite Leavis's insinuations on the matter, never actually makes). But the crucial point here is not only that Leavis is, evidently, unable to think of a real-world scientist whose creativity he admires; it is also that the intellectual horizons of *Little Dorrit* (arguably Dickens's greatest novel, as Leavis would probably agree) are so alienated from the scientific imagination that Dickens is quite unable to represent anything of Doyce's work. We are *told* that Doyce is a great inventor but never given any concrete sense of his inventing. Though Dickens has perhaps the largest representational range of any English writer after Shakespeare, it is not large enough to include the science and applied science that were such vital social forces in Dickens's own time and place. The character of Doyce, then, far from proving anything for Leavis's side, really amounts to an early or anticipatory instance of the disjunction between "the two cultures" that Snow notices: and this *despite* Dickens's abstractly positive attitude toward scientific inventing.

It might be objected, though, that Leavis, unlike Snow, never claims to speak with authority on both science and literature and that it is strictly as a literary critic that he ought to be judged. But here his blanknesses and evasions are perhaps even more disturbing. The curious windiness of the Richmond Lecture and its sequels largely results from the fact that a truly literary-critical response to Snow would foreground a principled defense of the modernism that Snow so distorts and undervalues: and yet this is exactly what Leavis does not do. He is, indeed, disabled from doing so by his general critical principles. Though Leavis is not flatly anti-modernist in Snow's fashion—he ardently admires Eliot and, of course, Lawrence—the great bulk of modernism does indeed lie outside Leavis's warmest sympathies. He recognizes writers like Yeats, Joyce, Pound, Marcel Proust, Franz Kafka, Bertolt Brecht, and Beckett either grudgingly or not at all, while, on the other hand, the essential Leavis canon (insofar as nineteenth- and twentieth-century literature is concerned) is occupied by such very different authors as Jane Austen, George Eliot, Nathaniel Hawthorne, Mark Twain, Dickens, Henry James, Lawrence at his most realistic and least modernist (hence Leavis's exaltation of *Women in Love* [1920] and his dismissal of *The Plumed Serpent* [1926] and *Lady Chatterley's Lover* [1928]), and, above all, the Leo Tolstoy of *Anna Karenina* (1875–1877). Indeed, if one were to select a single text, composed after the seventeenth century, that best exemplifies what Leavis values in literature, it would, almost certainly, be Tolstoy's greatest novel.[6]

Yet here we seem to hit on a perhaps unexpected point of agreement between Snow and Leavis: For scattered remarks in Snow's writings indicate that for him, too, Tolstoy represents the apex of modern literature. Though few would wish to dispute this shared enthusiasm for Tolstoy—probably the greatest of all literary realists—it provides a specific clue to a much larger underlying similarity between the otherwise so violently contrasting intellectual personalities of Snow and Leavis: namely, that, as their respective failures adequately to engage literary modernism may tend to imply, for both Snow and Leavis it is realistic prose fiction of the type that reached its most powerful expression in the nineteenth century that constitutes not only the greatest achievement in post–Renaissance letters, but, to a considerable degree, the essential model for what all modern literature ought to be. Leavis's bias toward realism has, indeed, been somewhat camouflaged by his early and influential role as a critical advocate for Eliot and Lawrence, a role that made him appear to be at least a fellow-traveler of the modernist revolution. Yet, as we have seen, Leavis's taste for modernism was always tentative and highly selective, and never really triumphed over his sense that realistic works like George Eliot's *Middlemarch* (1874), *Little Dorrit*, *Anna Karenina*, Henry James's *The Portrait of a Lady* (1908), Mark Twain's *Huckleberry Finn* (1884), and *Women in Love* provided the most reliable literary touchstones from the middle nineteenth century onwards. As for Snow, his critical insistence on the primacy of realism was considerably more blatant—in some circles, indeed, Snow's anti-modernist and pro-realist stance become almost scandalous during his career as a London book reviewer—but is most memorably recorded in his own fiction, the immense *Strangers and Brothers* cycle of novels. Leavis, I think, was perfectly right to be astounded at the inflated conventional reputation that this work once enjoyed, and to insist on the almost unreadable flatness of Snow's characters and situations; indeed, *Strangers and Brothers* provides a textbook Lukácsian example of the degeneration of high realism into a depthless and lifeless naturalism. What Leavis chose not to remark, however, was that Snow's novels are failed attempts to write precisely the *kind* of literature that he himself most approved. Almost perfectly antipathetic to one another, Snow and Leavis seem incapable of acknowledging their largest area of agreement: the notion that, whether literature is valued too little (as arguably for Snow) or too exclusively (as arguably for Leavis), and whether one is thinking of the brilliance of *Anna Karenina* or the banality of *Strangers and Brothers*, realistic prose fiction is the literature that matters.

How is the pro-realist ideology of Snow and Leavis connected to the inadequacy with which they argue the problem of the "two cultures"? I will not here pursue what nonetheless seems to me an intriguing fact: that, at least in English and the other Western European languages (for the situation may be different in Russian), the major realistic novelists seem seldom to have taken the kind of interest in science displayed by great poets from Virgil and Lucretius, through Dante and Milton, to Alfred Lord Tennyson and Auden. Instead, I will pursue a possibly more straightforward contention: that Snow's and Leavis's massive bias towards realism helped to blind them to the genre—science fiction—that could have shed some real light on their shared problem. Though Leavis's neglect of science fiction is entirely unsurprising—for in addition to his preference for realism one must recall his contempt for nearly all twentieth-century writing either American or putatively "popular" in provenance—it is more puzzling that Snow, the apostle of scientific culture and the follower of H.G. Wells, should have failed to notice, for example, the significance of the series of pioneering science fiction novels that Wells began in 1895 with *The Time Machine*. Despite his elaborate contempt for England's traditional literary culture, in his failure to appreciate science fiction Snow concurs with one of that culture's most disabling prejudices.

To be sure, we should not exaggerate the maturity of the science fiction tradition with regard either to literary or to scientific culture, especially vis-à-vis the defining revolutions of modernist literature and modern physics. Much science fiction, even by authors with some professional scientific training, sets fairly low standards of scientific rigor, while the number of science fiction novelists who have managed to write as though Joyce never wrote is downright embarrassing: A novel like Gregory Benford's *Timescape* (1980), which intervenes in cutting-edge physical speculation, is an exceptional masterpiece, as is Samuel Delany's *Dhalgren* (1975), one of the major achievements of the post–Joycean avant-garde. Yet not only is it as fair to let Benford and Delany represent twentieth-century science fiction as it is to let George Eliot and Tolstoy represent nineteenth-century realism, but, furthermore, *all* genuine science fiction, even when far below the level of its highest masterworks, must at least attempt to illuminate the issues raised by the concept of the "two cultures." After all, the fundamental problem announced by Snow is, in one sense, the response on the level of human feeling and perception to the changes, intellectual and practical, wrought by the development of science: and such is the concern too of nearly every science-fictional text. Indeed, one reliable test of whether a particular text is only weakly science-fictional is precisely whether it fails to establish any genuine connections between the "two cultures": as witness the innumerable dreary instances in which the reader is transported to a remote galaxy or a distant century only to witness an adventure story or a love story that might, in all essentials, have equally well (or better) been staged in the mundane here-and-now.

By contrast, strongly science-fictional works—i.e., those by which the genre is to be judged—interrogate the limits of the human in ways inaccessible (or less efficiently accessible) in the absence of scientifically based estrangement. I do not mean that scientific prediction or even speculation is the central aim of science fiction. On the contrary, the estrangements of the genre ultimately function to demystify our empirical here-and-now, and the great Ballardian maxim—that the future which matters in science fiction is never more than five minutes away—thus holds.[7] But such demystification, in strong science fiction, depends upon estrangements that in some way take the epistemological challenges of science seriously. The science in science fiction need not necessarily be empirically correct, and it may even incorporate a few discrete elements (like travel into the past) that scientists and scientifically oriented philosophers generally regard as impossible. But the general conceptual framework of science fiction is defined by the scientific project of producing rational, cognitive knowledge of the universe. And, in the finest works of scientific fiction, the disposition of plot, character, and theme are inextricably bound up with specific instances of scientific cognition, or, at least, the literary effect of scientific cognition. Thus, for example, the environmentalist insights of *Timescape* could hardly have been enforced so powerfully in the absence of the text's speculations on the nature of time enabled by quantum physics. Or, again, the demystifications of war in Joe Haldeman's *The Forever War* (1974), or of imperialism in Ursula K. Le Guin's *The Word for World Is Forest* (1972), or of species being itself in Octavia Butler's *Xenogenesis* trilogy (1987–1989), crucially depend upon possibilities of (respectively) time travel, space travel, and genetic engineering that are strictly unthinkable below a certain level of scientific understanding. Furthermore, science fiction can remind us—as Arnold, indeed, reminded Huxley—that the concept of science need not be always confined to the narrow English sense of the physical sciences but can also encompass everything suggested by the German word *Wissenschaft*: *Dhalgren* makes clear that urban sociology is a science, and Philip K. Dick's *The Man in the High Castle* (1962) and Joanna Russ's *The Two of Them* (1978) do much the same for political historiography and for gender studies, respectively. Indeed, one might go so far as to maintain that these texts by Delany, Dick, and Russ amount to substantial *contributions* to those fields of learning as well.

Adequately to display what might be termed the "bi-cultural" nature of science fiction would be fully to investigate the cognitive resources of the genre; and this would require a book—which, in fact, I have already written.[8] In conclusion here, I will only examine in a bit more detail two works less well-known than any mentioned above, for they are by an author who has only very recently emerged as one of our more interesting science fiction writers: Howard V. Hendrix's *Lightpaths* (1997) and *Standing Wave* (1998). The largest significance of these texts (each of which is a free-standing story but which together also constitute two-thirds of a trilogy in progress) is found, I think, in the recent history of the utopian novel. As is widely appreciated, such major works of the 1970s as Russ's *The Female Man* (1975), Le Guin's *The Dispossessed* (1974), Marge Piercy's *Woman on the Edge of Time* (1976), and Delany's *Triton* (1976; later retitled *Trouble on Triton*) represent the successful revival of the authentic utopia after decades of occlusion by the kind of negative utopia associated with the names of Yevgeny Zamyatin, (Aldous) Huxley, and George Orwell—a revival, however, that was itself largely occluded in the following decade, mainly by cyberpunk but also by the comeback of the more conventional negative utopia typified by Margaret Atwood's *The Handmaid's Tale* (1985)—and despite such brave exceptions as Delany's *Stars in My Pocket Like Grains of Sand* (1984). Hendrix, then, can be understood (along with more veteran authors like Piercy herself in *He, She and It* [1991], and Kim Stanley Robinson in the Mars trilogy [1993–1997]) as one of the writers who, in the 1990s, revived the utopian revival and insisted again on the indispensability of utopian speculation.

Lightpaths is set in an orbital complex that is authentically utopian, its society organized according to principles that, in view of the book's debt to *The Dispossessed*, might be called neo-Odonian. *Standing Wave*, a more wide-ranging if less intense and tightly organized novel, maintains a focus on this orbiting utopia (known as HOME, for High Orbital Manufacturing Enterprise) while also including views of other places, including some fascinating glimpses of a negative utopia based mainly on today's Christian Right. Ultimately, Hendrix's socio-political-economic speculations shade into metaphysical ones, as a post–Stapledonian materialist spirituality becomes the most encompassing world-view of the text. The point to be stressed here, however, is that both the politics and the metaphysics of these novels are concretized through a dynamic melding of the humanistic and the technical. In the context of utopia and of transcendence, Hendrix closely and "realistically" draws characters involved in ambiguous family relations, professional routine, resentful personal manipulation, sexual love, and much else. We see, for instance, how the personal ambivalence of a mother-son pair can be overdetermined, even in a utopia, by relations of bureaucracy. We see how the most violently bigoted forms of sub-fascist irrationalism may be closely linked to wholly understandable family tragedy. We glimpse the filiations between vegetarianism and certain varieties of sexual attraction, and between professional ambition and mind-altering drugs. Consistently, the light shone on such problems of what Leavis would call the human world is directly dependent on estrangements enabled by the novel's sophisticated handling of natural sciences from cosmology to botany, of human sciences like anthropology and political economy, and, above all (and in a way that owes much to William Gibson while finally, I think, going beyond him), of information science—a branch of learning that itself deconstructs the natural/human binary and so challenges any dichotomy of "two cultures." I end having hardly begun to do justice to Hendrix's work. But I think it incontestable that these novels, as works of genuine science fiction, provide both the kind of close human observation demanded by Leavis (though in a form beyond Leavis's comprehension) *and* the deeply progressive scientific and technological understanding that Snow finds so alien to the modern literary imagination.

Afterword

My analysis of the dispute between Snow and Leavis about "the two cultures" was originally delivered at the 1999 Eaton Conference, published in *Extrapolation* in 2001, and reprinted in a 2009 critical anthology (based on the original conference) edited by Gary Westfahl and the late (and much lamented) George Slusser. Today—in 2017—I find that, nearly a full generation after the original presentation, I remain willing to stand by what I wrote. I will devote this afterword only to correcting one misunderstanding to which the essay might, I think, give rise, and offering one further thought prompted by the longer historical perspective now available to us.

One of the essay's main arguments is that science fiction, as a literary form with a special relationship to scientific cognition, is a privileged genre for negotiating the gap between the scientific and literary cultures. Though I do not state or suggest that science fiction should therefore be understood as *equidistant* between the two cultures, or an equal synthesis of them, readers might misinterpret the essay to imply as much; and the essay does hardly anything to forestall such a misinterpretation. Indeed, the form of the term *science fiction* itself (possibly suggesting one part science and an equal part fiction) may conduce to such an error. But, grammatically, the substantive always takes priority over the adjective; and we should be clear that science fiction, as a form of literature, is primarily literary and only secondarily scientific in any sense of that term. Science fiction writers, after all, are *writers* by profession. Few have had any deeper involvement with science than that which can be attained by ordinarily intelligent amateurs, and many have lacked even that. Even among those with actual scientific training and most elaborately committed to scientific rationality, Arthur C. Clarke, for example, was never a real working scientist; and Isaac Asimov was one only briefly, near the beginning of his career. Gregory Benford, whom I briefly discuss in the essay, is—as a professor of physics with over a hundred scientific research papers to his credit—a rare exception among important authors of science fiction.

With regard to the Snow-Leavis controversy itself, I note an irony that seems more clearly accessible now than when I composed my conference paper. During the years of Snow's and Leavis's dueling lectures and papers, and long thereafter, one thing seemed fairly evident about the combatants' respective positions. Leavis—the quintessential literary Little Englander, nostalgic for the rural English communities of bygone days—appeared very much a man of the past, while Snow seemed just the opposite. As George Steiner put it in the work cited above: "Whereas Snow is immensely of the present, responsive in every way to what is new and jarring in our novel condition, Leavis has sought to bring time to a halt in a pastoral, Augustan dream of order."[9]

Yet, if Snow looked to posterity far more hopefully than Leavis did, posterity has been kinder to Leavis than to Snow. Both reputations declined somewhat after Leavis's death in 1978 and Snow's in 1980. In recent years, however, there has been a considerable revival of interest in Leavis's work. Since 2003, a Centre for Leavis Studies—succeeded by the Leavis Society—has given institutional form to global interest in Leavisite criticism; and Leavis's influence has extended far beyond this particular organization. It has become generally apparent, even to those who strongly dissent from much Leavisite doctrine, that Leavis, for all the omissions and narrowness in his work—failings I discuss in some detail and with some astringency in this essay—produced the most powerful and influential oeuvre of any English critic of the twentieth century. His is the work with which all subsequent serious criticism of English literature must begin, even if in disagreement. His attachment to the past, however unacceptable in so many ways, was also a vitalizing force in his thought. No English critic since Matthew Arnold—perhaps none since Dr. Johnson—has done as much to shape our understanding of English literature. As a critic of the English novel in particular, Leavis has not only no rival, but virtually no second.

Snow, meanwhile, has vanished *almost* without a trace. To some degree, admittedly, this is because his administrative work in the British Civil Service, to which he devoted much of his time and energy, is by nature anonymous and leaves no monuments behind. But Snow's novels, which were mainly responsible for his public reputation during his lifetime, are now as unread and unstudied as Leavis—who abominated them—could have wished. That the *Strangers and Brothers* sequence was once considered a modern classic, one sometimes mentioned in the same breath with the fiction of Faulkner or Proust, today seems merely bizarre—like learning that the poetic fame of Milton was once seriously rivaled by that of his older contemporary Francis Quarles. Snow may have thought he had the future "in his bones" (as he famously said of scientists in the Rede Lecture), but the actual future has not been much interested in Snow. If, nonetheless,

Snow's name seems unlikely to disappear completely, it is because of the Rede Lecture itself. Whatever one thinks of the way Snow addressed the problem he identified—even if one's view of the matter is as negative as Leavis's—Snow will always deserve credit for identifying and naming the problem of the two cultures: a problem that, as I discussed, is very much with us still and seems certain to remain with us in any conceivable future.

Notes

1. C.P. Snow, *The Two Cultures* (Cambridge: Cambridge University Press, 1993), and F.R. Leavis, *Nor Shall My Sword: Discourses on Pluralism, Compassion and Social Hope* (New York: Harper and Row, 1972). The former contains Snow's original Rede Lecture of 1959 and his essay of four years later, "The Two Cultures: A Second Look." The latter contains "Two Cultures? The Significance of Lord Snow," Leavis's Richmond Lecture of 1962 in which he delivered his first counterblast to Snow, plus five subsequent addresses and an introductory overview of the matter as Leavis saw it. Unless otherwise noted, parenthetical page references to Snow and Leavis are to these editions.

2. The key texts in the Huxley-Arnold debate are "Science and Culture," a lecture that Huxley gave in 1880 at the opening of Mason College, Birmingham (an institution established specifically to provide scientific training), and "Literature and Science," the Rede Lecture (!) that Arnold gave two years later in reply. I have designated Huxley and Arnold the intellectual grandfathers rather than fathers of Snow and Leavis, respectively, and it does seem possible to identify the pertinent individuals of the intervening generation. On one side, it is clearly H.G. Wells, who was Huxley's student and, much later, something of a mentor and hero to the young Snow. On the other side, the lines of descent are not quite so obvious; but Leslie Stephen, a Cambridge critic much admired by Leavis (and, incidentally, the father of Virginia Woolf), conveniently marks the point in English criticism between Arnold and Leavis.

3. *The Two Cultures*, 4–5; see also Snow, *Variety of Men* (New York: Scribner's, 1966), 4.

4. In "The Two Cultures: A Second Look," Snow does somewhat qualify the shallow positivism of his use of the second law (72). Still, Leavis (46–47) goes so far as to maintain that, on the evidence of his novels and his Rede Lecture, Snow's mind has enjoyed no real discipline either scientific or otherwise, and that science exists for him merely as a matter of external reference without psychological depth. Doubtless this, like so much in Leavis's assaults on Snow, is too harsh. Yet it may be recalled that, though Snow was professionally trained as a scientist, and though (as he later delighted to recall) he participated in the glory days of the Cavendish Laboratory under Rutherford during the 1920s and 1930s, he never became a scientist of real distinction; and he had abandoned scientific research altogether for more than two decades by the time of the Rede Lecture. Of course, he remained a vigorous propagandist for science and for what he took to be the scientific culture; but working scientists have by no means always felt well represented by Snow.

5. See George Steiner, *Language and Silence* (New York: Atheneum, 1970), 234: "What had been advertised as a responsible examination of the concept of 'the two cultures' dissolved—as so much else in Leavis's recent work has done—into a ceremonial dance before the dark god, D.H. Lawrence."

6. For instance: "*Anna Karenina* one of the great European novels?—it is, surely, *the* European novel. The completeness with which Tolstoy, with his genius, was a Russian of his time made him an incomparably representative European, and made the book into which his whole experience, his most comprehensive 'relatedness,' went what it is for us: the great novel of modern—of our—civilization" (Leavis, *Anna Karenina and Other Essays* [New York: Simon and Schuster, 1969], 32).

7. J.G. Ballard has been reported as saying, "The future in my work has never been more than five minutes away"—a remark that seems to me such a brilliant insight not only into Ballard's own fiction but into science fiction as a whole that I have generalized it into the "maxim" above. I have been unable to determine the original location of the quoted comment.

8. The advertisement is for Freedman, *Critical Theory and Science Fiction* (Hanover, NH: Wesleyan University Press, 2000).

9. Steiner, 233.

The Eaton Roll of Honor

This list, drawn from all 25 Eaton Conference programs and all 21 Eaton volumes, includes every individual who participated in an Eaton Conference as a speaker, panelist, coordinator, organizer, or special guest, as well as individuals who never attended conferences but contributed to Eaton volumes. We strove to make the list complete and accurate, but apologize in advance for any errors or omissions.

Elizabeth Aamot
Forrest J Ackerman
Brian W. Aldiss
Dina Al-Kassim
Paul Alkon
Kathryn Allan
Wayne Allen
Gwendolyn Alley
Alida Allison
Sarah M. Allison
Poul Anderson
Chad Andrews
Daniel Ante-Contreras
Rosemary Arbur
James W. Arnold
Meghan Astley
George Atkins
Brian Attebery
Stina Attebery
Jeremiah Axelrod
Daoine Bachran
J. Timothy Bagwell
Kenneth V. Bailey
Craig Baldwin
Katie Brewer Ball
Anindita Banerjee
Suparno Banerjee
Cate Bangs
Bradley Bankston
David Bañuelos
Celeste McConnell Barber
Bridgitte Barclay
Steve Barnes
Luana Barossi
Marleen S. Barr
Jean-Pierre Barricelli
Neil Barron
Gay Barton
Martha A. Bartter
Greg Bear
Michael Beehler
Max P. Belin
Karen Bellinfante
Gregory Benford
Steve Berman
Daniel Bernardi
Ratnakar Bhelkar
Peter Biskind
Mark Biswas
Irwin Blacker
Sterling Blake [Gregory Benford]
James P. Blaylock
Harold Bloom
Virginia Blum
Edra Bogle
Andŕe Bormanis
Mark Bould
Mark Brake
Leo Braudy
Thomas A. Brennan
Alan Brennert
Reginald Bretnor
Jeremy Brett
Paul Brians
Peter Brigg
David Brin
Charles N. Brown
Stephen P. Brown
Frank Bruno
Irving Buchen
Emma Bull
E. Jane Burns
Fred Burns
Judy Burns
Derek Burrill
Andrew M. Butler
Octavia E. Butler
Christopher J. Caes
Larry W. Caldwell
Patrice Caldwell
Andrew Calis
Ritch Calvin
Gerry Canavan
Townsend Carr
Paul A. Carter
Edwin F. Casebeer
Joseph Andrew Casper
Michael Cassutt
Danièle Chatelain
Elizabeth Chater
Paul Cheng
Todd Cherniawsky
Ria Cheyne
Thomas Clareson
Arthur C. Clarke
David Clayton
Cynthia Clegg
Michael Clifton
John Clute
Ron Cobb
Dylan Cole

Michael R. Collings
Helen Collins
Robert A. Collins
Emily Connelly
Melissa Conway
Bruce Cook
Brett Cooke
Robin Craig
John Cramer
Kathryn Cramer
Barry Crawford
Robert Crossley
Istvan Csicsery-Ronay
Stephen Cullenberg
Elizabeth Cummins
Ruth Curl
Scott Dalrymple
Jack Dann
David K. Danow
Joseph Dargue
Saul David
Elizabeth Davidson
Laurence Davies
Gareth Davies-Morris
Don Davis
Doug Davis
Sam Davis
Stefan Dechant
Nicole de Fee
Samuel R. Delany
Sharon Delmendo
Grant Dempsey
Grace Dillon
Thomas M. Disch
Stanley Donen
H. L. Drake
Pascal Ducommun
Jody Duncan
John S. Dunne
Scott Durham
Ollivier Dyens
John Dykstra
Neil Easterbrook
Grace Eckley
Cheryl Edelson
Doris Egan
Suzette Haden Elgin
Paul Elliot
Ted Elliott
Marissa Elliott-Baptiste
Harlan Ellison
Alan C. Elms
Langdon Elsbree
Matt Englund
Andrew Enstice
Zarah Ersoff
Dennis Etchison
Arthur B. Evans
Taylor Evans
Andrew Ferguson
Rachel Haywood Ferreira
Leslie Fiedler
Lucio Reis Filho
Nora Filipp
Sheila Finch
John Martin Fischer
Peter Fitting
Bud Foote
Robert L. Forward
A. Fowler-Wright
H. Bruce Franklin
Frank Kelly Freas
Laura Freas
Carl Freedman
Paweł Frelik
Adam Frisch
Sonja Fritzsche
Terri Frongia
Ann Garascia
Susan A. George
John Gerlach
David Gerrold
Sandra Gilbert
M. Elizabeth Ginway
Dana Gioia
Richard Gombert
Kathleen Ann Goonan
Vladimir Gopman
Andrew Gordon
Joan Gordon
Robert Gorsch
Chris Goto-Jones
Jean-Marc Gouanvic
Mimi Gramatky
John Grant
Kevin Grazier
Colin Greenland
Robert Griffin
Christine Grossman
Paul Guajardo
Susan Gubar
George R. Guffey
Eileen Gunn
James Gunn
Abhijit Gupta
Carl Gutierrez-Jones
Felipe Gutterriez
Patrick Gyger
Andrew Hageman
Alex Hajdu
Joe Haldeman
Jenni Halpin
Stephanie Hammer
Kirk Hampton
Arlen J. Hansen
Thomas Hanzo
Joan Haran
William Hardesty
Terry Harpold
Steven B. Harris
David G. Hartwell
Donald M. Hassler
George Hay
N. Katherine Hayles
Robert Heath
Ronald Heckelman
Michelle Heeg
Elyce Rae Helford
Karen Hellekson
Margo Hendricks
Howard V. Hendrix
Anthony J. Hicks
Jeff Hicks
David Higgins
Ed Higgins
Ingrid Hill
Rainer Hilscher
David Hinckley
Jane Hipoloto
Lacy Hodges
Karen A. Hohne
Veronica Hollinger
J. Michael Holquist
Neil Hook
Nalo Hopkinson
Sharman Horwood
Andrew Howe
Winona Howe
Yvonne Howell
Julian Hoxter
Marie-Hélène Huet
Elizabeth Anne Hull
Kathryn Hume
Richard Hunt
Robert Hunt
John Huntington
Ruth Jackson
Craig B. Jacobsen
Jake Jakaitis
Edward James
Fredric R. Jameson
Michael Jarvis
Larry Jasper
Emily Jiang
Joshua Johnson
Keith Johnson
Michael Johnson
Toby Braden Johnson

John Johnston
William B. Jones, Jr.
Jari Käkelä
Despina Kakoudaki
Matthew Wilhelm Kapell
Yuli Kargalitski
Beatrix Karthaus-Hunt
Jennifer Kavetsky
Bruce Kawin
Thomas Keeling
Fiona Kelleghan
Gary Kern
David Ketterer
De Witt Douglas Kilgore
Kyu Hyun Kim
Michael Joseph Klein
Dale Knickerbocker
Arthur Knight
Sharon D. King
Susan Knabe
Clayton Koelb
Ira Konigsberg
Kent T. Kraft
Susan Kray
Pekka Kuusisto
Lois Kuznets
Sha La Bare
Marc Laidlaw
Victoria Lamont
Geoffrey Landis
Brooks Landon
Jonathan Langford
Lizbeth Langston
Rob Latham
Nicholas Laudadio
Albert J. La Valley
David M. Lawrence
David Layton
Kristy L. Layton
Moshe Lazar
Bill Lee
Judith Lee
Regina Yung Lee
Simon Lee
David Leiby
Howard M. Lenhoff
Joseph Lenz
Dan Leopard
Christopher Leslie
Andrew Leung
Harry Levin
Michael Levy
Alex Lightman
Sandra Lindow
Mingming Liu
Donald Lloyd
Jean-Marc L'Officier
Brian Loftus
William Lomax
Alexis Lothian
Frances Louis
T.M. Lowe
Rowan Lozada-Aguilera
Roger Luckhurst
R. Jeffrey Lustig
Reinhart Lutz
Bradford Lyau
Justin Lynn
R.A. MacAvoy
Carol MacKay
Anthony Macias
Elisabeth Malartre
Daryl F. Mallett
Shawn Malley
Carl D. Malmgren
Miles Mancini
Geoff Mandel
Jean-Michel Margot
Melanie Marotta
Eugene Martin
Mark O. Martin
Simona Martini
Leon Marvell
Elizabeth Maslen
Noah Mass
Michelle Massé
Julia Mastro
Julian May
Larry McCaffery
Michael W. McClintock
Scott McCloud
Frank McConnell
Grant McCuen
Dennis McGucken
Kathleen McHugh
Maureen McHugh
Christopher McKitterick
Kimberley McMahon-Coleman
Willis McNeely
Regna Meenk
Hassan Melehy
Farah Mendlesohn
Ruben Mendoza
Steven E. Merritt
Ferne Merrylees
China Miéville
Larisa Mikhaylova
Joseph D. Miller
Walter James Miller
Marvin Minsky
David Mogen
Beth Mohlenhoff
Carlos Mondragon
Glyn Morgan
Mitchell Morris
José Manuel Mota
Katie Moylan
Christa Munro
Gladys Murphy
Graham J. Murphy
Hema Nair
Tetsuro Namba
Andrew Nash
Susan J. Navarette
Alex Naylor
Jess Nevins
Dianne Newell
Peter Nicholls
Capper Nichols
Phil Nichols
Ryan Nichols
Larry Niven
William F. Nolan
Kristin Noone
Maximillian E. Novak
Sean Nye
Erica Obey
Rockne S. O'Bannon
Robert O'Connor
Wendy Doniger O'Flaherty
Keren Omry
Peter Oppenheimer
Stanley Orr
Eric Otto
Michael Page
Eric Palfreyman
Chris Palmer
Anthony Parr
Patrick Parrinder
John S. Partington
Josh Pearson
Wendy Pearson
Louis Pedrotti
Noel Perrin
Mike Perschon
Jefferson M. Peters
James Peterson
Kirk Petruccelli
Mary Pharr
Kavita Philip
Amanda Phillips
Robert M. Philmus
Charles Platt
Kathleen Plummer
Frederik Pohl
David Porush
Stephen W. Potts

Tim Powers
Paul Price
Joel Primack
Gerald Prince
David Pringle
Eric S. Rabkin
Paula Rea Radisch
Amy J. Ransom
Lisa Raphals
Jack Rawlins
Julia D. Ree
John K. Reed
Steven L. Reinhart
Ricardo Reyna
John Rieder
Ellen Rigsby
Darcie Rives-East
Robin Roberts
Benjamin Robertson
Kim Stanley Robinson
Warren Rochelle
Alcena M.D. Rogan
Dennis Rohaytn
James Romm
Jorge Martins Rosa
Mark Rose
S.L. Rosen
Umberto Rossi
Dibs Roy
Rudy Rucker
Richard Rush
Claire Russell
W.M.S. Russell
Flavia Ruzi
Richard Saint-Gelais
Roger Sale
Roxanne Samer
David N. Samuelson
Marta Sanchez
Joe Sanders
Peter Sands
Nicolas Saucy
Valérie Savard
Andy Sawyer
Frank Scafella
Bradley Schauer
Stanley Schmidt
Robert E. Scholes
Oliver Scholl
Peter Schulman
Gray Scott
Scott Selisker
W.A. Senior
Lorenzo Servitje
Alexander Shafer
Patrick Sharp
Sharon Sharp
Steven Shaviro
Don Shay
Rebekah Sheldon
Will Shetterly
Lewis Shiner
Tom Shippey
Shane Shukis
Susan Shwartz
Giuliano Jorge Magalhães Silva
Robert Silverberg
Peter W. Sinnema
Joan Slonczewski
George Slusser
Stephanie A. Smith
Ward Smith
Brent Smith-Casanueva
Richard Sneary
Matthew Snyder
Vivian Sobchack
Zoë Sofoulis
S.P. Somtow
Kathleen Spencer
Norman Spinrad
Joshua Stein
Melissa Colleen Stevenson
Garrett Stewart
Ben Stoltzfus
Susan Stratton
Kyle Strohmaier
Robert Stromberg
Theodore Sturgeon
C.W. Sullivan III
Alfredo Suppia
Herbert Sussman
Craig Svonkin
Richard J. Terrile
Amanda Thibodeau
Derek Thiess
Anne-Marie Thomas
Pascal J. Thomas
G.R. Thompson
James Thrall
Julie Ha Tran
Naomi Turnbull
Arthur Campbell Turner
Harry Turtledove
Mary Turzillo
Gereon Uerz
Robert Van Cleave
A.E. van Vogt
Samuel Vasbinder
Jeff Verona
Arthur Versluis
Sherryl Vint
Jack G. Voller
Angela Wall
Jeffrey M. Wallmann
Robin Walz
Fengzhen Wang
Patricia S. Warrick
Janeen Webb
Batya Weinbaum
Mark Weinert
Linda Weintraub
Andrew Wenaus
Travis West
Gary Westfahl
Lynne Lundquist Westfahl
Clyde Wilcox
Kevin Wilcox
Gerry Williams
Lynn F. Williams
Nathaniel Williams
Jack Williamson
Jerome Winter
Robert Wise
David Wittenberg
Milton T. Wolf
Gary K. Wolfe
Robert Wood
Wong Kin Yuen
Seth Wolitz
Donald A. Wollheim
Karen Tei Yamashita
Lisa Yaszek
Mark Young
Ekaterina Yudina
Paul Zeitsev
Roger Zelazny
Allen Zhang

Bibliography

Adams, Douglas. *The Hitchhiker's Guide to the Galaxy*. 1979. *The More Than Complete Hitchhiker's Guide*. New York: Longmeadow, 1987.

Alderman, Naomi. "Dystopian Dreams: How Feminist Science Fiction Predicted the Future." *The Guardian*, March 25, 2017. At https://www.theguardian.com/books/2017/mar/25/dystopian-dreams-how-feminist-science-fiction-predicted-the-future.

Aldiss, Brian W. *Billion Year Spree: The True History of Science Fiction*. Garden City, New York: Doubleday, 1973.

_____, with David Wingrove. *Trillion Year Spree: The History of Science Fiction*. New York: Atheneum, 1986.

Aliens. TCF/Brandywine, 1986.

Alkon, Paul. *The Origins of Futuristic Fiction*. Athens: University of Georgia Press, 1987.

_____. *Science Fiction Before 1900: Imagination Discovers Technology*. New York: Twayne, 1994.

Amis, Kingsley. *New Maps of Hell*. New York: Harcourt, Brace, and World, 1960.

Anders, Charlie Jane. "How Richard Powers Made Science Fiction Book Covers Strange." Gizmodo, March 17, 2015. At http://io9.gizmodo.com/how-richard-powers-made-science-fiction-book-covers-str-1692015738.

Anderson, Poul. *Brain Wave*. 1954. *A Treasury of Great Science Fiction*. Volume 2. Ed. Anthony Boucher. Garden City, NY: Doubleday, 1959, 7–119.

Anthony, Piers, and Robert E. Margroff. *The Ring*. New York: Ace, 1968.

Armstrong, Michael. "How Science Fiction Failed Alaska and Prince William Sound." *Bulletin of the Science Fiction Writers of America*, 23 (Winter, 1989), 9.

Asimov, Isaac. *The Caves of Steel*. 1953. New York: Pyramid, 1962.

Bagdikian, Ben H. "The Lords of the Global Village." *Nation*, 248 (June 12, 1989), 805–820.

_____. *The Media Monopoly*. Boston: Beacon, 1983.

Ballard, J.G. *The Drowned World*. 1962. Harmondsworth: Penguin, 1965.

_____. "Thirteen to Centaurus." 1962. *The Best Short Stories of J.G. Ballard*. New York: Holt, Rinehart and Winston, 1978, 149–170.

Barr, Marleen S. "Duck, Donald: A Trump Exorcism." *Alternative Truths Anthology*. Ed. Bob Brown and Phyllis Irene Radford. Benton City, WA: B Cubed, 2017, 205–208

_____. "Into the Chappaqua Woods: Or A Spaceship from a Feminist Planet Lands on Trump's White House Lawn." *The Satirist*, March 2017. At https://www.thesatirist.com/stories/into-the-chappaqua-woods.html.

_____. *Oy Feminist Planets: A Fake Memoir*. Vancouver: NeoPoiesis, 2015.

_____. *Oy Pioneer!: A Novel*. Madison: University of Wisconsin Press, 2003.

_____. "Swan Song for Trump." *See the Elephant Magazine*. At http://www.metaphysicalcircus.com/swansong-for-trump-fiction-by-marleen-s-barr/.

_____. "Trump Dreams of Jeannie," *The Satirist*, December 2016. At http://www.thesatirist.com/stories/trump-dreams-of-jeannie.htmlhttp://www.thesatirist.com/stories/trump-dreams-of-jeannie.html.

_____. "Two Trump Heads Are Better Than One." *Writers Resist*, May 4, 2017. At http://www.writersresist.com/2017/05/04/two-trump-heads-are-better-than-one.

Barstow, Anne Llewellyn. *Witchcraze: A New History of the European Witch Hunts*. San Francisco: Harper/Collins, 1994.

Bass, T.J. "Rorqual Maru." 1971. *The 1973 Annual World's Best Science Fiction*. Ed. Donald A. Wollheim. New York: DAW, 1973, 150–182.

Baudrillard, Jean. *The Ecstasy of Communication*. Trans. Bernard and Caroline Schultze. Ed. Sylvere Lotringer. 1987. New York: Columbia University Press, 1988.

Baumgarten, Marjorie. Review of *Tomorrowland*. *Austin Chronicle*, May 22, 2015. At https://www.austinchronicle.com/calendar/film/2015-05-22/tomorrowland/.

Bear, Greg. *Blood Music*. New York: Arbor House, 1985. New York: Ace, 1986.

Beck, Robert N., Oscar H. Kapp, and Chin-Tu Chen. *Brain Imaging*. Project Proposal. Chicago: ANL Center for Imaging Science, no date.

Bedini, Silvio A. "The Evolution of Science Museums." *Technology and Culture*, 6 (Winter 1965), 1–29.

Beer, Gillian. *The Romance*. London: Methuen, 1970.

Benford, Gregory. "Aliens and Knowability: A Scientist's Perspective." *Bridges to Science Fiction*. Ed. George Slusser, George R. Guffey, and Mark Rose. Carbondale: Southern Illinois University Press, 1980), 53–63.

_____. *Deep Time: How Humanity Communicates Across Millennia*. New York: Avon, 1999.

_____. "In Alien Flesh." 1978. *In Alien Flesh*. New York: Tor, 1986, 3–32.

_____. "Is There a Technological Fix for the Human Condition?" *Hard Science Fiction*. Ed. George Slusser and Eric S. Rabkin. Carbondale: Southern Illinois University Press, 1986.

_____. "Science Fiction, Rhetoric, and Realities: Words to the Critic." *Fiction 2000: Cyberpunk and the Future of Narrative*. Ed. George Slusser and Tom Shippey. Athens: University of Georgia Press, 1992), 223–229.

_____. "Style, Substance, and Other Illusions." *Styles of Creation: Aesthetic Technique and the Creation of Fictional Worlds*. Ed. George Slusser and Eric S. Rabkin. Athens: University of Georgia Press, 1992, 47–57.

Benford, James, Gregory Benford, and Dominic Benford. "Messaging with Cost Optimized Interstellar Beacons." *Astrobiology*, 10:5 (July 2010), 475–490.

_____. "Searching for Cost Optimized Interstellar Beacons." *Astrobiology*, 10:5 (July 2010), 491–498.

Bergson, Henri. *Laughter. Comedy*. Ed. Wylie Sypher. Garden City, NY: Doubleday, 1956, 61–190. Translator Unidentified.

Bernal, J.D. *The World, the Flesh and the Devil*. 1929. London: Cape Editions, 1971.

Bernhardt, Todd. "Album of the Week—Andy's Take." Interview with Andy Partridge. XTC's Blog. At chalkhills.org/articles/XTCFans20100912.html.

Bernstein, Robert, author. Al Plastino, artist. "The Interplanetary Circus." 1961. *Superman vs. the Aliens: The Best of DC*, 5:42 (November 1983), 45–53.

Bérubé, Michael. "The Humanities, Declining? Not According to the Numbers." *The Chronicle of Higher Education* website, posted July 1, 2013. At http://www.chronicle.com/article/The-Humanities-Declining-Not/140093.

Bester, Alfred. *The Stars My Destination*. New York: Signet, 1957.

The Big Noise. Twentieth Century–Fox, 1944.

Blish, James, and Norman L. Knight. *A Torrent of Faces*. New York: Ace, 1967.

Brin, David. "The Self-Preventing Prophecy: How a Dose of Nightmare Can Help Tame Tomorrow's Perils." First posted at AOL's *iPlanet* (1999). At http://www.davidbrin.com/nonfiction/tomorrowsworld.html.

Brown, Fredric. "Arena." 1944. *The Science Fiction Hall of Fame, Volume I*. Ed. Robert Silverberg. 1970. New York: Avon, 1971, 281–309.

Brownlee, Marina S., Kevin Brownlee, and Stephen G. Nichols, eds. *The New Medievalism*. Baltimore: Johns Hopkins University Press, 1991.

Brownmiller, Susan. *Against Our Will: Men, Women and Rape*. New York: Simon & Schuster, 1975.

Brunner, John. *The Sheep Look Up*. 1972. New York: Del Rey/Ballantine, 1983.

_____. *Stand on Zanzibar*. 1968. New York: Ballantine, 1969.

Bukatman, Scott. *Terminal Identity: The Virtual Subject in Postmodern Science Fiction*. Durham, NC: Duke University Press, 1993.

Butler, Octavia E. *Parable of the Sower*. New York: Warner, 1995.

Campbell, John W., Jr. [as Don A. Stuart]. "Who Goes There?" *Astounding Science-Fiction*, 21:6 (August 1938), 60–98.

Canary, Robert H. "Science Fiction as Fictive History." *Extrapolation*, 16:1 (December 1974), 81–95.

Ĉapek, Karel. *The Makropoulos Secret*. 1922. Boston: International Pocket Library, 1975.

Carr, Terry. "The Dance of the Changer and the Three." 1968. *Nebula Awards Stories Four*. Ed. Poul Anderson. 1969. New York: Pocket, 1971, 38–52.

Carroll, Lewis. "Jabberwocky." 1871. *The Complete Works of Lewis Carroll*. New York: Random House, 153–154.

Cawelti, John G. *Adventure, Mystery, and Romance*. Chicago: University of Chicago Press, 1976.

Cherryh, C.J. *Downbelow Station*. New York: DAW, 1981.

Clarke, Arthur C. *Childhood's End*. New York: Ballantine, 1953.

_____. "The Food of the Gods." 1964. *The Wind from the Sun: Stories of the Space Age*. New York: Signet, 1973, 1972, 1–5.

Clavell, James. *Shogun*. New York: Atheneum, 1975.

Clute, John. "Great Illustrators." *SF: The Illustrated Encyclopedia*. New York: Dorling Kindersley, 1995, 240–241.

Coblentz, Stanton A. *After 12,000 Years*. *Amazing Stories Quarterly*, 2 (Spring 1929), 148–221.

Conklin, Groff. "Introduction." *The Graveyard Reader*. Ed. Conklin. New York: Ballantine, 1958, 7–8.

Conquest of Space. Paramount Pictures, 1955.

Cover, Arthur Byron. *Stationfall*. New York: Avon, 1989.

Crichton, Michael. *The Andromeda Strain*. New York: Dell, 1970.

Crossley, Robert. "Fiction and the Future." *College English*, 55 (1993), 908–918.

_____. *H.G. Wells*. Mercer Island, WA: Starmont, 1986.

Cunningham, Ann Marie. "Forecast for Science Fiction: We Have Seen the Future and It Is Feminine." *Mademoiselle* (February 1973), 140–141, 169–170.

Daitch, Susan. *The Colorist*. New York: Random House, 1989.

"Data's Day." *Star Trek: The Next Generation*. Los Angeles: KCOP, April 17, 1991.

Davis, John A. Richard Powers Art Blog. At richardpowersart.blogspot.com.

Davis, Kathe. Review of *Feminist Fabulation* and *A New Species*. *Extrapolation*, 35 (Spring 1994), 84–89.

Della Cava, Marco. "Tesla Announces New Self-Driving Cars." *USA Today*, October 19, 2016. At https://www.usatoday.com/story/tech/news/2016/10/19/tesla-announces-fully-self-driving-fleet/92430638/.

Dery, Mark. "Richard Powers's Pulp Surrealism." The Daily Beast, March 15, 2015. At http://www.thedailybeast.com/cover-story-richard-powerss-pulp-surrealism.

Di Fate, Vincent. "Foreword." *The Art of Richard Powers*. By Jane Frank. London: Paper Tiger, 2001, 6–10.

Disch, Thomas M. *Camp Concentration*. 1968. New York: Carroll and Graf, 1988.

Druillet, Philippe. *Delirius*. Paris: Dargaud, 1978.

_____. *Gail*. Paris: Dargaud, 1978.

_____. *Les 6 Voyages de Lone Sloane*. Paris: Dargaud, 1972.

Ehrenreich, Barbara, and Deirdre English. *Witches, Midwives, and Nurses: A History of Women Healers*. Old Westbury, New York: Feminist, 1973.

Elkins, Charles. "Science Fiction Versus Futurology: Dramatic Versus Rational Models." *Science-Fiction Studies*, 6:1 (March 1979), 20–31.

Estes, Leland L. "The Medical Origins of the European Witch Craze: A Hypothesis." *Journal of Social History*, 17 (1983), 271–284.

Farmer, Philip Jose. "Riders of the Purple Wage." 1967. *Dangerous Visions #1*. Ed. Harlan Ellison. New York: Berkley, 1969, 67–147.

Felperin, Howard. *Beyond Deconstruction: The Uses and Abuses of Literary Theory*. Oxford: Clarendon, 1985.

Flaubert. Gustave, and Philippe. Druillet. *Salammbo*. Paris: Dargaud, 1982.

The Fly. TCF/Brooksfilm, 1986.

Forward, Robert F. "When Science Writes the Fiction." *Hard Science Fiction*. Ed. George Slusser and Eric S. Rabkin. Carbondale: Southern Illinois University Press, 1986, 1–7.

Foster, Milton P., ed. *A Casebook on Gulliver Among the Houyhnhnms*. New York: Crowell, 1961.

Foucault, Michel. *The Order of Things*. New York: Vintage, 1973.

Frank, Jane. *The Art of Richard Powers*. London: Paper Tiger, 2001.

_____. *Science Fiction and Fantasy Artists of the Twentieth Century: A Biographical Dictionary*. Jefferson, NC: McFarland, 2009.

_____, and Howard Frank. *The Frank Collection: A Showcase of the World's Finest Fantastic Art*. London: Paper Tiger, 1999.

_____, and _____. *Great Fantasy Art Themes from the Frank Collection*. London: Paper Tiger, 2003.

Franklin, H. Bruce. *Robert A. Heinlein: America as Science Fiction*. Oxford: Oxford University Press, 1980.

_____. *War Stars: The Superweapon and the American Imagination*. Oxford: Oxford University Press, 1988.

Freedman, Carl. *Critical Theory and Science Fiction*. Hanove, NH: Wesleyan University Press, 2000.

Freud, Sigmund. *Civilization and Its Discontents*. 1930. Trans. James Strachey. New York: Norton, 1961.

_____. "Creative Writers and DayDreaming." *The Complete Psychological Works of Sigmund Freud*. Volume 9. Trans. under general editorship of James Strachey, with Anna Freud, Alix Stratchey, and Alan Tyson. 1908, London: Hogarth, 1959, 141–153.

Friedhoff, Richard Mark, and William Benzon. *Visualization: The Second Computer Revolution*. New York: Abrams, 1989.

Friedman, Robert I. "India's Shame: Sexual Slavery and Political Corruption Are Leading to an AIDS Catastrophe." *Nation*, April 8, 1996. At https://www.scribd.com/document/29618200/India-s-Shame-The-Nation.

Frissen, Jerry. Show and Tell: Le Blog de Jerry Frissen. At http://www.humano.com/blog/Le-Blog-de-Jerry-Frissen/1.

Frye, Northrop. *Anatomy of Criticism: Four Essays*. Princeton: Princeton University Press, 1957.

Gernsback, Hugo. *Ralph 124C 41+: A Romance of the Year 2660*. 1911–1912, 1925. Second Edition. New York: Frederick Fell, 1950.

Gerrold, David. *A Matter for Men*. New York: Timescape, 1983.

Gibson, William. *Count Zero*. New York: Ace, 1987.

_____. "The Gernsback Continuum." 1981. *Burning Chrome*. 1986. New York: Ace, 1987, 23–35.

_____. *Mona Lisa Overdrive*. New York: Bantam, 1988.

_____. *Neuromancer*. 1984. London: Grafton, 1986.

Gleick, Richard. *Genius: The Life and Science of Richard Feynman*. New York: Pantheon, 1992.

Green, Martin. *Science and the Shabby Curate of Poetry: Essays about the Two Cultures*. New York: Norton, 1965.

Green, Monica. "Women's Medical Practice and Health Care in Medieval Europe," *Signs*, 14 (Winter 1989), 434–473.
Greenblatt, Stephen. *Renaissance Self-Fashioning: From More to Shakespeare*. Chicago: University of Chicago Press, 1980.
Griffith, Mary. *Three Hundred Years Hence*. 1836. Philadelphia: Prime, 1950.
Grimm, Jacob, and Wilhelm Grimm. "Little Red-Cap." 1812. *Grimm's Household Tales, with the Author's Notes*. Volume 1. Trans. and ed. Margaret Hunt. London: George Bell, 1884.
Haldane, J.B.S. *Possible Worlds and Other Essays*. London: Chatto and Windus, 1927.
Harrison, Harry. *Make Room! Make Room!* New York: Berkley, 1966.
Hayles, N. Katherine. *Chaos Bound: Orderly Disorder in Contemporary Literature and Science*. Ithaca, NY: Cornell University Press, 1990.
Heilbrun, Carolyn G. "Why I Don't Read Science Fiction." *Women's Studies International Forum*, 7 (1984), 117–119.
Heinlein, Robert A. *Beyond This Horizon*. 1942, 1948. New York: Signet, 1960.
_____. *Orphans of the Sky*. 1963. New York: Berkley, 1970.
_____. "Science Fiction: Its Nature, Faults and Virtues." *The Science Fiction Novel: Imagination and Social Criticism*. Ed. Basil Davenport. Chicago: Advent, 1959, 14–48.
_____. *Stranger in a Strange Land*. New York: Putnam's, 1961. New York: Berkley, 1982.
_____. *Time Enough for Love*. New York: Berkley, 1973.
Hergé. *Objectif Lune*. 1953. Tournai: Casterman, 1981.
_____. *On a Marche sur la Lune*. 1954, Tournai: Casterman, 1981.
Hillegas, Mark R. "Second Thoughts on the Course in Science Fiction." *Science Fiction: The Academic Awakening*. Ed. Willis E. McNeely. Supplement to *CEA Critic*, 37 (November 1974), 15–17.
Hinsie, Leland E., and Robert J. Campbell. *Psychiatric Dictionary*. Fourth Edition. New York: Oxford University Press, 1970.
Hoban, Russell. *Riddley Walker*. 1980. New York: Pocket, 1982.
Hodgson, William Hope. *The House on the Borderland*. 1908. New York: Ace, 1962.
Holland, Norman N. Email to Marleen S. Barr. April 14, 2017.
Hollinger, Veronica. "A New Alliance of Postmodernism and Feminist Speculative Fiction." *Science-Fiction Studies*, 20 (July 1993), 272–276.
_____. "The Vampire and the Alien: Variations on the Outsider." *Science-Fiction Studies*, 16:2 (July 1989), 145–160.
Homer. *The Odyssey*. Trans. Robert Fitzgerald. 1961. Garden City, NY: Doubleday, 1963.
Hoyle, Fred. *The Black Cloud*. 1957. New York: Signet, 1959.
Hudson, Kenneth. *Museums of Influence*. Cambridge: Cambridge University Press, 1987.
Hume, David. *Dialogues Concerning Natural Religion*. 1779. Ed. Henry D. Aiken. New York: Hafner, 1948.
Hunter, Michael. "The Cabinet Institutionalized: The Royal Society's 'Repository' and Its Background." *The Origins of Museums: The Cabinet of Curiosities in Sixteenth and Seventeenth-Century Europe*. Ed. Oliver Impey and Arthur MacGregor. Oxford: Oxford University Press, 1985, 159–168.
Huntington, John. "Impossible Love in Science Fiction." *Raritan*, 4 (1984), 85–99.
_____. *The Logic of Fantasy: H.G. Wells and Science Fiction*. New York: Columbia University Press, 1982.
_____. "Newness, *Neuromancer*, and the End of Narrative." *Fictional Space: Essays on Contemporary Science Fiction*. Ed. Tom Shippey. Oxford: Blackwell, 1991, 59–75.
_____. "Science Fiction and the Future." *Science Fiction: A Collection of Critical Essays*. Ed. Mark Rose. Englewood Cliffs, NJ: Prentice-Hall, 1976, 156–166.
"Introduction." *Archaeologia, or Miscellaneous Tracts Relating to Antiquity, Published by the Society of Antiquaries of London*, 1 (1770), i–vi.
James, Henry. *The Art of the Novel*. New York: Scribner's, 1937.
Janowitz, Tama. *A Cannibal in Manhattan*. New York: Crown, 1987.
Jarzebski, Jerzy. "Stanislaw Lem, Rationalist and Visionary." *Science-Fiction Studies, Second Series*. Ed. R.D. Mullen and Darko Suvin. Boston: Gregg, 1978, 217–233.
Jeter, K.W. *Dr. Adder*. 1984. New York: Penguin/NAL, 1988.
Just Imagine. Twentieth Century–Fox, 1930.
Kael, Pauline. *Deeper into Movies*. New York: Bantam, 1974.
Ketterer, David. *Frankenstein's Creation: The Book, The Monster, and Human Reality*. Victoria: British Literary Studies, 1979.
_____. "Solaris and the Illegitimate Suns of Science Fiction." *Extrapolation*, 14 (December 1972), 73–89.
Keyes, Daniel. "Flowers for Algernon." 1959. *The Hugo Winners*. Volume 1. Ed. Isaac Asimov. Garden City, NY: Doubleday, 1962, 245–278.
Kilgour, Maggie. *From Communion to Cannibalism: An Anatomy of Metaphors of Incorporation*. Princeton: Princeton University Press, 1990.
King, Stephen. "Survivor Type." 1982. *Skeleton Crew*. 1985. New York: Signet, 1986, 407–426.
Kneale, J. Douglas. "Deconstruction." *The Johns Hopkins Guide to Literary Theory and Criticism*. Ed. Michael Groden and Martin Kreiswirth. Baltimore: Johns Hopkins University Press, 1994, 185–192.

Komatsu, Sakyo. "The Savage Mouth." 1978. Trans. Judith Merril. *The Best Japanese Science Fiction Stories.* Ed. John L. Apostolou and Martin H. Greenberg. New York: Dembner, 1989, 74–84.
Kristeva, Julia. "Joyful Revolt: Interview with Mary Zournazi." *Hope: New Philosophies for Change.* Ed. Zournazi. Trans. Peter Cowley. Annandale, NSW: Pluto Press, 2002, 64–77.
_____. *Powers of Horror: An Essay on Abjection.* Trans. Leon Roudiez. New York: Columbia University Press, 1982.
_____. "The Subject in Process." *The Tel Quel Reader.* Trans. and ed. Patrick Ffrench and Roland-François Lack. London: Routledge, 1998, 133–178.
Kroeber, Karl. *Romantic Fantasy and Science Fiction.* New Haven, CT: Yale University Press, 1988.
Kutner, C. Jerry. The Richard M. Powers Cyber Art Gallery. At home.earthlink.net/~cjk5/.
Kuttner, Henry, and C.L. Moore [as Lewis Padgett]. "Mimsy Were the Borogoves." *Astounding Science-Fiction,* 30:6 (February 1943), 52–69.
Lake, Jay. "On the Human Plan." *Lone Star Stories,* No. 31. 2009. At http://literary.erictmarin.com/archives/Issue%2031/plan.htm.
Landon, Brooks. "Styles of Invisibility: Sustaining the Transparent in Contemporary Prose Semblances." *Styles of Creation: Aesthetic Technique and the Creation of Fictional Worlds.* Ed. George Slusser and Eric S. Rabkin. Athens: University of Georgia Press, 1992, 245–257.
Leavis, F.R. *Anna Karenina and Other Essays.* New York: Simon & Schuster, 1969.
_____. *Nor Shall My Sword: Discourses on Pluralism, Compassion and Social Hope.* New York: Harper and Row, 1972.
Le Guin, Ursula K. "American Science Fiction and the Other." *Science-Fiction Studies,* 2:3 (November 1975), 208–210.
_____. "Nine Lives." 1969. *World's Best Science Fiction 1970.* Ed. Donald A. Wollheim and Terry Carr. New York: Ace, 1970, 302–327.
Leinster, Murray. *War with the Gizmos.* Greenwich, CT: Fawcett, 1958.
Lem, Stanislaw. *The Investigation.* 1959. Trans. Adele Milch. New York: Avon, 1976.
_____. *Memoirs Found in a Bathtub.* 1961. Trans. Michael Kandel and Christine Rose. New York: Seabury, 1973.
_____. *Solaris,* 1961. Trans. Joanna Kilmartin and Steve Cox. New York: Berkley, 1971. London: Arrow, 1973.
_____. *The Star Diaries.* 1957–1971. Trans. Michael Kandel. New York: Avon, 1977.
Lemaire, Anika. *Jacques Lacan.* Trans. David Macey. Boston: Routledge, 1979.
Locke, George. "Wells in Three Volumes? A Sketch of British Publishing in the 19th Century." *Science-Fiction Studies,* 3:3 (November 1976), 282–286.
Locke, John. *An Essay Concerning Humane Understanding.* 1689. Ed. Alexander Campbell Fraser. 1894. New York: Dover, 1959.
London, Jack. *The Scarlet Plague.* 1912. *The Science Fiction of Jack London.* Ed. Richard Gid Powers. Boston: Gregg, 1975.
Lord, Gabrielle. *Salt.* Victoria, Australia: Penguin Australia, 1990.
Lorraine, Lillith. "Into the 28th Century." *Science Wonder Quarterly,* 1 (Winter 1930), 250–267.
Lovecraft, H.P. "The Dunwich Horror." 1929. *The Best of H.P. Lovecraft.* New York: Ballantine, 1982.
Lukács, George. *The Historical Novel.* Trans. Hannah and Stanley Mitchell. London: Merlin, 1969.
_____. *The Theory of the Novel.* Trans. Anna Bostock. London: Merlin, 1971.
Luthi, Max. *Once Upon a Time: On the Nature of Fairy Tales.* 1962. Trans. Lee Chadeayne and Paul Gottwald, with Luthi's additions. New York: Frederick Ungar, 1970.
MacGregor, Arthur. "The Cabinet of Curiosities in Seventeenth-Century Britain." *The Origins of Museums: The Cabinet of Curiosities in Sixteenth and Seventeenth-Century Europe.* Ed. Oliver Impey and MacGregor. Oxford: Oxford University Press, 1985, 147–158.
MacLeod, Ian R. "Re-crossing the Styx." 2010. *The Year's Best Science Fiction: 28th Annual Collection.* Ed. Gardner Dozois. New York: St. Martin's, 2011), 119–131.
Merchant, Paul. *The Epic.* London: Methuen, 1971.
Mezières, Jean-Claude, and Pierre Christin. *Métro Châtelet, Direction Cassiopée.* Paris: Dargaud, 1980.
Miller, Edward. *That Noble Cabinet: A History of the British Museum.* London: Andre Deutsch, 1973.
Moebius. [Jean Giraud] "Arzach." *Oeuvres II.* Paris: Humanoides Associes, 1976.
Moore, C.L. "No Woman Born." 1944. *Treasury of Science Fiction.* Ed. Groff Conklin. 1948. New York: Bonanza, 1980, 164–201.
Moravec, Hans. *Mind Children: The Future of Robot and Human Intelligence.* Cambridge: Harvard University Press, 1989.
Mullen, R.D. "Blish, Van Vogt, and the Uses of Spengler." *Riverside Quarterly,* 3 (August 1968), 172–186.
Niven, Larry. *Neutron Star.* New York: Ballantine, 1968.
_____. *Tales of Known Space.* New York: Ballantine, 1975.
Nowlan, Philip Francis. *Armageddon 2419 A.D.* 1928. New York: Ace, 1962.
Ollier, Claude. *La Vie sur Epsilon.* Paris: Gallimard, 1972.
Orwell, George. *Nineteen Eighty-Four.* 1949. New York: Signet, 1961.

Parrinder, Patrick. "The Alien Encounter, Or, Ms. Brown and Mrs. Le Guin." *Science-Fiction Studies*, 17 (March 1979), 46–75.

_____. "Science Fiction and the Scientific World-View." *Science Fiction: A Critical Guide*. Ed. Parrinder. London: Longman, 1979, 67–88.

_____. "'You Must Have Seen a Lot of Changes': Fiction Beyond the Twenty-First Century." *Envisioning the Future: Science Fiction and the Next Millennium*. Ed. Marleen Barr. Middletown, CT: Wesleyan University Press, 2003, 173–190.

Pielke, Robert G. "Humans and Aliens: A Unique Relationship." *Mosaic*, 13 (1980), 29–40.

Piercy, Marge. "Marleen Barr's Lost and Found." *Lost in Space: Probing Feminist Science Fiction and Beyond*. By Marleen S. Barr. Chapel Hill: University of North Carolina Press, 1993, ix–xiii.

Plank, Robert. "Omnipotent Cannibals in *Stranger in a Strange Land*." *Robert A. Heinlein*. Ed. Joseph D. Olander and Martin Harry Greenberg. New York: Taplinger, 1978), 83–106.

Poe, Edgar Allan. "The Facts in the Case of M. Valdemar." 1845. *The Complete Tales and Poems of Edgar Allan Poe*. New York: Barnes & Noble, 1992, 656–663.

Pohl, Frederik. "The Tunnel Under the World." 1954. *The Best of Frederik Pohl*. New York: Del Rey/Ballantine, 1975, 1–34.

_____, and C.M. Kornbluth. *The Space Merchants*. New York: Ballantine, 1953.

Politzer, Heinz. *Franz Kafka: Parable and Paradox*. Ithaca, NY: Cornell University Press, 1966.

Powers, Richard M. *Spacetimewarp Paintings*. Garden City, NY: Doubleday, 1983.

Poynor, Rick. "Unearthly Powers: Surrealism and Science Fiction." Design Observer, May 19, 2011. At http://designobserver.com/feature/unearthly-powers-surrealism-and-sf/27128.

Propp, Vladimir. *Morphology of the Folktale*. 1928. Trans. Lawrence Scott. Bloomington: Indiana University Press, 1958. Austin: University of Texas Press, 1975.

Pynchon, Thomas. "Introduction." *Slow Learner*. Boston: Little, Brown, 1984, 1–23.

Rahner, Karl. *The Practice of Faith: A Handbook of Contemporary Spirituality*. New York: Crossroad, 1983.

Rawson, Claude J. "Cannibalism and Fiction: Reflections on Narrative Form and 'Extreme' Situations." *Genre*, 10:4 (Winter 1977), 667–711

_____. "Cannibalism and Fiction, Part II: Love and Eating in Fielding, Mailer, Genet, and Wittig." *Genre*, 11:2 (Summer 1978), 227–313.

ReaderCon 5. Cambridge, MA: privately printed, 1992. Souvenir book.

Regis, Ed. *Great Mambo Chicken and the Transhuman Condition: Science Slightly Over the Edge*. Reading, MA: Addison-Wesley, 1990.

Reich, Robert. "As the World Turns." *New Republic*, 200 (May 1, 1989), 23, 26–28.

Richard M. Powers. Pinterest. At pinterest.com/jbc85/richard-m-powers/.

Richard Powers. The Internet Speculative Fiction Database. At http://www.isfdb.org/cgi-bin/ea.cgi?1811.

Robinson, Spider. "Melancholy Elephants." *Analog: Science Fiction/Science Fact*, 52 (June 1982), 132–143.

Rohde, Sean. The Richard M. Powers Compendium. At http://powerscompendium.tumblr.com/.

Rose, Mark. *Alien Encounters: Anatomy of Science Fiction*. Cambridge: Harvard University Press, 1981.

St. Charles, Girard. "A Being." The Richard M. Powers Cyber Art Gallery. At http://home.earthlink.net/~cjk5/poem.html.

Sanders, Scott. "The Artist of Hunger." *Isaac Asimov's Science Fiction Magazine*, 7:7 (July 1983), 44–62.

The SF Encyclopedia Picture Gallery. The Encyclopedia of Science Fiction. At http://sf-encyclopedia.uk/gallery.php.

Shakespeare, William. *King Lear*. New York: Signet, 1963.

Shaw, George Bernard. *Back to Methuselah*. New York: Brentano's, 1921.

Sheckley, Robert. "The People Trap." *The People Trap and Other Pitfalls, Snares, Devices and Delusions, as Well as Two Sniggles and a Contrivance*. New York: Dell, 1968, 7–26.

Shelley, Mary. *Frankenstein, Or, The Modern Prometheus*. 1831. Ed. Johanna M. Smith. Boston: Bedford, 1992.

_____. *The Last Man*. 1826. Ed. Hugh J. Luke, Jr. Lincoln: University of Nebraska Press, 1965. London: Hogarth, 1985.

Shippey, Tom. "The Critique of America in Contemporary Science Fiction." *Foundation: The Review of Science Fiction*, No. 61 (Summer 1994), 36–49.

_____. "Introduction." *The Oxford Book of Science Fiction Stories*. Ed. Shippey. Oxford: Oxford University Press, 1992), ix–xxvi.

_____. "Learning to Read Science Fiction." *Fictional Space: Essays on Contemporary Science Fiction*. Ed. Shippey. Oxford: Blackwell, 1991, 1–33.

_____. "Response to Three Papers on 'Philology: Whence and Whither' Given by Drs Utz, Macgillivray, and Zolkowski, at Kalamazoo, 4th May 2002." *The Heroic Age: A Journal of Early Medieval Northwestern Europe*, No. 11 (May 2008). At http://www.heroicage.org/issues/11/foruma.php#shippey.

Silverberg, Robert. "Sundance." 1969. *The Road to Science Fiction, Volume 3: From Heinlein to Here*. Ed. James Gunn. 1979. Clarkston, GA: White Wolf, 1996, 461–473.

Sladek, John L. "The Happy Breed." 1967. *Dangerous Visions #3*. Ed. Harlan Ellison. New York: Berkley, 1969, 79–100.

Slesar, Henry. "Ersatz." 1967. *Dangerous Visions #3*. Ed. Harlan Ellison. New York: Berkley, 1969, 63–70.
Slusser, George. "Introduction: The Iconology of Science Fiction and Fantasy Art." *Unearthly Visions: Approaches to Science Fiction and Fantasy Art*. Ed. Gary Westfahl, Slusser, and Kathleen Church Plummer. Westport, CT: Greenwood, 2002, 1–15.
Smith, Martin Cruz. *Gorky Park*. New York: Random House, 1981.
Snow, C.P. *The Two Cultures*. Cambridge: Cambridge University Press, 1993.
_____. *Variety of Men*. New York: Scribner's, 1966.
Sobchack, Vivian. "Abject Times: Temporality and the Science Fiction Film in Post–9/11 America." *Reality Unbound: New Departures in Science Fiction Cinema*. Ed. Aidan Power, Delia González de Reufels, Rasmus Greiner, and Winfried Pauleit. Berlin: Bertz + Fischer, 2017), 12–33.
_____. *The Limits of Infinity: The American Science Fiction Film*. Cranbury, NJ: A.S. Barnes, 1980.
Soylent Green. Metro-Goldwyn-Mayer, 1973.
Spengler, Oswald. *The Decline of the West*. Two volumes. 1918. Trans. Charles Francis Atkinson. London: Allen & Irwin, 1926–1928.
Spenser, Edmund. *The Faerie Queene. Poetical Works*. Ed. J.C. Smith and E. de Selincourt. London: Oxford University Press, 1970, 1–406.
Spinrad, Norman. *Journals of the Plague Years*. New York: Bantam, 1995.
Stableford, Brian. *Scientific Romance in Britain, 1890–1950*. London: Fourth Estate, 1985.
Stapledon, Olaf. *Last and First Men and Star Maker: Two Science Fiction Novels by Olaf Stapledon*. 1930, 1937. New York: Dover, 1968.
"The Stars of Modern SF Pick the Best Science Fiction." *The Guardian*, May 14, 2011. At https://www.theguardian.com/books/2011/may/14/science-fiction-authors-choice.
Steiner, George. *Language and Silence*. New York: Atheneum, 1970.
Stevens, Wallace. "Esthétique du Mal." *Transport to Summer*. New York: Knopf, 1951, 52–53.
Stevenson, Robert Louis. *Memories and Portraits*. London: Heinemann, 1924.
Stewart, George R. *Earth Abides*. 1949. New York: Fawcett Crest, 1971.
Sturgeon, Theodore. *More Than Human*. New York: Ballantine, 1953.
Suchariktul, Somtow. "Rabid in Mallworld." *Isaac Asimov's Science Fiction Magazine*, 4 (June 1980), 20–44.
Suvin, Darko. "Afterword." *Solaris*. By Stanislaw Lem. Trans. Joanna Kilmartin and Steve Cox. New York: Berkley, 1971, 212–223.
_____. *Metamorphoses of Science Fiction: On the Poetics and History of a Literary Genre*. New Haven, CT: Yale University Press, 1979.
_____. "On the Poetics of the Science Fiction Genre." 1972. *Science Fiction: A Collection of Critical Essays*. Ed. Mark Rose. Englewood Cliffs, NJ: Prentice-Hall, 1976, 57–71.
Swanwick, Michael. *Vacuum Flowers*. 1987. New York: Ace, 1988.
Swift, Jonathan. *Gulliver's Travels*. 1726. Ed. Martin Price. Indianapolis: Bobbs-Merrill, 1963.
_____. *A Modest Proposal*. 1729. *The Writings of Jonathan Swift*. Ed. Robert A. Greenberg and William B. Piper. New York: Norton, 1973), 502–509.
The Thing. U/Turman Focter Productions, 1982.
The Thing (from Another World). Winchester Pictures, 1951.
THX 1138. American Zoetrope, 1969.
Tidhar, Lavie. "Vladimir Chong Chooses to Die." *The Year's Best Science Fiction: 32nd Annual Collection*. Ed. Gardner Dozois. New York: St. Martin's, 2015, 199–209.
Tiptree, James, Jr. [Alice Sheldon] "Morality Meat." 1985. *Crown of Stars*. New York: Tor, 1990, 69–95.
Todorov, Tzvetan. *Grammaire du Décaméron*. The Hague: Mouton, 1969.
Tolkien, J.R.R. *The Fellowship of the Ring*. 1954. New York: Ballantine, 1965.
Tolstoy, Alexsey. *Aelita, or The Decline of Mars*. Trans. unidentified. 1923. Ann Arbor, MI: Ardis, 1985.
2001: A Space Odyssey. Metro-Goldwyn-Mayer, 1968.
Van Vogt, A.E. *Slan*. 1940, 1946. New York: Ballantine, 1961.
_____. *The World of Null-A*. 1945. New York: Simon & Schuster, 1948.
Verne, Jules. *Autour de la Lune*. Paris: J. Hetzel, 1870.
_____. *De la Terre à la Lune: Trajet Direct en 97 Heures 20 Minutes*. Paris: J. Hetzel, 1865.
Vesser, H. Aram. *The New Historicism*. New York: Routledge, 1988.
Vick, Karl. "Bill Targets Bacteria." *Washington Post*, January 29, 1996. At https://www.washingtonpost.com/archive/local/1996/01/29/bill-targets-bacteria/f4d6079d-916e-4e58-a0b5-cb47736d3e07/?utm_term=.0c1175b7a0d3.
_____. "Man Gets Hands on Bubonic Plague Germ, but That's No Crime." *Washington Post*, December 30, 1995. At https://www.washingtonpost.com/archive/local/1995/12/30/man-gets-hands-on-bubonic-plague-germ-but-thats-no-crime/6053d93a-cc24-4abe-80c0-70fe0993ea21/?utm_term=.5688ef93b884.
Weinbaum, Stanley G. "A Martian Odyssey." 1933. *The Science Fiction Hall of Fame, Volume 1*. Ed. Robert Silverberg. 1970. New York: Avon, 1971, 13–39.
Weinberg, Robert. *A Biographical Dictionary of Science Fiction and Fantasy Artists*. Westport, CT: Greenwood, 1988.

Welch, Martin. "The Ashmolean as Described by Its Earliest Visitors." *Tradescant's Rarities: Essays on the Foundation of the Ashmolean Museum, 1683, With a Catalogue of the Surviving Early Collections.* Ed. Arthur MacGregor. Oxford: Oxford University Press, 1983, 59–69.

Wells, H.G. *The Definitive Time Machine: A Critical Edition of H.G. Wells's Scientific Romance.* Intro. and notes Harry M. Geduld. Bloomington: University of Indiana Press, 1987.

_____. "Fiction About the Future." Typescript, Wells Collection, University of Illinois Library. Unpublished talk broadcast over Australian radio, December 29, 1938.

_____. *The Island of Doctor Moreau: A Variorum Text.* Ed. Robert Philmus. Athens: University of Georgia Press, 1993.

_____. *Things to Come.* New York: Macmillan, 1935.

_____. *The Time Machine.* 1895. Atlantic Edition of *The Works of H.G. Wells.* Volume I. New York: Scribner's, 1924. London: Heinemann, 1949. New York: Bantam, 1982. Also in *Three Prophetic Novels of H.G. Wells.* Ed. E.F. Bleiler. New York: Dover, 1960, 263–335.

_____. *When the Sleeper Wakes. Three Prophetic Novels of H.G. Wells.* Ed. E.F. Bleiler. New York: Dover, 1960, 1–187.

Westfahl, Gary. "Artists in Wonderland: Toward a True History of Science Fiction Art." *Unearthly Visions: Approaches to Science Fiction and Fantasy Art.* Ed. Westfahl, George Slusser, and Kathleen Church Plummer. Westport, CT: Greenwood, 2002, 19–38.

Whitehead, Ralph, Jr. "Class Acts: America's Changing Middle Class Faces Polarization and Problems." *Utne Reader*, No. 37 (January-February 1990), 158–161.

Wilde, Oscar. *The Picture of Dorian Gray.* 1891. New York: Dell, 1968.

Wilson, Simon. *Surrealist Painting.* London: Phaidon, 1991.

Wittfogel, Karl August. *Oriental Despotism: A Comparative Study of Total Power.* New Haven, CT: Yale University Press, 1957.

Wittlin, Alma Stephanie. *The Museum: Its History and Its Tasks in Education.* London: Routledge, 1949.

Wolfe, Gary K. Review of *Feminist Fabulation. Locus*, 31 (September 1993), 25–26, 70.

Wolfe, Gene. *The Shadow of the Torturer.* 1980. New York: Timescape, 1981.

Wordsworth, William. "The Recluse." *The Prelude, with a Selection from the Shorter Poems, the Sonnets, The Recluse, and The Excursion.* Ed. Carlos Baker. New York: Holt, Rinehart and Winston, 1948.

"Wow-Art." At www.wow-art.com.

Zamiatin, Yevgeny. *We.* 1924. Trans. Mira Ginsburg. New York: Viking, 1972.

Zelazny, Roger. *Sign of Chaos.* New York: Arbor House, 1987.

Žižek, Slajov. *For They Know Not What They Do.* London: Verso, 1991.

About the Contributors

Paul **Alkon** is the Leo S. Bing Professor Emeritus of English and American Literature at the University of Southern California. His books on science fiction include *Origins of Futuristic Fiction*, *Science Fiction Before 1900*, and *Winston Churchill's Imagination*.

Poul **Anderson** was an acclaimed writer of science fiction and fantasy. He won seven Hugo Awards and three Nebula Awards, was proclaimed a Science Fiction Research Association Grand Master, and was inducted into the Science Fiction and Fantasy Hall of Fame in 2000. He died in 2001.

Marleen S. **Barr** teaches English at the City University of New York and is known for pioneering work in feminist science fiction. She won the Science Fiction Research Association's Pilgrim Award for lifetime achievement in science fiction criticism. She has written numerous books, edited anthologies, and coedited the science fiction issue of *PMLA*.

Gregory **Benford** is a fellow of the American Physical Society and received the Lord Prize in science, the Asimov Prize for fiction, and the United Nations Medal in Literature. His fiction and nonfiction have won many awards, and he has published 32 novels, 4 volumes of nonfiction, more than 200 short stories and several hundred scientific papers in various fields.

David **Brin** is an astrophysicist whose international best-selling novels include *The Postman*, *Earth*, *Existence*, and the *Uplift Series*. He serves on advisory boards and speaks or consults on a wide range of topics. His nonfiction book about the information age, *The Transparent Society*, won the Freedom of Speech Award of the American Library Association.

Danièle **Chatelain** is a professor of French at the University of Redlands and the author of *Perceiving and Telling*. She has published several essays with George Slusser, notably "Conveying Unknown Worlds." She is the coeditor of *H.G. Wells's Perennial Time Machine* and coauthor and translator of critical editions of multiple authors' works.

Robert **Crossley** is an emeritus professor of English at the University of Massachusetts, Boston. He is the author of *Olaf Stapledon*, the standard biography of its subject. His most recent book is *Imagining Mars*.

H. Bruce **Franklin** is the author or editor of 19 books on American history and culture. His early university SF classes and groundbreaking *Future Perfect* helped open academia to science fiction. He has been awarded the 1981 Eaton Award, the Science Fiction Research Association's Pioneer Award, and its Pilgrim Award for lifetime scholarship.

Carl **Freedman** is the author of many books, articles, and reviews, and is the William A. Read Professor of English Literature and distinguished research master at Louisiana State University. He began attending Eaton Conferences in 1989.

Kirk **Hampton** has published two novels in the style of "Wakean science fantasy," *The Moonhare* and *Lisho*, and four articles on science fiction with Carol MacKay. For 10 years he produced and starred in a weekly cable television show for Public Access in Austin, Texas.

N. Katherine **Hayles** is the James B. Duke Professor of Literature at Duke University. She teaches and writes on literature, science and technology in the 20th and 21st centuries. She is the author of *Unthought*.

Howard V. **Hendrix** is a professor at California State University, Fresno, and holds a Ph.D. in English literature from the University of California, Riverside. He has published numerous novels, collections of stories, and works of nonfiction, as well as articles, reviews, and editorials. He was western regional director and vice president of the Science Fiction and Fantasy Writers of America.

John **Huntington** is an emeritus professor of English at the University of Illinois and participated in many Eaton Conferences. His book, *The Logic of Fantasy*, won the Eaton Award. His essay in this volume is one of numerous Eaton presentations.

Fredric R. **Jameson** is the Knut Schmidt-Nielsen Professor of Comparative Literature, professor of romance studies and director of the Institute for Critical Theory at Duke University. He has written over 30 books and received the 2008 Holberg International Prize and the 2012 Modern Language Association Lifetime Achievement Award for scholarship.

Carol **MacKay** is a distinguished teaching professor of English at the University of Texas, Austin. She has edited volumes on William Makepeace Thackeray, Charles Dickens, and Annie Besant, and is the author of *Soliloquy in Nineteenth-Century Fiction* and *Creative Negativity*.

Frank **McConnell** was a professor of English at the University of California, Santa Barbara, and was a mainstay of the Eaton Conference until his death in 1999. He is the author of 13 books, including *The Science Fiction of H.G. Wells*, and several hundred essays. He served on the Pulitzer Prize Committee for fiction.

Joseph D. **Miller** is a professor and chair of pharmacology at the American University of the Caribbean. He received his Ph.D. from the University of Texas and was formerly a NASA space shuttle project director. He was involved in Eaton Conferences for many years, contributing numerous critical essays to conference volumes.

Patrick **Parrinder** is an emeritus professor of English at the University of Reading and president of the H.G. Wells Society. His book *Shadows of the Future* won the Eaton Award. He is general editor of the *Oxford History of the Novel in English* and seventeen H.G. Wells volumes published by Penguin Classics.

Stephen W. **Potts** works with the Arthur C. Clarke Center for Human Imagination and taught genre fiction and popular culture at the University of California, San Diego. He has written scholarly articles and books, fiction, editorials and reviews, including the anthology *Chasing Shadows* and a collection of critical essays on *The Hobbit*.

Eric S. **Rabkin** is the University of Michigan Arthur F. Thurnau Professor Emeritus, professor emeritus of English language and literature, and professor emeritus of art and design. He has authored over 20 books, and his "Fantasy and Science Fiction" was the world's first writing-intensive massive open online course. He received the Golden Apple Award for outstanding teacher at UM and the Science Fiction Research Association's Pilgrim Award for lifetime achievement in SF criticism.

Tom **Shippey** is the author of many articles on science fiction. He collaborated with Harry Harrison on two alternate history trilogies and acted as judge for the John W. Campbell, Jr., Award almost from its inception. He has taught Oxford and Harvard and is well known for books on J.R.R. Tolkien and medieval studies.

George **Slusser** was a professor emeritus of comparative literature at the University of California, Riverside, and was renowned for coediting numerous volumes of essays on science fiction and fantasy, including 21 Eaton volumes. With his wife Danièle Chatelain, he translated and edited works by numerous authors and several author studies. He received the Science Fiction Research Associatino's Pilgrim Award for lifetime achievement in SF criticism.

Vivian **Sobchack** is a professor emerita at the University of California, Los Angeles' department of film, television and digital media. She is the author of *The Address of the Eye* and *Carnal Thoughts* and editor of two collections. She received the Society for Cinema and Media Studies' Distinguished Career Achievement Award and the Science Fiction Research Association's Pilgrim Award for lifetime achievement in SF criticism.

Gary **Westfahl** is the author, editor, or coeditor of 26 books, including the Hugo Award–nominated *Science Fiction Quotations.* He is an adjunct professor at the University of La Verne in California. He received the Science Fiction Research Association's Pilgrim Award for lifetime achievement in SF criticism.

Index

www.ingramcontent.com/pod-product-compliance
Lightning Source LLC
Chambersburg PA
CBHW081547300426
44116CB00015B/2781
* 9 7 8 1 4 7 6 6 6 9 2 8 1 *